# The Devil's Final Battle

## How the Current Rejection of the Message of Fatima Causes the Present Crisis in the Church and the World

*Compiled and Edited by*

**Father Paul Kramer, B.Ph., M.Div., S.T.L. (Cand.)**

and the editorial staff of The Missionary Association

In the Third Secret (of Fatima) it is foretold, among other things, that the great apostasy in the Church will begin at the top.

... Cardinal Mario Luigi Ciappi

**ADVANCED READING COPY—UNCORRECTED PROOF**

ISBN 0-9663046-5-9
6.25 x 9.25 — 278 pages

Ordering information:
1-800-954-8737

The Missionary Association
7 High Street
Terryville, Conn. 06786

ISBN 0-9663046-5-9

The Missionary Association
7 High Street
Terryville, Conn. 06786
U.S.A.

Printed in Canada

*This book is respectfully dedicated to*
***Our Lady of Fatima***
*and to all Cardinals, patriarchs, bishops, priests,*
*religious and lay persons*
*who have dedicated themselves*
*in humility and love to Her service.*

"In the Third Secret it is foretold, among other things, that the great apostasy in the Church will begin *at the top*."

... Cardinal Mario Luigi Ciappi, Pope John Paul II's personal papal theologian

"It [the Third Secret] has nothing to do with Gorbachev. The Blessed Virgin was alerting us against apostasy in the Church."

... Cardinal Oddi, March 17, 1990, in the journal *Il Sabato*

"Through some crack the smoke of satan has entered into the Church of God."

... Pope Paul VI

"We must admit realistically and with feelings of deep pain, that Christians today in large measure feel lost, confused, perplexed and even disappointed; ideas opposed to the truth which has been revealed and always taught are being scattered abroad in abundance; heresies, in the full and proper sense of the word, have been spread in the area of dogma and morals, creating doubts, confusions and rebellion; the liturgy has been tampered with; immersed in an intellectual and moral relativism and therefore in permissiveness, Christians are tempted by atheism, agnosticism, vaguely moral enlightenment and by a sociological Christianity devoid of defined dogmas or an objective morality."

... Pope John Paul II

"She (the Blessed Virgin Mary) told me that the devil is in the mood for engaging in a decisive battle against the Virgin. And a decisive battle is the final battle where one side will be victorious and the other side will suffer defeat. Also from now on we must choose sides. Either we are for God or we are for the devil. There is no other possibility."

... Sister Lucy of Fatima

# Table of Contents

# The Devil's Final Battle

## Preface

The hypothetical man on the street would be surprised to learn that the terrorist attack of September 11, 2001 and the sexual scandal now wracking the Catholic Church are closely related events. But they are indeed closely related. The relation becomes apparent when the two events are viewed through the prism of the Message of Fatima.

It is often said that as the Church goes, so goes the world. That, in essence, is what the Mother of God cautioned when She came to Fatima, Portugal, 85 years ago, in a series of apparitions authenticated by a public miracle without precedent in world history. Since that time the prophetic admonitions in the Message of Fatima have all been fulfilled to the letter—save for one: the annihilation of various nations, which the Virgin of Fatima warned would be the ultimate consequence of failing to honor Her requests.

The Fatima apparitions have been deemed authentic by a series of Popes and are now commemorated in the *Roman Missal* by the decree of Pope John Paul II. And yet, in what must be seen as a mystery of iniquity, the Virgin's simple requests remain unfulfilled due to conscious decisions by some of the highest-ranking prelates in the Catholic Church. The result, just as She predicted, is an ever-deepening crisis in the Church and the world, accompanied by a growing sense, even among non-Catholics, that we are witnessing the beginning of an apocalypse.

This book was originally conceived as a compilation of some of the more important writings and speeches on Fatima in recent years.[1] It was hoped that collecting these works under one cover would give them wider distribution and longer shelf life. But this concept was soon supplanted by a better one—recasting the articles and speeches as an integral book with a coherent overall theme. With the authors' permission, Father Paul Kramer and the editorial staff of the Missionary Association sculpted the articles and speeches (adding much new material) into a work unlike anything ever published about Fatima.

It was in the process of assessing and augmenting the material that something remarkable happened: a theme emerged entirely on its own, as if by Providence. In approaching the subject of the Fatima Message from different angles, the various speakers and writers had all converged on one conclusion: the events at Fatima represent a heavenly focal point in the battle now raging for the Church and the world. Both the crisis in the Church and the crisis in the world center around the divine truths summed up with heavenly concision in the Fatima apparitions. In the fulfillment of the Message of Fatima lies the end of these twin crises. In the denial of that Message lies, in great measure, the origin and the augmentation of both.

The astounding events at Fatima were not some useless spectacle, for God does not engage in useless spectacles. The Mother of God came to earth with our present circumstances clearly in view, and with the solicitude of a mother She offered us a way out—the way chosen by God Himself for our time. That being the case, one cannot understand the state of the Church and the world today without understanding what happened at Fatima.

One must also understand the strange and systematic effort by certain Catholic churchmen to obstruct fulfillment of the heavenly imperatives of the Fatima Message, including the consecration of Russia to the Immaculate Heart of Mary, the miraculous conversion of Russia to Catholicism, and the consequent triumph of the Immaculate Heart in a period of world peace. The central importance of Fatima in the scheme of current world events is only demonstrated by the recent, almost frantic, efforts of certain Vatican officials to "deconstruct" and "demythologize" Fatima in order to avoid giving offense to various elements outside the Church—especially the Russian Orthodox, whose implacable opposition to Rome is as intense as ever after forty years of useless "ecumenical dialogue" with Vatican representatives. The pages that follow present evidence against the most prominent churchmen involved in this campaign against Fatima, laying at their feet a large portion of the blame for the ecclesial crisis and the world crisis we must all face.

To those who say that our undertaking to expose their campaign against Fatima is scandalous, we can only reply with the words of the Virgin Herself: "If My requests are heeded, Russia will be converted, and there will be peace; if not, she will spread her errors throughout the world, causing wars and persecutions of the Church. The good will be martyred; the Holy Father will have much to suffer; various nations will be annihilated." Russia has not converted. Russia's errors, including the holocaust of "legalized" abortion, have spread throughout the world. There is no peace. And today even unbelievers live in fear of the annihilation of nations. To echo the words of Pope St. Gregory the Great, it is better that scandal arise than that the truth be hidden—especially when, as in this case, the truth could avert global disaster.

We submit this work to the judgment of the Holy Catholic Church and to the judgment of you, the reader. We submit this work publicly because numerous private entreaties spread over more than five years to high Church authorities have all been unavailing. Meanwhile, the men who surround an increasingly frail Pope render him effectively incapable of responding to petitions from rank-and-file clergy and laity. At this very moment a papal deathwatch is underway, with would-be successors to the papal throne maneuvering for positions of advantage at the next conclave. As the decades-long episcopal cover-up of sexual scandals among the priesthood demonstrates, in present circumstances the public forum is the *only* forum open to Catholics who seek redress of just grievances affecting the whole Church.

Our motivation in presenting this book is that of loyal sons and daughters of the Church, who know and love the Faith and believe in conscience that the current course being followed by certain Church leaders is gravely mistaken, as recent events should make clear to any objective observer. If we have erred in any of our facts, logic or conclusions or committed any injustice, it would then be the duty of anyone and everyone who reads this book to offer us, not invective or baseless denunciations, but legitimate correction based upon *facts*—for our own sake and the sake of the Church. But if what we report, present and demonstrate is true and just, then another duty arises for each person: the duty to *act* upon the evidence we present—now, while there is still time.

Terryville, Connecticut
July 13, 2002
85th Anniversary of the Fatima Secret

## Footnote:

1. Among the principal sources of this book are: "Are There Two Original Manuscripts on the Third Secret?", Andrew M. Cesanek *(The Fatima Crusader,* Issue 64, Spring 2000); "Cardinal Ratzinger's Third Secret", Father Gregory Hesse (*The Fatima Crusader*, Issue 66, Winter 2001); "Chronology of a Cover-up", Father Paul Kramer (published on www.fatima.org); "Freemasonry and the Subversion of the Church (the *Alta Vendita*)", John Vennari (Transcript of speech from Fatima Conference in Rome, October 2001); "It Doesn't Add Up", John Vennari (*The Fatima Crusader*, Issue 70, Spring 2002); "Let us Hear the Witness for Heaven's Sake" (*The Fatima Crusader*, Issue 70, Spring 2002); "Lucy and the Pirates", Mark Fellows (*The Fatima Crusader*, Issue 70, Spring 2002); "The Lying Press Conference of June 26, 2000", Father Paul Kramer (Transcript of speech from Fatima Conference in Rome, October 2001); "Our Lady of Fatima vs. the Desire to Destroy our Catholic Heritage", John Vennari (Transcript of speech, Fatima Rally Against Terrorism, New York, Nov. 2001); "The 'Party Line' and its Relationship to Fatima", Father Paul Kramer (Transcript of speech from Fatima Conference in Rome, October 2001); "Pope John Paul II Gives Us the Key to the Real Third Secret" (Three Part series, *The Fatima Crusader,* Issues 67-69); "The Stalinization of the Catholic Church" (Transcript of speech from Fatima Conference in Rome, October 2001); "The Third Secret" (Transcript of speech from Fatima Conference in Rome, October 2001).

# Introduction

A great crime has been committed against the Catholic Church and the world at large. The perpetrators of this crime are men who hold high offices in the Catholic hierarchy; their names will be introduced in the course of this presentation.

The victims of this crime include you and your loved ones. The consequences of the crime have already been catastrophic, and if those responsible are not turned from their current course very soon, the ultimate result will be nothing short of apocalyptic in its dimensions. Indeed, even unbelievers have the sense today that the world is heading toward an apocalypse. The commission of this crime is one of the principal reasons that this is so.

The subject matter of the crime that concerns us is commonly known as the Message of Fatima. In 1917 the Mother of God consigned to three saintly children at Fatima, Portugal a message of utmost urgency for the Church and mankind; a message authenticated by an unprecedented public miracle predicted three months in advance and witnessed by 70,000 people; a message whose prophecies of future world events have thus far been fulfilled to the letter; a message pronounced worthy of belief by the highest authorities of the Catholic Church; a message whose authenticity is attested to by a succession of Popes, including the reigning Pope, who has himself alluded repeatedly to the apocalyptic elements of the message.

The nature of the crime is a systematic attempt, since the year 1960, to conceal, misrepresent and deny the authenticity of this message even as its alarming prophecies are being fulfilled before our very eyes. As we will prove, this attempt to murder the Message of Fatima has been perpetrated by none other than Churchmen at the very summit of the Catholic hierarchy—men who belong to the Vatican apparatus that surrounds an ailing and increasingly debilitated Pope.

Every crime has a motive, assuming the criminal is not insane. The men involved in this crime are not insane, and we believe they do have a motive. While motive may sometimes be difficult to prove, the evidence of motive in this case is abundant.

Without presuming that the perpetrators are conscious enemies of the Church (although some of them may well be), based on the evidence it appears that the probable motive for the crime is this: The perpetrators recognize that the contents of the Message of Fatima, as understood in the traditional Catholic sense, cannot coexist with decisions made since the Second Vatican Council (1962-65), decisions which they unswervingly carry out, to change the entire orientation of the Catholic Church. This change of orientation would (if it were possible) convert the Catholic Church from a divine institution that directs its earthly activity toward the eternal salvation of souls, to a mere co-participant with human organizations in the building up of a utopian world "brotherhood" between men of all religions or no religion at all.

This new orientation of the Church pursues a vision of the world as illusory as it is contrary to the Church's divine commission to make disciples of all nations, baptizing them in the name of the Father, the Son and the Holy Ghost. This new orientation is, in fact, the cherished goal of those organized forces which have been conspiring against the Church for nearly 300 years, and whose activities stand exposed and condemned in more papal pronouncements than have been issued on any other single subject in Church history.

Both direct and circumstantial evidence of the crime indicate that it extends to the deliberate concealment of that part of the Message of Fatima which predicts precisely this attempt to change the orientation of the Church, and the ruinous consequences of that attempt. The hidden portion of the Message, commonly known as the Third Secret of Fatima, would thus be a heavenly indictment of decisions made and actions taken by the very men who have perpetrated this crime.

The evidence shows that the crime also extends to tampering with the last surviving witness to the Fatima Message, Sister Lucia dos Santos. Sister Lucy has been subjected to secret "interviews" and other forms of pressure in an effort to alter her unvarying testimony on the authentic content of the Message, which stands in the way of the perpetrators' pursuit of the new orientation of the Church.

This is the crime, and this is the motive. Now it is our burden to prove both. We will endeavor to do so in the succeeding pages, using the very statements of the accused, the testimony of other witnesses, and a great deal of other evidence to establish their guilt. And when we are done presenting the evidence, we shall ask you, the reader, to render a verdict. Not a verdict in the legal sense, for we have no right to constitute ourselves an ecclesiastical court. We mean, rather, a verdict representing the conscientious belief of members of the faithful that good grounds exist for investigation of the crime we allege here, and for its prosecution by the highest authority in the Church: the Supreme Pontiff, John Paul II, or his successor, as the case may be.

We shall ask you, then, to render a verdict that amounts to a kind of indictment of the accused for the crime alleged. We shall also ask for your help in handing up that indictment to the Pope, in keeping with the God-given right of the faithful—infallibly defined by the First Vatican Council and guaranteed by Church law—to petition the Supreme Pontiff directly and immediately for the redress of just grievances in the Church. In making these requests we have in mind as well the teaching of Saint Thomas Aquinas, and the unanimous teaching of the doctors and theologians of the Church, that "if the faith were endangered, a subject ought to rebuke his prelate even publicly."

In considering the evidence we are about to present, we ask you to keep one overarching principle in mind: As Saint Thomas teaches, there is no argument against a fact—*contra factum non argumentum est.* If a statement is contrary to fact, then no authority on earth can expect us to believe it. Thus, for example, if a high-ranking prelate in the Vatican were to issue a decree that Catholics must believe that the Eiffel Tower is located in Saint Peter's Square, that would not make it so, and we would be obliged to reject the decree. For the *fact* is that the Eiffel Tower is located in Paris, and there is no argument against that fact. Therefore, *no man, no matter what his authority, can demand that we believe something that is manifestly contrary to fact*.

As you shall see, however, the crime involving Fatima is largely an attempt by certain men who enjoy high offices in the Church to impose upon Catholics an understanding of the Message of Fatima that is plainly contrary to fact—as, for example, the claim by these men that a consecration of Russia to the Immaculate Heart of Mary can be accomplished by consecrating the world, while deliberately avoiding any mention of Russia.

As the Church itself teaches (cf. Vatican I and John Paul II's encyclical *Fides et Ratio*), the faith does not conflict with reason. Catholics are not expected to suspend the use of their reason, their common sense, in order to be Catholics. That would not be faith, but blindness—the blindness of the Pharisees. And so it is with the Message of Fatima. No matter what some men in the Vatican would prefer, *the Church* does not expect us to believe nonsense when it comes to what the Message really means.

We ask you, then, to use your *common sense*, to keep an open mind, to consider the evidence dispassionately, and then decide. Indeed, you *must* decide. For if the charge we have made is true, then what is at stake in this case is nothing less than the salvation of millions of souls (possibly including your own), the welfare of the Church and the survival of civilization itself in this age of humanity. For no other reason did the Mother of God deliver the Message of Fatima to our increasingly endangered world.

# Chapter 1

## The Message and the Miracle

God does not waste miracles. Throughout salvation history—from Joshua, to Moses, to the Twelve Apostles, to the saints of the Catholic Church down through the centuries—God has granted miracles for one overriding purpose: to serve as a divine credential for a witness who invokes the miracle in His name. When God chooses a witness, and then associates an authentic miracle with the testimony of that witness, we can know for certain that the witness is worthy of belief. God does not grant miracles to vouch for unreliable witnesses; God does not *choose* unreliable witnesses.

No, God does not waste miracles. Much less does God waste a public miracle witnessed by 70,000 people, believers and unbelievers alike, which occurred at precisely the moment predicted three months earlier by three witnesses whose testimony had been doubted: Lucia dos Santos (known to the world as Lucy), and her cousins, Francisco and Jacinta Marto.[1]

It is October 13, 1917. In a humble field known as the Cova da Iria in Fatima some 70,000 people have assembled to await the happening of a miracle. This in itself is astounding. For never before in salvation history has a visionary predicted months in advance that a public miracle would occur at a precise time and place. Never before has a vast crowd assembled to witness a predicted public miracle. Yet that is exactly what was happening on this day.

Why this day? Because Lucia dos Santos and her cousins Francisco and Jacinta had been receiving apparitions from "the Lady" on the thirteenth of each month since the previous May. The Lady had been appearing to them above a holm-oak tree in the Cova, and with each apparition the crowds had grown. But doubts about the veracity of the seers had also grown, as well as mockery and persecution of the seers and their families at a time when Portugal was under the control of an atheistic and Masonic political regime.

And then, on July 13, 1917, the Lady had shown them something which would terrify them and change them forever, making them into saints who would spend their lives (in the case of Francisco and Jacinta, very brief lives) praying and making sacrifices for sinners. As Lucy recounts in testimony the Catholic Church has deemed worthy of belief, the Lady showed them hell:

> She opened Her hands once more, as She had done during the two previous months. The rays of light seemed to penetrate the earth, and we saw as it were a sea of fire. Plunged in this fire were demons and souls [of the damned] in human form, like transparent burning embers, all blackened or burnished bronze, floating about in the conflagration, now raised into the air by the flames that issued from within themselves together with great clouds of smoke, now falling

back on every side like sparks in huge fires, without weight or equilibrium, amid shrieks and groans of pain and despair, which horrified us and made us tremble with fear. (It must have been this sight which caused me to cry out, as people say they heard me). The demons could be distinguished [from the souls of the damned] by their terrifying and repellent likeness to frightful and unknown animals, black and transparent like burning coals.[2] This vision lasted but an instant. How can we ever be grateful enough to our kind heavenly Mother, Who had already prepared us by promising, in the first apparition, to take us to Heaven. Otherwise, I think we would have died of fear and terror.[3]

Having shown the children the fate of the damned, which is considered the first part of the Great Secret of Fatima, the Lady then confided to the children the second part. Everyone, including those members of the Vatican apparatus who are the focus of this presentation, agrees that the second part of the Secret, as recorded in Sister Lucy's diaries, is as follows:

> You have seen hell where the souls of poor sinners go. To save them, God wishes to establish in the world devotion to My Immaculate Heart. If what I say to you is done, many souls will be saved and there will be peace. The war is going to end; but if people do not cease offending God, a worse one will break out during the reign of Pius XI. When you see a night illumined by an unknown light, know that this is the great sign given you by God that He is about to punish the world for its crimes, by means of war, famine, and persecutions against the Church and of the Holy Father.
>
> To prevent this, I shall come to ask for the Consecration of Russia to My Immaculate Heart, and the Communion of Reparation on the First Saturdays. If My requests are heeded, Russia will be converted, and there will be peace; if not, she will spread her errors throughout the world, causing wars and persecutions of the Church. The good will be martyred, the Holy Father will have much to suffer, various nations will be annihilated. In the end, My Immaculate Heart will triumph. The Holy Father will consecrate Russia to Me, and she will be converted, and a period of peace will be granted to the world. In Portugal the dogma of the Faith will always be preserved etc. Do not tell this to anybody. Francisco, yes, you may tell him.[4]

The basic elements of this astonishing Message are these:

- Many souls go to hell because of the sins they commit.
- To save them, God wishes to establish throughout the world the uniquely Catholic devotion to the Immaculate Heart of Mary.
- This is to be accomplished by consecrating the nation of Russia to the Immaculate Heart of Mary (in conjunction with the

Communions of Reparation on the first Saturdays of each month), whereupon Russia will be converted to the Catholic faith.

- If this is done, many souls will be saved and there will be peace.
- If it is *not* done, Russia will spread its errors throughout the world. There will be wars, famine, persecutions of the Church, and martyrdom of the good. The Holy Father will have much to suffer. And if Our Lady's requests are still not obeyed, then various nations will be annihilated.
- Nevertheless, "In the end, My Immaculate Heart will triumph. The Holy Father will consecrate Russia to Me, which will be converted, and a period of peace will be given to mankind."

To these things, the Lady added an urgent request that Catholics include in their recitation of the Rosary at the end of each decade, the following prayer: "O my Jesus, forgive us our sins, save us from the fires of hell. Lead all souls to Heaven, especially those most in need." In obedience to the Lady's request, and as a testament to the authenticity of Her apparitions at Fatima, the Church included this prayer in the Rosary, and Catholics recite it to this day.

The Church has also adopted the First Saturday devotion of the Communion of Reparation, which the Lady explained thusly: "I promise to help at the hour of death, with all the graces needed for salvation, whoever on the First Saturday of five consecutive months shall: confess and receive Holy Communion, recite five decades of the Holy Rosary, and keep Me company for fifteen minutes while meditating on the fifteen mysteries of the Rosary, with the intention of making reparation to Me."

We pause here to note in passing (for further discussion later) the curious phrase at the end of the first two parts of the Secret: "In Portugal the dogma of the Faith will always be preserved etc." The incomplete phrase, ending with "etc.", appears in Sister Lucy's fourth memoir of the apparitions. It clearly introduces a heavenly prediction, containing further words of Our Lady not recorded, about the state of adherence to Catholic dogma in the Church at large, distinguished from Portugal in particular, where the dogma of the Faith will always be preserved.

Standing alone, the observation about adherence to Catholic dogma in Portugal appears gratuitous and quite senseless, for the phrase does not at all follow logically from the first two parts of the Secret. Every recognized Fatima scholar concluded from this that the phrase represents the beginning of a third part of the Secret—what came to be known simply as the Third Secret of Fatima. As we shall see, Lucy was so terrified by its contents that even after she was ordered to write it down in October of 1943, she was unable to do so until the subsequent apparition on January 2, 1944 in which Our Lady assured her that it ought to be done. And yet, to this day, the Vatican has never revealed the words of the Virgin which clearly follow "In Portugal the dogma of the

Faith will always be preserved etc." The "etc." remains a secret. This ongoing concealment is a key element of the crime that is the subject of this book.

Having received from Heaven itself a message with obviously profound importance for the Church and all humanity, Lucy knew that she and her cousins needed a divine credential if they were to be believed. During the apparition on July 13, Sister Lucy asked the Lady "to tell us who You are, and to work a miracle, so that everybody will believe that You are appearing to us." And the Lady replied: "Continue to come here every month. In October I will tell you who I am and what I want, and I will perform a miracle for all to see and believe."[5] The Lady repeated this promise in further apparitions to Lucy and the other seers on August 19 and again, at the Cova, on September 13.

And so the people had assembled in a great crowd at the Cova on October 13. And at precisely the hour predicted in July—12 noon solar time, and 1:30 p.m. by the clock in Portugal—it begins. Lucy suddenly tells the people in the crowd to shut their umbrellas in the midst of a drenching rain which has turned the Cova to mud. She then goes into an ecstasy, and the Lady, appearing again, first tells Lucy who She is and what She wants, just as She had promised: "I want a chapel to be built here in My honor. I am the Lady of the Rosary." The Lady is the Mother of God, the Virgin Mary, who will henceforth also be known under the title Our Lady of Fatima, one of many bestowed upon the Blessed Virgin by the Church. The chapel, of course, was built, and then rebuilt after being blown up on March 6, 1922 by a bomb placed there by the friends of the Tinsmith, a nickname for the Masonic mayor of Ourem.[6]

And then the Miracle began. We recount here the testimony of a reporter who cannot possibly be accused of partiality in this matter and for a good reason! We refer to Avelino de Almeida, the chief editor of *O Seculo*, the large "liberal" anticlerical and Masonic daily newspaper of Lisbon. He writes:

> From the road, where the carriages were crowded together and where hundreds of persons had stayed for want of sufficient courage to advance across the muddy ground, we saw the huge crowd turn towards the sun which appeared at its zenith, clear of the clouds. It resembled a disc of silver, and it was possible to stare at it without the least discomfort. It did not burn the eyes. It did not blind. We would say that it produced an eclipse. Then a tremendous cry rang out, and the crowd nearest us were heard to shout: "Miracle! Miracle! ... Marvel! ... Marvel!" Before the dazzled eyes of the people, whose attitude transported us to biblical times, and who, dumbfounded, heads uncovered, contemplated the blue of the sky, the sun trembled, it made strange and abrupt movements, outside of all cosmic laws, "the sun danced", according to the typical expression of the peasants ...[7]

Attacked violently by all the anticlerical press, Avelino de Almeida renewed his testimony, fifteen days later, in his review, *Ilustração Portuguesa*.

This time he illustrated his account with a dozen photographs of the huge ecstatic crowd, and repeated as a refrain throughout his article: "I saw ... I saw ... I saw." And he concluded fortuitously: "Miracle, as the people shouted? Natural phenomenon, as the experts say? For the moment, that does not concern me, I am only saying what I saw... The rest is a matter for Science and the Church."[8]

Saturday, October 13 begins for the pilgrims as a walk of penance because it had rained the whole preceding night. Now, this "almost sudden change of weather, with the dusty roads transformed into muddy quagmires by a pelting rain, causing to replace abruptly, for a day, the sweetness of autumn with the biting rigors of winter, did not succeed in moving them, to make them give up or despair."[9]

In comparing the numerous accounts of witnesses, we can distinguish the diverse aspects and the result of the astounding phenomena seen by all. For each one of the phenomena, it would be possible to line up some ten pages of witnesses which would constitute in themselves an impressive book.

Here is the first marvelous fact described by Dr. Almeida Garrett:

> It must have been 1:30 p.m. when there arose at the exact spot where the children were, a column of smoke, thin, fine and bluish, which extended up to perhaps two meters above their heads, and evaporated at that height. This phenomenon, perfectly visible to the naked eye, lasted for a few seconds. Not having noted how long it had lasted, I cannot say whether it was more or less than a minute. The smoke dissipated abruptly, and after some time, it came back to occur a second time, then a third time ...[10]

Whereas "the low and heavy sky had a very dark color, laden with moisture, [which] released an abundant and long lasting rain," during the time of the apparition, the rain stopped totally. Abruptly the sky cleared: "The sun triumphantly pierced the thick bed of clouds hiding it until then, and shone intensely." (Dr. Almeida Garrett) This abrupt change of weather took all the eyewitnesses by surprise: "It was a day of heavy and continuous rain. But a few minutes before the miracle, it stopped raining." (Alfredo da Silva Santos)

And this testimony from a physician, a man of science, concerning the inexplicable silvering of the sun, allowing it to be viewed directly without harm to the eyes:

> "Suddenly I heard the uproar of thousands of voices, and I saw the whole multitude spread out in that vast space at my feet ... turn their backs to that spot where, until then, all their expectations focused, and look at the sun on the other side ... I turned around, too, toward the point commanding their gazes, and I could see the sun, like a very clear disc, with its sharp edge, which gleamed without hurting the sight ... It could not be confused with the sun seen through a fog (there was no fog at that moment), for it was neither veiled, nor dim. At Fatima, it kept its light and heat, and stood out clearly in the sky, with

a sharp edge, like a large gaming table. The most astonishing thing was to be able to stare at the solar disc for a long time, brilliant with light and heat, without hurting the eyes, or damaging the retina." (Dr. Almeida Garrett)[11]

In the same vein this testimony by the editor-in-chief of *O Seculo*:

"And then we witnessed a unique spectacle, an incredible spectacle, unbelievable if you did not witness it. From above the road ... We see the immense crowd turn towards the sun, which appeared at its zenith, clear of the clouds. It looked like a plate of dull silver, and it was possible to stare at it without the least discomfort. It did not burn the eyes. It did not blind. One might say that an eclipse had occurred." (Article of October 15, 1917)

And likewise: "The people could look at the sun as we look at the moon." (Maria do Carmo)[12]

One could multiply endlessly the testimonies about the ensuing solar phenomena, witnessed even by the secular editor-in-chief of an anticlerical newspaper. Consider these:

"It shook and trembled; it seemed like a wheel of fire." (Maria da Capelinha)[13]

"The sun turned like a fire wheel, taking on all the colors of the rainbow." (Maria do Carmo)[14]

"It appeared like a globe of snow turning on itself." (Father Lourenço)[15]

"The pearl-like disc had a giddy motion. This was not the twinkling of a star in all its brilliance. It turned on itself with impetuous speed." (Dr. Almeida Garrett)[16]

"At a certain moment, the sun stopped and then began again to dance, to spin; it stopped again, and began again to dance." (Ti Marto)[17]

"The sun took on all the colors of the rainbow. Everything assumed those same colors: our faces, our clothes, the earth itself." (Maria do Carmo)[18]

"A light, whose colors changed from one moment to the next, was reflected on the people and on things." (Dr. Pereira Gens)[19]

What happened next constitutes the most terrifying aspect of the Miracle, and one with profound implications for our era, in which man has perfected the ability to destroy the whole world with fire from the sky: the sun appeared to detach itself from the sky and plunge toward the earth.

"We suddenly heard a clamor, like a cry of anguish of that entire crowd. The sun, in fact, keeping its rapid movement of rotation, seemed to free itself from the firmament and blood-red, to plunge towards the earth, threatening to crush us with its fiery mass. Those were some terrifying seconds." (Dr. Almeida Garrett)[20]

"I saw the sun turn and it seemed to descend. It was like a bicycle wheel." (John Carreira)[21]

"The sun began to dance and, at a certain moment, it appeared to detach itself from the firmament and to rush forward on us, like a fire wheel." (Alfredo da Silva Santos)[22]

"I saw it perfectly descending as if it came to crash on the earth. It seemed to detach itself from the sky and rush toward us. It maintained itself at a short distance above our heads; but that sort of attack was of very short duration... It seemed very near the people and it continued to turn in the opposite direction." (Maria do Carmo)[23]

"Suddenly, the sun appeared with its circumference well-defined. It came down as if to the height of the clouds and began to whirl giddily upon itself like a captive ball of fire. With some interruptions, this lasted about eight minutes." (Father Pereira da Silva)[24]

"It suddenly seemed to come down in a zig-zag, menacing the earth." (Father Lourenço)[25]

"Seeing the sun falling on us ..." (Father John Gomes)[26]

"Finally, the sun stopped and everybody breathed a sigh of relief ..." (Maria da Capelinha)[27]

"From those thousands of mouths I heard shouts of joy and love to the Most Holy Virgin. And then I believed. I had the certainty of not having been the victim of a suggestion. I had seen the sun as I would never see it again." (Mario Godinho, an engineer)[28]

Another astonishing fact: all those people, who were for the most part soaked to the bone, verified with joy and amazement that they were dry. The fact is attested to in the canonical process for Jacinta and Francisco, who were ultimately beatified on May 13, 2000.

"The moment one would least expect it, our clothes were totally dry." (Maria do Carmo)[29]

"My suit dried in an instant." (John Carreira)[30]

The academician Marques da Cruz testified as follows:

This enormous multitude was drenched, for it had rained unceasingly since dawn. But—though this may appear incredible—after the great miracle everyone felt comfortable, and found his garments quite dry, a subject of general wonder ... The truth of this fact has been guaranteed with the greatest sincerity by dozens and dozens of persons of absolute trustworthiness, whom I have known intimately from childhood, and who are still alive (1937), as well as by persons from various districts of the country who were present.[31]

And finally, there were also moral miracles of the conversions of many people. In his book, *Meet the Witnesses*, John Haffert writes:

> The captain of the regiment of soldiers on the mountain that day—with orders to prevent the gathering of the crowd—was converted instantly. Apparently so were hundreds of other unbelievers, as their testimony will show.[32]
>
> "There was an unbeliever there who had spent the morning mocking the 'simpletons' who had gone off to Fatima just to see an ordinary girl. He now seemed paralyzed, his eyes fixed on the sun. He began to tremble from head to foot, and lifting up his arms, fell on his knees in the mud, crying out to God." (Father Lourenço)[33]
>
> "I live eighteen miles from Fatima. And in May of 1917 we were told about the extraordinary apparitions, but the news came to us mixed up with the fantasy of the people. Naturally I did not believe. I sincerely supposed it was only (the) imagination of someone. ... At my mother's request, I went once more to Cova da Iria in August at the time of the apparitions. Once more I came back discouraged and disappointed. But that time, something extraordinary happened. My mother, who had had a large tumor in one of her eyes for many years, was cured. The doctors who had attended her said they could not explain such a cure. Still I did not believe in the apparitions. Finally, and again at my mother's request, I went to the Cova da Iria once more on the thirteenth of October. ... In spite of what had happened to my mother, I was disappointed and did not believe in the apparitions. So I sat inside my car. Then all at once I noticed that everybody looked at the sky. Natural curiosity attracted my attention, and I got out of the car and looked at the sky, too. ... From those hundreds of mouths I heard words of belief and of love to the Blessed Virgin. And then I believed." (Mario Godinho, an engineer)[34]

A number of other cases of cures and conversions are documented in, among other places, the following books: *Documentação Crítica de Fátima* and *Fatima from the Beginning*.[35]

To those who would say the miracle was a product of "mass hysteria" at the scene, God Himself arranged a ready rebuttal: the phenomenon could be admired from beyond Fatima. Perfectly credible witnesses, who were very far from the Cova da Iria, related having seen the unprecedented spectacle of the dance of the sun, exactly like the 70,000 pilgrims gathered around the holm-oak where the Virgin had appeared.[36]

In the small village of Alburitel, situated about ten miles from Fatima, the whole town was able to enjoy the vision of the solar prodigy. The testimony frequently quoted is that of Father Inacio Lourenço, because it is the most detailed. But what he relates having seen, all the villagers, questioned by the investigators, confirmed seeing it exactly the same way.

The witnesses of the event were indeed innumerable, their testimonies agree and we are flooded with the documents they have left us.[37]

In the first place, numerous accounts appeared at once in the Portuguese press. It is noteworthy that the first to provide testimony were the anticlerical reporters. The three articles of Avelino de Almeida—the one of October 13, immediately before the event; the other of October 15, edited at Vila Nova de Ourem on the evening of the 13th; and a third article of October 29—merit a special mention. In spite of the jeering tone and Voltarian irony which inspire in part the first article, in spite of the expected anticlerical tones which still appear in the article of the 15th, these texts from a talented reporter, one who besides, is honest and conscientious, are historical documents of prime importance[38]. But he was not the only one to relate the facts, for other reporters were present at the Cova da Iria.

Next there were the official investigations. In November 1917, at the request of Bishop de Lima Vidal, who was then directing the diocese of Lisbon, the parish priest of Fatima led his investigation and questioned several witnesses of the parish. Unfortunately, he transcribed only four depositions!

The investigations of the historians fortunately compensated for the negligence of the official investigators. The report of Father Formigao, who obtained from Dr. José Maria de Almeida Garrett, professor at the Faculty of Sciences of Coimbra, a very thorough account, is the most scientific report in our possession[39]. In addition, we have the reports of Father da Fonseca (whose work was done in order to verify the points disputed by Father Dhanis,[40] who refused to examine the evidence), Father de Marchi, Canon Barthas, Father Dias Coelho and Father Richard.

In 1977, to commemorate the sixtieth anniversary of the last apparition, it was still possible to assemble in Fatima more than thirty persons who had been present at the solar prodigy and who could reveal their memories. Thanks to those numerous testimonies, it is possible to reconstruct a precise running commentary, allowing us to relive, hour-by-hour and minute-by-minute, this decisive day, assuredly one of the most important in the history of the world. Indeed, the evidence of the solar miracle on October 13, 1917 was so overwhelming that in 1952 even Hollywood vouched for its authenticity by releasing a classic film (starring Gilbert Roland) entitled "The Miracle of Our Lady of Fatima", which is still being sold on videotape today.

Why was this day so important? Because it was the day on which a heavenly Message from the Mother of God was authenticated beyond any reasonable doubt; a message which, more than 84 years later, stands at the heart of the perilous situation of the Church and the world at this very moment in human history, offering us a way out.

# Chapter 2

## The Long Opposition Begins

Even a cursory reading of the first two parts of the Great Secret in the Message of Fatima reveals that it is a heavenly challenge to the powers of the world, whose hold on even Catholic Portugal had been increasing since the beginning of the 20th Century.

Recalling the text of the Secret set forth in the first chapter, it is obvious that what Heaven has proposed therein would be anathema to the Masonic regime in Portugal, and indeed to all of the organized forces against the Church which, at the beginning of the last century, were plotting (by their own admission, as we shall see) a final assault upon the Catholic citadel. The basic elements of the Message constitute a veritable charter of opposition to these forces: saving souls from hell; the establishment throughout the world of a Catholic devotion to the Immaculate Heart of Mary; the consecration of Russia to that Immaculate Heart, and Russia's consequent conversion to Catholicism; world peace borne of the triumph of the Immaculate Heart.

The Message of Fatima is important for the salvation of souls; that much is completely obvious. But somewhat less obvious—and this is what will come to infuriate both the external and internal enemies of the Church—the Message and Our Lady's appearance are also very important for the correct ordering of human society. If mankind heeds the Virgin's message, then peace among individuals, families, cities and countries, and in fact the whole world, can be achieved in the form of *Catholic social order*. (We shall see in the next chapter that this social order is not some utopian dream, but a thing which has been achieved even in the 20th Century—in Portugal, through its Consecration to the Immaculate Heart of Mary in 1931.) To be sure, Original Sin would remain, but we would see a period in human history like that prophesied by Isaias, who, under divine inspiration, envisioned a time when men would make war no more, would learn the art of war no more, but would beat their swords into plowshares.[1] The tendency of man toward sin would be vastly ameliorated and controlled by the beneficent influence of the Church and Her sacraments. And who, looking upon the world today, could seriously argue that even the worst "excesses" of men in the Catholic social order that once existed in pre-"Reformation" Europe are anything at all when compared with the evil and violence which have been virtually institutionalized in every nation in our time—first and foremost the endless holocaust of "legalized" abortion.

The implications flowing from the simple text of the Great Secret of Fatima are plain enough to anyone of minimal intelligence: Such a plan for peace in the world could only be achieved if enough individuals, at every level of society, cooperated. The plan could succeed, even then, only if it were based on the designs of the Creator of mankind, Who has anointed Jesus Christ, the Redeemer of mankind, as King of kings and Lord of lords (Apoc. 19:16). Jesus is King, not only of individuals but also of societies and the whole world. Therefore, if this plan of the Blessed Virgin Mary, Who is Queen of Heaven and of earth, is to work, mankind must acknowledge the sovereign Kingship of Christ over all mankind as it is exercised through His Catholic Church. That men will, in fact, be moved to do so in sufficient numbers—first in Russia and then elsewhere—is the very miracle promised by the Virgin if Her requests are honored.

One can understand that the prince of this world, as Jesus Christ referred to the devil, would not accept easily the proposed destruction of his flourishing kingdom here on earth. Nor would this peace plan from Heaven be accepted by those men, associations and secret societies whose power and ill-gotten riches would be forfeited if the plan were put into effect and the conversion of Russia and the triumph of the Immaculate Heart—and thus of the Catholic Faith—were to follow.

With this background we can better appreciate why fierce opposition to the Message of Fatima arose even while the apparitions were going on, and why it continues to this day, enlisting even men within the Church as opponents of the requests of the Virgin.

At the time of the Fatima apparitions, the Mayor of Ourem, the county seat to which Fatima and Aljustrel (the village where the children who had seen Our Lady lived) belonged, was Arturo de Oliveira Santos, a blacksmith by trade, who professed no belief in God. His formal education had been slight, and his ambitions were large. Arturo Santos was a self-propelled and intrepid young man, who became the editor of the *Ouriense*, a local gazette in which his anti-monarchial and anti-religious opinions were expressed with bitter zeal and with some talent. At twenty-six he joined the Grand Orient Masonic Lodge at Leiria.

As the great Catholic historian, William Thomas Walsh, points out, Santos became indoctrinated with the esoteric lore of a syncretistic and naturalistic religion which had been the main opponent of the Catholic Church in modern times, and which had already boasted that, by planning and carrying out the Portuguese revolution of 1910, it had taken a long step toward the total elimination of Christianity in the Iberian Peninsula. Walsh further informs us that in 1911 the Grand Orient chief, Magahaes Lima, predicted that in a few years no young man would wish to study for the priesthood in Portugal, while the prominent Portuguese Mason Alfonso Costa assured all his brethren, and some delegates from the French lodges, that one more generation would see the finish of Catholicism, "the principal cause of the sad condition into which our country has fallen". Indeed there was much evidence to support the prediction, but not the accusation.

Professor Walsh goes on to note that in 1911 the new masters of Portugal seized Church property, scattered, imprisoned and exiled hundreds of priests and nuns, and gave the Cardinal Patriarch of Lisbon five days to leave that city, never to return. Refugee priests and religious fled to France and elsewhere. Some knelt at Lourdes and prayed to the Mother of God to help their unhappy country, once proud to call itself "The Land of Holy Mary", now a spectacle of unbelief and anarchy, with a new revolution every month.

Arturo Santos founded a new Masonic lodge in Ourem, where he had moved his blacksmith shop, and by 1917 he had become its president. Through friends in his brotherhood, he was able to become Mayor of Ourem. This title carried with it the corollary titles of President of the town Administration and of the Chamber, and Deputy Judge of Commerce. With all these honors and their companion authority, Senhor Santos became the most feared and influential man in his section of Portugal.

During his administration, fewer and fewer people went to Mass and the Sacraments, there were more divorces, and there were not so many children. When he arrested six priests and held them incommunicado for eight days, the leading Catholic laymen in the Council and the Chamber were too busy making profitable compromises so they did not have time to protest loudly enough to be heard. To the blacksmith and his friends the fight for "progress and enlightenment", as they preferred to describe their conflict with the Catholic Church, was all but won.[2]

By August of 1917 all Portugal knew the story of the Apparitions at Fatima, although in a variety of versions. The journalists of the anti-religious press enjoyed writing comical versions of the story. As Father de Marchi records the attitude of the anti-religious press, they claimed that: "these children were the puppets of the Jesuits. Not the Jesuits? Well, then, the clergy in general, or the Pope, in particular—luring ignorant and unwary people to the Cova da Iria, in order to fleece them of their money. They didn't have any money? Well, then, of their political allegiance, so that the humane fabric of the enlightened Republic could be sabotaged to the advantage of Rome and Reaction. The press enjoyed its jolly excursions. The Freemasons were delighted."[3] All loyal supporters of the reigning New Order found the situation increasingly humorous.

But Arturo Santos, the Mayor of Ourem, did not find it so humorous because the open manifestation of religion was happening in his own county. Some of his constituents already believed that Our Lady was appearing at Fatima, and he could not think what explanations he could provide his political colleagues if this Christian religious manifestation, which was contrary to the Mayor's hopes of building a Godless Republic, continued to thrive in his own county. So he decided to bring the heavy fist of the law down upon the three seers.

On August 11, 1917, the Mayor of Ourem ordered the parents of the three children to present them for trial at the City Hall. Ti Marto, the father of Jacinta and Francisco, said, "There's no sense in taking such young children before a court of that kind. Besides, it's three leagues, and that's too far for them to walk. And they don't know how to ride on a beast. I'm not going to do it. And I'll go over and tell the Administrator why." His wife Olimpia agreed.

Lucy's father, Antonio, however was inclined to agree with his wife Maria Rosa that if Lucy was lying, it would be a good thing to have her taught a lesson, while if she was telling the truth (and they doubted she was), then Our Lady would take care of her. Antonio put his daughter on the back of a burro (she fell off 3 times on the way) and they set off on the journey to see the Mayor. Ti Marto left his children at home and went by himself to speak on their behalf. Before the journey, Jacinta said to Lucy, "Never mind. If they kill you, you just tell them that I am like you, and Francisco more so, and that we want to die too. And now I will go with Francisco to the well to pray very hard for you."

The Mayor asked Lucy if she had seen a Lady at the Cova da Iria, and who she thought it was. He demanded that she tell him the secret that Our Lady had confided to the children, and promise never to return to the Cova da Iria again. Lucy refused to tell him the secret and to make such a promise. (Our Lady had asked the children to return to the Cova da Iria on the 13th day of each month, and they had promised to go there at the appointed time and date for the next 3 visits as well.) Then the Mayor asked Antonio if the people in Fatima believed the story, and he replied, "Oh no, sir! All this is just women's tales."

"And what do you say?" the Mayor asked Ti Marto. "I am here at your command," he replied, "and my children say the same things I do." "Then you think it is true?" "Yes, sir, I believe what they say."

The bystanders laughed. The Mayor made a gesture of dismissal and one of his men told them to go. The Mayor followed them to the door and said to Lucy, "If you don't tell that secret, it will cost you your life!" Then Lucy and her father and Ti Marto returned to Aljustrel.

In the evening of August 12, three policemen summoned the children to the house of Ti Marto, where the Mayor was waiting for them in person. He told the children that death might be the penalty for not revealing the Great Secret they had learned on July 13. The children refused to tell it, on the grounds that they could not disobey Our Lady. "Never mind," whispered Jacinta to the others. "If they kill us, so much the better, for then we shall see Jesus and Our Lady."

On the morning of August 13, Ti Marto was out working in the fields. He came into the house to wash the soil off his hands. There was a crowd of people around the house, who had come to be present at the apparition that was to take place that day at the Cova da Iria. His wife Olimpia was upset and she pointed towards the living room. Ti Marto went into the living room, and as we read in his own account of it to Father de Marchi: "Who should I see but the Mayor himself. Even then, I suppose, I wasn't very polite to him, because I saw a priest was there too, and I went first to shake hands with the priest. Then I said to the Mayor, 'I did not expect to see you here, sir.' "

The Mayor said he would take the children to the Cova da Iria in his wagon, and he said it would give them time to talk to the parish priest at Fatima, who, he said, wanted to question them. The children and their parents had misgivings about his suggestion of taking them in his wagon, but they complied. He took them first to see the parish priest at Fatima, and then, instead of taking them to the Cova da Iria, people saw him crack the whip and make the horse bolt off down the road in the opposite direction. He took them to Ourem, and locked them in a room in his house.

There were about fifteen thousand people at the Cova da Iria, and everyone wondered where the children were. At the time Our Lady was to appear, a number of supernatural manifestations occurred that were also noticed by the crowd at Her other apparitions at Fatima, which convinced many people, even unbelievers, that She had arrived. But the children were not there to receive Her message. Then some people arrived with the news that the Mayor of Ourem had kidnaped the children and had taken them first to the parish priest of Fatima and then to his own house at Ourem. The crowd quickly concluded that the two had conspired together in the kidnaping, which they felt had "spoiled the apparition and disappointed the Mother of God." Bitter voices were raised against the Mayor and the parish priest. But Ti Marto persuaded the crowd not to take revenge. "Boys, take it easy! Don't hurt anyone! Whoever deserves punishment will receive it. All this is (allowed) by the power of the One above!"

The next morning the Mayor of Ourem again interrogated the children, who again said they had seen a beautiful Lady, and again refused to tell him the Secret, even when he threatened them with life imprisonment, torture and death. The Mayor was resolved to obtain from the children some sort of admission that would end the religious manifestation taking place in his county. So he then had them thrown into the town jail, with its dark and bad-smelling cells with iron bars. They were put into the common room where most of the prisoners were herded together. The children were frightened and sad, especially the seven-year-old Jacinta, who thought she would never see her parents again. But they reassured one another, reminding each other of what Our Lady had told them about Heaven, and they offered their sufferings for the conversion of sinners. The children prayed the Rosary in the prison, and the convicts joined in the prayers.

Some time later, the Mayor had the children brought before him by a policeman, and he made a final demand for the Secret. Then, since they again refused to tell it, he told them they would be boiled alive in oil. He shouted a command, and a guard opened a door. He asked the guard if the oil was good and hot, and he replied it was. Then he ordered the guard to throw the youngest, Jacinta, into the boiling oil first. The guard seized the child and carried her away. A guard saw Francisco moving his lips silently, and he asked him what he was saying. "An Ave Maria", Francisco replied, "so my little sister will not be afraid." Lucy and Francisco were convinced that the guard would soon come back to kill them too. Francisco said to Lucy, "What do we care if they kill us? We'll go right to Heaven."

Later the guard came back to the room where the children were being questioned by the Mayor, and informed Lucy and Francisco that Jacinta had been boiled in oil since she would not reveal the Secret. And the Mayor tried to persuade the remaining two children to reveal the Secret or the same thing would happen to them. Since they would not reveal the Secret, Francisco was taken away to the same fate. Afterwards, the guard came for Lucy. Even though she believed that Francisco and Jacinta had been killed for not revealing the Secret, she too would rather die than reveal the Secret the Blessed Virgin had entrusted to her. So she also was taken under the custody of the guard to what she thought was certain death.

It turned out that Jacinta had simply been led to another room, and Francisco and Lucy, when it was their turn to be "boiled in oil", were led to the same room, and they were all together again. It had just been a trick to frighten them into revealing the secret. Lucy, writing in her memoirs, recalling the incident, informs us that she was certain, as were her two cousins, that they were about to be martyred at the hands of the Mayor.

The next morning, with another interrogation, the Mayor still was unable to get them to reveal the Secret. So he admitted it was no use, and ordered them sent back to Fatima. It was August 15, the Feast of the Assumption of Our Lady.

That the Masonic mayor of Ourem would go so far as to threaten three little children with a horrible death in order to prevent people from believing and openly manifesting their faith in God, His Holy Mother and the Catholic Church, gives some indication of the extent to which the Freemasons would go in their desperation to level the Church once and for all and erect in its place their Godless Republic—not only in Portugal, but throughout the whole world.

# Chapter 3

## Heaven's Peace Plan in Microcosm

The "enlightened" minds of the "modern world" scoff at the notion that a simple public ceremony consecrating Russia to the Immaculate Heart of Mary could produce the conversion of that nation, and with it enormous benefits to the whole world, including peace among nations. But then, the "modern world" scoffs at miracles in general, and indeed at the divine claims of the Church whose saints have performed miracles in such abundance.

But a consecration of Russia is precisely what God had ordained in the very Message He authenticated with the solar miracle of October 13, 1917—a message which, we hasten to point out again, has received the approbation of the Catholic Church's highest authorities, including a series of Popes since the time of the apparitions at Fatima. As we will see, in 2002 the currently reigning Pope even decreed that the Feast of the Virgin of Fatima be included in the Church's universal calendar of liturgical feast days, for inclusion in the *Third Typical Edition of the Roman Missal*. Thus, the Magisterium formally validates the authenticity of the apparitions.

We recall that in the Message of July 13, 1917, Our Lady had promised Lucy that "I shall come to ask for the Consecration of Russia to My Immaculate Heart and the Communion of Reparation on the first Saturdays." True to Her word, the Virgin appeared again to Lucy on June 13, 1929 in Tuy, Spain, where Lucy—now Sister Lucia dos Santos, a Dorothean nun (she would not become a Carmelite until 1948)—was in prayer in the convent chapel during the Holy Hour of Adoration and Reparation. Even among the annals of recognized heavenly apparitions to the saints of the Catholic Church, this one was extraordinary.

We will let Sister Lucy recount the apparition in her own simple but quite dramatic words—and remember that here also we are dealing with an apparition that the Church, including the currently reigning Pope, has pronounced worthy of belief:

> I had requested and obtained permission from my superiors and confessor to make the Holy Hour from 11:00 p.m. until midnight from Thursday to Friday. Being alone one night, I knelt down before the Communion rail in the middle of the chapel to say the prayers of the Angel, lying prostrate. Feeling tired, I got up and knelt, and continued to say them with my arms in the form of a cross.
>
> The only light came from the sanctuary lamp. Suddenly a supernatural light illumined the whole chapel and on the altar appeared a cross of light which reached to the ceiling. In a brighter part could be seen, on the upper part of the Cross, the face of a Man and His body to the

waist. On His breast was an equally luminous dove, and nailed to the Cross, the body of another Man.

A little below the waist, suspended in mid-air, was to be seen a Chalice and a large Host onto Which fell some drops of Blood from the face of the Crucified and from a wound in His breast. These drops ran down over the Host and fell into the Chalice. Under the right arm of the Cross was Our Lady (Our Lady of Fatima with Her Immaculate Heart in Her hand) ... Under the left arm (of the Cross), some big letters, as it were of crystal-clear water running down over the altar, formed these words: "Grace and Mercy".

I understood that it was the mystery of the Most Holy Trinity that was shown to me ...[1]

Frère Michel has rightly called this apparition "the Trinitarian Theophany". As with the Miracle of the Sun, there is nothing else like it in the history of the world. Thus did God Himself signify the singular importance of what Our Lady was about to tell Sister Lucy:

> The moment has come *when God asks* the Holy Father to make, in union with all the bishops of the world, the consecration of Russia to My Immaculate Heart, promising to save it by this means.

*God Himself* had requested this. Sister Lucy had been in the presence not merely of the Mother of God, but the Most Holy Trinity. Of course, Sister Lucy immediately conveyed the divine request to her confessor, Father Gonçalves, as reflected in her published correspondence with him.[2]

For at least the next seventy years Sister Lucy—the same Lucy who would not deny the truth even though threatened with a horrible death by the Masonic Mayor of Ourem—gave the same testimony: Our Lady, as God's messenger, had requested the public consecration of Russia in a ceremony to be conducted jointly by the Pope and all the world's bishops. The persistent effort by certain persons to change that testimony for the sake of human respect (to avoid offending the Russians), and to serve a new orientation of the Church, is the crux of the great Fatima controversy that persists to this day, and which has prompted this book. We shall return to this point in due course.

As if to demonstrate the efficacy of the Consecration the Virgin had requested, God saw fit to allow a demonstration project, as it were, in Portugal. On the anniversary of the first apparition at Fatima, May 13, 1931, and in the presence of 300,000 faithful who came to Fatima for the event, the bishops of Portugal solemnly consecrated their nation to the Immaculate Heart of Mary. These good bishops placed Portugal under the protection of Our Lady to preserve that nation from the Communist contagion that was sweeping through Europe, and especially Spain. Indeed, the Virgin's prophecy of the spread of Russia's errors throughout the world was already being fulfilled with relentless exactitude. And who, in July of 1917, could have foreseen the emergence of world communism out of Russia—months before the Bolshevik revolution and Lenin's ascent to power? Only Heaven could have foreseen it; only the Mother of God, informed by Her Divine Son.

As a result of this (1931) Consecration Portugal experienced a three-fold miracle. Here, we will give only the barest details.

There was, first of all, a magnificent Catholic Renaissance, a great rebirth of Catholic life so striking that those who lived through it attributed it unquestionably to the work of God. During this period, Portugal enjoyed a drastic upsurge in priestly vocations. The number of religious almost quadrupled in 10 years. Religious communities rose likewise. There was a vast renewal of Christian life, which showed itself in many areas, including the development of a Catholic press, Catholic radio, pilgrimages, spiritual retreats, and a robust movement of Catholic Action that was integrated into the framework of diocesan and parish life.

This Catholic Renaissance was of such magnitude that in 1942 the bishops of Portugal declared in a Collective Pastoral Letter: "Anybody who would have closed his eyes twenty-five years ago and opened them now would no longer recognize Portugal, so vast is the transformation worked by the modest and invisible factor of the apparition of the Blessed Virgin at Fatima. Really, Our Lady wishes to save Portugal."[3]

There was also a miracle of political and social reform, in accordance with Catholic social principles. Shortly after the 1931 Consecration, a Catholic leader in Portugal ascended to power, Antonio Salazar, who inaugurated a Catholic, counter-revolutionary program. He strove to create, as much as possible, a Catholic social order wherein the laws of government and social institutions harmonize with the law of Christ, His Gospel and His Church.[4] A fierce adversary of socialism and liberalism, he was opposed to "everything which diminishes or dissolves the family."[5]

President Salazar did not simply talk a good line; he enacted legislation to protect the family, including laws that frowned upon divorce. Article 24 read "In harmony with the essential properties of Catholic marriages: It is understood that by the very fact of the celebration of a canonical marriage, the spouses renounce the legal right to ask for a divorce."[6] The effect of this law was that Catholic marriages did not diminish in number, but increased. So that by 1960—a very critical year, as we shall see—nearly 91 percent of all marriages in the country were canonical marriages.

In addition to these astonishing religious and political changes, there was a twofold miracle of peace. Portugal was preserved from the Communist terror, especially from the Spanish Civil War which was raging next door. Portugal was also preserved from the devastations of World War II.

Regarding the Spanish Civil War, the Portuguese bishops had vowed in 1936 that if Our Lady protected Portugal, they would express their gratitude by renewing the National Consecration to the Immaculate Heart of Mary. True to their word, on May 13, 1938, they renewed the Consecration of Portugal to the Immaculate Heart in thanksgiving for Our Lady's protection. Cardinal Cerejeira acknowledged publicly: "Since Our Lady of Fatima appeared in 1917

... A special blessing of God has descended upon the land of Portugal ... especially if we review the two years which have gone since our vow, one cannot fail to recognize that the invisible hand of God has protected Portugal, sparing it the scourge of war and the leprosy of atheistic communism."

Even Pope Pius XII expressed astonishment that Portugal was spared the horrors of the Spanish Civil War and the Communist menace. In an address to the Portuguese people, the Pope spoke of "the Red Peril, so menacing and so close to you, and yet avoided in such an unexpected manner."[7]

The Portuguese passed this first danger unscathed, but immediately there was a second staring them in the face. World War II was about to break out. In yet another fulfillment of the Virgin's prophecy of July 13, 1917, the war would begin "in the reign of Pius XI," following "a night illumined by an unknown light ..."

On February 6, 1939, seven months before the declaration of war, Sister Lucy wrote to her bishop, Msgr. da Silva. She told him that war was imminent, but then spoke of a miraculous promise. She said "in this horrible war, Portugal would be spared because of the national consecration to the Immaculate Heart of Mary made by the bishops."[8]

And Portugal *was* spared the horrors of war, the details of which are too numerous to here recount.[9] Even more remarkable, Sister Lucy wrote to Pope Pius XII on December 2, 1940, to tell him that Portugal was receiving special protection during the war that other nations would have received if the bishops would have consecrated their nations to the Immaculate Heart of Mary. She wrote: "Most Holy Father, Our Lord promises a special protection to our country in this war, due to the consecration of the nation, by the Portuguese prelates, to the Immaculate Heart of Mary; as proof of the graces that would have been granted to other nations, had they also consecrated themselves to Her."[10]

Likewise, Portugal's Cardinal Cerejeira did not hesitate to attribute to Our Lady of Fatima the great graces that She had obtained for Portugal during this time. On May 13, 1942 he said: "To express what has been going on here for twenty-five years, the Portuguese vocabulary has but one word: miracle. Yes, we are convinced that we owe the wonderful transformation of Portugal to the protection of the Most Holy Virgin."[11]

Cardinal Cerejeira maintained what we will maintain throughout this presentation: that the miraculous blessings Our Lady obtained for Portugal as a heavenly reward for the 1931 consecration of that nation were only a foretaste of what She will do for the entire world, once Russia is also properly consecrated to Her Immaculate Heart.[12] As the Cardinal said:

> What has taken place in Portugal proclaims the miracle. And it foreshadows what the Immaculate Heart of Mary has prepared for the world.[13]

It is not hard to understand why Portugal at this time has been called the "Showcase of Our Lady". And the triple miracle of Portugal is but a preview of how Russia and the world will look after the Collegial Consecration of Russia. The miraculous example of Portugal is also helpful to us as a gauge by which we can judge the present. If we contrast the threefold miracle of Portugal with the present condition of Russia and the world, it is obvious that the consecration of Russia has yet to be achieved. (We shall return to this point in a later chapter.)

For men with high offices in the Church to take actions that impede the consecration of Russia, thereby denying to the Church and the world the heavenly bounty Mary's intercession obtained for Portugal, is not only a monumental folly but also an incalculable crime. It is this crime that has motivated the publication of this book.

# Chapter 4

## The Third Secret

Precisely as predicted by the Virgin in 1917, World War II had erupted during the reign of Pius XI, while Josef Stalin was liquidating Catholics and exporting world communism from Soviet Russia.

### So Terrible She Could Not Write It Down

In June of 1943, Sister Lucy, now age 36, had come down with pleurisy. This development greatly alarmed Bishop da Silva of Leiria-Fatima and Canon Galamba, his close friend and advisor. They both feared that Sister Lucy would die without writing down the Third Secret. By September 1943 they suggested to her that she write it down, but she had declined to comply with the suggestion because she did not wish to take responsibility for such an initiative on her own. She stated that she would, however, obey an express command from Bishop da Silva. Sister Lucy was gravely concerned that, without a formal command from her bishop, she did not yet have Our Lord's permission to reveal the Third Secret.

In mid-October 1943, during a visit to Sister Lucy at the convent in Tuy, Spain (about 250 miles from Fatima and near the Portuguese border), Bishop da Silva gave Sister Lucy a formal order to write down the Secret. Sister Lucy then attempted to obey the bishop's command, but was unable to do so for the next two and a half months.

### The Virgin Herself Instructs Sister Lucy to Reveal the Secret

Finally, on January 2, 1944 the Blessed Virgin Mary appeared to Lucy again, to strengthen her and confirm that it is indeed God's will that she reveal the final part of the Secret. Only then was Sister Lucy able to overcome her trepidation and write down the Third Secret of Fatima.[1] But even so, it was not until January 9, 1944 that Sister Lucy wrote the following note to Bishop da Silva, informing him that the Secret had finally been committed to paper:

> I have written what you asked me; God willed to try me a little, but finally this was indeed His will: (the text) is sealed in an envelope and it [the sealed envelope] is in the notebooks ...[2]

### A Single Sheet of Paper

It was thus immediately apparent that the Secret involved two documents: one sealed in the envelope, and the other contained in Sister Lucy's notebook. (Why else would she have turned over the notebook as well as the sealed envelope?) We shall focus for the time being on what was sealed in the envelope.

Lucy was still so filled with trepidation over the contents of the Secret that she would entrust her note in the sealed envelope (along with the notebook) to no one but a bishop for carrying to Bishop da Silva. On June 17, 1944, Sister Lucy left Tuy, crossed the River Minho, and arrived at Asilo Fonseca where she handed to Archbishop Manuel Maria Ferreira da Silva (the Archbishop of Gurza) the notebook in which she had inserted the envelope containing the Secret. That same day, Archbishop da Silva delivered the Secret to Bishop José Alves Correia da Silva (the Bishop of Leiria) at his country home not far from Braga. Then, the Bishop of Leiria took the Secret to the Episcopal Palace in Leiria. These details will be very important in view of what is set forth in the Vatican commentary on the Third Secret ultimately published on June 26, 2000.

From the first, the unanimous testimony was that the Third Secret is written in the form of a letter on a single sheet of paper. Father Joaquin Alonso (the official archivist of the papers on the Fatima apparitions) reports that both Sister Lucy and Cardinal Ottaviani stated that the Secret was written on a single sheet of paper:

> Lucy tells us that she wrote it on a sheet of paper. Cardinal Ottaviani, who has read it, tells us the same thing: 'She wrote it on a sheet of paper ...'.[3]

Cardinal Ottaviani, as Prefect of the Congregation for the Doctrine of the Faith in 1967, stated that he had read the Third Secret and that it was written on a single sheet of paper. He testified to this fact on February 11, 1967, during a press conference at the time of a meeting of the Pontifical Marian Academy in Rome. Cardinal Ottaviani stated:

> And then, what did she [Lucy] do to obey the Most Holy Virgin? She wrote on a sheet of paper, in Portuguese, what the Holy Virgin had asked her to tell ...[4]

Cardinal Ottaviani is a witness to this fact. In the same press conference, he states:

> I, who have had the grace and the gift to read the text of the Secret—although I too am held to secrecy because I am bound by the Secret ...[5]

We also have the testimony of Bishop Venancio, who was then the Auxiliary Bishop of Leiria-Fatima, that he was ordered by Bishop da Silva in mid-March 1957 to bring copies of all Sister Lucy's writings—including the original of the Third Secret—to the Apostolic Nuncio at Lisbon for transferral to Rome. Before bringing Lucy's writings to the Nuncio, Bishop Venancio looked at the envelope containing the Third Secret while holding it up to the light and saw that the Secret was "written on a small sheet of paper".[6] Frère Michel first identifies the nature of this testimony:

However, thanks to the disclosures of Bishop Venancio, at the time Auxiliary Bishop of Leiria and intimately involved with these events, we now have many reliable facts which we will take care not to neglect. I myself received them from the mouth of Bishop Venancio on February 13, 1984, at Fatima. The former Bishop of Fatima repeated to me on this subject, almost word for word, what he had already said previously to Father Caillon, who gave a very detailed account of it in his conferences.[7]

Here now is Bishop Venancio's testimony, according to Frère Michel:

> Bishop Venancio related that once he was by himself, he took the great envelope of the Secret and tried to look through it and see the contents. In the bishop's large envelope he discerned a smaller envelope, that of Lucy, and inside this envelope *an ordinary sheet of paper* with margins on each side of three quarters of a centimeter. He took the trouble to note the size of everything. Thus the final Secret of Fatima was written on a small sheet of paper.[8] [emphasis added]

The evidence further shows that this single sheet of paper contained some 20-25 lines of text. On this point the testimonies of Sister Lucy, Cardinal Ottaviani, Bishop Venancio, Father Alonso, Frère Michel and Frère François all agree:

> ... we are just as certain that the twenty or thirty lines of the third Secret ...[9]

> The final Secret of Fatima, written on a small sheet of paper, is therefore not very long. Probably twenty to twenty-five lines ...[10]

> Bishop Venancio looked "at the envelope [containing the Third Secret] while holding it up to the light. He could see inside a little sheet of which he measured the exact size. We thus know that the Third Secret is not very long, probably 20 to 25 lines ..."[11]

## Written in the Form of a Letter

Equally clear is that the Third Secret was written down in the form of a letter to Bishop da Silva. Sister Lucy herself tells us that the Third Secret was written as a letter. On this point we have the written testimony of Father Jongen who, on February 3-4, 1946, interrogated Sister Lucy as follows:

> 'You have already made known two parts of the Secret. When will the time arrive for the third part?' 'I communicated the third part in a *letter* to the Bishop of Leiria,' she answered.[12] [emphasis added]

Next we have the decisive words of Canon Galamba:

> When the bishop refused to open the *letter*, Lucy made him promise that it would definitely be opened and read to the world either at her death or in 1960, whichever would come first.[13] [emphasis added]

## To Be Revealed to the World by 1960

Why 1960? In 1955 Cardinal Ottaviani asked her why it was not to be opened before 1960. She told him, "because then it will seem clearer (mais claro)." Sister Lucy had made the Bishop of Fatima-Leiria promise that the Secret would be read to the world at her death, but in no event later than 1960, "because the Blessed Virgin wishes it so."[14] And from Canon Barthas: "Moreover, it [the Third Secret] will soon be known, since Sister Lucy affirms that Our Lady wills that it can be published beginning in 1960."

This testimony introduces a third crucial fact concerning the Secret: that it was to be revealed by 1960. Indeed, in February 1960, the Patriarch of Lisbon would declare:

> Bishop da Silva enclosed (the envelope sealed by Lucy) in another envelope on which he indicated that the *letter* had to be opened in 1960 by himself, Bishop José Correia da Silva, if he was still alive, or if not, by the Cardinal Patriarch of Lisbon.[15] [emphasis added]

Father Alonso tells us:

> Other bishops also spoke—and with authority—about the year 1960 as the date indicated for opening the famous *letter*. Thus, when the then titular Bishop of Tiava, and Auxiliary Bishop of Lisbon asked Lucy when the Secret was to be opened, he always received the same answer: in 1960.[16] [emphasis added]

And in 1959, Bishop Venancio, the new Bishop of Leiria, declared:

> I think that the *letter* will not be opened before 1960. Sister Lucy had asked that it should not be opened before her death, or not before 1960. We are now in 1959 and Sister Lucy is in good health.[17] [emphasis added]

Finally, we have the Vatican announcement of February 8, 1960 (appearing in a communiqué of the Portuguese news agency A.N.I.), concerning the decision to suppress the Secret—a document to which we shall return in Chapter 6. The Vatican announcement states:

> ... it is most likely that the *letter* will never be opened, in which Sister Lucy wrote down the *words which Our Lady confided* as a secret to the three shepherds of the Cova da Iria.[18] [emphasis added]

Thus far all the evidence points to the following: a secret written down in the form of a letter on a single sheet of paper, containing 20-25 lines of handwritten text, with 3/4 centimeter margins on each side; a secret to be revealed not later than 1960, and in that year, particularly, because "it will be much clearer (mais claro)" then.

It was this document that Bishop Venancio transferred to the Papal Nuncio, who then transferred it to the Holy Office (now known as the Congregation for the Doctrine of the Faith) in 1957:

Arriving at the Vatican on April 16, 1957, the Secret undoubtedly was placed by Pope Pius XII in his personal desk, inside a small wooden box, bearing the inscription *Secretum Sancti Officii* (Secret of the Holy Office).[19]

It is important to note that the Pope was the head of the Holy Office prior to Pope Paul VI reorganizing the Vatican in 1967. Therefore, it was quite appropriate for the Pope to retain the Third Secret in his possession and for the box containing it to be labeled "Secret of the Holy Office". With the Pope being the head of the Holy Office, this box became part of the Holy Office archives. Bear these crucial facts in mind for later consideration.

## A Prediction of Apostasy in the Church

What about the contents of the Secret? We return now to the telltale phrase "In Portugal the dogma of the Faith will always be preserved etc." which, as noted in a previous chapter, appears at the end of the integral text of the first two parts of the Great Secret in Lucy's Fourth Memoir.

On this point we must consider the crucial testimony of Fr. Joseph Schweigl, who was entrusted by Pope Pius XII with a secret mission: to interrogate Sister Lucy about the Third Secret. This he did at the Carmel of Coimbra on September 2, 1952. Upon his return to Rome, Father Schweigl went to his residence at the Russicum and said to a colleague the following day:

> I cannot reveal anything of what I learned at Fatima concerning the Third Secret, but I can say that it has two parts: one concerns the Pope; the other logically (although I must say nothing) would have to be the continuation of the words: 'In Portugal, the dogma of the Faith will always be preserved.'[20]

Thus is confirmed the conclusion that one part of the Secret is indeed a continuation of the phrase whose completion the Vatican has yet to reveal: "In Portugal the dogma of the Faith will always be preserved etc."

This conclusion is corroborated by many other witnesses, including the following:

## Father Fuentes

On December 26, 1957, Father Fuentes interviewed Sister Lucy. The interview was published in 1958 with an imprimatur of his Archbishop, Archbishop Sanchez of Vera Cruz, Mexico. Among other things, Sister Lucy told Father Fuentes the following:

> Father, the Most Holy Virgin is very sad because no one has paid any attention to Her message, neither the good nor the bad. The good continue on their way but without giving any importance to Her message. The bad, not seeing the punishment of God falling upon them, continue their life of sin without even caring about the message. But believe me,

Father, God will chastise the world and this will be in a terrible manner. The punishment from Heaven is imminent.

Father, how much time is there before 1960 arrives? It will be very sad for everyone, not one person will rejoice at all if beforehand the world does not pray and do penance. I am not able to give any other details because it is still a secret. ...

This is the Third part of the Message of Our Lady which will remain secret until 1960.

Tell them, Father, that many times, the most Holy Virgin told my cousins Francisco and Jacinta, as well as myself, that many nations will disappear from the face of the earth. She said that Russia will be the instrument of chastisement chosen by Heaven to punish the world if we do not obtain beforehand the conversion of that poor nation.

Father, the devil is in the mood for engaging in a decisive battle against the Blessed Virgin. And the devil knows what it is that most offends God and which in a short space of time will gain for him the greatest number of souls. *Thus, the devil does everything to overcome souls consecrated to God, because in this way, the devil will succeed in leaving souls of the faithful abandoned by their leaders, thereby the more easily will he seize them.*

That which afflicts the Immaculate Heart of Mary and the Heart of Jesus is *the fall of religious and priestly souls*. The devil knows that *religious and priests who fall away from their beautiful vocation drag numerous souls to hell. ... The devil wishes to take possession of consecrated souls*. He tries to corrupt them in order to lull to sleep the souls of laypeople and thereby lead them to final impenitence.[21]

## Father Alonso

Before his death in 1981, Father Joaquin Alonso, who for sixteen years was the official archivist of Fatima, testified as follows:

It is therefore completely probable that the text makes concrete references to the crisis of faith within the Church and to the negligence of the pastors themselves [and the] internal struggles in the very bosom of the Church and of grave pastoral negligence of the upper hierarchy.[22]

In the period preceding the great triumph of the Immaculate Heart of Mary, terrible things are to happen. These form the content of the third part of the Secret. What are they? If 'in Portugal the dogma of the Faith will always be preserved,'... *it can be clearly deduced from this that in other parts of the Church these dogmas are going to become obscure or even lost altogether.*[23]

Does the unpublished text speak of concrete circumstances? It is very possible that it speaks not only of a real crisis of the faith in the Church during this in-between period, but like the secret of La Salette, for example, there are more concrete references to the internal struggles of Catholics or to the fall of priests and religious. *Perhaps it even refers to the failures of the upper hierarchy of the Church.* For that matter, none of this is foreign to other communications Sister Lucy has had on this subject.[24]

## Cardinal Ratzinger

On November 11, 1984, Cardinal Ratzinger, head of the Congregation for the Doctrine of the Faith, gave an interview in *Jesus* magazine, a publication of the Pauline Sisters. The interview is entitled "Here is Why the Faith is in Crisis," and was published with the Cardinal's explicit permission. In this interview Cardinal Ratzinger admits that a crisis of faith is affecting the Church around the world. In this context, he reveals that he has read the Third Secret and that the Secret refers to "dangers threatening the faith and the life of the Christian and therefore (the life) of the world."

The Cardinal thus confirms Father Alonso's thesis that the Secret pertains to widespread apostasy in the Church. Cardinal Ratzinger says in the same interview that the Secret also refers to "the importance of the *Novissimi* [the Last Times/the Last Things]" and that "If it is not published, at least for now, it is to avoid confusing religious prophecy with sensationalism ..." The Cardinal further reveals that "the things contained in this 'Third Secret' correspond to what has been announced in Scripture and has been said again and again in many other Marian apparitions, first of all that of Fatima ..."[25]

## Bishop Amaral

In complete accord with Cardinal Ratzinger is Bishop Amaral—the third Bishop of Fatima. In a speech in Vienna, Austria on September 10, 1984, he said the following:

> Its content concerns only our faith. To identify the [Third] Secret with catastrophic announcements or with a nuclear holocaust is to deform the meaning of the message. *The loss of faith of a continent is worse than the annihilation of a nation*; and it is true that faith is continually diminishing in Europe.[26] [Emphasis added]

## Cardinal Oddi

On March 17, 1990 Cardinal Oddi gave the following testimony to Italian journalist Lucio Brunelli in the journal *Il Sabato*:

> It [the Third Secret] has nothing to do with Gorbachev. The Blessed Virgin was alerting us against apostasy in the Church.

## Cardinal Ciappi

To these witnesses we must add the testimony of Cardinal Mario Luigi Ciappi, who was nothing less than Pope John Paul II's own personal papal theologian. In a personal communication to a Professor Baumgartner in Salzburg, Cardinal Ciappi revealed that:

In the Third Secret it is foretold, among other things, that the great apostasy in the Church will begin *at the top*.[27]

All of these testimonies are consistent with the repeated remarks of Sister Lucy herself—not only to Fr. Fuentes, as quoted above, but to many other reliable witnesses. Although bound to secrecy concerning the precise contents of the Third Secret, her remarks to reliable witnesses are full of references to Churchmen "being fooled by false doctrine"; to a "diabolical disorientation" afflicting "so many persons who occupy places of responsibility" in the Church; to "priests and consecrated souls" who "are so deceived and misled" because "the devil has succeeded in infiltrating evil under cover of good ... leading into error and deceiving souls having a heavy responsibility through the place which they occupy ... They are blind men guiding other blind men," and so on.[28]

## Pius XII Confirms the Secret's Prediction of Apostasy

But perhaps the most remarkable testimony of all on this score, although it is of indirect relevance, is that of Msgr. Eugenio Pacelli, before he became Pope Pius XII and while he was still serving as Vatican Secretary of State during the reign of Pius XI. Speaking even before Sister Lucy had committed the Third Secret to paper, the future Pius XII made an astonishing prophecy about a coming upheaval in the Church:

> I am worried by the Blessed Virgin's messages to Lucy of Fatima. This persistence of Mary about the dangers which menace the Church is a divine warning against the suicide of altering the Faith, in Her liturgy, Her theology and Her soul. ... I hear all around me innovators who wish to dismantle the Sacred Chapel, destroy the universal flame of the Church, reject her ornaments and make her feel remorse for her historical past.

Pius XII's biographer, Msgr. Roche, noted that at this moment in the conversation, according to a Count Galeazzi, "the gaze of the Pope, seen through the lenses of his glasses, became supernatural, and there emanated from his tall and slender body an irresistible mystical force." Pius XII then said (in answer to an objection from a curial Cardinal):

> A day will come when the civilized world will deny its God, when the Church will doubt as Peter doubted. She will be tempted to believe that man has become God. In our churches, Christians will search in vain for the red lamp where God awaits them. Like Mary Magdalene, weeping before the empty tomb, they will ask, "Where have they taken Him?"[29]

It is quite remarkable that the future Pope would relate this apparently supernatural intuition of coming devastation in the Church specifically to "the Blessed Virgin's messages to Lucy of Fatima" and "this persistence of Mary about the dangers which menace the Church." The prediction would be utterly senseless if it had been based on the first two parts of the Great Secret, which make no mention of such things as "the suicide of altering the Faith, in Her liturgy, Her theology and Her soul" or "innovators who wish to dismantle the Sacred Chapel, destroy the universal flame of the Church, reject her ornaments and make her feel remorse for her historical past." Nor is there any indication whatsoever in the first two parts that "In our churches, Christians will search in vain for the red lamp where God awaits them."

How did the future Pope Pius XII know these things? Clearly, he was given a supernatural glimpse, or had direct knowledge, that some hitherto undisclosed portion of "the Blessed Virgin's messages to Sister Lucy of Fatima" revealed these future events in the Church.

In short, every single testimony pertaining to the contents of the Third Secret, from 1944 until at least 1984 (the date of the Ratzinger interview) confirms that it points to a catastrophic loss of faith and discipline in the Church, representing a breakthrough for the forces arrayed against her for so long—the "innovators" that the future Pius XII heard "all around me," clamoring for the dismantling of the Sacred Chapel and changes in the liturgy and Catholic theology.

As we will show, that breakthrough began in 1960, precisely the year when (as Sister Lucy had insisted) the third part of the Secret should be revealed. But before we return to that fateful year, when the great crime we speak of first began, we must first discuss the motive that preceded the crime. This will we now endeavor to do.

# Chapter 5

## A Motive Emerges

As we charged in the Introduction, the crime against the Church and the world which we intend to prove in this book involves "a systematic attempt, since the year 1960, to conceal, misrepresent and deny the authenticity of this message—the Message of Fatima—even as its alarming prophecies are being fulfilled before our very eyes."

But why would men in the highest positions of authority in the Church commit such a crime? As Aristotle observed, in order to understand an action one must look to the motive. That is what we shall do in this chapter.

To be sure, proving motive is always a difficult business; for one cannot read another man's mind, much less judge the state of his soul. In arriving at a conclusion as to motive you, like any jury in a merely civil case, can only base your decision on the external actions of the accused, in light of the surrounding circumstances. When a jury finds that a man has murdered his wife for the motive of obtaining insurance money, for example, it makes its finding of motive based on a reasonable inference drawn from the surrounding circumstances. Rarely would the killer in such a case openly admit "I killed her for the insurance." Instead, motive would be inferred from such things as the husband's recent purchase of a very large insurance policy on the wife.

Now, no one would accuse a jury of "rash judgment" in inferring from the circumstances that the husband in our hypothetical case harbored the intention of killing his wife for money. In the case of Fatima, too, motive can be deduced from circumstances; it is not "rash judgment" to reach a reasonable conclusion about motive based on what the accused themselves have said and done. Moreover, as we will demonstrate in this case we have the equivalent of an admission as to motive. The accused have been quite explicit about what they approve and what they intend concerning the crime at issue.

### A New and Ruinous Orientation of the Church

As we charged in the Introduction, the motive in this case arises from the recognition by the accused that the Message of Fatima, understood in a traditional Catholic sense, cannot be reconciled with decisions they have taken since the Second Vatican Council to change the entire orientation of the Catholic Church. That is, the Message stands in the way of their effort to do precisely what the future Pius XII foresaw in his moment of supernatural clarity: to remake the Church into an institution oriented toward the world. We recall once again those prophetic words of Msgr. Pacelli (the future Pope Pius XII), uttered in the light of the Message of Fatima:

I am worried by the Blessed Virgin's messages to Lucy of Fatima. This persistence of Mary about the dangers which menace the Church is a divine warning against the suicide of altering the Faith, in Her liturgy, Her theology and Her soul. ... I hear all around me innovators who wish to dismantle the Sacred Chapel, destroy the universal flame of the Church, reject her ornaments and make her feel remorse for her historical past.

A day will come when the civilized world will deny its God, when the Church will doubt as Peter doubted. She will be tempted to believe that man has become God. In our churches, Christians will search in vain for the red lamp where God awaits them. Like Mary Magdalene, weeping before the empty tomb, they will ask, "Where have they taken Him?"

In the Introduction we also noted that this great change of orientation in the Church—in "her liturgy, her theology, her soul", as the future Pius XII put it—was the long-cherished goal of the organized forces that have been plotting against the Church for centuries; the same forces that were at work in Portugal in 1917, but were repelled by the Consecration of that nation to the Immaculate Heart of Mary in 1931. To repel those forces throughout the world was the very reason Heaven itself sent the Mother of God to Fatima to prescribe the Consecration of Russia. Those forces were soon to become the prime weapon of Satan's long war against the Church. Truly, the outcome of the war against the Church in our time hinges on the battle over fulfillment of the Fatima Message.

Our presentation of the evidence of the motive in this case—namely, a desire to impose upon the Church a new orientation to the exclusion of the Message of Fatima—requires some considerable historical background, which we will now present.

## The Goal of Organized Freemasonry: To Neutralize and "Instrumentalize" the Catholic Church

As we have seen with the example of Portugal in 1917, the forces of Masonry (and their Communist fellow travelers) conspired to prevent the Message of Fatima from finding its fulfillment in Portugal. The Message was called a fraud or a childish delusion; the seers themselves were persecuted and even threatened with death. Such was the hatred of these forces for the Catholic Church and the Virgin Mother of God.

And so it is with these forces in the world at large today. One need not descend into the fever swamps of conspiracy theory to know that before 1960, the Popes issued more condemnations and warnings about the plotting of the Freemasons and the communists against the Church than on any other single subject in Church history.

On this point, one cannot fail to consider the infamous *Permanent Instruction of the Alta Vendita*, a Masonic document that mapped out an entire plan for the infiltration and corruption of the Catholic Church in the 20th Century.[1] While it has become fashionable since the Second Vatican Council to scoff at the existence of such a conspiracy, it must be noted that the secret papers of the Alta Vendita (an Italian secret society), including the *Permanent Instruction*, fell into the hands of Pope Gregory XVI. The *Permanent Instruction* was published at the request of Blessed Pope Pius IX by Cardinal Cretineau-Joly in his work *The Roman Church and Revolution.*[2] With his brief of approbation of February 25, 1861 (addressed to the author) Pope Pius IX guaranteed the authenticity of the *Permanent Instruction* and the other Masonic papers, but he did not allow anyone to divulge the true names of the members of the Alta Vendita implicated in the documents. Pope Leo XIII had likewise requested their publication. Both Popes acted, no doubt, in order to prevent such a tragedy from taking place. These great Pontiffs knew that such a calamity was far from impossible. (Pius XII also knew it, as we can see from his prophetic remarks while he was still Vatican Secretary of State.)

The full text of the *Permanent Instruction* is also contained in Msgr. George E. Dillon's book, *Grand Orient Freemasonry Unmasked.*[3] When Pope Leo XIII was presented with a copy of Msgr. Dillon's book, he was so impressed that he ordered an Italian version to be completed and published at the Pope's own expense.[4]

The Alta Vendita was the highest lodge of the Carbonari, an Italian secret society with links to Freemasonry and which, along with Freemasonry, was condemned by the Catholic Church.[5] The estimable Catholic historian Father E. Cahill, SJ, who is hardly a "conspiracy nut", states in his work *Freemasonry and the Anti-Christian Movement* that the Alta Vendita was "commonly supposed to have been at the time the governing center of European Freemasonry."[6] The Carbonari were most active in Italy and France.

In his book *Athanasius and the Church of Our Time* (1974), Bishop Rudolph Graber, another objective and quite unimpeachable authority writing after the Second Vatican Council, quoted a prominent Freemason who declared that "the goal (of Freemasonry) is no longer the destruction of the Church, but to make use of it by infiltrating it."[7] In other words, since Freemasonry cannot completely obliterate Christ's Church, it plans not only to eradicate the influence of Catholicism in society, but to use the Church's structure as an instrument of "renewal," "progress" and "enlightenment"—that is, a means of furthering many of its own principles and goals.

Discussing the Masonic vision of society and the world, Bishop Graber introduces the concept of synarchy: "What we are faced with here is the sum-total of the secret forces of all the 'orders' and schools which have joined together to set up an invisible world government. In the political sense, synarchy aims at the integration of all the financial and social forces which the world government, under socialist leadership naturally, has to support and promote. Catholicism, like all religions, would consequently be absorbed into a universal syncretism. Far from being suppressed, it would be integrated, a course which is already being steered in the principle of fellowship between clerics (of various religions)."

The strategy advanced in the *Permanent Instruction* to achieve this aim is astonishing in its audacity and cunning. From the start, the document tells of a process that will take decades to accomplish. Those who drew up the document knew that they would not see its fulfillment. They were inaugurating a work that would be carried on by succeeding generations of the initiated. The *Permanent Instruction* says, "In our ranks the soldier dies and the struggle goes on."

The *Instruction* called for the dissemination of liberal ideas and axioms throughout society and within the institutions of the Catholic Church so that laity, seminarians, clerics and prelates would, over the years, gradually be imbued with progressive principles. In time, this new mentality would be so pervasive that priests would be ordained, bishops consecrated, and Cardinals nominated whose thinking was in step with the modern thought rooted in the "Principles of 1789" (i.e. the principles of Freemasonry which inspired the French Revolution)—namely, pluralism, the equality of all religions, separation of Church and State, unbridled freedom of speech, and so forth.

Eventually, a Pope would be elected from these ranks who would lead the Church on the path of "enlightenment and renewal". It must be stressed that it was not their aim to place a Freemason on the Chair of Peter. Their goal was to effect an environment that would eventually produce a Pope and a hierarchy won over to the ideas of liberal Catholicism, *all the while believing themselves to be faithful Catholics*.

These liberalized Catholic leaders, then, would no longer oppose the modern ideas of the revolution (as had been the consistent practice of the Popes from 1789 until 1958, who unanimously condemned these liberal principles), but would amalgamate or "baptize" them into the Church. The end result would be a Catholic clergy and laity marching under the banner of the "enlightenment", all the while thinking they are marching under the banner of the Apostolic keys.

No doubt with the *Permanent Instruction* in mind, in *Humanum Genus*, Leo XIII called upon Catholic leaders to "tear off the mask from Freemasonry and make plain to all what it really is."[8] The publication of these documents of the Alta Vendita was a means of "tearing off the mask".

Lest there be any claim that we have mischaracterized the *Permanent Instruction*, we now quote from it at considerable length. What follows is not the entire *Instruction*, but the section that is most pertinent to our proof. The document reads:

> The Pope, whoever he is, will never come to the secret societies; it is up to the secret societies to take the first step toward the Church, with the aim of conquering both of them.
>
> The task that we are going to undertake is not the work of a day, or of a month, or of a year; it may last several years, perhaps a century; but in our ranks the soldier dies and the struggle goes on.

We do not intend to win the Popes to our cause, to make them neophytes of our principles, propagators of our ideas. That would be a ridiculous dream; and if events turn out in some way, if Cardinals or prelates, for example, of their own free will or by surprise, should enter into a part of our secrets, this is not at all an incentive for desiring their elevation to the See of Peter. That elevation would ruin us. Ambition alone would have led them to apostasy, the requirements of power would force them to sacrifice us. What we must ask for, what we should look for and wait for, as the Jews wait for the Messiah, is a Pope according to our needs ...

With that we shall march more securely towards the assault on the Church than with the pamphlets of our brethren in France and even the gold of England. Do you want to know the reason for this? It is that with this, in order to shatter the high rock on which God has built His Church, we no longer need Hannnibalian vinegar, or need gunpowder, or even need our arms. We have the little finger of the successor of Peter engaged in the ploy, and this little finger is as good, for this crusade, as all the Urban II's and all the Saint Bernards in Christendom.

We have no doubt that we will arrive at this supreme end of our efforts. But when? But how? The unknown is not yet revealed. Nevertheless, as nothing should turn us aside from the plan drawn up, and on the contrary everything should tend to this, as if as early as tomorrow success were going to crown the work that is barely sketched, we wish, in this instruction, which will remain secret for the mere initiates, to give the officials in charge of the supreme Vente some advice that they should instill in all the brethren, in the form of instruction or of a memorandum ...

Now then, to assure ourselves a Pope of the required dimensions, it is a question first of shaping him ... for this Pope, a generation worthy of the reign we are dreaming of. Leave old people and those of a mature age aside; go to the youth, and if it is possible, even to the children ... You will contrive for yourselves, at little cost, a reputation as good Catholics and pure patriots.

This reputation will put access to our doctrines into the midst of the young clergy, as well as deeply into the monasteries. In a few years, by the force of things, this young clergy will have overrun all the functions; they will form the sovereign's council, they will be called to choose a Pontiff who should reign. And this Pontiff, like most of his contemporaries, will be necessarily more or less imbued with the Italian and humanitarian principles that we are going to begin to put into circulation. It is a small grain of black mustard that we are entrusting to the ground; but the sunshine of justice will develop it up to the highest power, and you will see one day what a rich harvest this small seed will produce.

In the path that we are laying out for our brethren, there are found great obstacles to conquer, difficulties of more than one kind to master.

They will triumph over them by experience and by clearsightedness; but the goal is so splendid that it is important to put all the sails to the wind in order to reach it. You want to revolutionize Italy, look for the Pope whose portrait we have just drawn. You wish to establish the reign of the chosen ones on the throne of the prostitute of Babylon, let the Clergy march under your standard, always believing that they are marching under the banner of the apostolic keys. You intend to make the last vestige of tyrants and the oppressors disappear; lay your snares like Simon Bar-Jona; lay them in the sacristies, the seminaries, and the monasteries rather than at the bottom of the sea: and if you do not hurry, we promise you a catch more miraculous than his. The fisher of fish became the fisher of men; you will bring friends around the apostolic Chair. You will have preached a revolution in tiara and in cope, marching with the cross and the banner, a revolution that will need to be only a little bit urged on to set fire to the four corners of the world.[9]

## The Rise of Liberal Catholicism

As we have noted, the goal of Freemasonry was not to destroy the Church, which the Masons knew was impossible, but to neutralize and *instrumentalize* the Church—that is, to make the human element of the Church into an instrument for the advance of Freemasonic goals, by inducing the Church's members to embrace liberal ideas. A liberalized hierarchy would readily lend itself to the work of establishing the Masonic ideal of a new world order (*novus ordo seclorum*)—a false pan-religious "brotherhood" in which the Church abandons her claim to be the sole ark of salvation and ceases her opposition to the forces of the world. The first stage of this process was manifested in the 19th Century, by which time society had become increasingly permeated with the liberal principles of the French Revolution. Even in the mid-1800s this program was already causing great detriment to the Catholic Faith and the Catholic State. The supposedly "kinder and gentler" notions of pluralism, religious indifferentism, a democracy which believes all authority comes from the people, false notions of liberty, interfaith gatherings, separation of Church and State and other novelties were gripping the minds of post-enlightenment Europe, infecting statesmen and churchmen alike.

## The Condemnation of Liberal Catholicism

The Popes of the 19th and early 20th Centuries waged war against these dangerous trends in full battle-dress. With a presence of mind rooted in the uncompromised certitude of Faith, these Popes were not taken in. They knew that evil principles, no matter how honorable they may appear, cannot bear good fruit, and that these were evil principles at their worst, since they were rooted not only in heresy, but apostasy. Like commanding generals who recognize the duty to hold their ground at all cost, these Popes aimed powerful cannons at the errors of the modern world and fired incessantly. The encyclicals were their cannonballs and they never missed their target.

The most devastating blast came in the form of Blessed Pope Pius IX's monumental *Syllabus of Errors*, which he appended to his encyclical *Quanta Cura* (1864). When the smoke cleared, all involved in the battle were in no doubt as to who was on what side. The line of demarcation had been drawn clearly. In the *Syllabus*, Blessed Pius IX condemned the principal errors of the modern world, not because they were modern, but because these new ideas were rooted in pantheistic naturalism and, therefore, were incompatible with Catholic doctrine, as well as being destructive to society.

The teachings in the *Syllabus* were counter-liberalism, and the principles of liberalism were counter-syllabus. This was clearly recognized by all parties. Father Denis Fahey referred to this showdown as "Pius IX vs. the Pantheistic Deification of Man."[10] Speaking for the other side, the French Freemason Ferdinand Buissont declared likewise, "A school cannot remain neutral between the *Syllabus* and the *Declaration of the Rights of Man*."[11]

Yet the 19th Century saw a new breed of Catholic who sought a utopian compromise between the two. These men looked for what they believed to be "good" in the principles of 1789 and tried to introduce them into the Church. Many clergymen, infected by the spirit of the age, were caught up in a net that had been "cast into the sacristies and into the seminaries" by Freemasonry. These men came to be known as liberal Catholics. Blessed Pope Pius IX regarded them with absolute horror. He said these "liberal Catholics" were the "worst enemies of the Church". In a letter to the French deputation headed by the Bishop of Nevers on June 18, 1871, Blessed Pius IX declared:

> That which I fear is not the Commune of Paris—no—that which I fear is Liberal Catholicism ... I have said so more than forty times, and I repeat it to you now, through the love that I bear you. The real scourge of France is Liberal Catholicism, which endeavors to unite two principles as repugnant to each other as fire and water."[12]

## The Rise of Modernism

Yet in spite of this, the numbers of liberal Catholics steadily increased. The crisis reached a peak around the turn of the century when the liberalism of 1789 that had been "blowin' in the wind" swirled into the tornado of modernism. Fr. Vincent Miceli identified this heresy as such by describing modernism's "trinity of parents". He wrote: "Its religious ancestor is the Protestant Reformation ... its philosophical parent is the Enlightenment ... its political pedigree comes from the French Revolution."[13]

What is meant by "modernism"? Modernism is nothing more or less than a synthesis or combination of all the errors of Liberal Catholicism into a comprehensive philosophical and theological system whose effect is to undermine the integrity of the entire Catholic faith. While a complete examination of the vast modernist system of thought is far beyond the scope of this book, it suffices for our purposes to say that, by various subtle errors, the modernist denies or undermines the divinity and divine revelation of Christ, the founding of the one true Church by Him, and the absolute immutability of

Catholic doctrine (which the modernist claims can "evolve" according to changing circumstances). The modernist also embraces and promotes the liberal notions of "free speech," "freedom of conscience," and the error of religious indifferentism, which holds that all religions are more or less good and praiseworthy because they all arise from a so-called "religious sense" in man—an error which, of course, implicitly denies the reality of Original Sin by suggesting that all men can be truly religious and can find salvation in the various religions they invent without need of Baptism, Faith and the sacraments of the Catholic Church.

## Saint Pius X Puts Down the Modernist Revolt

Pope St. Pius X, who ascended to the Papal throne in 1903, recognized modernism as a most deadly plague that must be arrested. St. Pius X waged war on modernism by systematically isolating, defining and condemning its many erroneous propositions. In particular, St. Pius X issued a monumental encyclical against modernism (*Pascendi*) and a *Syllabus* of modernist errors (*Lamentabili*). In his encyclical *Pascendi* this great Pope wrote: "There is no part of Catholic truth which they leave untouched, none that they do not strive to corrupt." In the same encyclical he called modernism "the synthesis of all heresies," declaring that the most important obligation of the Pope is to insure the purity and integrity of Catholic doctrine, and that if he did nothing, then he would have failed in his essential duty.[14]

But St. Pius X did not stop there. A few years after *Pascendi*, recognizing that the modernists had to be crushed before they rose up and caused havoc in the Church, this sainted Pope issued his letter *Sacrorum antistitum*, which mandated the Anti-Modernist Oath to be sworn by all priests and teachers. He oversaw the purging of modernists from the seminaries and universities and excommunicated the stubborn and unrepentant. St. Pius X knew that nothing less than the very nature of the Church was under attack by the modernists, who in their audacity were now acting openly for the overthrow of Catholic Dogma and Tradition:

> [T]he gravity of the evil is daily growing and must be checked at any cost. We are no longer dealing, as at the beginning, with opponents 'in sheep's clothing', but with open and bare-faced enemies in our very household, who, having made a pact with the chief foes of the Church [i.e. Freemasons, Liberals, Protestants, Jews, Muslims, etc.], are bent on overthrowing the Faith ... They want to renovate it as if it were consumed by old age, increase it and *adapt it to worldly tastes, progress and comforts*, as if it were opposed not just to the frivolity of a few, but to the good of society. ... There will never be enough vigilance and firmness on the part of those entrusted with the faithful safe-keeping of the sacred deposit of evangelical doctrine and ecclesiastical tradition, in order to oppose these onslaughts against it.[15]

St. Pius X effectively halted the spread of modernism in his day. It is reported, however, that when he was congratulated for eradicating this grave error, Pius X immediately responded that despite all his efforts, he had not succeeded in killing this beast, but had only driven it underground. He warned that if Church leaders were not vigilant, it would return in the future more virulent than ever.[16] As we are about to see, St. Pius X's prediction has come true—with a vengeance.

## Modernism Begins to Rise Again

A little-known drama that unfolded during the reign of Pope Pius XI demonstrates that the underground current of Modernist thought was alive and well in the immediate post-St. Pius X period.

Father Raymond Dulac relates that at the secret consistory of May 23, 1923, Pope Pius XI questioned the thirty Cardinals of the Curia on the timeliness of summoning an ecumenical council. In attendance were illustrious prelates such as Merry del Val, De Lai, Gasparri, Boggiani and Billot. The Cardinals advised against it. Cardinal Billot warned, "The existence of profound differences in the midst of the episcopacy itself cannot be concealed ... [They] run the risk of giving place to discussions that will be prolonged indefinitely."

Boggiani recalled the Modernist theories from which, he said, a part of the clergy and of the bishops are not exempt. "This mentality can incline certain Fathers to present motions, to introduce methods incompatible with Catholic traditions."

Billot was even more precise. He expressed his fear of seeing the council "maneuvered" by "the worst enemies of the Church, the Modernists, who are already getting ready, as certain indications show, to bring forth the revolution in the Church, a new 1789."[17]

## Masonic Predictions of a Modernist Breakthrough at an Ecumenical Council

In discouraging the idea of a Council for such reasons, these Cardinals showed themselves more apt at recognizing the "signs of the times" than all the post-Vatican II theologians combined. Yet their caution may have been rooted in something deeper. They may also have been haunted by the writings of the infamous illuminé, the excommunicated Canon Roca (1830-1893) who preached revolution and Church "reform", and who predicted in amazingly precise detail the subversion of the Church that would be brought about by a Council.

In *Athanasius and the Church of Our Time,* Bishop Graber quotes Roca's prediction of a "newly illuminated church" which would be influenced by the "socialism of Jesus".[18] In the mid-19th Century, Roca predicted that "The new church, which might not be able to retain anything of Scholastic doctrine and the original form of the former Church, will nevertheless receive consecration and canonical jurisdiction from Rome." Roca also, amazingly enough, predicted the liturgical "reform" after Vatican II: "[T]he divine cult in the form directed by the liturgy, ceremonial, ritual and regulations of the Roman Church will shortly undergo a transformation *at an ecumenical council,* which will restore to it the venerable simplicity of the golden age of the Apostles in accordance with the dictates of conscience and modern civilization."

Roca foretold that through this council will come "a perfect accord between the ideals of modern civilization and the ideal of Christ and His Gospel. This will be the consecration of the New Social Order and the solemn baptism of modern civilization." In other words, this council would usher in the triumph of the Masonic plan for subversion of the Church. Roca also spoke of the future of the Papacy. He wrote "There is a sacrifice in the offing which represents a solemn act of expiation ... The Papacy will fall; it will die under the hallowed knife *which the fathers of the last council will forge*. The papal caesar is a host [victim] crowned for the sacrifice." Roca enthusiastically predicted nothing short of a "new religion, new dogma, new ritual, new priesthood." He called the new priests "progressists" and speaks of the "suppression" of the soutane [cassock] and the "marriage of priests."[19]

Pointing to the writings of the French heresiarch, Abbé Melinge (who used the pseudonym Dr. Alta), Bishop Graber warned of a revolutionary program of "the replacement of the Roman faith by a 'pluri-confessional' pontificate, able to adapt to a polyvalent ecumenism, such as we are seeing established today in the intercelebration of priests and Protestant pastors." (Melinge was referring to certain renegade priests; today, however, the Pope himself conducts joint services, including Vespers, with Protestant "bishops.")[20]

Chilling echos of Roca, Melinge and the Alta Vendita are to be found in the words of the Rosicrucian, Dr. Rudolph Steiner who declared in 1910 "We need a council and a Pope to proclaim it."[21]

## The Masonic Alliance with Communism

It must be noted that in their striving toward these goals the Masons were the kin of the communists, who were plotting alongside them for the overthrow of both Church and State. As Pope Leo XIII observed in *Humanum Genus* (1884), his monumental encyclical on the threat posed by the Masonic societies: "Yea, this change and overthrow is deliberately planned and put forward by many associations of communists and socialists; and to their undertakings the sect of Freemasons is not hostile, but greatly favors their designs, and holds in common with them their chief opinions."

As we have since learned from numerous independent witnesses, Communist infiltration of the Church[22] began as early as the 1930s. Lenin himself (the very founder of Russian Communism) declared in the 1920's that he would infiltrate the Catholic Church, particularly the Vatican. The historical evidence on this score was recently summarized in the venerable periodical *Chrisitian Order*:

> Ex-Communist and celebrated convert Douglas Hyde revealed long ago that in the 1930s the Communist leadership issued a worldwide directive about infiltrating the Catholic Church. While in the early 1950s,

Mrs. Bella Dodd was also providing detailed explanations of the Communist subversion of the Church. Speaking as a former high ranking official of the American Communist Party, Mrs. Dodd said: "*In the 1930s we put eleven hundred men into the priesthood in order to destroy the Church from within.*" The idea was for these men to be ordained and progress to positions of influence and authority as Monsignors and Bishops. A dozen years before Vatican II she stated that: "*Right now they are in the highest places in the Church*"—where they were working to bring about change in order to weaken the Church's effectiveness against Communism. She also said that these changes would be so drastic that "*you will not recognize the Catholic Church.*"[23]

As *Christian Order* points out, the existence of a communist conspiracy to infiltrate the Church has been confirmed abundantly not only by former communists Dodd and Hyde, but also by Soviet defectors:

> Ex-KGB officer Anatoliy Golitsyn, who defected in 1961 and in 1984 forecast with 94% accuracy all the astonishing developments in the Communist Bloc since that time, confirmed several years ago that this "penetration of the Catholic and other churches is part of the Party's 'general line' [i.e. unchanged policy] in the struggle against religion." In fact, hundreds of files smuggled into the West by former KGB archivist Vassili Mitrokhin and published in 1999 tell a similar tale, about the KGB cultivating the closest possible relationships with 'progressive' Catholics and financing their activities. One of the leftist organs identified was the small Italian Catholic press agency *Adista*, which for decades has promoted every imaginable post-conciliar cause or "reform" and whose Director was named in *The Mitrokhin Archive* as a paid KGB agent.

Mrs. Dodd, who converted to the Faith shortly before her death, was legal counsel to the Communist Party of the United States. She gave voluminous testimony on Communist infiltration of Church and state before the House UnAmerican Activities Committee in the 1950s. As if to atone for her role in subverting the Church, Dodd delivered a series of lectures at Fordham University and elsewhere during the years leading up to Vatican II. *Christian Order* recounts the testimony of a monk who attended one of those lectures in the early 1950s:

> I listened to that woman for four hours and she had my hair standing on end. Everything she said has been fulfilled to the letter. You would think she was the world's greatest prophet, but she was no prophet. She was merely exposing the step-by-step battle plan of Communist subversion of the Catholic Church. She explained that of all the world's religions, the Catholic Church was the only one feared by the Communists, for it was its only effective opponent. *The whole idea was to destroy, not the institution of the Church, but rather the Faith of the people, and even use the institution of the Church, if possible, to destroy the Faith through the promotion of a pseudo-religion: something that resembled*

*Catholicism but was not the real thing*. Once the Faith was destroyed, she explained that there would be *a guilt complex introduced into the Church*. ... to label the 'Church of the past' as being oppressive, authoritarian, full of prejudices, arrogant in claiming to be the sole possessor of truth, and responsible for the divisions of religious bodies throughout the centuries. This would be necessary in order to shame Church leaders into an '*openness to the world*,' and to a *more flexible attitude toward all religions and philosophies*. The Communists would then exploit this openness in order to undermine the Church.[24]

Now, if the enemies of the Church were to succeed in their plans, which we have just outlined, we would see these things happening in the Church:

- First, there would be, as Roca predicted, an upheaval *at an ecumenical council* of such magnitude that the entire world would realize that the Catholic Church had undergone a revolution in line with modern ideas. It would be clear to all that an "updating" of the Church had taken place.
- Second, a new "theology" would be introduced that would tend to contradict previous teachings.
- Third, the Freemasons and Communists themselves would voice their cockle-doodle of triumph, believing that the Catholic Church had finally "seen the light" on such points as pluralism, the secular state, equality of religions, and whatever other compromises had been achieved.
- Fourth, as the result of this subversion, the new orientation of the Church would come to take precedence over the very dogmas and traditions of the Church in Her teaching and practice—including the Message of Fatima, which would have to be "revised" or buried to accommodate the new orientation.

It now remains for us to demonstrate the extent to which this design for subversion of the Church has come to pass, and how it has given rise to the motive for the grave crime committed: the attempt to nullify the authentic Message of Fatima. By this crime the accused have left the Church and the world exposed to the gravest possible dangers, including the annihilation of various nations and the loss of millions of souls. Truly, this is a crime not only against the Church but against humanity.

# Chapter 6

## The Motive Takes Hold

Around 1948, Pope Pius XII, at the request of the staunchly orthodox Cardinal Ruffini, considered calling a general Council and even spent a few years making the necessary preparations. There is evidence that progressive elements in Rome eventually dissuaded Pius XII from bringing it to realization since this Council showed definite signs of being in line with *Humani Generis* and its condemnation of modernist errors. Like this great 1950 encyclical, the new Council would combat "false opinions which threaten to undermine the foundations of Catholic doctrine."[1]

At the same time, the "errors of Russia" to which the Virgin of Fatima referred were penetrating the Church itself. Various Catholic religious orders were being infiltrated. For example, the so-called "Catholic Priest Worker" movement was so clearly infiltrated by Communists that Pope Pius XII called for an end to it in the 1950's.

Tragically, Pope Pius XII became convinced that he was too advanced in years to shoulder the momentous task of a Council to combat the swelling ranks of the Church's enemies, and he resigned himself to the decision that "this will be for my successor."[2] Pope Pius died on October 9, 1958.

And now we have arrived very near to the critical year in our case. We have arrived at 1958, two years before 1960—the year in which the Third Secret was to be disclosed in accordance with the wishes of the Virgin of Fatima, as Sister Lucy had testified. Throughout the Pontificate of Pope Pius XII, the Holy Office, under the able leadership of Cardinal Ottaviani, maintained a safe Catholic landscape by keeping the wild horses of modernism firmly corralled. Many of today's modernist theologians disdainfully recount how they and their friends had been "muzzled" during this period.

Yet even Ottaviani could not prevent what was to happen in 1958. A new type of Pope "whom the progressives believed to favor their cause"[3] would ascend to the Pontifical Chair and would force a reluctant Ottaviani to remove the latch, open the corral and brace himself for the stampede. However, such a state of affairs was not unforeseen. At the news of the death of Pius XII, the old Dom Lambert Beauduin, a friend of Roncalli's (the future John XXIII) confided to Father Bouyer: "If they elect Roncalli, everything would be saved; he would be capable of calling a council and of consecrating ecumenism."[4]

### A Council is Called as the Message of Fatima Comes Under Attack

And so it happened just as Dom Lambert foretold. Roncalli was elected and, as Pope John XXIII, called a Council and consecrated ecumenism. The "revolution in tiara and cope" predicted by the Alta Vendita was underway.

And one of the first acts of the revolution was to dispense with the Third Secret of Fatima. Contrary to the expectations of the whole world, on February 8, 1960 (just over a year after the Council had been called), the Vatican issued the following anonymous announcement through the A.N.I. press agency:

> Vatican City, February 8, 1960 (A.N.I.) – It is probable that the "Secret of Fatima" will never be made public. In Vatican circles highly worthy of belief, they have just declared to the representative of United Press International that it is most likely the letter will never be opened, in which Sister Lucy wrote down the words which the Virgin Mary addressed to the three shepherds of the Cova da Iria ... It is most probable that the "Secret of Fatima" will remain forever under absolute seal.

And in the same communiqué we find the first direct attack from Vatican sources on the credibility of the Message of Fatima as a whole:

> Although the Church recognizes the Fatima apparitions, she does not pledge herself to guarantee the veracity of the words which the three shepherds claim to have heard from Our Lady.

*Claim* to have heard? Could there be any doubt about the veracity of their testimony after the Miracle of the Sun? Could there be any question that they had been given an authentic prophecy from Heaven in view of the complete fulfillment of every prediction in the Message thus far—from the imminent end of World War I, to the spread of Russia's errors, to World War II and the election of Pius XI?

Here we see the first focused attack on the Message of Fatima from within the Vatican apparatus, as the Vatican begins, in 1960, to pursue a new orientation of the Church that will arise (as we shall soon see) at the Second Vatican Council. Consider these developments surrounding the February 8, 1960 communiqué:

- The communiqué publicly questions the veracity of Lucy, Jacinta, and Francisco.
- From 1960 forward, Sister Lucy is silenced on orders of the Vatican apparatus,[5] so she could not defend herself from the implied accusation that her testimony is unreliable.
- The documents in the official Fatima archives, which Father Alonso will compile between 1965 and 1976, (more than 5,000 documents in 24 volumes) will be barred from publication, even though these documents confirm that the Fatima prophecies in the first two parts of the Secret (the election of Pius XI, the coming of World War II, the spread of Communism throughout the world, etc.) had been revealed privately by Sr. Lucy long before their fulfillment, and that her testimony was utterly accurate and reliable.

*The crime had begun*. And now the motive for the crime—the desire to change the orientation of the Church away from the Catholic certitudes of the Message of Fatima and toward an "enlightened" accommodation to the world—would develop in earnest with the commencement of the Second Vatican Council on October 11, 1962. We recall again the words of Sister Lucy that Our Lady wished the Third Secret to be released in 1960 because it "will be clearer (mais claro) then." Now it would become very clear indeed.

## The "Errors of Russia" Infiltrate the Church

First, just before the Council's commencement, there would be another betrayal of the Message of Fatima, a sign of many unprecedented things to come. In the spring of 1962, in Metz, France, Cardinal Eugene Tisserant had a meeting with none other than Metropolitan Nikodim of the Russian Orthodox Church—a KGB operative, as were the other Orthodox prelates. At this meeting Tisserant and Nikodim negotiated what came to be known as the Metz Pact, or more popularly, the Vatican-Moscow Agreement.[6] The existence of the Vatican-Moscow Agreement is an irrefutable historical fact attested to in all of its details by Monsignor Roche, who was Cardinal Tisserant's personal secretary.

In substance, the agreement was as follows: Pope John, according to his fond wish, would be "favored" by the attendance of two Russian Orthodox observers at the Council. In return, the Catholic Church would agree that the Second Vatican Council would refrain from any condemnation of Soviet Communism or Soviet Russia. In essence, the Council would compromise the moral liberty of the Catholic Church by pretending that the most systematized form of human evil in human history did not exist—even though, at the very moment the Council opened, the Soviets were persecuting, imprisoning and murdering millions of Catholics.

Her liberty thus constrained in a bargain with Communists, the Council failed even to mention Communism. By this failure the Council departed from the teaching of Pope Leo XIII, Blessed Pius IX, Saint Pius X and also Pope Pius XI, who reminded the Church that we could not refrain from condemning this incomparable evil. As he said in *Divini Redemptoris*,

> This all too imminent danger, venerable brethren, as you have already surmised is Bolshevistic and atheistic Communism which aims at upsetting the social order and undermining the very foundations of Christian civilization. In the face of such a threat the Catholic Church *could not and does not remain silent*. This Apostolic See above all has *not refrained from raising its voice* for it knows that its proper and special mission is to defend truth, justice and all those eternal values which communism ignores or attacks.[7]

And yet the Council would say not one word about Soviet Communism, but would instead begin a "dialogue" with the very forces the Church once opposed.

Why did this happen? It was surely no "coincidence" that the Council's silence about Communism synchronized perfectly with the Communist infiltration of the Catholic Church which, as we showed in a previous chapter, had been revealed just before Vatican II by key witnesses with no motive to lie (Dodd, Hyde, Golitsyn, Mitrokhin and others). Even without such testimonies, our common sense should tell us that the forces of Communism (working alongside those of Freemasonry) would inevitably attempt to destroy the Catholic Church from within. Satan is intelligent enough to know that the Catholic Church is the one citadel he must storm in his effort to conquer the whole world for the kingdom of darkness.

This, then, was the state of affairs in the Church at the very moment that the Second Vatican Council was wrongly constrained to observe its shameful silence on the evil of Communism. And, needless to say, under the Vatican-Moscow Agreement, the Consecration of Soviet Russia to the Immaculate Heart by the Council Fathers, in order to bring about its conversion, would be absolutely out of the question. This early shift toward a new orientation of the Church, which the Council would accelerate in a most dramatic fashion, was already in conflict with the Message of Fatima.

And so it has been ever since the meeting in Metz, which marked the beginning of the conciliar and post-conciliar pursuit of *Ostpolitik*, the policy implemented by the Vatican Secretary of State under which the Church has ceased all condemnation and opposition to Communist regimes in favor of "dialogue" and "quiet diplomacy"—a policy which to this day has silenced the Vatican concerning the vicious persecution of the Church in Red China.

Thus on October 12, 1962, two representative priests of the Orthodox church debarked from a plane at Fiumicino Airport and attended the Second Vatican Council. The Council began with Orthodox observers watching its proceedings, making sure that the Vatican-Moscow Agreement was observed. The written intervention of 450 Council Fathers against Communism was mysteriously "lost" after being delivered to the Secretariat of the Council, and Council Fathers who stood up to denounce Communism were politely told to sit down and be quiet.[8]

The Church's own leaders had lowered the drawbridge to the Communists, at the same time Communists and Freemasons were attempting to destroy her from within by (to recall the predictions of Bella Dodd)

- encouraging "the promotion of a pseudo-religion: something that resembled Catholicism but was not the real thing,"
- labelling "the 'Church of the past' as being oppressive, authoritarian, full of prejudices, arrogant in claiming to be the sole possessor of truth, and responsible for the divisions of religious bodies throughout the centuries,"
- shaming Church leaders into "an 'openness to the world,' and to a more flexible attitude toward all religions and philosophies."

And finally, as Dodd predicted, "The Communists would then exploit this openness in order to undermine the Church."

This grand effort at subversion would involve, first and foremost, the breakthrough of modernist "theology" at an ecumenical council—just as Canon Roca and the other illumines of Freemasonry had boasted.

### The Neo-Modernists Triumph at Vatican II

On October 13, 1962, the day after the two communist observers arrived at the Council, and on the very anniversary of the Miracle of the Sun at Fatima, the history of the Church and the world was profoundly changed by the smallest of events. Cardinal Liénart of Belgium seized the microphone in a famous incident and demanded that the candidates proposed by the Roman Curia to chair the drafting commissions at the Council be set aside and that a new slate of candidates be drawn up. The demand was acceded to and the election postponed. When the election was finally held, liberals were elected to majorities and near-majorities on the conciliar commissions—many of them from among the very "innovators" decried by Pius XII. The traditionally formulated preparatory schemas for the Council were discarded and the Council began literally without a written agenda, leaving the way open for entirely new documents to be written by the liberals.

It is well known and superbly documented[9] that a clique of liberal *periti* (experts) and bishops then proceeded to hijack Vatican II with an agenda to remake the Church into their own image through the implementation of a "new theology". Both critics and defenders of Vatican II are in agreement on this point. In his book *Vatican II Revisited*, Bishop Aloysius J. Wycislo (a rhapsodic advocate of the Vatican II revolution) declares with giddy enthusiasm that "theologians and biblical scholars who had been 'under a cloud' for years surfaced as *periti* (theological experts advising the bishops at the Council), and their post-Vatican II books and commentaries became popular reading."[10]

He noted that "Pope Pius XII's encyclical *Humani Generis* had ... a devastating effect on the work of a number of pre-conciliar theologians",[11] and explains that "During the early preparation of the Council, those theologians (mainly French, with some Germans) whose activities had been restricted by Pope Pius XII, were still under a cloud. Pope John quietly lifted the ban affecting some of the most influential ones. Yet a number remained suspect to the officials of the Holy Office."[12]

On this point, the eyewitness testimony of Msgr. Rudolf Bandas, himself a conciliar *peritus*, is of decisive importance to our case:

> No doubt good Pope John thought that these suspect theologians would rectify their ideas and perform a genuine service to the Church. But exactly the opposite happened. Supported by certain Rhine Council Fathers, and often acting in a manner positively boorish, they turned around and exclaimed: "Behold, we are named experts, our ideas stand approved." ... When I entered my tribunal at the Council, on the first day

> of the fourth session, the first announcement, emanating from the Secretary of State, was the following: "No more periti will be appointed." But it was too late. The great confusion was underway. It was already apparent that *neither Trent nor Vatican I nor any encyclical would be permitted to impede its advance.*[13]

Indeed, Pope John XXIII himself was happy to announce that beginning with this Council the Church would, quite inexplicably, cease condemning error and stop all her worrying about the dire condition of the world:

> Nowadays ... the spouse of Christ prefers to make use of the medicine of mercy rather than the arms of severity. She considers that she meets the needs of the present day by demonstrating the validity of her teaching rather than by issuing condemnations. ... We feel we must disagree with those prophets of gloom, who are always forecasting disaster, as though the end of the world was at hand.[14]

But Pope John XXIII's optimism was quite at odds with the profound alarm over the state of the world to be seen in the many pronouncements of his immediate predecessors (not to mention in the Message of Fatima itself). Consider these few examples:

St. Pius X:

> We felt a sort of terror considering the disastrous conditions of humanity at the present hour. Can we ignore such a profound and grave evil, which at this moment much more than in the past is working away at its very marrow and leading it to its ruin? ... Truly whoever ponders these things *must necessarily and firmly fear* whether such a perversion of minds is not the sign of announcing, and the beginning of the last times ... *[E Supremi]*.

Pius XI:

> With God and Jesus Christ excluded from political life, with authority derived not from God but from man, ... the chief reason of the distinction between ruler and subject has been eliminated. The result is that society is *tottering to its ruin* because it no longer has a secure and solid foundation *[Quas Primas]*.

Pius XII (*after* the end of WWII):

> We are overwhelmed with sadness and anguish, seeing that the wickedness of perverse men has reached a degree of impiety that is *unbelievable and absolutely unknown in other times* [Letter of February 11, 1949].

> Venerable brethren, you are well aware that almost the whole human race is today allowing itself to be driven into two opposing camps, for Christ or against Christ. *The human race is involved today in a supreme*

*crisis,* which will issue in its salvation by Christ, or in its destruction [*Evangeli Praecones,* 1951].

To be sure, there would be countless battles at Vatican II between the International Group of Fathers who fought to uphold the dogmas of the Faith and Catholic Tradition, and the progressive Rhine group. Tragically, however, it was the liberal and modernist element that prevailed, let loose by Pope John XXIII's optimism that the truth would prevail of its own force without the aid of any medicinal condemnations by the Magisterium. Wycislo sings the praises of triumphant progressives such as Hans Küng, Karl Rahner, John Courtney Murray, Yves Congar, Henri de Lubac, Edward Schillebeeckx and Gregory Baum, who had been considered suspect before the Council (for good reason) and are now the leading lights of post-Vatican II theology.[15]

In effect, those whom Pope Pius XII considered unfit to be walking the streets of Catholicism were now in control of the town. And as if to crown their achievements, the *Oath Against Modernism* and the *Index of Forbidden Books* were both quietly suppressed shortly after the close of the Council—a decision Bishop Graber called "incomprehensible."[16] St. Pius X had predicted correctly. Lack of vigilance in authority had provoked modernism to return with a vengeance.

## Two Prominent Examples of "Rehabilitated" Neo-Modernists

Let us consider two examples of the "new" theologians who were let loose upon the Church to do their work of destruction: Dominque Chenu and Hans Küng.

Chenu was an advocate of the New Theology made famous by Henri de Lubac. Chenu was issued a condemnation for his progressive ideas in 1942 under Pope Pius XII.[17] His book *Une ecole de theologie* was placed on the Index of Forbidden Books and he lost his rectorship at the Dominican College of Le Saluchoir.[18] Father David Greenstock, writing in the 1950 *Thomist* against the New Theology of Chenu and de Lubac, explained the dangers of their system and the reason for their condemnation. Greenstock pointed out that the partisans of the New Theology reject Aristotelian-Thomistic philosophy in favor of modern philosophies. This must be done, they claim, in order to appeal to "modern man" who finds Thomistic philosophy "irrelevant". The result is that Catholic theology is knocked off of its firm, philosophical foundation and shifted onto the fluid philosophical systems of the 20th Century, most of which are founded upon atheism and agnosticism.

Chenu also rejected the unchangeableness of Catholic doctrine, claiming that the source of all theology is not immutable dogma, but rather the vital life[19] of the Church in its members, which cannot be separated from history. Thus, strictly speaking, says Greenstock, Chenu held that "theology is the life of the members of the Church, rather than a series of conclusions drawn from revealed data with the aid of reason"—a principle that is slippery, imprecise and erroneous. As a result, Chenu held that religion can change with the times, and should change with the times, according to the demands of circumstances.

Greenstock explained that the partisans of this New Theology are both unorthodox and deceitful. "The main contention of the partisan of this new movement," wrote Greenstock, "is that theology, to remain alive, must move with the times. At the same time, they are very careful to repeat all the fundamental propositions of traditional theology, almost as if there was no intention of any attack against it. This is very true of such writers as Fathers de Lubac, Daniélou, Rahner, ... All of whom are undoubtedly at the very center of this movement."[20]

The eminent Dominican theologian, Father Reginald Garrigou-LaGrange, writing in his famous 1946 essay "Where is the New Theology Taking Us?",[21] demonstrated that the purveyors of the New Theology (Blondel, de Lubac, Chenu) pervert entirely the concept of the immutability of Truth. Thus, he warned, the New Theology can only lead in one direction—straight back to Modernism.

While all this was going on, Father Chenu and Father de Lubac were receiving behind-the-scenes protection and encouragement from Cardinal Suhard, Archbishop of Paris. Suhard told Chenu not to worry because "In twenty years, everyone in the Church will be talking like you." As we can see, the Cardinal accurately predicted the invasion of the Church by neo-modernist thinking. Most Churchmen today *do* talk like Chenu. In the early 1960s, Father Chenu was one of many radical theologians who were invited to Vatican II by Pope John XXIII. In the end, thanks to the Council's progressivist orientation, Father Chenu saw many of his formally condemned theories advanced as part of Vatican II's new teachings, especially within *Gaudium et Spes*. Chenu relates joyfully that the very points for which his work was condemned in 1942 are the same exact points now promoted by members of the hierarchy in the name of the Council.[22]

As for Hans Küng, this "leading-light" of the post-conciliar period had worked closely at the Council with other radicals such as Congar, Ratzinger, Rahner and Schillebeeckx. In the 1970s, however, because Küng had gone "too far", he was censored by the Vatican for certain heretical views, including the following: rejection of the Church's infallibility; the claim that bishops do not receive their teaching authority from Christ; the suggestion that any baptized layperson has the power to confect the Holy Eucharist; the denial that Christ is "consubstantial" with the Father; the undermining of doctrines (unspecified) concerning the Virgin Mary.[23]

It needs to be pointed out that these are only *some* of Küng's heretical views, but they were the only ones mentioned within the Vatican's sanctions. Thus, in effect, the Vatican left Küng's other heterodox tenets untouched. For example, in one of his most famous books entitled *On Being a Christian*, Hans Küng:

- denies the Divinity of Christ (p. 130)

- dismisses the miracles of the Gospel (p. 233)
- denies the bodily resurrection of Jesus (p. 350)
- denies that Christ founded an institutional Church (p. 109)
- denies that the Mass is the re-presentation of Calvary (p. 323).[24]

Küng has never retracted these unorthodox and heretical statements. Moreover, Küng has publicly called for a revision of Church teaching on issues such as papal infallibility, birth control, mandatory celibacy of priests, and women in the priesthood. Despite this blatant rejection of Church teaching, the only penalty that the Vatican ever inflicted against Küng was that he was "not allowed" to be considered a Catholic theologian, and as such, was not allowed to teach theology in a Catholic university. This "penalty" was circumvented when the University of Tübiginin, Küng's home campus, retained Küng as a teaching professor and simply restructured part of the University so that Küng, a great celebrity, may continue teaching in that part of the University which is now chartered as a "secular" school.

Meanwhile, the Vatican has never condemned Küng as a heretic, never excommunicated him (as canon law provides), never ordered that his books be removed from libraries in Catholic seminaries and universities (where they are now found in abundance), never prevented him from being a guest-lecturer at Catholic institutions, never obstructed him from publishing articles in *Concilium* or other progressivist "Catholic" publications. Father Hans Küng is not even suspended. Rather, to this day, Küng remains a priest in good standing in the diocese of Basle, with no other canonical penalties leveled against him.

This means that a priest who continues to vomit his heretical poison upon anyone within reach is still allowed to conduct public liturgy, preach and give advice in the confessional. The Vatican's Congregation for the Clergy, under Cardinal Castrillón Hoyos, leaves him untouched. So, despite the feeble Vatican "condemnation", Küng retains access to a wide variety of influential "pipelines" to disseminate his poisonous doctrine throughout the Church. In fact, it is said that Hans Küng's "theological breakthroughs" on the nature of the Church are what provided the "theological foundation" that made possible the 1999 "Lutheran-Catholic" Accord.

Further, in 1998, Vatican Secretary of State Cardinal Sodano, the most powerful Cardinal in the Church, praised Küng in a public speech at the Lateran, in which he lauded Küng's "beautiful pages dedicated to the Christian mystery".[25] Cardinal Sodano also referred to Küng as "the German theologian" even though Küng had been supposedly stripped of that title. (This is the same Cardinal Angelo Sodano who is ultimately behind the present persecution of Father Nicholas Gruner and his Fatima apostolate, as we shall see.)

Now, the 1942 condemnation that the Vatican leveled at Chenu was much more severe than what was hurled at Küng. Yet Chenu not only survived, but became a leading light of the Conciliar Church without ever changing his erroneous views. The same is true of Rahner, Congar, de Lubac and von

Balthasar, all of whom were theologically suspect before the Council but came to enjoy great prestige—even though they never abandoned a single one of their heterodox opinions. Even the likes of Küng has reason to believe that whatever mild condemnation he suffers is just a temporary inconvenience, an annoying setback, a fate meted out to all true "prophets." Just as Chenu saw his heretical views eventually win the day thanks to a revolutionary Council, so likewise Küng may fill his breast with the hope that his errors will, in the not-so-distant future, eventually emerge as "mainstream" Catholicism *de facto,* even if not by any actual teaching of the authentic Magisterium, which could never bind the Church to such errors.

## The Neo-Modernists Hail the "New" Church of Vatican II

With good reason, then, have progressivists such as Cardinal Suenens, Küng, Louis Bouyer and Yves Congar celebrated Vatican II as a Revolution, as the death of one era and the beginning of a new:

- Cardinal Suenens, who wielded great influence over Pope Paul VI, and who is a darling to those in the Church who call themselves "Charismatics", rejoiced that Vatican II marked the end of the Tridentine epoch and the end of the era of Vatican I.[26]
- Hans Küng gloated, "Compared to the post-Tridentine epoch of the Counter-reformation, Vatican Council II represents in its fundamental characteristics, a 180 degree turn ... It is a new Church that has sprung up since Vatican II."[27]
- Father Bouyer, a French *peritus* at the Council, exclaimed with relish that the anti-Protestant, anti-Modernist aspect of the Catholic Church "might as well die."[28]
- Likewise, the Rome-based Jesuit magazine, *La Civiltà Cattolica,* also exclaimed joyfully, "With Vatican Council II, the Tridentine age was brought to a close for the Church."[29]

These statements are especially audacious when we consider that the Councils of Trent and Vatican I are dogmatic Councils whose teachings can never be changed, disregarded, or reinterpreted in the name of a "deeper understanding". The First Vatican Council declared infallibly:

> The meaning of Sacred Dogmas, which must always be preserved, is that which our Holy Mother the Church has determined. Never is it permissible to depart from this in the name of a deeper understanding.[30]

Modernists, however, as Pope Saint Pius X warned, do not accept anything as fixed or unchanging. Their chief principle is the "evolution of dogma". They champion the notion that religion must change for the sake of changing times. In this respect, as in many others, the prime movers of Vatican II reveal themselves as men steeped in the error of Modernism.

## Masons and Communists Rejoice

Along with the neo-modernists, the Masons and communists have rejoiced at the Council's outcome. Just as the authors of the *Permanent Instruction of the Alta Vendita* had hoped, just as the Communist infiltrators spoken of by Bella Dodd had hoped, the notions of liberal culture had finally won adherence among the major players in the Catholic hierarchy. Freemasons and Communists have celebrated the astounding turn of events wrought by the Council. They rejoice that Catholics have finally "seen the light," and that many of their Masonic principles have been sanctioned by the Church.

For example, Yves Marsaudon of the Scottish Rite, in his book *Ecumenism Viewed by a Traditional Freemason* praised the ecumenism nurtured at Vatican II. He said:

> Catholics ... must not forget that all roads lead to God. And they will have to accept that this courageous idea of freethinking, which we can really call a revolution, pouring forth from our Masonic lodges, has spread magnificently over the dome of St. Peter's.[31]

Yves Marsaudon was delighted to add that "One can say that ecumenism is the legitimate son of Freemasonry."[32]

The post-Vatican II spirit of doubt and revolution obviously warmed the heart of French Freemason Jacques Mitterand, who wrote approvingly:

> Something has changed within the Church, and replies given by the Pope to the most urgent questions such as priestly celibacy and birth control, are hotly debated within the Church itself; the word of the Sovereign Pontiff is questioned by bishops, by priests, by the faithful. For a Freemason, a man who questions dogma is already a Freemason without an apron.[33]

Marcel Prelot, a senator for the Doubs region in France, is probably the most accurate in describing what has really taken place. He wrote:

> We had struggled for a century and a half to bring our opinions to prevail within the Church and had not succeeded. Finally, there came Vatican II and we triumphed. From then on the propositions and principles of liberal Catholicism have been definitively and officially accepted by Holy Church.[34]

The Communists were equally delighted with the results of the Council. As the Italian Communist Party declared at its 11th Party Congress in 1964: "The extraordinary 'awakening' of the Council, which is rightly compared with the Estates General of 1789, has shown the whole world that the old politico-religious Bastille is shaken to its foundations."[35] *L'Unita,* the official publication of the Italian Communist Party, brazenly gave advice to Pope Paul VI regarding Archbishop Marcel Lefebvre, who led traditionalist opposition to the conciliar liberals and had militated for a conciliar condemnation of Communism: "Be conscious of the danger that Lefebvre represents. And continue the magnificent movement of approach begun with the ecumenism of Vatican II."[36]

## A Whole New "Orientation" for the Church

The public exclamations of delight over Vatican II from neo-modernist luminaries, communists and Masons should not be surprising. It was obvious to anyone who had eyes to see that the Second Vatican Council appeared to embrace ideas that had been condemned by Pope Blessed Pius IX in the *Syllabus of Errors*, but were in step *with Modernist thought*. (As we will discuss further, Cardinal Ratzinger himself has described certain aspects of the Council's teaching as a "countersyllabus".) This did not happen by accident, but by design. The progressivists at Vatican II sought to avoid direct statements which would easily be seen as condemned Modernist errors. They also deliberately planted ambiguities in the Council texts which they intended to exploit after the Council.[37]

By utilizing deliberate ambiguities, the Council documents promoted an ecumenism that had been condemned by Pope Pius XI, a religious liberty for false sects that had been condemned by the 19th Century Popes (especially Blessed Pope Pius IX), a new liturgy along the lines of Protestantism and ecumenism that Archbishop Bugnini[38] called "a major conquest of the Catholic Church", a collegiality that strikes at the heart of the Papal primacy, and a "new attitude toward the world"—especially in one of the most radical of all the Council documents, *Gaudium et Spes*. Even Cardinal Ratzinger has admitted that *Gaudium et Spes* is permeated by the spirit of Teilhard de Chardin.[39]

The result of all this was nothing short of an entirely new orientation of the Church, or what Pope Paul VI called an "opening to the world." As Pope Paul VI himself was forced to admit, however, the opening to the world proved to be a disastrous miscalculation.

## Pope Paul VI Admits that the Church Has Been Invaded By Worldly Thinking

As Pope Paul VI himself admitted only eight years after the Council, "the opening to the world has become a veritable invasion of the Church by worldly thinking. We have perhaps been too weak and imprudent." Only three years after the Council, Paul VI had admitted that "The Church is in a disturbed period of self-criticism, or what could better be called self-demolition."[40] And in 1972, in perhaps the most astonishing remark ever made by a Roman Pontiff, Paul VI lamented that "from somewhere or other the smoke of Satan has entered the temple of God."[41]

Let us consider some of the manifest reasons for Pope Paul VI's astounding admissions.

## The Church "Opens" Itself to "Dialogue" with Communist and Masonic Enemies

With Vatican II began the large enterprise of collaboration with the forces of the world, the great opening to the world. Nowhere is this more apparent than in *Gaudium et Spes* itself, which declares: "By unremitting study they"—meaning every priest in the Catholic Church, every bishop, every member of the hierarchy—"should fit themselves to do their part in establishing dialogue with the world and with men of all shades of opinion".

Now the objection will be raised: What is wrong with peaceful collaboration and dialogue with men of all shades of opinion in those areas in which the Church can find some sort of basic agreement? Here again the pre-conciliar Popes warned us about one of the devil's snares and delusions under the appearance of good. Speaking precisely about this call to collaborate and dialogue with Communists in causes which are supposedly common to all mankind—which is really the devil's call for the Church to lay down her arms and join the enemy—Pope Pius XI warned as follows in *Divini Redemptoris*:

> In the beginning Communism showed itself for what it was in all its perversity. But very soon it realized that it was alienating people. It has, therefore, changed its tactics and strives to entice the multitudes by trickery in various forms, hiding its real designs behind ideas that are in themselves good and attractive. Under various names that do not suggest Communism, they try perfidiously to worm their way even into professedly Catholic and religious organizations. They invite Catholics to collaborate with them in the realm of so-called humanitarianism and charity. And at times make proposals that are in perfect harmony with the Christian spirit and the doctrine of the Church. See to it faithful brethren that the Faithful do not allow themselves to be deceived. ***Communism is intrinsically evil, and no one who would save Christian civilization may collaborate with it in any undertaking whatsoever***.[42]

Pius XI could not have been clearer about the duty to shun "dialogue" and collaboration with Communists. And why? The Italians have a saying: *Dimmi con chi vai, e ti diro che sei*—"Tell me who you go with and I will tell you what you are." As Pius XI recognized, if one associates with a certain class of people, one will inevitably be influenced to become as they are, in spite of oneself. If one collaborates with the forces of the world they will tend to seduce him; he will become like them. If the Church opens itself to the world in the sense of ceasing her opposition to the powers that she once opposed, and if she says instead that the Church will now collaborate and dialogue with her enemies, her members will, in time, become like those they once opposed. And the opening to the world will result in the Church becoming like the world.

## The Church "Reconciles" Itself with Liberalism

Those "conservatives" who deny that Vatican II constitutes a break with tradition, or that it contradicts prior teaching, have failed to listen to the very movers and shakers of the Council, who shamelessly acknowledge the truth. Yves Congar, one of the Council's "experts" and chief among the artisans of the Council's reforms, remarked with quiet satisfaction that "The Church has had, peacefully, its October revolution."[43] Congar also admitted, as if it were something to be proud of, that Vatican II's *Declaration on Religious Liberty* is contrary to the *Syllabus* of Pope Pius IX.[44] He said:

> It cannot be denied that the affirmation of religious liberty by Vatican II says materially something other than what the *Syllabus* of 1864 said, and even just about the opposite of propositions 16, 17 and 19 of this document.[45]

Congar thus blithely suggests that Vatican II has undone an infallible papal condemnation of error.

Most noteworthy are the statements of the progressivist Cardinal Suenens, one of the most liberal prelates of this century, himself a Council Father, who spoke glowingly of the old regimes that have come crashing down. The words he used in praise of the Council are supremely telling, perhaps the most chilling and the most damning of all. Suenens declared "Vatican II is the French Revolution of the Church."[46]

And, only a few years ago, none other than Cardinal Ratzinger, apparently unruffled by such admissions, added one of his own. According to him, the Vatican II text *Gaudium et Spes* is nothing less than a "*counter*-Syllabus". He said:

> If it is desirable to offer a diagnosis of the text (*Gaudium et Spes)* as a whole, we might say that (in conjunction with the texts on religious liberty, and world religions) it is a revision of the *Syllabus* of Pius IX, *a kind of countersyllabus* ... Let us be content to say here that the text serves as a *countersyllabus* and, as such, represents on the part of the Church, *an attempt at an official reconciliation with the new era inaugurated in 1789*. ... the *one-sidedness* of the position adopted by the Church under Pius IX and Pius X in response to the situation created by the new phase of history inaugurated by the French Revolution was, to a large extent, *corrected via facti*, especially in Central Europe, but there was still no basic statement of the relationship that should exist between the Church and the world that had come into existence after 1789. In fact, *an attitude that was largely pre-revolutionary continued to exist in countries with strong Catholic majorities*. Hardly anyone will deny today that the Spanish and Italian Concordat strove to preserve *too much of a view of the world that no longer corresponded to the facts*. Hardly anyone will deny today that, in the field of education and with respect to the historico-critical method in modern science, anachronisms existed that corresponded closely to this adherence to *an obsolete Church-state relationship*.[47]

Consider the sheer audacity of a Cardinal calling two of the greatest Popes in Church history "one-sided" in their efforts to protect the Church from the errors of liberalism and modernism! According to Cardinal Ratzinger himself, at Vatican II the Church made an "attempt" to "correct" and "counter" the teaching of Blessed Pius IX and Saint Pius X, and to reconcile itself instead *with the French Revolution* and the Enlightenment.

*But this was the very goal of the* Permanent Instruction, *Masonry's blueprint for subversion of the Church!* That is precisely why, in his *Syllabus of Errors*, Blessed Pius IX condemned the proposition that "The Roman Pontiff can and ought to reconcile himself and come to terms with progress, liberalism and modern civilization." (Condemned Proposition #80). And Saint Pius X, in his apostolic letter *Notre Charge Apostolique*, condemned the Sillon movement in France, rebuking its members because "They do not fear to make blasphemous reconciliations between the Gospel and the Revolution."

But according to Ratzinger, "*there can be no return to the Syllabus*, which may have marked the first stage in the confrontation with liberalism but cannot be the last stage."[48] And what is this last "stage" in the "confrontation with liberalism"? Apparently, in Ratzinger's view, it is the Church's *acceptance* of the very ideas she once condemned! Confronting liberalism by *reconciling* with it? What sort of double-talk is this? Ratzinger's "confrontation" with liberalism is nothing more than an abject surrender.

Moreover, in the opinion of Cardinal Ratzinger, not only the condemnations of liberalism in the *Syllabus* of Blessed Pius IX but also the anti-modernist teaching of Saint Pius X in *Pascendi* must now be considered outdated. In 1990, the Congregation for the Doctrine of the Faith issued an "Instruction on the Theologian's Ecclesiastical Vocation." In explaining the Instruction to the press, Cardinal Ratzinger claimed that certain teachings of the Magisterium were "not considered to be the final word on the subject as such, but serve rather as a mooring in the problem, and, above all, as an expression of pastoral prudence, a kind of *temporary disposition*."[49] As examples of these "temporary dispositions," Ratzinger cited "the statements of the Popes during the last century on religious freedom, as well as the anti-modernist decisions at the beginning of this century ..."[50]—that is, the anti-modernist teaching of Saint Pius X in the early 1900s.

These comments by Cardinal Ratzinger should disturb any Catholic, not only because they admit that the Council embraced a cherished goal of the Church's enemies, but because they come from the very man who, as the head of the Sacred Congregation for the Doctrine of the Faith (CDF), is supposed to be in charge of *guarding* the purity of Catholic doctrine. And this, as we shall soon show, is the same man who has led the charge to do away with the traditional Catholic understanding of the Message of Fatima.

## The Teaching that the Roman Catholic Church Is Exclusively the One True Church of Christ Is Abandoned

As the attempt to reconcile the Church with the principles of the French Revolution would neutralize the Church's once fierce opposition to the errors of the modern age, so would the "ecumenical venture" launched at the Council soon bring about the *de facto* abandonment of all efforts to convert Protestants and schismatics to the Catholic faith—as in the conversion of Russia.

At the same time the Council embraced the "ecumenical movement"—only 35 years after Pius XI had condemned it in his encyclical *Mortalium Animos*—the Council's document *Lumen Gentium* threw into confusion the whole doctrine of the Catholic Church as the one true Church. According to *Lumen Gentium* "the Church of Christ ... *subsists* in the Catholic Church."

This causes bewilderment. Why doesn't the document clearly proclaim what the Catholic Church has always taught, as seen in the encyclicals of Pius XII—namely, that the one true Church of Christ *is* the Catholic Church?[51] Why employ a term favorable to the progressivist error that the Church of Christ is actually *bigger* than the Catholic Church, so that schismatic and Protestant sects are "in some mysterious way" part of (or linked with) the Church of Christ? This error, based upon Vatican II's use of the word "subsists", is trumpeted by Father Avery Dulles, recently made a Cardinal by Pope John Paul II:

> ***The Church of Jesus Christ is not exclusively identical to the Roman Catholic Church***. It does indeed subsist in Roman Catholicism, but it *is also present in varying modes and degrees in other Christian communities* to the extent that *they too are what God initiated in Jesus* and are obedient to the inspirations of Christ's Spirit. As a result of their common sharing in the reality of the one Church, the several Christian communities already have with one another a real but imperfect communion.[52]

Likewise, Cardinal Ratzinger once again embraces the views of the "new theology." In an interview with the German newspaper *Frankfurter Allgemeine*, Ratzinger said the following:

> When the Council Fathers replaced the word "is" with the word "subsistit" (subsists), they did so for a very precise reason. The concept expressed by "is" (to be) is far broader than that expressed by "to subsist." "To subsist" is a very precise way of being, that is, to be as a subject, which exists in itself. Thus the Council Fathers meant to say that *the being of the Church as such is a broader entity than the Roman Catholic Church*, but within the latter it acquires, in an incomparable way, the character of a true and proper subject.[53]

Ratzinger claims that the Council Fathers *intended* to say that the "being" of the Church is broader than the Catholic Church, but his claim is false. The generality of the Council Fathers had no intention of contradicting the teaching of Pius XII that the Church of Christ *is* the Catholic Church, not some vague "entity" that is "broader" than the Catholic Church.

In truth, it was *Ratzinger's* intention to use ambiguity to undermine the traditional teaching that the one and only Church of Christ *is* the Catholic Church—an intention he shared with his fellow partisans of the "new theology" at Vatican II. We know this because it was Father Ratzinger himself, serving as a theological *peritus* at the Council, who introduced the term "subsistit" (subsists) into the drafting of the conciliar document *Lumen Gentium*. He inserted this term at the suggestion of a *Protestant minister*, Pastor Schmidt, from Germany.

If the reader finds Ratzinger's explanation of the use of the term "subsistit" (subsists) to be confusing, know that it was *meant* to be. "Subsists" and "is" can, however, mean the very same thing, contrary to what Ratzinger suggests. For the sake of the precision that should characterize any conciliar document, the Council ought to have stated clearly that "The Church of Christ subsists *only* in the Catholic Church." But as Father Edward Schillebeeckx, another conciliar *peritus*, admitted, his liberal confreres had deliberately inserted ambiguities into the conciliar texts,[54] knowing that they would later be able to interpret them in a heterodox manner after the Council.

That is precisely what Cardinal Ratzinger now does with the ambiguous term "subsistit" (subsists). Indeed, the original German text of the above-quoted interview in *Frankfurter Allgemeine* shows that Ratzinger is even more radical in his departure from the teaching of Pius XII: "... die Konzilsväter das *von Pius XII gebrauchte* Wort 'ist' durch 'subsistit' ersetzten"—literally, "... the Council Fathers replaced the word 'is,' *used by Pius XII*, with 'subsistit.'" That is, Cardinal Ratzinger admits that Vatican II *replaced* the terminology of Pius XII—thanks to none other than Cardinal Ratzinger and his Protestant minister friend! Even worse, the original German of the interview also states: "So wollten die Väter sagen: Das Sein der Kirche als solches *reicht viel weiter* als die römisch-katholische Kirche,"—literally, "Thus the Fathers meant to say: the being of the Church as such *extends much further* than the Roman Catholic Church."[55] Thus, Dulles and Ratzinger flatly contradict the perennial Catholic teaching that the Church of Christ *exists exclusively in* the Catholic Church. Yet their view is now the common interpretation of Vatican II.

Here we see a prime example of how the "new theologians" at Vatican II have passed the theological football to themselves, while pretending that it was the "Council" that threw the pass.

## The Church No Longer Seeks the Conversion and Return of Heretics and Schismatics

With this new view of "the Church of Christ" as something much bigger than the Roman Catholic Church, it is no wonder that after 40 years of "ecumenical activity" even Vatican prelates now openly repudiate the return of Protestants and schismatics to Rome.

For example, there was the recent statement of Cardinal Walter Kasper, the former secretary of the Church's most prominent post-conciliar heretic, Hans Küng. Kasper, whose modernist views are well-known throughout the Church, was made a Cardinal by Pope John Paul II in February 2001 and now enjoys the rank of Prefect of the Vatican's Pontifical Council for Promoting Christian Unity. Kasper said:

> ... today we no longer understand ecumenism in the sense of a return, by which the others would 'be converted' and return to being 'Catholics'. This was expressly abandoned at Vatican II.[56]

In fact, Kasper's statement scorns the thrice-defined infallible dogma that "outside the Church there is no salvation."[57] For example, there is Pope Eugene IV's infallible *ex cathedra* declaration that "none of those existing outside the Catholic Church, not only pagans, but also Jews, heretics, and schismatics, can ever be partakers of eternal life, but that they are to go into the eternal fire 'which was prepared for the devil and his angels,' (Mt. 25:41) unless before death they are joined with Her; ... no one, even if he pour out his blood for the Name of Christ, can be saved unless they abide within the bosom and unity of the Catholic Church."[58]

Kasper's view also flatly contradicts the constant teaching of the Church that the only way to Christian unity is *the return of the dissidents* to the Catholic Church through their conversion. In the 1949 admonition of the Holy Office of Pius XII concerning the "ecumenical movement," the bishops were warned that in any "ecumenical" discussions they might authorize, the Protestant interlocutors must be presented with "the Catholic truth" and "the teaching of the Encyclicals of the Roman Pontiffs on the return of the dissidents to the Church."[59] The Catholic doctrine of the return of the dissidents was stressed again by Pius XII himself on December 20, 1949: "The Catholic doctrine will have to be proposed and exposed totally and integrally: what the Catholic Church teaches about the true nature and means of justification, about the constitution of the Church, about the primacy of the jurisdiction of the Roman Pontiff, about the only true union which is accomplished with *the return of the dissidents* to the only true Church of Christ, must not be passed over in silence or covered over in ambiguous words."[60]

At least Kasper says openly what most of today's prelates seem to believe anyway, but will neither confirm nor deny. Kasper's "policy" is based on a total repudiation of the Church's solemn teaching on the return of the dissidents, and it implicitly denies the dogma that there is no salvation outside the Catholic Church. Yet Kasper's policy actually represents the prevailing "spirit of Vatican II." This was confirmed by none other than Cardinal Ratzinger, when he was still Father Ratzinger, in his 1966 book *Theological Highlights of Vatican II.* In *Theological Highlights* Ratzinger claims that the Council had given the Church *a new orientation toward non-Catholics*, which dispenses with any call for their conversion:

> The Catholic Church has no right to absorb the other Churches ... [A] basic unity—of Churches that remain Churches, yet become one Church—*must replace the idea of conversion*, even though conversion retains its meaningfulness for those in conscience motivated to seek it.[61]

Now, Cardinal Ratzinger wrote this book during the Council. As a co-worker with Karl Rahner, he was heavily involved with drafting the conciliar documents. He is in a position to tell us what were the actual intentions of the "architects" of Vatican II, which is not to be confused with the intention of the Council Fathers themselves. And he declares that the teaching of Vatican II, according to those who drew up the documents, was that conversion is an option.[62] That is, the non-Catholic need not convert to the true Church—either for salvation or for unity.

This view is no less radical than that of Father Edward Schillebeeckx, another progressivist Council *peritus*, who was investigated by the Vatican after the Council (but never disciplined) for his open denial of various Catholic dogmas. Schillebeeckx exulted that "At Vatican II, the Catholic Church officially abandoned its monopoly over the Christian religion."[63]

Likewise, a "Catholic" journal from the Rome-based International Jewish-Christian Documentation Service (SIDIC)[64] spoke of Vatican II's new orientation toward non-Catholics. In 1999 it spotlighted what it considers to be the "main problem" with so-called "traditional Catholics", including Archbishop Lefebvre:

> Lefebvre's refusal to accept ecumenism originates in clear teachings from the Magisterium: the encyclical *Satis Cognitum* of Leo XIII (1896); the encyclical *Mortalium Animos* of Pius XI (1928); the Dec. 20, 1949, Instruction of the Holy Office regarding ecumenism. The only ecumenism accepted by Lefebvre and his followers is that which strives for the ***unconditional return*** of the members of other confessions to the one Church of Christ, the Roman Catholic Church. ***This hardened sectarianism is precisely the kind of logic which Vatican II***, through profound reflection on the nature of the Church, ***refused to accept*** ...[65]

The novel claim that non-Catholics need not convert because they are "in some mysterious way" part of the Church of Christ[66] scorns the Church's perennial teaching on the necessity of non-Catholics to abandon their errors and return to the one true Church of Jesus Christ, as the pre-conciliar Popes unanimously taught.

Even more disturbing are reported cases of Vatican Cardinals *actively discouraging* non-Catholics who desire to convert to Catholicism. *Catholic Family News* published the story of Father Linus Dragu Popian, who had been raised in the Romanian Orthodox religion. In 1975 he risked his life to escape Communist Romania and presented himself as a seminarian to the Vatican, expressing his wish to convert to Catholicism. The then-Secretary of State, Cardinal Villot, and other Vatican Cardinals were horrified. They told young Popian that he must not flee Communism and must not become Catholic, because this would damage the Vatican's relations with Communist Romania and the Romanian Orthodox Church.[67]

Little has changed in Rome since then. Bishop Fellay of the Society of St. Pius X related in a recent interview that he had met a schismatic [Orthodox] bishop who wanted to convert to the Catholic Church. Bishop Fellay advised him to deal directly with Rome. When the Orthodox bishop told the Vatican he wanted to become a Catholic, "panic ensued. The following day, Cardinal Neves, Prefect of the Congregation of Bishops said to the schismatic bishop, 'Your Excellency, it is not necessary to convert. Since the Council, things have changed! There's no need to convert any more.'"[68]

This deliberate refusal to allow a schismatic Orthodox bishop to return to Rome is completely in line with the Balamand Declaration of 1993, negotiated between certain Vatican officials and various Orthodox churches. In this document the Vatican's representative (Cardinal Cassidy of the Pontifical Council for "Christian Unity") actually agreed that, owing to "radically altered perspectives and thus attitudes" engendered by Vatican II, the Catholic Church will train new priests "to pave the way for future relations between the two churches, passing beyond *the outdated ecclesiology of return to the Catholic Church*."[69] The claim that the Magisterium's constant teaching on the return of the dissidents (heretics and schismatics) to the one true Church as the only means of true Christian unity could become "outdated" is heretical. This outrageous statement flatly denies the infallible dogmatic teaching of the Church:

> There is but one universal Church of the faithful, outside which no one at all is saved. (Pope Innocent III, Fourth Lateran Council, 1215.)
>
> We declare, say, define, and pronounce that it is absolutely necessary for the salvation of every human creature to be subject to the Roman Pontiff. (Pope Boniface VIII, the Bull *Unam Sanctam*, 1302.)
>
> The most Holy Roman Church firmly believes, professes and preaches that none of those existing outside the Catholic Church, not only pagans, but also Jews and heretics and schismatics, can have a share in life eternal; but that they will go into the eternal fire which was prepared for the devil and his angels, unless before death they are joined with Her; and that so important is the unity of this ecclesiastical body that only those remaining within this unity can profit by the sacraments of the Church unto salvation, and they alone can receive an eternal recompense for their

> fasts, their almsgivings, their other works of Christian piety and the duties of a Christian soldier. No one, let his almsgiving be as great as it may, no one, even if he pour out his blood for the Name of Christ, can be saved, unless he remain within the bosom and the unity of the Catholic Church. (Pope Eugene IV, the Bull *Cantate Domino*, 1442.)

Thus, in defiance of a thrice-defined truth of the Catholic faith, a Vatican-negotiated agreement declares that the conversion of Russia called for by Our Lady of Fatima is nothing but "outdated ecclesiology"! This in itself should give any Catholic pause.

## The Social Kingship of Christ Abandoned

As a consequence of the Church's unprecedented new orientation since Vatican II, there has been a *de facto* abandonment of the Church's constant teaching on the Social Kingship of Christ. According to this teaching, not only individual men, but all nations, are obliged to submit to Christ and conform themselves to His teaching. It is the teaching of Christ, not "dialogue" with unbelievers, that will bring peace to the world; it is His Church that must serve as the chief instrument of world peace. The constant teaching of the Church on this doctrine is summed up with admirable concision by Pius XI in his encyclical *Ubi Arcano Dei*:

> Since the Church is the safe and sure guide to conscience, for to her safekeeping alone there has been confided the doctrines and the promise of the assistance of Christ, she is able not only to bring about at the present hour a peace that is truly the peace of Christ, but can, *better than any other agency which We know of*, contribute greatly to the securing of the same peace for the future, to making war impossible in the future. For the Church teaches (*she alone* has been given by God the mandate and the right to teach with authority) that not only our acts as individuals *but also as groups and as nations* must conform to the eternal law of God. In fact, it is much more important that the acts of a nation follow God's law, since on the nation rests a much greater responsibility for the consequences of its acts than on the individual. *When, therefore, governments and nations follow in all their activities, whether they be national or international, the dictates of conscience grounded in the teachings, precepts, and example of Jesus Christ, and which are binding on each and every individual, then only can we have faith in one another's word and trust in the peaceful solution of the difficulties and controversies which may grow out of differences in point of view or from clash of interests.*[70]

Speaking of efforts to obtain world peace through a League of Nations, Pius XI declared:

> An attempt in this direction has already and is now being made; its results, however, are almost negligible and, especially so, as far as they can be said to affect those major questions which divide seriously and serve to arouse nations one against the other. *No merely human institution*

> *of today can be as successful in devising a set of international laws which will be in harmony with world conditions as the Middle Ages were in the possession of that true League of Nations, Christianity*. It cannot be denied that in the Middle Ages this law was often violated; still it always existed as an ideal, according to which one might judge the acts of nations, and a beacon light calling those who had lost their way back to the safe road.[71]

In order to reinforce this teaching, Pius XI inaugurated the Feast of Christ the King with his encyclical *Quas Primas*:

> It was surely right, then, in view of the common teaching of the sacred books, that the Catholic Church, which is the kingdom of Christ on earth, destined to be spread among all men and all nations, should with every token of veneration salute Her Author and Founder in Her annual liturgy as King and Lord, and as King of kings. ... [T]he empire of our Redeemer embraces all men. To use the words of Our immortal predecessor, Pope Leo XIII: "His empire includes not only Catholic nations, not only baptized persons who, though of right belonging to the Church, have been led astray by error, or have been cut off from Her by schism, but also all those who are outside the Christian faith; so that truly the whole of mankind is subject to the power of Jesus Christ." *Nor is there any difference in this matter between the individual and the family or the State; for all men, whether collectively or individually, are under the dominion of Christ*.[72]

## The "Civilization of Love" Replaces the Conversion of Pagans

After Vatican II, however, the Social Kingship of Christ was replaced by something called the "civilization of love"—a term coined by Paul VI to describe the utopian notion that "dialogue with the world" would lead to a world brotherhood of religions that would not at all be explicitly Christian. The slogan "civilization of love" has been repeated incessantly since then. As Pope John Paul II described this novel notion in his address for the World Day of Peace in 2001:

> Dialogue leads to a recognition of diversity and opens the mind to the mutual acceptance and genuine collaboration demanded by the human family's basic vocation to unity. As such, dialogue is a privileged means for building *the civilization of love and peace* that my revered predecessor Paul VI indicated *as the ideal* to inspire cultural, social, political and economic life *in our time. ... The different religions too can and ought to contribute decisively to this process*. My many encounters with representatives of other religions—I recall especially the meeting in Assisi in 1986 and in Saint Peter's Square in 1999—have made me more confident that mutual openness between the followers of the various religions can greatly serve the cause of peace and *the common good of the human family*.[73]

Even the current Pope has been led to think that interreligious prayer meetings such as those at Assisi in 1986 and 2002 are among the very means by which this utopian notion is supposed to be realized. Yet the mere sight of such spectacles would have horrified Pius XI and every one of his predecessors. Meanwhile, the Social Kingship of Christ in a Catholic social order is *de facto* excluded from the new orientation.

Of course, the Church's new "ecumenical" and "interreligious" orientation cannot possibly be reconciled with the Message of Fatima, and this explains why, beginning with Vatican II, an effort has been made to revise the Message in keeping with the new orientation, if not to bury it completely.

### Must Catholics Accept the New Orientation of the Church?

Of course, Catholics have the right, even the duty, to resist this new orientation arising from the ambiguities of the Council and the opinions of the "new theology", which conflict with the perennial and infallible Magisterium. For years, Catholics have labored under the misconception that they must accept the *pastoral* Council, Vatican II, with the same assent of faith that they owe to dogmatic Councils. This, however, is not the case. The Council Fathers repeatedly referred to Vatican II as a *pastoral* Council. That is, it was a Council that dealt not with *defining* the Faith, but with measures in the realm of practical and prudential judgment—such as the launching of the "ecumenical venture." The Council's own document, the Preliminary Note (in Latin, *Nota Praevia*) to *Lumen Gentium*, states this clearly: "In view of the conciliar practice and *pastoral purpose* of the present Council, the sacred Synod defines matters of faith and morals as binding on the Church only when the Synod itself openly declares so."[74] No matters of faith and morals were defined "as binding on the Church" concerning the new "ecumenical orientation", nor as to any of the other novel "pastoral" formulations in the language of the conciliar documents.

That Vatican II was inferior in authority to a dogmatic council is confirmed by the testimony of the Council Father, Bishop Thomas Morris. At his own request, this testimony was not unsealed until after his death:

> I was relieved when we were told that this Council was not aiming at defining or giving final statements on doctrine, because a statement on doctrine has to be very carefully formulated and I would have regarded the Council documents as tentative and liable to be reformed.[75]

Then there is the important testimony from the Council's Secretary, Archbishop (later Cardinal) Pericle Felici. At the close of Vatican II, the bishops asked Archbishop Felici for that which the theologians call the "theological note" of the Council—that is, the doctrinal "weight" of its teachings. Felici replied:

In view of conciliar practice and the pastoral purpose of the present Council, this sacred Synod defines matters of faith or morals as binding on the Church only when the Synod itself openly declares so.[76]

He also said:

We have to distinguish according to the *schemas* and the chapters those which have already been the subject of dogmatic definitions in the past; ***as for the declarations which have a novel character, we have to make reservations.***[77]

Pope Paul VI himself observed that "Given the Council's pastoral character, it avoided pronouncing in an extraordinary manner, dogmas endowed with the note of infallibility."[78]

Thus, unlike a dogmatic Council, Vatican II does not demand an unqualified assent of faith. The Council's verbose and ambiguous documents are not on a par with the doctrinal pronouncements of past councils. Vatican II's novelties are not unconditionally binding on the faithful, nor did the Council itself ever say that they were.

And yet the ambiguous teachings of the Council, and the Church's new post-conciliar orientation, have resulted in nothing less than what Cardinal Ratzinger himself has termed the "demolition of bastions" in the Church—including, as we shall see, the demolition of the Message of Fatima. As we will now demonstrate, this destructive undertaking has largely fulfilled the dreams of the Church's enemies, and the prophetic warnings of the Message of Fatima as reported by Pope Pius XII.

# Chapter 7

## The Demolition of Bastions

No wonder the Church's worst enemies have been so delighted with the Council and the radical changes it introduced. They are also no doubt quite pleased with the sudden and catastrophic ecclesial collapse in every department following Vatican II. Every available statistic shows that the sudden and dramatic changes ushered in by Vatican II have been accompanied by equally sudden and dramatic declines in the number of priests and religious, the number of new ordinations, the number of seminarians and the number of conversions and baptisms. Immediately after Vatican II some *50,000 priests defected,* and today there remain approximately 50,000 fewer Catholic priests than there were *thirty-one years ago*. In 1997 there were fewer baptisms in the United States than there were in 1970.[1]

Even Cardinal Ratzinger has spoken of "*a continuing process of decay* that has gone on largely on the basis of appeals to the Council, and thus has discredited the Council in the eyes of many people."[2] Yet Cardinal Ratzinger, along with the others who have presided over this debacle, insists—incredibly enough—that we need more of the same, more of the new orientation of Vatican II:

> Does this mean the Council itself must be revoked? Certainly not. It means only that the real reception of the Council has *not yet even begun*. What devastated the Church after the Council was not the Council but the refusal to accept it. ... The task, therefore, is not to suppress the Council but to *discover the real Council* and to deepen its *true intention* in the light of present experience.[3]

Going even further, and citing as his authority one of the very neo-modernist theologians who have helped produce this disaster for the Church, Cardinal Ratzinger declared:

> The fact is, as Hans Urs von Balthasar pointed out as early as 1952, that ... She [the Church] must relinquish many of the things that have hitherto spelled security for her and that she has taken for granted. *She must demolish longstanding bastions* and trust solely the shield of faith.[4]

The Cardinal's call for "demolition of longstanding bastions" in the Church is perhaps the most damning admission of all concerning the revolutionary new orientation of the Church brought on by the Second Vatican Council. For what could the Cardinal mean by "*longstanding* bastions" if not the Church's traditional defenses against her enemies—what the Cardinal himself condescendingly describes as "many of the things that have hitherto spelled *security* for her and that she has taken for granted"? The Cardinal admits that he wishes to *demolish* the very things that give the Church security! The

Church must, in the Cardinal's strange view of things, trust "solely in the shield of faith." But what does *that* mean? How can Catholics hold on to their faith unless it is kept secure by the very bastions the Cardinal wishes to demolish?

By citing "new theologian" Hans Urs von Balthasar as his authority for this "demolition of bastions", the Cardinal himself blesses the "new theology" in its project of tearing down the Church's traditional theology, with its clear and precise definitions of the truths that Catholics must believe. In the Cardinal's call to *demolish* the Church's "longstanding bastions", we see clearly what can only be called a "desire to destroy." That phrase is taken from a book by the Catholic writer Atila Sinke Guimarães, entitled *Animus Delendi* (Latin for "the desire to destroy"). Guimarães shows that the conciliar and post-conciliar "reformers" of the Church are motivated by a mentality that sees the destruction of the "old" Church as "tragic but necessary" for the Church's "growth and renewal" in the "modern world."

How are the "bastions" to be demolished? Our Lady says the *dogma* of Faith will be preserved in Portugal. Dogmas are in themselves bastions of the Church. Obviously, then, the demolition of bastions will involve the undermining of dogmatic definitions, even as lip-service is paid to the dogmas by the neo-modernist "new theologians" who are doing the undermining. Dogmas can be undermined in these ways: 1) simply ignore them, and they will cease to exist for all practical purposes; 2) replace clear terms with ambiguous terms—e.g. "is" with "subsist"; 3) dismiss dogma as "outdated theology"; 4) pretend there is no such thing as infallible dogmatic definitions which every Catholic must believe, just as they are written; and 5) where the dogma of no salvation outside the Church is concerned, simply refer incessantly to non-Catholics as "believers" or "Christians."

What precisely are the bastions that, in the view of "reformers" like Ratzinger, must be demolished? We recall again what Pius XII accurately predicted in his inspired comments about the coming crisis in the Church:

> I am worried by the Blessed Virgin's messages to Lucy of Fatima. This persistence of Mary about *the dangers which menace the Church* is a divine warning against the suicide of altering the Faith, in Her *liturgy,* Her *theology,* and Her *soul.* … I hear all around me innovators who wish to *dismantle* the Sacred Chapel, *destroy* the universal flame of the Church, *reject* her ornaments and make her feel remorse for her historical past.

Pius XII identified three elements of the Church that the "innovators" wished to alter: her liturgy, her theology and her soul (i.e. her very nature). Notice that Pius XII, basing himself on the Fatima Message, as well as what he had witnessed personally in the Church at that time, spoke of a coming attempt to *dismantle, destroy* and *reject* these things in the Church. In other words, the "demolition of bastions."

## The Demolition of the Liturgy

Before Vatican II the Popes, even including Pope John XXIII, unanimously defended the Church's ancient Latin liturgy against innovation, recognizing that the immutable Latin language was a barrier against heresy, as Pope Pius XII taught in his monumental encyclical on the liturgy, *Mediator Dei*. Indeed, the Protestant "reformers" of the 16th Century hated nothing more than the traditional Catholic Mass in Latin, the Damasian-Gregorian liturgy which was the center of the life of the Church from at least the 4th Century (and probably earlier) until the liturgical "reform" of Pope Paul VI in 1969.

Nowhere can the desire to destroy, the demolition of bastions, be seen more clearly than in Pope Paul's explanation of his decision to suppress the traditional Latin Mass of more than 1,500 years' standing and replace it with a newly concocted rite of Mass in the vernacular—a totally unprecedented action his predecessors would have regarded as absolutely unthinkable:

> It is here that the greatest newness is going to be noticed, the newness of language. No longer Latin, but the spoken language will be the principal language of the Mass. The introduction of the vernacular will certainly be a great sacrifice for those who know the beauty, the power, and the expressive sacrality of Latin. We are parting with the speech of the Christian centuries; *we are becoming like profane intruders in the literary preserve of sacred utterance*. We will lose a great part of that stupendous and incomparable artistic and spiritual thing, the Gregorian chant. We have reason for regret, reason almost for bewilderment. What can we put in the place of that language of the angels? We are giving up something of priceless worth. Why? *What is more precious than these loftiest of our Church's values*?

What indeed *is* more precious than "these loftiest of our Church's values"? According to Paul VI what was more precious was an appeal to "modern man", whom the Pope apparently viewed as so obtuse as to be unable to make heads or tails of Latin prayers in the *Roman Missal*, even if the same Missal included vernacular translations alongside the Latin. Paul VI continued by answering his own question:

> The answer will seem banal, almost prosaic. Yet it is a good answer because it is human, it is apostolic. Understanding of prayer is more important than the silken garments in which it is royally dressed. Participation by the people is worth more—particularly participation by *modern people*, so fond of plain language which is easily understood and converted into everyday speech.[5]

Paul VI's speech is a blueprint for what has happened to the entire Church since the Council. The conciliar and post-conciliar changes—all without precedent in Church history—are the work of *profane intruders* who labor to destroy something of *priceless worth*, to *demolish bastions* that had been standing for centuries—not only in the sacred liturgy, but in the perennial teaching of the Church. It is no accident that Vatican II caused unprecedented destruction, since the Council's prime movers were planning destruction all along.

## The Demolition of Theology

In the December 19, 1946 edition of *L'Osservatore Romano*, Pope Pius XII (targeting the heterodox theories of modernists like Chenu and de Lubac) warned that what was being trumpeted as a "new theology" would end up undermining the Faith:

> There is a good deal of talk (but without the necessary clarity of concept) about a 'new theology', which must be in constant transformation, following the example of all other things in the world, which are in a constant state of flux and movement, without ever reaching their term. If we were to accept such an opinion, what would become of the unchangeable dogmas of the Catholic Faith; and what would become of the unity and stability of that Faith?[6]

As we have seen, Pope John XXIII disregarded Pius XII's warning; at Vatican II Pope John rehabilitated the very proponents of the "new theology" who were under suspicion of heresy during the pontificate of Pius XII. To recall the testimony of Msgr. Bandas: "No doubt good Pope John thought that these suspect theologians would rectify their ideas and perform a genuine service to the Church. But exactly the opposite happened. ... The great confusion was underway. It was already apparent that *neither Trent nor Vatican I nor any encyclical would be permitted to impede its advance*."

Now, what have been the effects of the "new theology" upon the Church? Today, in the name of Vatican II, we are told—

- that the Church must dialogue and collaborate with Communists, Muslims, heretics, schismatics, and other objective enemies of the faith;
- that the Church's constant pre-conciliar teaching against Liberalism (as seen in the *Syllabus* of Blessed Pius IX) and against Modernism (as seen in *Pascendi* by St. Pius X) is "one-sided" and outdated;
- that the Church (as Cardinal Ratzinger claims) must "attempt" a "reconciliation" with the principles of the French Revolution;
- that the "Church of Christ" is larger than the Catholic Church;
- that Protestants and schismatics need no longer convert and return to the Catholic Church for salvation or even for unity.

The Church's enemies in the neo-modernist, Freemasonic and Communist camps have seen their theological dreams largely come true.

## The Demolition of the Church's Soul

The future Pius XII was not speaking idly when, in the light of the Message of Fatima, he predicted the coming attempt to alter not only the Church's liturgy and theology, but *her very soul*—what she *is*. Of course, this design can never succeed completely, because Our Lord promised that the gates of hell would not prevail against His Church. But this divine promise does not exclude the Church's human element suffering the gravest possible wounds from her enemies, short of a final death. It was the prospect of such grave injuries to the Church that so alarmed Pius XII, especially in light of the Fatima prophecies.

And indeed Pius' worst fears have been realized in the post-conciliar period, in which we have witnessed an effort to change the Church from the sole ark of salvation, outside of which no one is saved, into a mere collaborator with other "churches and ecclesial communities", non-Christian religions and even atheists in building up a utopian "civilization of love." In this "civilization of love" the salvation of souls from hell—which is no longer mentioned—is replaced by a new form of "salvation": salvation through world "brotherhood" and world "peace." This is the very notion which Freemasonry has been promoting for the past three centuries.

In keeping with this Freemasonic notion of "salvation" through the "brotherhood of man" (understood in a secular, non-Christian sense), many Catholic churchmen now tell us that we must respect the various Protestant and schismatic sects as partners in "ecumenical dialogue" and the "search for Christian unity." In keeping with this new notion, there are joint ecumenical "liturgies" between Catholics, Protestants and schismatic Orthodox churches to demonstrate the supposed "partial communion" between "all Christians." To be sure, the executors of the new orientation of the Catholic Church still allow that she is the most perfect of all churches, but the claim that the Catholic Church is *the one true Church*, to the complete exclusion of all others, has *de facto* been abandoned by all but a remnant of faithful Catholics, who are considered "rigid sectarians" and "pre-conciliar" for simply believing what Catholics always believed before 1965.

But "Christian unity" is only a step toward pan-religious unity in the world brotherhood. At the same time "Christian unity" is being promoted by pan-Christian activities which the great pre-conciliar Popes would have regarded as sacrileges, "interreligious dialogue" has made the Church more "open" to the "value" of non-Christian religions, whose followers would no longer be regarded as being in need of faith and Baptism to save their souls. Karl Rahner's "anonymous Christianity"—which holds that the sincere followers of any religion can be, and probably are, "Christians" without even knowing it—has become the *de facto* theology of the Church. Accordingly, there would be pan-religious prayer meetings in which the members of all religions gather together to pray for peace and to demonstrate their "unity" as members of the human family, without any of them being told that they are in danger of damnation without Baptism, faith in Christ and membership in His Church. In the "reformed" Good Friday liturgy, Catholics (for the first time in the Church's liturgical history) no longer pray publicly for the conversion and salvation of the souls of those outside the Catholic Church.

As anyone can see, the replacement of the Social Kingship of Christ with the "civilization of love" has totally neutralized the Catholic Church, which no longer serves as the center of the world's moral and spiritual authority, as she was meant to be by her divine Founder.

The progressivist theologians who advanced this new orientation of the Church have formed almost two generations of Catholic laity and clergy. The works of Rahner, Küng, Schillebeeckx, Congar, de Lubac, von Balthasar, and their disciples now dominate the teaching-texts of Catholic seminaries and universities. For the past 35 years, the progressivist tenets of these men have served as the principal formation for priests, religious, theologians, and Catholic college students. Thus, we have now reached a stage where prelates prefer Rahner's theology to that of Saint Robert Bellarmine, for example, who is a canonized saint and Doctor of the Church, or Saint Thomas Aquinas, the great Doctor and one of the greatest saints in Church history. The teaching of Bellarmine and Aquinas—indeed, the teaching of all the Popes before Vatican II—tends to be accepted only in accordance with the spin given it by Rahner and the other "new theologians." The same is true of most professors in Catholic colleges and seminaries.

This process of attempting to change the very soul and theology of the Church, as Pope Pius XII feared, has involved not only the "ecumenical venture" and "interreligious dialogue", but also an endless series of apologies from Catholic churchmen, high and low, for the Church's past "triumphalism" in claiming to be the sole repository of divine revelation, and the supposed sins of her deceased members against other "Christians" and other cultures. This was precisely what Pius XII predicted when he spoke of the innovators who would "make her [the Church] feel remorse for her historical past."

## The Enemy's Predictions Fulfilled

We now summarize the close correspondence between what we have seen happen in the post-conciliar Church and the goals of both Freemasonry (as revealed by Roca and various Freemasons, many quoted by Bishop Graber, and *The Permanent Instruction*) and Communism (as attested to by Bella Dodd and other ex-Communists):

- The radical revision of the Roman liturgy following an ecumenical council. (Roca)
- An accord between "the ideals of modern civilization and the ideal of Christ and His Gospel. This will be the consecration of the New Social Order and the solemn baptism of modern civilization"—that is, the overall liberalization of Catholic churchmen in accordance with the same false principles condemned in the *Syllabus* of Blessed Pius IX. (Roca, Melinge, *The Permanent Instruction of the Alta Vendita*)
- The emergence of a "pluri-confessional pontificate, able to adapt to a polyvalent ecumenism, such as we are seeing established today in

the intercelebration of priests and Protestant pastors"—only today, the Pope himself celebrates joint liturgies with Protestant clerics.[7] (Roca, Melinge)

- The introduction of a "*guilt complex into the Church* ... to label the 'Church of the past' as being oppressive, authoritarian, full of prejudices, arrogant in claiming to be the sole possessor of truth, and responsible for the divisions of religious bodies throughout the centuries." (Dodd)
- The "opening up" of the Church to the world and to a more "flexible" attitude toward all religions and philosophies. (Dodd)
- The use of this new orientation to undermine the Church, without actually destroying it. (Dodd, Watson, the Soviet defectors and *The Permanent Instruction*)

And all of these developments were predicted by the future Pope Pius XII in remarks he related specifically to "the Blessed Virgin's messages to Lucy of Fatima" and "this persistence of Mary about the dangers which menace the Church."

## The Passion of the Church

Thus, the passion that our Holy Church is presently suffering is really no great mystery. By recklessly ignoring the Popes of the past, by abandoning condemnations of error, by "rehabilitating" suspect theologians and making them heroes of the Church, by abolishing the *Index of Forbidden Books* and the Holy Office, by doing away with the traditional Catholic liturgy which was a barrier against heresy, by pronouncing the anti-liberal teaching of Blessed Pius IX and the anti-modernist teaching of Saint Pius X as "one-sided" and "outdated"—in short, by ruthlessly and systematically stripping the Church of almost all her defenses—our present Church leaders have demolished nearly all the bastions that once protected the Church from infiltration and corruption, thus creating a compromised structure that we can now see collapsing upon itself in scandal, corruption, disobedience, and loss of faith.

Yet our Church leaders continue to insist that the disastrous process of change responsible for this *admitted* invasion and auto-demolition of the Church be continued full steam ahead. This is precisely why Cardinal Ratzinger, many years after Vatican II, declared that the Church "must demolish longstanding bastions."[8]

As we have demonstrated, all of this was predicted by the Church's enemies. Bishop Graber, commenting on the post-conciliar crisis in light of the Masons' own predictions of what they would soon succeed in doing, declared:

> If in the face of these unambiguous admissions [by Masons, etc.] anyone still holds to the opinion that the events in the Church [since Vatican II] are marginal phenomena or transitional difficulties which will die down of their own accord in time, he is simply beyond hope. *But all the greater is the responsibility of the leading men in the Church* if they do

> not occupy themselves with these questions and imagine that everything can be repaired by patching it up here and there.[9]

But it is these very "leading men of the Church" who are the subject of our case. Yet we hasten to say, once again, that we do not claim that every churchman who promotes novel practices, such as ecumenism, is deliberately acting as an enemy of the Church. The renowned priest of the 19th Century, Father Frederick Faber, was a true prophet when he said in a remarkable sermon preached at Pentecost, 1861 in the London Oratory:

> We must remember that if all the manifestly good men were on one side and all the manifestly bad men were on the other, there would be no danger of anyone, least of all the elect, being deceived by lying wonders. It is the good men, once good, we must hope good still, who are to do the work of anti-christ and so sadly to crucify the Lord afresh ... ***Bear in mind this feature of the last days, that this deceitfulness arises from good men being on the wrong side.*** [10]

As we will proceed to prove, the men who concern us *are* on the wrong side. In their "demolition of bastions" in the Catholic Church through the imposition of her new orientation—or what Cardinal Ratzinger called the Council's "attempt at an official reconciliation" with "the new era" begun by the French Revolution—they have necessarily arrayed themselves against the Message of Fatima. For there is nothing more integrally Catholic, nothing more opposed to the spirit of "the new era", nothing more inimical to the conciliar ecumenism, nothing more opposed to the tearing down of Catholic bastions, than the Virgin Mary's call for the consecration of Russia to Her Immaculate Heart, Russia's consequent conversion to the Catholic Faith, and the glorious triumph of the Immaculate Heart throughout the world in a Catholic social order.

## The Message of Fatima: A Final Bastion

From what we have said thus far it should be apparent that the Message of Fatima, in its sheer Catholic integrity, cannot coexist with the new vision of the Church foisted upon us by those with a "desire to destroy" through the "demolition of bastions." This destruction has happened precisely because the vast program of Vatican II's *aggiornamento* runs contrary to the Catholic truths that permeate the Fatima Message.

Our Lady did not come to Fatima to demolish bastions in the Church, but rather to exhort the members of the Church to defend her bastions in the coming crisis. She did not preach "ecumenism" or "interreligious dialogue", but the constant and unchanging teaching of the Church: that there is no salvation outside Her. When Our Lady came to Fatima, She did not give us any "new theology"; nor did She give us any "new understanding" of doctrine that would conflict in any way with the constant teaching of the Magisterium.

What do we see in the Message of Fatima? We see the key doctrines of our Faith reinforced, the very doctrines that have come under the fiercest attack in our time.[11] When the Mother of God came to Fatima—

- She spoke of the doctrine of Heaven;
- She spoke of the doctrine of Hell;
- She showed the children Hell;
- She spoke of the doctrine of Purgatory;
- She spoke of the doctrine of the Holy Eucharist;
- She spoke of the doctrine of the Sacrament of Penance.
- And She also spoke, indirectly, of the Social Kingship of Jesus Christ when She conveyed Heaven's command that Russia be consecrated to Her Immaculate Heart and *converted* to the Catholic religion—the very thing the Vatican's negotiators described as "outdated ecclesiology" in the Balamand Declaration.

## A Motive Clearly Exposed

In conclusion, for those who unswervingly pursue the new orientation of the Church, the Message of Fatima can only represent another bastion that must be demolished. That is why, as Pius XII revealed in his prophetic remarks, the Virgin's messages to Sister Lucy concerned "the dangers which menace the Church." Although it is not revealed in those portions of the Message of Fatima that we have thus far been allowed to see, Pius XII spoke of "a divine warning" at Fatima about the "innovators all around me" who would bring grave harm to the Church through the "alteration of the faith, in her liturgy, her theology and her soul."

We now see, clearly exposed, the motive for the crime which is the subject of this book. *There is a fundamental opposition between the "new" Church ushered in by Vatican II and the Church of all time, as represented by the Message of Fatima.* The Message of Fatima is a heavenly roadblock in the path of those who are determined to bulldoze the bastions of the old Church so that they can erect a new, more "enlightened" Church on the rubble.

These two competing visions of the Church—the vision of a "new" Church and the vision of the Church of all time as seen at Fatima—cannot coexist. One vision must yield to the other. The men who are the subject of this book have (explicitly or implicitly) made their choice concerning which vision of the Church must, to their way of thinking, govern. They have chosen the new vision—the new orientation of the Church initiated at Metz and at Vatican II. *In that choice lies their motive, and in that motive lies our understanding of their otherwise inexplicable actions against the Message of Fatima.*

Putting aside for the moment the question of the subjective motives of the proponents of this new orientation—who speak for themselves in the statements we have presented—it cannot be denied that objectively their actions are scandalous, suicidal to the Church (in a relative sense, of course) and harmful to millions of souls. Thus, their actions constitute a crime, no matter what the perpetrators may intend subjectively, because one can commit a crime through recklessness or culpable negligence without consciously intending harm. For just as a man who sincerely believes it is right to murder someone is nonetheless guilty of murder, so are those who have harmed the Church—even with the best of intentions—guilty of a crime against Her. It is the difference between what the law calls a specific intent to cause harm to another, and a general intent to do an act that one should know will cause harm, even if one does not subjectively intend harm. In other words, the law punishes deliberate acts committed by one who should have known better than to commit the act.

For some of those responsible for this disaster, it may be a misguided sense of "enlightenment"—"doing evil under the guise of good" or a "diabolical disorientation" in the leadership of the Church, to quote the words of Sister Lucy herself. With these men, it is a case of "blind men guiding other blind men" as Sister Lucy said,[12] referring to what Jesus said in the Gospel (Mt. 15:14), "the blind leading the blind." It is also a case of the blind refusing to admit that they are blind. Some of these men may, in fact, have convinced themselves that what they are doing is best for the Church, even though it is manifestly ruinous.

In any case, we will show that the accused are, objectively speaking, guilty of a terrible crime against the Church and the world through their participation in a veritable conspiracy to frustrate the fulfillment of the authentic Message of Fatima. Let God be the judge of their souls. Their objective words and deeds, however, judge themselves in the external forum of history.

What is more, the actions of these men can be judged by the light of the Church's own infallible teaching, which (as we have shown) they have openly declared "outdated" or "corrected" in accordance with the "modern" way of thinking and the "new theology." The results of this departure from infallible teachings are evil, as the current condition of the Church should demonstrate to anyone. Catholics must judge an evil to be evil when they see it, rather than pretending it is good merely because certain figures in authority insist it is good. "Woe to you that call evil good, and good evil ..." (Isaias 5:20).

We shall now examine how the motive we have established has animated the recent effort by the Vatican apparatus to bury the Message of Fatima once and for all.

# Chapter 8

## The Message of Fatima versus the Party Line

What has been the overall effect of the sudden, unprecedented and quite dramatic changes in the Church which began with Vatican II? As Catholic writers have observed, what Catholics have witnessed over the past 40 years represents a kind of "Stalinization of the Roman Catholic Church" that bears an eerie resemblance to what was called at the time "the Adaptation" of Russian Orthodoxy to the demands of the Stalinist regime.

The subversion of the Orthodox Church by Stalin is certainly among the developments in Russia foreseen by the Virgin of Fatima. This is precisely why She came to call for the consecration of Russia to Her Immaculate Heart: so that Russia would embrace the one true religion and the one true Church, not the schismatic Orthodox Church which was founded in human rebellion against Rome when it left the Mystical Body of Christ over 500 years ago, and thus was constitutionally incapable of avoiding its total Adaptation to Stalinism.

The Orthodox Adaptation began officially when the Metropolitan Sergius of the Russian Orthodox Church published an "Appeal" in *Isvestia* on August 19, 1927. The Appeal of Sergius, as it came to be known, set forth a new basis for the activity of the Russian Orthodox Church. The Russian layman Boris Talantov described this as "an Adaptation to the atheistic reality of the U.S.S.R." In other words, the church had to find a way of living, so the argument goes, with the "atheistic reality" of Stalinist Russia. So Sergius proposed what came to be known in shorthand as the Adaptation.

The Adaptation consisted first and foremost of a false separation between the so-called spiritual needs of man, the purely religious needs of man, and his socio-political needs. In other words, a separation of Church and State. The church was to satisfy the purely religious needs of the citizens of the Soviet Union but without touching on the socio-political structure which had been erected by the Communist Party.

The Adaptation required a new administration of the church in Russia according to guidelines which were set forth after the appeal of Sergius was published. Basically this came down to an agreement not to criticize the official ideology of the Soviet Union under Stalin. And this would be reflected in all of the activities of the church. Any opposition by the Russian Orthodox Church to the Soviet regime would henceforth be considered a deviation from pure religious activity and a form of counter-revolution which was no longer to be permitted or countenanced.

In effect the Orthodox Church, through its silence, became an arm of the Soviet state. In fact, Sergius would go on to defend it and even call for the condemnation and the sentencing to concentration camps of his own fellow Orthodox for so-called counter-revolutionary activities. Talantov, who condemned the whole Adaptation, described it this way: "In actual fact all religious activity was reduced to external rites. The church preaching of those clergymen who held strictly to the Adaptation was totally remote from life and therefore had no influence whatever on hearers. As a result of this, the intellectual, social and family life of believers, and the raising of the younger generation, remained outside church influence. One cannot worship Christ and at the same time in social and family life tell lies, do what is unjust, use violence, and dream of an earthly paradise."[1]

This, then, is what the Adaptation involved: The church would be silent about the evils of the Stalinist regime. It would become a purely "spiritual" community "in the abstract", would no longer voice opposition to the regime, would no longer condemn the errors and lies of Communism, and would thus become the Church of Silence, as Christianity behind the Iron Curtain was often called.

The Appeal of Sergius caused a split in the Russian Orthodox Church. The real believers who rejected the Adaptation, who denounced the Appeal and who remained attached to the Metropolitan Joseph rather than Sergius, were arrested and sent to concentration camps. Boris Talantov himself would eventually die in prison, as a political prisoner of the Stalinist regime. Meanwhile, the Church of Silence, in effect, was transformed into an organ of the KGB. Stalin decimated the Russian Orthodox Church; all of the real Orthodox believers were sent off to concentration camps or executed and replaced by KGB operatives.

Shortly before Talantov died in August of 1967, he wrote as follows about the Adaptation:

> The Adaptation to atheism implanted by Metropolitan Sergius has concluded (been completed by) the betrayal of the Orthodox Russian Church on the part of Metropolitan Nikodim and other official representatives of the Moscow Patriarch based abroad. This betrayal irrefutably proved by the documents cited must be made known to all believers in Russia and abroad because such an activity of the Patriarchate, relying on cooperation with the KGB, represents a great danger for all believers. In truth, the atheistic leaders of the Russian people and the princes of the Church have gathered together against the Lord and His Church.[2]

Here Talantov refers to the same Metropolitan Nikodim who induced the Vatican to enter into the Vatican-Moscow Agreement, under which (as we showed in a previous chapter) the Catholic Church was forced to remain silent about Communism at Vatican II. Thus, *the same Orthodox prelate who betrayed the Orthodox Church was instrumental in an agreement by which the Catholic Church was also betrayed.* At Vatican II certain Catholic churchmen, cooperating with Nikodim, agreed that *the Catholic Church, too, would become a Church of Silence.*

And since the Council, the Catholic Church has unquestionably fallen silent not only as to the errors of Communism—which the Church has completely ceased condemning, even in Red China, which viciously persecutes the Church—but also as to the errors of the world at large. We recall that in his opening address to the Council, Pope John freely admitted that the Council (and the Church after him) would no longer condemn errors but would open itself to the world in a "positive" presentation of her teaching to "men of good will." What followed, as Pope Paul VI himself admitted, was not the hoped-for conversion of "men of good will" but what Paul VI himself called "a veritable invasion of the Church by worldly thinking." In other words, to the extent that this is possible in the Catholic Church (which can never completely fail in her mission), there has been a kind of *Sergian Adaptation of Roman Catholicism.*

Now, in keeping with this Adaptation of the Catholic Church, by the year 2000 the Message of Fatima had been firmly subjugated to the demands of the new orientation. It had already been determined by certain members of the Vatican apparatus that Russia was not to be mentioned in any consecration ceremony the Pope might undertake in response to the Virgin's requests. In the November 2000 issue of *Inside the Vatican*, a leading Cardinal, identified only as "one of the Pope's closest advisors," is quoted to the effect that "Rome fears the Russian Orthodox might regard it as an 'offense' if Rome were to make specific mention of Russia in such a prayer, as if Russia especially is in need of help when the whole world, including the post-Christian West, faces profound problems ..." The same Cardinal-advisor added: "Let us beware of becoming too literal-minded."

In other words, "Rome"—meaning a few members of the Vatican apparatus who advise the Pope—has decided not to honor the specific request of Our Lady of Fatima for fear of giving offense to the Russian Orthodox. "Rome" does not wish to give the impression that Russia should be converted to the Catholic Faith through its consecration to the Immaculate Heart of Mary, for this would be quite contrary to the new "ecumenical dialogue" launched by Vatican II. The consecration and conversion of Russia called for by the Mother of God would also be contrary to the Vatican's diplomatic agreement (in the 1993 Balamand Declaration) that the return of the Orthodox to Rome is "outdated ecclesiology"—a claim that, as we have shown, flatly contradicts the infallibly defined Catholic dogma that heretics and schismatics cannot be saved outside the Catholic Church. In keeping with this blatant departure from Catholic teaching, the Vatican's own apostolic administrator for Russia, Archbishop Tadeusz Kondrusiewicz, stated publicly in January of 1998 that "The Second Vatican Council has declared that the Orthodox Church is our Sister Church and has the same means for salvation. So there is no reason to have a policy of proselytism."[3]

Given this *de facto* abandonment of the Church's constant teaching that heretics, schismatics, Jews and pagans must be added to the Catholic flock if they are to be saved, a consecration of Russia to the Immaculate Heart to bring about the conversion of Russia would, of course, be out of the question—at least so far as those who promote the new orientation of the Church are concerned.

Thus, on May 13, 1982 and again on March 25, 1984, the Pope had consecrated the *world* to the Immaculate Heart, but with no mention of Russia. In neither case had the bishops of the world participated. Thus, neither of the two requirements attested to by Sister Lucy throughout her life had been met. Clearly recognizing this, the Pope himself had made telltale remarks during and after the 1984 ceremony. During the ceremony, before 250,000 people in Saint Peter's Square, he spontaneously added to the prepared text the following: "Enlighten especially the peoples of which You Yourself *are awaiting* our consecration and confiding."[4] Hours after the ceremony, as reported in the Italian Catholic bishops' newspaper *Avvenire*, the Holy Father prayed inside St. Peter's, before 10,000 witnesses, asking Our Lady to bless "those peoples for whom You Yourself *are awaiting* our act of consecration and entrusting."[5] Russia has not been consecrated to the Immaculate Heart, and the Pope knows it. Evidently persuaded by his advisers, the Pope had told Bishop Cordes, head of the Pontifical Council of the Laity, that he had omitted any mention of Russia because "it would be interpreted as a provocation by the Soviet leaders."[6]

## The Emergence of the "Party Line" on Fatima

But the faithful would not simply abandon the Consecration of Russia, for it was obvious that during the period 1984-2000 Russia had failed to experience the religious conversion the Virgin had promised as the fruit of a proper consecration to the Immaculate Heart. Quite the contrary, despite certain political changes, Russia's spiritual, moral and material condition had only deteriorated since the "consecration" of 1984.

Consider these proofs, which provide only a sketch of the gravity of Russia's situation as of the year 2000 (and it has only become worse since then, as we shall see):

- Some 16 years after the Consecration, Russia has the highest abortion rate in the world. Fr. Daniel Maurer, CJD, who spent the last eight years in Russia, says that statistically, the average Russian woman will have eight abortions in her childbearing years—though Fr. Maurer believes the actual number is about 12 abortions per woman. He has spoken to women who have had as many as 25 abortions. A major reason for these dreadful figures is that other contraception methods (which are immoral anyway) have not been introduced in Russia, nor are they trusted. This leaves abortion as the "cheapest way to limit the family size". *Presently in Russia, abortions are free, but births are not.*[7]

- The Russian birth rate is plummeting and Russia's population is dropping at the rate of 700,000 people each year—an unprecedented event in a civilized nation during "peacetime."[8]
- Russia has the highest alcohol consumption in the world.[9]
- Satanism, occultism and witchcraft are on the rise in Russia, as even the Russian Orthodox patriarch, Alexy II, publicly admits.[10]
- Homosexuality is rampant in Moscow and throughout the country. In fact, in April 1993, nine years after the 1984 "consecration", Boris Yeltsin had allowed homosexuality to be de-criminalized. Homosexuality is now "legal" in Russia.[11]
- Russia is a leading world center for the distribution of child pornography. The *Associated Press* reported on a Moscow-based child pornography ring linked to another child pornography ring in Texas. To quote AP: "Russian law does not distinguish between child pornography and pornography involving adults, and treats the production and distribution of either as a minor crime, said Dmitry Chepchugov, head of the Russian Interior Ministry's department for high technology crimes. Russian police often complain about the legal chaos that has turned Russia into an international center of child pornography production. '***Unfortunately, Russia has turned into a world trash bin of child pornography***,' Chepchugov told reporters in Moscow."[12]
- Russians now avidly watch "reality-based" TV. On the most vile "reality-based" shows, cameras film the intimate personal lives of Russian "couples," including their sexual activity. Despite grumbles of disapproval from old hard-line Communists, Russian viewers "cannot get enough" of this pornography. The program "boasts an audience share of more than 50% and thousands of Russians have endured sub-zero temperatures and queued for more than an hour to catch a glimpse of it through a window of the flat. Millions have logged on to the website, which has crashed frequently under the weight of traffic."[13]
- As for the standing of the Catholic Church, in 1997 Russia enacted a new law on "freedom of conscience" which gave privileged status to Russian Orthodoxy, Islam, Judaism and Buddhism as Russia's "traditional religions," while requiring Catholic parishes to obtain approval from local bureaucrats for their very existence. As a result:
- The miniscule Catholic priesthood in Russia, some 200 priests, consists almost entirely of foreign-born clerics many of whom are given only three-month entry visas, while businessmen receive six-month visas.[14]

- There are a mere ten Russian-born priests in the whole country—five in Siberia and five in Kazakhstan. Ninety-five percent of the priests and nuns in Russia are foreign born. In Archbishop Bukovsky's frank opinion the Catholic Church "is small ... and will always be small."[15]
- Catholics comprise less than one-half of one percent of the Russian population, and Russian Muslims outnumber Catholics by more than 10-to-1. According to a report by Radio Free Europe, in Russia Catholicism is seen as "a kind of unexplainable eccentricity — why should a Russian be Catholic?"[16]
- According to the Vatican, there are 500,000 Catholics in Russia, and most of these are in Siberia, where Stalin sent their grandparents.[17]

Given this kind of evidence, the question whether the Consecration of Russia had been done in the manner requested by Our Lady of Fatima was simply not going to go away. Therefore, from the perspective of the executors of the Church's new orientation—the Church's Adaptation to the world—something had to be done about Fatima. And, in particular, something had to be done about a Canadian priest by the name of Father Nicholas Gruner, whose Fatima apostolate had become a sounding board for millions of Catholics who were convinced that the Consecration of Russia had been derailed by the plans of certain men in the Vatican. Quite simply, Fatima and "the Fatima priest" had to be buried once and for all.

The process began as early as 1988, when, Frère François recounts: "[A]n order came from the Vatican addressed to the authorities of Fatima, to Sister Lucy, to diverse ecclesiastics, including Father Messias Coelho, and a French priest [evidently Fr. Pierre Caillon] very much devoted to Our Lady, ordering everyone to cease pestering the Holy Father with the Consecration of Russia." Fatima devotee Father Caillon confirmed the issuance of this order: "An order came from Rome, obliging everyone to say and think: 'The Consecration is done. The Pope having done all that he can, Heaven has deigned to agree to this gesture.'"[18] It was around this time, 1988-1989, that many Fatima Apostolates who had maintained that the consecration of Russia had not been done suddenly reversed themselves and declared that the 1984 consecration fulfilled the desires of Heaven. Sadly, even Father Caillon soon afterwards changed his testimony and began to say that the 1984 Consecration had fulfilled the Virgin's requests.

It was also at this time that typewritten and computer-generated letters, purportedly from Sister Lucy, began to circulate. Typical of the manifestly incredible letters was the one dated November 8, 1989, to a Mr. Noelker, which contains the statement by "Sister Lucy" that Pope Paul VI consecrated the world to the Immaculate Heart during his brief visit to Fatima in 1967—a consecration that never happened, as Sister Lucy certainly knew because she witnessed the entire visit.[19]

Thus emerged *the Party Line* on the Message of Fatima. What, precisely, do we mean by "the Party Line"? Vladimir Ilyich Lenin once said: "The lie is sacred and deception will be our principal weapon." Thus it was no surprise that *Pravda,* when it was the official organ of the Soviet Communist Party, was filled with lies, even though the Russian word *Pravda* means "truth." A newspaper whose name is "truth" was always filled with lies, because, as Lenin said, "the lie is sacred and deception will be our principal weapon".

Now, a liar will not convince anyone of his lies if he wears a big placard on his chest that says "Liar!" Not even a fool would believe such a man. For the liar to convince people that his lies are truth, the *truth must be redefined*. This is what is meant by Lenin's phrase "the lie is sacred ..." The lie becomes the "truth" and is slavishly adhered to in place of the truth. As Scripture says, pronouncing the curse in the book of Isaias, "Woe to you that call evil good, and good evil: that put darkness *for* light, and light *for* darkness". [Is. 5:20] The darkness of falsehood is given the appearance of the light of truth, and this is one of the principal errors of Russia.

But this trick of turning a lie into the "truth" did not originate with Russia, or with the Communists; it originated with the devil, who is the Father of Lies. St. Paul speaks of the devil under the guise of the angel of light. To be more specific, he refers to the Gospel of our Lord Jesus Christ: "But though we, or an angel from heaven, preach a gospel to you besides that which we have preached to you, let him be anathema." [Gal. 1:8] It is the devil, appearing under the guise of an angel of light, who gives the appearance of truth in order to deceive by means of the lie. This is where the error "the lie is sacred" and "falsehood is truth" originated.

Father Paul Kramer relates a conversation he had with General Daniel Graham, a general in the US Army. "General Graham said that he had once been in Russia with a Soviet official and the Soviet official asked him, 'Don't you want peace?' And the General answered: 'No! Because I know how you define peace. I do not want that kind of peace.' As they were conversing, they drove by a huge billboard that showed soldiers with their rifles. On the billboard was the caption: 'Pobieda kommunista eta mir'. Which is, in English, 'Communist Victory is Peace.'"

According to Marxist teaching, the Communist State wages war to make revolution and uses every possible means of deception—total war—in order to subjugate the entire world to Communism. And once total war has been waged and Communism is victorious over the entire planet, then there is the Communist version of "peace". But what is peace *in reality*? It is best defined by St. Augustine: "Peace is the tranquillity of order." Which definition is correct? It is not a matter of subjective evaluation. St. Thomas Aquinas explains: *"ens et verum convertunter",* which is a scholastic way of saying that truth is convertible with reality. That which is objectively *real* is, for that very reason, objectively *true*. In other words, truth is that which *is,* whereas a lie is that which *is not*. That which *is not* cannot be true. Therefore, if someone declares, for example, that white is black, the claim that white is black is a lie—no matter how high the authority of the one making the claim.

According to Marxist doctrine, however, *truth is that which promotes the Communist revolution.* And what is it that promotes the Communist revolution? It is whatever has been decided to be the Party Line. *What the Party dictates to be true becomes the "truth" even if, in reality, it is a lie*. Thus, if the Party Line is that black is white, then that is what all Party members must believe, simply because it has been decided by the Party that black is white.

Just as there has been a kind of "Stalinization" of the Church, in the sense of an Adaptation of the Church to the world, so also must there be a kind of Stalinist Party Line on Fatima—a version of Fatima dictated from on high to which all the members of the Church of the post-conciliar Adaptation must adhere. In essence, the Party Line on Fatima comes down to this: The "Consecration of Russia" is over and done with, and everyone must cease asking for it. We have "peace" as predicted by Our Lady of Fatima. Russia is undergoing the "conversion" Our Lady promised. Therefore—so the Party Line goes—nothing in the Message of Fatima remains to be accomplished, and Fatima now belongs to the past.

As we shall see, all of the terms in quotation marks—"consecration of Russia", "peace" and "conversion"—have been redefined to accommodate the Party Line on Fatima. Where Fatima is concerned, we are now being asked to believe the equivalent of "black is white," for that is the Party Line.

## The Dictatorship of the Vatican Secretary of State

Now every Party Line requires a dictator, a head of the Party, to impose it. From where, exactly, within the Vatican apparatus did the Party Line on Fatima originate? The evidence is overwhelming that it originated with the Vatican Secretary of State. On this point some brief background is in order.

First of all, in the proper state of things—what Augustine called "the tranquillity of order" or peace—the Church is not a dictatorship. Dictatorship is a barbaric institution. As Euripides says "among the barbarians all are slaves but one." Our Lord said "the princes of the Gentiles lord it over" their subjects. [Mt. 20:25] He said to His apostles "with you it is not to be this way." Yet the tranquillity of order—the peace of the Church—has been disturbed enormously in the post-conciliar period. What we see in the Church today is that the hierarchs of the Roman Curia (*not* the Pope, but a few of his Vatican ministers) lord it over their subjects with an oriental despotism. To be more precise, they lord it over *certain* subjects, who buck the Party Line, while the Church at large suffers from a near-collapse of faith and discipline which these same potentates ignore.

How did this come to pass? Since the restructuring of the Roman Curia, around 1967, by order of Pope Paul VI—which was actually designed and carried out by Cardinal Jean Villot—the heads of the various Roman dicasteries have been able to behave like dictators. Before the Second Vatican

Council, the Roman Curia was structured as a monarchy. The Pope was the Prefect of the Holy Office, while the Cardinal in charge of the day-to-day business of the Holy Office was the second-in-command. The other dicasteries were of lower rank. And while having their own authority and jurisdiction, again in accordance with that principle of subsidiarity,[20] they were subordinate to the Holy Office, and the Holy Office was directly under the Pope. This arrangement was entirely in keeping with the Divine Constitution of the Church. The Pope, the Vicar of Jesus Christ on earth, was at the head of the chain of command.

But after Vatican II, Cardinal Villot engineered the restructuring of the Roman Curia. Long before Gorbachev announced his program of *perestroika* in the Soviet Union, the Church underwent its own *perestroika* in the Roman Curia. The Holy Office was renamed—but far more significant, the Holy Office lost its supreme position in the Curia. The Curia was restructured in such a manner that the Cardinal Secretary of State was placed over all the other dicasteries, including the former Holy Office. Renamed and restructured, it was now called the Congregation for the Doctrine of the Faith (CDF), and the Pope was no longer the Prefect. But it (the CDF) is now under a Cardinal Prefect (today it is Cardinal Ratzinger) and he is under the authority of the Secretary of State.

According to the previous arrangement under the Pope and his Holy Office, faith and morals were the preeminent factors determining curial policies. In the post-conciliar arrangement, however, under the Cardinal Secretary of State and his dicastery, the Secretariat of State, it is *the Party Line* —the politics of the Secretary of State—that is the supreme determining factor in the formulation of Church policies. Even the former Holy Office, now the CDF, is subordinate to the Secretary of State. As a result of this restructuring, the Holy Father, the Supreme Pontiff, is reduced to a figurehead who gives his approval, as a rubber stamp, to rulings presented to him as a *fait accompli. The Pope has been reduced to a figurehead in the service of the dictatorship of the Secretary of State.*[21]

In the Masonic registry required by Italian law, one did find the name of Jean Villot—the same Villot who oversaw the curial reorganization. After Cardinal Villot died, in his private library was found a handwritten message from the Grand Master of Villot's Masonic Lodge, praising Villot for upholding Masonic traditions.[22] As a French priest living in Rome said: "At least in one area he was traditional."

## The Use of False "Obedience" to Impose the Party Line

In 1917, the very year Our Lady appeared at Fatima, Saint Maximilian Kolbe was in Rome, where he saw the Masons showing their open hostility to the Catholic Church and carrying placards announcing their intention to infiltrate the Vatican so that satan would rule from the Vatican and the Pope would be his slave.[23] They also boasted at the same time that they would destroy the Church. The intention of the Masons to destroy the Church fits in perfectly with the well-known Masonic dictum, "We will destroy the Church *by means of holy obedience*." As we showed in an earlier chapter, Bishop Graber of Regensburg, Germany, collected other such testimonies of Masonic luminaries, and the *Permanent Instruction of the Alta Vendita* itself boldly declared "let the Clergy march under your standard, always believing that they are marching under the banner of the apostolic keys." That is, the demand for "obedience" would be used in dictatorial fashion to undermine true obedience and the faith itself.

And the curial reorganization of 1967 would be instrumental in accomplishing that aim by subjecting the whole Church to the Party Line of the Secretary of State—including the Party Line on Fatima—under the guise of a false "obedience" to an authority who has clearly exceeded the bounds established by God Himself. As we will demonstrate shortly, it was Cardinal Sodano who literally dictated the "interpretation" of the visional aspect of the Third Secret of Fatima, which has been published without the Virgin's own words to explain it.

## The Secretary of State Targets the Message of Fatima

This brings us to the precise role of the Secretary of State in imposing the Party Line with respect to Fatima. As we have noted, this process would involve the Message of Fatima in general and, in particular, perhaps its foremost proponent in the Church: the Fatima apostolate of Father Nicholas Gruner.

As early as 1989, the Secretary of State at the time, Cardinal Casaroli (the great "architect" of *Ostpolitik*) had communicated to Father Gruner's bishop at the time, His Excellency Gerardo Pierro of the Diocese of Avellino, Italy, what the Bishop had called "worried signals" about Father Gruner's Fatima apostolate. Father Gruner had been ordained in Avellino in 1976 for a Franciscan community that did not form as expected. Since 1978 he had been residing in Canada with the Bishop's permission, where he had become the leader of a small Fatima apostolate that had since grown into the largest of its kind in the world. But after the Party Line concerning the "consecration" of 1984 had been imposed by the anonymous order of 1988, it was inevitable that Father Gruner's apostolate and the Secretary of State would collide—just as the traditional orientation and the new orientation of the Church have collided after Vatican II.

The basic technique for trying to get rid of Father Gruner had been to create a bogus canonical scenario in which, having been ordered to find some other bishop to incardinate him outside of Avellino, Father Gruner's incardination anywhere else would be blocked through unprecedented arm-twisting behind the scenes, so that Father Gruner would be forced to "return" to Avellino and abandon his apostolate. Having blocked Father Gruner's incardination by three successive benevolent bishops who were friends of Fatima, the Vatican apparatus (in a complex proceeding beyond the scope of this book[24]) had finally lowered the boom: Father Gruner must "return" to Avellino or be "suspended" for "disobedience." In essence, Father Gruner was under a threat of "suspension" for having failed to do what his very accusers had systematically prevented him from doing—namely, find another bishop to incardinate him.[25]

As Father Gruner's various canonical appeals from these unprecedented actions against him wended their way through Vatican tribunals, his Fatima apostolate continued to flourish. By the year 2000 the apostolate, particularly through its journal *The Fatima Crusader*, had become the strongest and most persistent voice in the Church for both the Consecration of Russia and disclosure of the Third Secret.

Furthermore, the Pope himself had complicated the Fatima picture with his decision to beatify Jacinta and Francisco in a ceremony at Fatima on May 13, 2000. His intention to beatify the two children was made known as early as June of 1999, and this development had clearly triggered an internal struggle within the Vatican apparatus. This is shown by the curious on-again, off-again nature of the beatification ceremony, which is most unusual for the Vatican. First, the Secretary of State, Cardinal Angelo Sodano, announced in October 1999 that the beatification of Jacinta and Francisco would take place on April 9, 2000 in St. Peter's Square, along with four other beatifications. The Patriarch of Lisbon is quoted in the Portuguese press as having been informed by the Vatican that it was "quite impossible" for the Pope to come to Fatima for the children's beatification and that the question was "closed." The Patriarch told Portuguese journalists that he was convinced this "impossibility" of the Pope coming to Fatima was exclusively due to a decision by none other than the Vatican Secretary of State.

But the Pope had other ideas. In November of 1999 His Holiness—obviously bypassing Cardinal Sodano—informed Bishop Serafim, the Bishop of Fatima, directly that he should announce that the Pope would indeed come to Fatima on May 13 to perform the beatifications. Bishop Serafim did not make the new announcement until December 1999. And then, in March of 2000, the Bishop also let it slip that "the Pope will do something special for Fatima." This prompted furious speculation in the press that the Pope was, at last, going to reveal the Third Secret. Bishop Serafim was immediately rebuked in public by the Cardinal Patriarch of Lisbon, possibly under orders from somebody in the employ of the Vatican Secretary of State, who did not wish anyone to know that the Pope was contemplating revelation of the Secret. But the proverbial cat was out of the proverbial bag.[26]

And so the Pope went to Fatima on May 13, 2000 to beatify Jacinta and Francisco. The papal appearance was a kind of living demonstration of the conflict between the two visions of the Church we have been discussing. Evoking the Church of all time, the Pope delivered a sermon after the beatifications. In this sermon many things the Church seemed to have forgotten over the past forty years were suddenly recalled again:

> *According to the divine plan*, "a woman clothed with the sun" (Apoc. 12:1) came down from Heaven to this earth to visit the privileged children of the Father. She speaks to them with a mother's voice and heart: She asks them to offer themselves as victims of reparation, saying that She was ready to lead them safely to God. ...
>
> Later Francisco, one of the three privileged children, exclaimed: "We were burning in that light which is God and we were not consumed. What is God like? It is impossible to say. In fact we will never be able to tell people". God: a light that burns without consuming. *Moses had the same experience when he saw God in the burning bush. ...*
>
> "Another portent appeared in Heaven; behold, a great red dragon" (Apoc. 12:3). These words from the first reading of the Mass make us think of the great struggle between good and evil, showing how, when man puts God aside, he cannot achieve happiness, but ends up destroying himself. ...
>
> The Message of Fatima is a call to conversion, alerting humanity ***to have nothing to do with the "dragon" whose "tail swept down a third of the stars of heaven***, and cast them to the earth" (Apoc. 12:4).
>
> Man's final goal is Heaven, his true home, where the heavenly Father awaits everyone with His merciful love. God does not want anyone to be lost; that is why 2,000 years ago He sent His Son to earth, "to seek and to save the lost" (Lk. 19:10). ...
>
> In Her motherly concern, the Blessed Virgin came here to Fatima to ask men and women "to stop offending God, Our Lord, who is already too much offended". It is a mother's sorrow that compels Her to speak; *the destiny of Her children is at stake*. For this reason She asks the little shepherds: "Pray, pray much and make sacrifices for sinners; *many souls go to hell because they have no one to pray and make sacrifices for them*".

The Pope's direct linkage of the Message of Fatima with the Book of the Apocalypse, and his likening of the Fatima seers' encounter with God to that of Moses before the Burning Bush, comprised a stunning papal authentication of the Fatima apparitions as divinely given prophecies for our time. All of a sudden, Fatima was squarely before the eyes of the whole Church again.

There was, first of all, the Pope's astonishing reference to the Message of Fatima as a Biblical moment, the very fulfillment of chapter 12, verse 1 of the Apocalypse, which speaks of the "Woman clothed with the sun." Here John Paul II echoed Paul VI, who, in his apostolic letter *Signum magnum*, delivered at Fatima on May 13, 1967, declared:

> The great sign which the Apostle John saw in Heaven, "a woman clothed with the sun," is interpreted by the sacred Liturgy, not without foundation, as referring to the most Blessed Mary, the mother of all men

by the grace of Christ the Redeemer. ... On the occasion of the religious ceremonies which are taking place at this time in honor of the Virgin Mother of God in Fatima, Portugal, where She is venerated by countless numbers of the faithful for Her motherly and compassionate heart, we wish to call the attention of all sons of the Church once more to the indissoluble link between the spiritual motherhood of Mary ... and the duties of redeemed men toward Her, the Mother of the Church.

Even more astonishing, in his sermon John Paul II had explicitly linked the Message of Fatima to Apocalypse, chapter 3, verse 4, which prophesies that the "tail of the dragon" will sweep one-third of the stars from Heaven and cast them down to the earth. As Father Gruner would later note: "In the language of the Bible, the "stars of Heaven" are those who are set in the heavens to illumine the way for others to go to Heaven. This passage has been classically interpreted in Catholic commentaries to mean that one-third of the clergy—i.e. Cardinals, bishops, priests—fall from their consecrated state and are actually working for the devil." For example, the *Haydock Commentary* to the *Douay-Rheims Bible* notes that the image of one-third of the stars of Heaven has been interpreted to refer to "bishops and eminent persons who fall under the weight of persecution and apostatized ... The devil is always ready, as far as God permits him, to make war against the Church and the faithful servants of God."

In this connection Father Gruner, Gerry Matatics and others have cited the commentary on Apoc. 12:3-4 by Father Herman B. Kramer, in *The Book of Destiny*—published with an *imprimatur*, providentially enough, in 1956, only six years before the opening of Vatican II. In reference to the symbol of one-third of the stars of Heaven, Father Herman Kramer notes: "This is one-third of the clergy" and that "'one-third' of the stars shall follow the dragon"—meaning one-third of the clergy, who are the "stars", the consecrated souls in the Church.[27] That is, one-third of the Catholic clergy will be in the service of the devil, working to destroy the Church from within. Father Herman Kramer's commentary points out that the red dragon—a sign of the devil which could also symbolize Communism because red is Communism's emblematic color—brings the Church into great distress by undermining it from within.

The commentary goes on to say that, by means of these apostate clergy, the devil will probably enforce upon the Church "the acceptance of unchristian morals, false doctrines, *compromise with error,* or obedience to the civil rulers in violation of conscience." In addition, he suggests that "The symbolic meaning of the dragon's tail may reveal that the clergy who are ripe for apostasy will hold the influential positions in the Church, having won preferment by hypocrisy, deceit and flattery." The clergy who will follow the dragon — i.e. the devil — would include those "who neglected to preach the truth or to admonish the sinner by a good example, but rather sought popularity by being lax and the slaves of human respect," as well as those "who fear for their own interests and will not remonstrate against evil practices in the Church" and bishops "who abhor upright priests who dare to tell the truth".[28] Father Herman Kramer also observes as follows concerning the state of the Catholic Church in the times prophesied by Apoc. 12:3-4:

> *"The apostolic democracy founded by Our Lord may have given way to an absolute monarchy, in which the episcopate rules with oriental despotism. The priests may be reduced to a state of servility and fawning sycophancy. The rule by reason, justice and love may have been supplanted by the absolute will of the bishop, whose every act and word are to be accepted without question, without recourse to fact, truth or justice. Conscience may have lost its right to guide the actions of the priests and may stand ignored or condemned. Diplomacy, expediency and other trickery may be upheld as the greatest virtues."*[29]

But none of this is mentioned in those parts of the Message of Fatima which have thus far been revealed. Had the Pope, then, with his startling reference to Apocalypse 12:3-4, just given the world a glimpse into the contents of the Third Secret? Would he now reveal the Secret in its entirety?

But, alas, the sermon ends. It is not the Pope who will discuss the Third Secret. As quickly as it began, the Pope's momentary return to the vision of the Church of all time is over, and a chief exponent of the new vision rises to his feet. It is Cardinal Angelo Sodano, the Vatican Secretary of State—the same Cardinal Sodano who had tried, but failed, to prevent the Pope from going to Fatima to beatify Jacinta and Francisco. For some strange reason it is Sodano, not the Pope, who will announce that the Pope has decided to reveal the Third Secret of Fatima:

> On the solemn occasion of his visit to Fatima, His Holiness has directed me to make an announcement to you. As you know, the purpose of his visit to Fatima has been to beatify the two "little shepherds". Nevertheless he also wishes his pilgrimage to be a renewed gesture of gratitude to Our Lady for Her protection during these years of his papacy. This protection seems also to be linked to the so-called "third part" of the secret of Fatima.

And then what had seemed so strange suddenly became quite explicable. Cardinal Sodano's task would be to prepare the faithful to accept the notion that the Message of Fatima, including the Third Secret, was now to be considered a thing of the past. The process would begin with the Cardinal's "interpretation" of the Third Secret:

> That text contains a prophetic vision similar to those found in Sacred Scripture, which do not describe with photographic clarity the details of future events, but rather synthesize and condense against a unified background of events spread out over time in a succession and a duration which are not specified. As a result, the text *must be interpreted in a symbolic key*. ...

> According to the interpretation of the "little shepherds", which was also recently confirmed by Sister Lucia, the "Bishop clothed in white" who prays for all the faithful is the Pope. As he makes his way with great effort towards the Cross amid the corpses of those who were martyred (bishops, priests, men and women religious and many lay persons), he too falls to the ground, *apparently* dead, under a burst of gunfire.

As the faithful will soon learn, this is simply a lie. The "Bishop dressed in White" in the vision is not "apparently dead" but *is killed*—as the text of the vision clearly states—in the manner of a military execution, along with many bishops, priests and religious, outside a half-ruined city.

Why, then, insert the word "apparently" into the "interpretation"? Cardinal Sodano immediately tips his hand:

> After the assassination attempt of 13 May 1981, it appeared evident to His Holiness that it was "a motherly hand which guided the bullet's path", enabling the "dying Pope" to halt "at the threshold of death". ...
>
> The successive events of 1989 led, both in the Soviet Union and in a number of countries of Eastern Europe, to the fall of the Communist regime which promoted atheism. ...
>
> Even if the events to which the third part of the Secret of Fatima refers *now seem part of the past*, Our Lady's call to conversion and penance, issued at the beginning of the Twentieth Century, remains timely and urgent today.

Quite simply, Sodano was preparing the way for an "interpretation" of the Message of Fatima that would bury it once and for all: the Message culminated with the 1981 assassination attempt and the "fall of Communism" in 1989—events which "now seem part of the past." To insure this result, a "commentary" would be prepared before the actual text of the Third Secret would be released:

> In order that the faithful may better receive the message of Our Lady of Fatima, the Pope has charged the Congregation for the Doctrine of the Faith with making public the third part of the secret, after the preparation of an appropriate commentary.

But why had this commentary not been ready in time for the May 13 ceremony? After all, news of the Third Secret's impending disclosure had been circulating since at least March of 2000. In that month, Bishop Seraphim had announced that the Pope had told him during a visit to Rome that the Pope would "do something special for Fatima"[30] when he went there for the beatification ceremony in May 2000.

Curiously enough, the Pope had urged Bishop Serafim to say nothing about this while he was in Rome, but to wait until he returned to Fatima. But the subject was on the Pope's mind since the previous November, so why had no "commentary" been prepared during the period November 1999 to May

2000? Surely, such a commentary could easily have been completed in that time.

Two conclusions suggest themselves. Either the Pope had not told Cardinal Sodano of his intention concerning disclosure of the Third Secret—in which case the Pope does not trust Sodano—or the Pope did tell Sodano, whereupon Sodano assumed that he would somehow be able to prevent disclosure at the May 13, 2000 ceremony. This would explain why Sodano had not arranged for a commentary beforehand: he thought it would not be needed because he would be able to prevent any disclosure of the Third Secret. But the Pope had pressed ahead, and now the Secret had to be "managed" in such a way that the question of Fatima could be laid to rest.

## A Press Conference to Announce the Sodano Party Line

We thus arrive at the fateful date of June 26, 2000. On this date the Third Secret is "disclosed" at a Vatican press conference, along with a commentary prepared by Cardinal Ratzinger and Monsignor Tarcisio Bertone, Secretary of the CDF, entitled *The Message of Fatima* (hereafter referred to as *TMF*). In *TMF* the Party Line on Fatima would be officially promulgated—by the direct command of Cardinal Angelo Sodano.

First of all, the faithful were told that the following text of a vision seen by Sister Lucy is all there is to the Third Secret of Fatima:

> After the two parts which I have already explained, at the left of Our Lady and a little above, we saw an Angel with a flaming sword in his left hand; flashing, it gave out flames that looked as though they would set the world on fire; but they died out in contact with the splendour that Our Lady radiated towards him from her right hand: pointing to the earth with his right hand, the Angel cried out in a loud voice: 'Penance, Penance, Penance!'. And we saw in an immense light that is God: 'something similar to how people appear in a mirror when they pass in front of it' a Bishop dressed in White 'we had the impression that it was the Holy Father'. Other Bishops, Priests, men and women Religious going up a steep mountain, at the top of which there was a big Cross of rough-hewn trunks as of a cork-tree with the bark; before reaching there the Holy Father passed through a big city half in ruins and half trembling with halting step, afflicted with pain and sorrow, he prayed for the souls of the corpses he met on his way; having reached the top of the mountain, on his knees at the foot of the big Cross he was killed by a group of soldiers who fired bullets and arrows at him, and in the same way there died one after another the other Bishops, Priests, men and women Religious, and various lay people of different ranks and positions. Beneath the two arms of the Cross there were two Angels, each with a crystal aspersorium in his hand, in which they gathered up the blood of the Martyrs and with it sprinkled the souls that were making their way to God.

The immediate reaction of millions of Catholics could be summarized in two words: *That's it*? Clearly, something was amiss, since nothing in this text corresponded to what Cardinal Ratzinger himself had said about the Third Secret in 1984—a point to which we shall return shortly. Nor did it contain anything that would have explained its mysterious suppression since 1960.

Most important, this ambiguous vision, written down on four sheets of notebook paper, contained no words of Our Lady. In particular, it contained nothing that would complete the famous phrase spoken by Our Lady at the conclusion of the recorded portion of the Message of Fatima as faithfully transcribed by Sister Lucy in her memoirs: "In Portugal the dogma of the faith will always be preserved etc." Sister Lucy had added this phrase, including the "etc.", to her fourth memoir as part of the integral text of the Message. This addition had led every reputable Fatima scholar to conclude that it signaled the beginning of the unrecorded Third Secret, and that the Third Secret pertained to a widespread dogmatic crisis in the Church outside of Portugal. Clearly, the Virgin had more to say that was not written down because Sister Lucy had been instructed to keep it secret—until, as we have seen, 1960.

In a curious maneuver, however, *TMF* had avoided any discussion of the telltale phrase by taking the text of the Message of Fatima from Sister Lucy's *third* memoir, where the phrase does not appear. *TMF* justifies this as follows: "For the account of the first two parts of the 'secret', which have already been published and are therefore known, we have chosen the text written by Sister Lucia in the *Third* Memoir of 31 August 1941; some *annotations* were added in the *Fourth* Memoir of 8 December 1941." Annotations? The key phrase concerning the preservation of dogma in Portugal was no "annotation" but *an integral part of the spoken words of Our Lady*, after which She had said: "Tell this to no one. Yes, you may tell Francisco."

Having deceptively mischaracterized an integral part of the Message of Fatima as an "annotation", *TMF* then buries it in a footnote that is never mentioned again: "In the 'Fourth Memoir' Sister Lucia adds: 'In Portugal, the dogma of the faith will always be preserved, etc. ...'."

Why are Sodano/Ratzinger/Bertone so leery of this key phrase that they would so obviously go out of their way to avoid it by using an earlier and *less complete* memoir of the text of the Message? If there is nothing to hide in this phrase, why not simply use the Fourth Memoir and attempt an explanation of what the phrase means? Why did the authors of *TMF* so obviously *pretend* that the phrase is a mere "annotation", when they know full well that it appears in the integral text as part of the spoken words of the Mother of God? We shall return to this suspicious behavior in a later chapter.

Another grounds for suspicion was that the vision of the "Bishop dressed in White" was not at all the one-page "*letter* ... in which Sister Lucy wrote down the *words which Our Lady confided* as a secret to the three shepherds of the Cova da Iria"—as the Vatican itself had described it in the aforementioned 1960 press release. The text of the vision spans *four pages* of what appear to be ruled notebook paper.

Another suspicious circumstance is that on June 26 Cardinal Sodano's falsehood of May 13 was clearly exposed: the Pope *is killed* by soldiers who fire upon him as he kneels at the foot of a large wooden Cross outside a half-ruined city. The Pope is not "apparently dead", as Sodano had falsely asserted in May; the Pope *is* dead. The vision, whatever it means, clearly has absolutely nothing to do with the 1981 assassination attempt. The faithful had already been duped in May, and now the process of duping them was clearly continuing.

The dozens of discrepancies raised by this text—prompting Catholics around the world to doubt that we have received the Secret in its entirety—will be addressed in a later chapter. For now, we consider the Ratzinger/Bertone "commentary" in *TMF* on the Fatima Message as a whole.

## Cardinal Sodano Dictates the "Interpretation" of the Third Secret

First of all, *TMF* is a virtual admission that the "interpretation" of the Message of Fatima which Cardinal Ratzinger and Msgr. Bertone will "attempt" (to use Cardinal Ratzinger's word) has been dictated by none other than Cardinal Sodano. No fewer than four times, *TMF* states that it is following *Sodano's* "interpretation" of the Third Secret—namely, that Fatima belongs to the past:

> Before attempting an interpretation, the main lines of which can be found in the statement read by *Cardinal Sodano* on May 13 of this year …
>
> For this reason the figurative language of the vision is symbolic. In this regard *Cardinal Sodano* stated …
>
> As is clear from the documentation presented here, the interpretation offered by *Cardinal Sodano*, in his statement on 13 May, was first put personally to Sister Lucia. …
>
> First of all, *we must affirm with Cardinal Sodano* that the events to which the Third Secret of Fatima refers now seem *part of the past*.

And just in case the reader still has not gotten the point, the basic aim of *TMF* is driven home once again:

> Insofar as individual events are described, *they belong to the past*.

Is it not curious that the interpretation of the Virgin of Fatima's vital message to the world had been given over, not to the Pope, nor even to the Congregation for the Doctrine of the Faith (which was merely aping Cardinal Sodano's opinion), but to the *Vatican Secretary of State*? What authority does Cardinal Sodano have to impose his view upon the Church? None, of course. But Cardinal Sodano had arrogated that authority to himself in keeping the overall post-conciliar ascendancy of the Vatican Secretary of State to the status of *de facto* Pope when it comes to the daily governance of Church affairs.

## Cardinal Ratzinger Executes the Sodano Party Line

Returning to the "commentary" with these facts in mind, one can see that the press conference of June 26, 2000 had one overriding purpose: to carry out Cardinal Sodano's order concerning the "correct" interpretation of the Message of Fatima. By the time the reporters left that room, the Message of Fatima—all of it—was to be buried. And once buried, the Message would no longer impede Cardinal Sodano and his collaborators in their relentless pursuit of the Church's new, post-Fatima orientation, which includes (as we shall see) the important Church business of lauding, dining and hobnobbing at the Vatican with the likes of Mikhail Gorbachev, having the Pope apologize to the Red Chinese regime, pressuring Romanian Catholics to surrender to the Orthodox church the local Catholic Church's rights to the properties stolen by Josef Stalin, and other such "triumphs" of Vatican diplomacy.

In other words, every last holdout in the Church must be brought along to the Vatican's new way of thinking and speaking to the world, which does not square well with Our Lady of Fatima's prophecy of the *triumph* of Her Immaculate Heart, the spread of *devotion* to Her Immaculate Heart and the consequent *conversion* of Russia through the intervention of the Immaculate Heart. This sort of talk just won't do anymore, even if it does come from the Mother of God. So, the precise task entrusted to Cardinal Ratzinger and Msgr. Bertone on June 26 was to find a way to detach the faithful once and for all from the explicitly Catholic aspects of the Message of Fatima, which all too clearly remind us of the "triumphal" Church of the "pre-conciliar dark age". As the *Los Angeles Times* would observe in its headline of June 27, 2000: "Catholic Church Unveils Third Secret: The Vatican's Top Theologian Gently Debunks a Nun's Account of Her 1917 Vision That Fueled Decades of Speculation." The effort was so blatant that even a secular newspaper could not help but notice it. Let us provide the proof of this crime against the Virgin of Fatima and the saintly seers God chose to receive Her message.

First there was Cardinal Ratzinger's attempt in *TMF* to dispose of the *triumph* of the Immaculate Heart:

> I would like finally to mention another key expression of the "secret" which has become justly famous: "my Immaculate Heart will triumph". What does this mean? The Heart open to God, purified by contemplation of God, is stronger than guns and weapons of every kind. The *fiat* of Mary, the word of her heart, has changed the history of the world, because it brought the Saviour into the world—because, thanks to her *Yes,* God could become man in our world and remains so for all time.

The attentive reader will notice immediately that Cardinal Ratzinger has conveniently removed the first three words from the Virgin's prophecy: *In the end.* This clearly deliberate censorship of the very Mother of God was necessary for Cardinal Ratzinger's revisionist "interpretation" along the lines dictated by Sodano: namely, that Fatima belongs to the past.

Thus, "*In the end,* My Immaculate Heart will triumph" is—after the expedient removal of the first three words—now to be understood as follows: "2,000 years ago My Immaculate Heart triumphed." Our Lady's prophecy of what *will* happen *in the end* is blatantly falsified into a mere acknowledgment of what had already happened 20 centuries ago at the *beginning* of Christian history. Four future events—the triumph of the Immaculate Heart, the consecration of Russia, Russia's conversion, and the resulting period of peace in the world—are cunningly converted into one event 2,000 years ago!

This tampering with a message God Himself sent to earth through His Blessed Mother should cause any member of the faithful to rise up and demand justice in the name of Heaven. But Cardinal Ratzinger's butchery of the Message of Fatima does not end here; it is far worse than even this. Concerning Our Lady's call to establish *devotion* to Her Immaculate Heart throughout the world as "God wishes," Cardinal Ratzinger offered this mockery:

> According to Matthew 5:8, the 'immaculate heart' is a heart which, with God's grace, has come to perfect interior unity and therefore 'sees God.' To be 'devoted' to the Immaculate Heart of Mary means therefore to embrace this attitude of heart, which makes the *fiat*—your will be done—the defining centre of one's whole life.

Notice, first of all, the quotation marks Cardinal Ratzinger places around *devoted* and *immaculate heart*, which he strips of its upper-case I—a sure sign these words are about to acquire a new meaning.

Thus, "God wishes to establish in the world devotion to My Immaculate Heart" is now to be understood as: "God wishes everyone to do His will." In fact, everyone whose heart is open to God's will acquires an "immaculate heart" of his own. So, devotion to the Immaculate Heart of Mary means opening one's *own* heart to God, not spreading devotion to *Her* heart in order to make the world (especially Russia) Catholic. Immaculate with a capital I becomes immaculate with a lower-case i, and Her Heart becomes everyone's heart, at least potentially. As a magician would say: "Presto, change-o!"

There is, of course, only one word to describe the demotion of the one and only Immaculate Heart—conceived without Original Sin and guilty of no personal sin whatsoever—to the level of the heart of any person who turns away from his sins and finds interior unity with God. The word is *blasphemy*. More will be said about this particular outrage in the next chapter.

The *conversion* of Russia was a bit more difficult to make disappear. There is not much one can say to obscure the Mother of God's very clear statement that "the Holy Father will consecrate Russia to Me, which *will be converted*." But the conversion of Russia is no longer acceptable to the Vatican apparatus, as we have already shown. The solution was simply to avoid any discussion of the subject in *TMF*, although Our Lady's words are quoted without comment. The conversion of Russia? What conversion?

The crowning insult was Cardinal Ratzinger's citation of only one "authority" on Fatima in *TMF*: the Flemish theologian Edouard Dhanis, S.J., whom Cardinal Ratzinger identifies as an "eminent scholar" on Fatima. Cardinal Ratzinger of course knows that Dhanis, a modernist Jesuit, made a veritable career out of casting doubt on the Fatima apparitions. Dhanis proposed that everything in the Secret of Fatima beyond a call for prayer and penance was cobbled together in the minds of the three children from things they had seen or heard in their own lives. Dhanis thus categorized as "Fatima II" all those things which the "eminent scholar" arbitrarily rejected as fabrications—without ever once interviewing Sister Lucy or studying the official Fatima archives.

As Dhanis put it: "All things considered, it is not easy to state precisely what degree of credence is to be given to the accounts of Sister Lucy. Without questioning her sincerity, or the sound judgment she shows in daily life, one may judge it prudent to use her writings only with reservations. ... Let us observe also that a good person can be sincere and prove to have good judgment in everyday life, but have a *propensity for unconscious fabrication* in a certain area, or in any case, a tendency to relate old memories of twenty years ago with embellishments and considerable modifications."[31]

Dhanis, who refused to examine the official Fatima archives, cast doubt on every aspect of the Message of Fatima which did not accord with his neo-modernist leanings: the prayer taught by the Angel he called "inexact"; the vision of hell he called an "exaggeratedly medieval representation"; the prophecy of "a night illumined by an unknown light" heralding the advent of World War II he described as "grounds for suspicion." And as for the consecration of Russia, Dhanis flatly declared that: "Russia could not be consecrated by the Pope, without this act taking on the air of a challenge, both in regard to the separated hierarchy, as well as the Union of Soviet Socialist Republics. *This would make the consecration practically unrealizable* ..." Thus, Dhanis declared that the consecration of Russia would be "morally impossible by reason of the reactions it would normally provoke."[32]

Dhanis' deconstruction of the Message of Fatima is a typical example of how modernists undermine Catholic truths based upon premises they themselves invent. Since (invented premise) the consecration of Russia is morally impossible, how could Our Lady of Fatima have requested it? Having thus stacked the deck against Sister Lucy, Dhanis states the "inevitable" conclusion: "But could the Most Holy Virgin have requested a consecration which, taken according to the rigor of the terms, would be practically unrealizable? ... This question indeed seems to call for a *negative response*. ... Thus, it hardly seems probable that Our Lady asked for the consecration of Russia. ..." Based entirely on the premise Dhanis invented, Sister Lucy's testimony is pronounced a fraud.

These are the views which Cardinal Ratzinger endorsed in his "commentary" by praising Dhanis as an "eminent scholar" on Fatima. And Cardinal Ratzinger, following the line of Dhanis, suggests that the Third

Secret in particular consists of "images which Lucia may have seen in devotional books and which draw their inspiration from long-standing intuitions of faith." In other words, who can really say which parts of the Third Secret are authentic and which are merely personal memories or "intuitions"? And if that were true of the Third Secret, it would also be true of the rest of the Message of Fatima.

Cardinal Ratzinger's stealthy attempt to undermine Sister Lucy's credibility, while professing great respect for the Message of Fatima, will be taken up again in the following chapter. Here it suffices to say that Cardinal Ratzinger's evident agreement with Dhanis that all the specifically prophetic elements of the Message are unreliable serves to disqualify him from making any "interpretation" of the Third Secret, or any other part of the Fatima Message. Quite simply, Cardinal Ratzinger *does not believe* that the Mother of God called for the consecration of Russia, the conversion of Russia to the Catholic Faith, the triumph of the Immaculate Heart, and the establishment of the specifically Catholic devotion to *the one and only* Immaculate Heart throughout the world. That being the case, the Cardinal had a duty to reveal his bias and abstain from the matter, instead of pretending to give an "interpretation" that is really an attempt to debunk and discredit that which he purports to "interpret."

What was left of the Message of Fatima after Cardinal Ratzinger and Bertone got done with it on June 26? On this point, Cardinal Ratzinger and Dhanis agree: "What remains was already evident when we began our reflections on the text of the 'secret': the exhortation to prayer as the path of 'salvation for souls' (*sic*) and, likewise, the summons to penance and conversion." On June 26, 2000 the Message of Fatima became Fatima Lite: a watered-down prescription for personal piety without any specific relevance to the future.

For *this* the Mother of God came to earth and called down the Miracle of the Sun? It is interesting to note that even in presenting this minimalist version of the Message, Cardinal Ratzinger could not write about salvation for souls without bracketing those words with the same squeamish quotation marks he used to distance himself from the words *devotion*, *triumph* and *immaculate* in his commentary. It seems even Fatima Lite is not quite light enough in Catholic content for the ecumenical palates of modern Churchmen.

As for Our Lady's prophetic warning that "various nations will be annihilated" if the consecration of Russia were not done, this we are apparently supposed to forget. There will be no annihilation of nations, "Fatima is all in the past." Cardinal Sodano says as much. Cardinal Ratzinger agrees.

## The Party Line on the Consecration of Russia

We have mentioned Archbishop Bertone's role in *TMF*. His principal contributions to the farce were two:

First, Bertone issued the "command" (binding, of course, on no one) that the faithful must cease asking for the Consecration of Russia: "Hence any further discussion or request [of the Consecration] is without basis."

To support this claim, Bertone cited exactly one piece of evidence: the manifestly fake "letter of November 8, 1989" from "Sister Lucy" to Mr. Noelker, which we have already mentioned—the same letter in which "Sister Lucy" writes about a consecration of the world by Pope Paul VI at Fatima which she never witnessed because it never happened. Tellingly enough, Bertone fails to identify the addressee of the letter. Nor does he provide the world with a copy to examine, lest anyone notice the fatal blunder concerning Pope Paul's nonexistent "consecration of the world." Even more telling, *TMF* contains absolutely no direct testimony by Sister Lucy herself concerning the Consecration, even though Bertone himself had interviewed her about the Third Secret only two months earlier, and she was readily available to Cardinal Ratzinger and the entire Vatican apparatus during the beatification ceremony in May.

Small wonder. *TMF*'s version of the "consecration of Russia" —which is to say Cardinal Sodano's version—flatly contradicts a lifetime of testimony to the contrary by Sister Lucy. We consider a few examples here.

Over 55 years ago, on July 15, 1946, the eminent author and historian, William Thomas Walsh interviewed Sister Lucy, which is recounted in his important work, *Our Lady of Fatima,* which sold over one million copies. At this interview, which appears at the book's end, Mr. Walsh asked her pointed questions about the correct procedure for the Collegial Consecration:

> Finally we came to the important subject of the second July secret, of which so many different and conflicting versions have been published. Lucia made it plain that Our Lady did not ask for the consecration of *the world* to Her Immaculate Heart. What She demanded specifically was the consecration of *Russia.* She did not comment, of course, on the fact that Pope Pius XII had consecrated the world, not Russia, to the Immaculate Heart in 1942. But she said more than once, and with deliberate emphasis: 'What Our Lady wants is that the Pope and all the bishops in the world shall consecrate Russia to Her Immaculate Heart on one special day. If this is done, She will convert Russia and there will be peace. If it is not done, the errors of Russia will spread through every country in the world'.[33]

Sister Lucy is clear and forthright. The collegial consecration requested by Heaven is the Consecration of *Russia,* not the *world,* which must be done by the Pope in union with the world's bishops on the same day.

Then there is the little-known revelation of Our Lady to Sister Lucy in the early 1950s, which is recounted in *Il Pellegrinaggio Della Meraviglie,* published under the auspices of the Italian episcopate. The Virgin Mary appeared to Sister Lucy in May 1952 and said "Make it known to the Holy Father that I am always awaiting the Consecration of Russia to My Immaculate Heart. Without the Consecration, Russia will not be able to convert, nor will the world have peace."[34]

Thus, 10 years after Pope Pius XII's 1942 Consecration of the world, we have the report of Our Lady reminding Sister Lucy that Russia will not be converted, nor will there be peace, unless Russia is consecrated by name.

Thirty years later, in 1982, Sister Lucy's testimony remains steadfast. On May 12, 1982, the day before the attempted 1982 consecration, the Vatican's own *L'Osservatore Romano* published an interview of Sister Lucy by Father Umberto Maria Pasquale, a Salesian priest, during which she told Father Umberto that Our Lady had never requested the Consecration of the world, but *only* the Consecration of Russia:

> At a certain moment I said to her: "Sister, I should like to ask you a question. If you cannot answer me, let it be. But if you can answer it, I would be most grateful to you ... Has Our Lady ever spoken to you about the Consecration of ***the world*** to Her Immaculate Heart?"
>
> "***No,*** Father Umberto! ***Never!*** At the Cova da Iria in 1917 Our Lady had promised: ***I shall come to ask for the Consecration of Russia*** **...** In 1929, at Tuy, as She had promised, Our Lady came back to tell me that the moment had come to ask the Holy Father for the Consecration of ***that country*** (Russia)."

This testimony was confirmed by Sister Lucy in a handwritten letter to Father Umberto, which the priest also published. (See photographic reproduction below.) A translation of the letter reads:

> Reverend Father Umberto, in replying to your question, I will clarify: Our Lady of Fatima, in Her request, referred only to the Consecration of Russia ... — *Coimbra 13 IV - 1980 (signed) Sister Lucia*

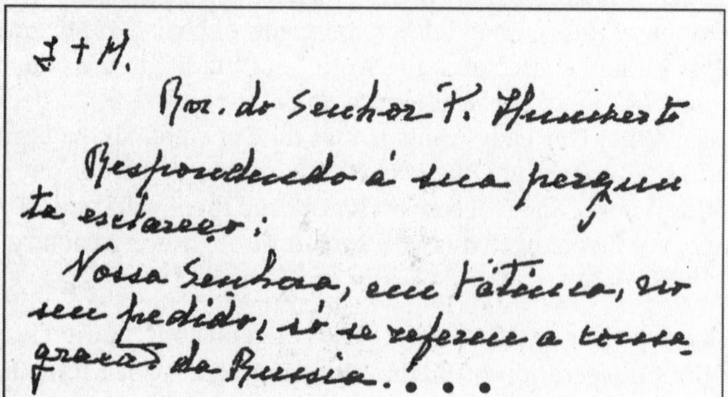
J + M.

Rev.do Senhor P. Humberto

Respondendo à sua pergunta esclareço:

Nossa Senhora, em Fátima, no seu pedido, só se referiu a consagração da Russia...

Coimbra 13 IV-1980

Ir. Lucia

Again, on March 19, 1983, at the request of the Holy Father, Sister Lucy met with the Papal Nuncio, Archbishop Portalupi, Dr. Lacerda, and Father Messias Coelho. During this meeting, Sister Lucy confirmed that Pope John Paul's Consecration of 1982 did not fulfill the requests of Our Lady. Sister Lucy said:

> In the act of offering of May 13, 1982, Russia did not appear as being the object of the consecration. And each bishop did not organize in his own diocese a public and solemn ceremony of reparation and Consecration of Russia. Pope John Paul II simply renewed the consecration of the world executed by Pius XII on October 31, 1942. From this consecration we can expect some benefits, but not the conversion of Russia.[35]

She concluded, "The Consecration of Russia *has not been done as Our Lady had demanded it.* I was not able to say it because I did not have the permission of the Holy See."[36]

A year later, on March 25, 1984, Pope John Paul II made an act of offering wherein he again consecrated "the world", not Russia. As with the 1982 Consecration, "each bishop did not organize in his own diocese a public and solemn ceremony of reparation and consecration of Russia". Concerning this ceremony Frère François writes: "In the months which followed the act of offering of March 25, 1984, which was only a renewal of the act of 1982, the principal scholars of Fatima agreed in saying that the consecration of Russia had not yet been done as Heaven wished it."[37]

Such was also the conviction of Father Antonio Maria Martins,[38] and of Father Messias Coelho who, on the eve of March 25, 1984, had announced in *Mensagem de Fátima,* of which he is the publisher-editor, "Consecration of Russia: It will not be done yet this time." He further explained, "It is certain the more contains the less. Apparently therefore, the 'Consecration of the world' will perhaps give the impression of having the power to take the place of consecrating specifically Russia. However, the problem cannot be resolved in logical terms, nor even in the light of systematic theology."[39]

These theologians based their statements not only on the bald fact that a consecration of Russia needs to mention the word "Russia", but also on the testimony of Sister Lucy herself.

On Thursday, March 22, 1984, two days before the Act of Offering, the Carmel of Coimbra was celebrating Sister Lucy's seventy-seventh birthday. She received on that day, as was her custom, her old friend Mrs. Eugenia Pestana. After extending good wishes to her Carmelite friend, Mrs. Pestana asked, "Then Lucy, Sunday is the Consecration?" Sister Lucy, who had already received and read the text of the Pope's consecration formula made a negative sign and declared "That consecration cannot have a decisive character."[40]

The "decisive character" which is the stamp of the proper consecration is the miraculous conversion of Russia. Although the new "ecumenical orientation" of the Church has confused the issue, the conversion of Russia means conversion to *Catholicism*. This is not only a matter of common sense, but it is also found in the testimony of Father Joaquin Alonso, probably the foremost Fatima expert of the 20th Century. Father Alonso, who had many interviews with Sister Lucy, wrote in 1976:

> ... we should affirm that Lucia always thought that the '*conversion*' of Russia is not to be limited to the return of the Russian people to the Orthodox Christian religions, rejecting the Marxist atheism of the Soviets, but rather, it refers purely, plainly and simply to the total, integral conversion of Russia to the one true Church of Christ, the Catholic Church.[41]

In a 1985 interview in *Sol de Fatima*, Sister Lucy was asked if the Pope fulfilled the request of Our Lady when he consecrated the world in 1984. Sister Lucy replied: *"There was no participation of all the bishops, and there was no mention of Russia."* She was then asked, *"So the consecration was not done as requested by Our Lady?"* to which she replied: *"No. Many bishops attached no importance to this act."*[42]

Even Father Rene Laurentin, a comrade of the progressivists, admitted in 1986 that "Sister Lucy remains unsatisfied[43] ... Lucy seems to think that the Consecration has 'not been made' as Our Lady wanted it."[44]

Then on July 20, 1987, Sister Lucy was interviewed quickly outside her convent while voting. Here she told journalist Enrique Romero that the Consecration of Russia has not been done as requested.[45]

More of Sister Lucy's affirmations that the 1984 consecration did not fulfill Heaven's conditions could be cited,[46] but the point is made: Msgr. Bertone and Cardinal Ratzinger, following Sodano's Party Line, were relying *entirely* on a single, manifestly bogus letter to overcome more than fifty years of unwavering testimony by Sister Lucy on Heaven's requirements for an effectual consecration of Russia. They had not dared to ask Sister Lucy about the matter themselves—or, if they had, she had not provided answers consistent with the Party Line.[47]

## The Party Line on Fatima and World Peace

This brings us to Msgr. Bertone's second contribution to the farce. It came in the form of this statement:

> The decision of His Holiness Pope John Paul II to make public the third part of the "secret" of Fatima brings to an end a period of history marked by tragic human lust for power and evil, yet pervaded by the merciful love of God and the watchful care of the Mother of Jesus and of the Church.

It is difficult to find words to express the offensiveness of this absurd claim. Here Sodano's Party Line seriously proposes that an entire era of human lust for power and evil has been brought to an end with the Vatican's "disclosure" of the ambiguous vision of the "Bishop dressed in White." In which case, why did the Vatican wait forty years to bring on world peace, when all it had to do, according to Msgr. Bertone, was stage a press conference in 1960 to publish the ambiguous vision of the "Bishop dressed in White"?

Cardinal Sodano evidently recognized that he must provide the faithful with some sort of counterfeit to take the place of the triumph of the Immaculate Heart, which had never materialized following the 1984 "consecration of Russia." The press conference of June 26, 2000 was thus presented as the great culmination of the Message of Fatima!

Somehow Msgr. Bertone and Cardinal Ratzinger alike had managed to ignore the obvious implications of Sister Lucy's letter to the Pope of May 12, 1982, which they themselves had (in part) photographically reproduced in *TMF*:

> And if we have not yet seen the complete fulfillment of the final part of this prophecy, *we are going towards it with great strides*.[48] If we do not reject the path of sin, hatred, revenge, injustice, violations of the rights of the human person, immorality and violence, etc. And let us not say that it is God who is punishing us in this way; on the contrary *it is people themselves who are preparing their own punishment*.

This 1982 letter makes *absolutely no reference* to the 1981 assassination attempt; much less does it characterize the attempt as any sort of fulfillment of the Third Secret. Clearly, a year after the attempt Sister Lucy remained worried about a global chastisement in consequence of the Church's failure to heed the imperatives of the Fatima Message. She clearly did not have in view the triumph of the Immaculate Heart, but rather the annihilation of nations.

Also very curious is that the same letter from Sister Lucy (which Ratzinger and Bertone tell us was addressed to Pope John Paul II) contains the phrase: "The third part of the secret that *you are so anxious to know* (que tanto ansiais por conhecer)". Why would the Pope be "so anxious to know" the third part of the Secret if he already had the text in his possession at the Vatican, where it has been lodged since 1957? Why would His Holiness be "so anxious to know" what he had already read in 1981 (as Bertone/Ratzinger claim), or as early as 1978, as papal spokesman Joaquin Navarro-Valls told the Portuguese press?

It is highly suspicious that the phrase "you are so anxious to know" is deleted *from every Vatican translation of the original Portuguese letter* in the various language versions of the Cardinal Ratzinger/Bertone commentary. Even the Portuguese language version of *TMF* omits the phase "you are so anxious to know" from the *Portuguese* typeset reproduction of the original letter. Clearly, the Vatican apparatus wanted to avoid a storm of questions about how the Pope could be anxious to know something he already knew. But by the time reporters could compare their translations with the original Portuguese letter, the press conference was over and no further questions could be asked.

Two conclusions are possible: Either the letter was not really written to the Pope, or there was something more to the Secret which the Pope really did not know as of May 12, 1982, the date of the purported letter from Sister Lucy. As Sir Walter Scott's famous aphorism goes: "Oh what a tangled web we weave, when first we practice to deceive."[49] The first lie—that Fatima belongs to the past—leads to a tangled web of other lies in order to cover up the first.

## Targeting Father Gruner

But there was more to be done in this campaign to bury Fatima in the past. What about "the Fatima priest", whose apostolate's publications and broadcasts were persistently and quite effectively hammering home the point that the Vatican apparatus, pursuing its new vision of the Church, had turned its back on the Virgin's requests? At the end of the June 26 press conference, Cardinal Ratzinger went out of his way to mention Father Nicholas Gruner by name, stating that Father Gruner must be "submissive to the Magisterium" on the question of the Consecration of Russia, which (so the Party Line goes) was now over and done with. But the Magisterium—the authoritative teaching office of the Church—had taught nothing of the kind. There was only the Sodano Interpretation of Fatima, and *TMF*'s non-binding "attempt" to explain away all of the specific prophetic content of the Fatima Message[50] (leaving only prayer and penance).

Ratcheting up this persecution, the Vatican's Congregation for the Clergy had, only days before the June 26 press conference, sent Father Gruner a letter containing the astounding threat that he would be excommunicated from the Catholic Church. This letter was followed up with a communiqué to the bishops of the Philippines (where Father Gruner's apostolate is strongly supported), advising that Father Gruner would be excommunicated unless (among other things demanded) he "reconciled himself to Church authorities"—that is, return to the Diocese of Avellino, close down his apostolate and bow to the Party Line on Fatima. For his own part, the Bishop of Avellino had never needed Father Gruner's services, never supported him financially since 1978, and had never taken any steps to secure a proper immigration visa for the "return" to Avellino. The Bishop of Avellino was nothing but a pawn in the Secretary of State's chess game. (We will have more to say about this travesty in later chapters.)

In his remarks about Father Gruner at the end of the June 26 press conference, Cardinal Ratzinger had also noted that Father Gruner was no doubt suffering from *angoscia*—the Italian word for extreme mental anguish. Cardinal Ratzinger obviously knew of the threat of excommunication, which would indeed cause *angoscia* in any faithful priest who loves the Church. But Father Gruner's plight is only emblematic of the plight of the Church as a whole in the post-conciliar epoch: a priest who has committed no offense against faith and morals is personally threatened with excommunication by the very head of the Congregation for the Clergy, while throughout the Church predators in Roman collars molest altar boys or spread heresy, while their bishops hide them and protect them from any punishment, and the Congregation for the Clergy does nothing.

What is to explain this outrageous disparity of justice? There seems to us only one sensible explanation, based on what we have shown thus far: In the Catholic Church of the post-conciliar Adaptation the one unforgivable offense, just as in Stalinist Russia, is to buck the Party Line. And Father Gruner had bucked the Party Line on Fatima.

## Exit Our Lady, Enter Gorbachev

We have claimed that this mockery and obscuration of the Fatima Message—the Party Line on Fatima—was intended to bury it once and for all, so that Cardinal Sodano could get on with his pursuit of the Church's new orientation. Here is the explicit proof:

Fatima having been "gently debunked" (to quote the *Los Angeles Times*) by Cardinal Ratzinger and Msgr. Bertone on June 26, the Vatican apparatus, led by Cardinal Sodano, immediately got down to what it considers the serious business of the Church. The very next day Mikhail Gorbachev was seated as a guest of honor between Cardinals Sodano and Silvestrini at a Vatican "press conference." What was the purpose of this press conference? It was called to celebrate one of the key elements of the Church's new orientation: *Ostpolitik*, the policy of "dialogue" and accommodation with Communist regimes (including Red China) that persecute the Church. The immediate occasion for the press conference was the posthumous publication of the memoirs of Cardinal Casaroli, the grand architect of *Ostpolitik* and Cardinal Sodano's predecessor in enforcing the Party Line of the Secretary of State.[51]

In true Stalinist fashion, no questions from the press were permitted at this curious "press conference"—a press conference with no questions from the press! Evidently the Vatican wanted to be sure that no one bucked the Party Line with any questions about Fatima, or why the Vatican was honoring the likes of Mikhail Gorbachev, a man who admits he is still a Leninist and whose tax-free foundations are promoting the use of abortion and contraception to eliminate four billion people from the world's population.[52] This is not even to mention this blood-drenched character's public defense of the Soviet invasion of Afghanistan when he was still head of the Soviet Communist Party—a genocidal campaign that included planting bombs disguised as toys, so that Afghan children would have their limbs and heads blown off.[53]

Could there be a more dramatic demonstration of the fundamental opposition between the Church of all time and the Church of the Adaptation? On June 26, 2000 Our Lady of Fatima was shown the door, Her heavenly message audaciously censored and revised by men who would dare to consign it to oblivion. Then, a day later, Mikhail Gorbachev entered the Vatican to celebrate the Church's new orientation, as implemented by the late Cardinal Casaroli and by his successor, Cardinal Sodano.

Gorbachev, leader of the culture of death, was honored by the Vatican again on November 4, 2000 when he addressed the Pope and other prelates at the "Jubilee of Politicians"—a dinner gala for about 5,000 of the world's rulers of godless secular republics. The photographers captured the Pope listening very attentively to a speech by this key promoter of the abortion holocaust.[54] This grotesque mixture of a Jubilee—a spiritual tradition in the Church derived from an Old Testament custom—with speeches by pro-abortion politicians on secular matters, is only typical of the new orientation, which constantly seeks to merge the Church with the world in the great Adaptation of Roman Catholicism to "modern civilization".

# Chapter 9

## Enforcing the New Orientation in a "Post-Fatima" Church

The months following the June 26 press conference witnessed an acceleration in the campaign to impose the new orientation on the Message of Fatima and the Church at large.

For example, on June 29, 2000, only two days after the Gorbachev farce, a seemingly unrelated but actually quite relevant event took place. Cardinal Castrillón Hoyos issued a letter in his capacity as the head of the Ecclesia Dei Commission, which is supposed to insure access to the traditional Latin Mass for those who seek it. The letter announces something quite remarkable at a time of general lack of discipline in the Church: The General Chapter (meeting) of the Priestly Fraternity of St. Peter (chartered by John Paul II to serve the needs of traditional Catholics who have not welcomed the changes in the Church) will be suppressed. Its election will not be held. The Fraternity's priestly members will not be allowed to re-elect as their superior Father Josef Bisig, who was expected to be nominated and re-elected by an overwhelming majority at the Chapter. Cardinal Castrillón Hoyos would simply impose upon the Fraternity a candidate more to his liking. Further, the rectors of the Fraternity's two seminaries would be removed and replaced with more liberal-minded priests.

The rationale for the Cardinal's actions is stated in his letter:

> You know quite well that your seminary is observed by many people in the Church and that it must be exemplary in all respects. In particular, it is required to avoid and combat *a certain spirit of rebellion against the present-day Church*, which spirit easily finds followers among the young students, who like all young people already are inclined to extreme and rigorous positions.[1]

In a later interview in *30 Days* magazine, the Cardinal further explained that he was only helping the Fraternity "to strike a balance between their original charism and the outcome of their insertion *within the ecclesial reality of today*."[2]

Consider these two phrases together: "a spirit of rebellion against the present-day Church", and "their insertion within the ecclesial reality of today". Now, the seminarians of the Priestly Fraternity are baptized Catholics. They were born and raised in the "mainstream" Catholic Church. They were not members of the supposedly "schismatic" Society of St. Pius X founded by Archbishop Marcel Lefebvre, known for his resistance to the post-conciliar changes. No, they were young men who came from the "mainstream" of the

Church and joined the Fraternity's seminaries to be formed in a traditional manner and to celebrate the traditional Latin Mass.

And yet these young men, who have never gone into schism (so-called), are being told that nonetheless they must be inserted into the "present-day Church" and "the ecclesial reality of today". But if they are already Catholics, then what is this thing into which they are being "inserted"? Is it the Holy Catholic Church? Clearly, it is not. What the Cardinal is speaking of—whether he knows this explicitly or not—is *the Church of the Adaptation*; the Church of the new orientation. We know this because the priests and seminarians of the papally chartered Fraternity of Saint Peter are indubitably Catholics, so that if they are being inserted into anything it is not the Holy Catholic Church but something else.

And that is why we speak of the Stalinization of the Church. It is not as if the Church has been completely overthrown and has ceased entirely to be what she was, for this is impossible, given the promise of Our Lord that the gates of hell would not prevail against His Church. Rather, a sort of Trojan Horse has been set up inside the Church—a church within the Church; a collection of novel practices and attitudes—never before seen in Church history—that now wishes to insist that *it* is the Church. And whomever wishes to get along in the Church today, the Holy Catholic Church, must consent to be inserted into this "ecclesial reality of today" *within* the perennial ecclesial reality of the Church. The "ecclesial reality of today" is only a temporary phenomenon that God will surely rectify because of the untold damage it has caused the Church; but Cardinal Castrillón and his collaborators, carrying the overall Party Line of the Church's new orientation, wish to pretend that it will be a permanent thing.

One could not ask for a better proof of the existence of the Church's new orientation—her Stalinist Adaptation, as it were—than the Cardinal's brutal suppression of the Priestly Fraternity. Such actions would never be taken against the Jesuits or the other priestly orders that have been undermining the Church since Vatican II. Why? Because these morally and doctrinally corrupt orders *adhere to the Adaptation, to the Party Line, to the new orientation*. In the current crisis, the only thing the Vatican is willing to enforce with immediate and vigorous action is the Adaptation of the Church to the world—not sound doctrine, not sound practice, which are flouted throughout the Church with virtual impunity—but only the Adaptation.

In September of 2000 we encounter yet another dramatic example of the Church's Adaptation. From September 12-19, 2000, Cardinal Roger Etchegaray was in Red China to attend "a Symposium on Religions and Peace". While there he celebrated Mass in the presence of the schismatic bishops of the Catholic Patriotic Association (CPA). The Mass was celebrated in the Shrine of Our Lady Help of Christians, which the Red Chinese regime has stolen from the true Catholic Church in China.[3]

The CPA was formed in the 1950's to replace the Catholic Church after "Chairman Mao" declared the Catholic Church "illegal" in Red China. The CPA is thus a human organization created by a Communist government and set up as a "church" which Chinese Catholics *must* join, forsaking the Roman Catholic Church, whose very existence has been declared "illegal" by the Red Chinese regime. *The CPA constitution explicitly rejects submission to the Pope and declares the CPA to be autonomous from Rome.* The CPA bishops and priests, therefore, are all schismatics by definition.

Over 100 bishops have been consecrated illicitly by the CPA without a papal mandate, in direct violation of the Code of Canon Law; worse still, those illicitly consecrated bishops publicly declared their primary allegiance to the Communist regime of China while disavowing (in the CPA Constitution) any allegiance or submission to the Pope. As a result, these illicit bishops, and those who consecrated them, would be excommunicated *latae sententiae* (automatically), even if they were members of the Catholic Church, which they are not. In 1994 the CPA bishops issued a so-called pastoral letter in which they endorsed China's population control policy, including forced abortions on all women who have one child already, calling upon Chinese Catholics to support this abomination.

In short, the CPA is a Communist-created, Communist-controlled, blatantly schismatic, blatantly heretical, pro-abortion organization, created by the devil himself, acting through Mao Tse-tung and his successor "President" Jiang. And yet the Vatican has declared no schism, nor any excommunication of these Communist-controlled, pro-abortion clergy. Instead, Cardinal Etchegaray went to China and celebrated Mass in the presence of CPA bishops in a Marian Shrine which the CPA, with the aid of Communist goons, stole from the Catholic Church and the Catholic faithful. Cardinal Etchegaray even stated that he "recognized the fidelity to the Pope of the Catholics of the official church [i.e., the CPA]". *Fidelity* to the Pope on the part of bishops who endorse forced abortion and whose Communist-controlled association rejects the papal primacy in its very constitution? What sort of nonsense is this?

While Cardinal Etchegaray was in China, an 82-year-old Catholic priest in the "underground" Catholic Church, which remains in union with Rome, was beaten into a coma and carted off to jail by "security" police.[4] In accordance with *Ostpolitik*, the Vatican has issued no protest over the nearly fatal beating of this priest, nor any protest over the arrest, imprisonment and torture of loyal Catholic priests, bishops and laity by the Red Chinese regime. The Vatican apparatus is still chained to the Church's new orientation—"dialogue" with the Church's enemies and silence even in the face of blatant torture and persecution of faithful Catholics. This is the fruit of the new orientation's abandonment of righteous opposition to evil. And this policy of the Adaptation of the Church will, in the long run, have the intended effect on millions more, who will apostasize and lose their faith, because the Vatican apparatus will no longer stand up and oppose evil with the righteous anger of old.

Here too we see the disparity of treatment as between traditional Catholics who in any way present an obstacle to the new orientation, and those who embrace the new orientation wholly and entirely. In contrast with the Vatican's pandering to the CPA, Archbishop Marcel Lefebvre was publicly pronounced both excommunicated and schismatic in a *motu proprio* prepared for the Pope's signature within 48 hours of Archbishop Lefebvre's consecration of four bishops without a papal mandate[5]—an action the Archbishop took in an effort (however misguided some may think it to be) to maintain Catholic tradition in a Church that appears to have gone mad.

The Red Chinese procure (through former Catholic bishops) the consecration of 100 bishops without a papal mandate for their pro-abortion "church" and the Vatican takes no punitive action. Quite the contrary, it sends a Cardinal (no less) as a representative to hobnob with some of the illicit bishops! Yet, when Archbishop Lefebvre consecrates four bishops to serve Catholic Tradition, he is immediately cast into outer darkness by the same Vatican apparatus, even though Archbishop Lefebvre and the four newly consecrated bishops consistently professed their loyalty to the Pope whom they were attempting to serve by preserving traditional Catholic practice and belief. Why this striking disparity of treatment? The answer is that Archbishop Lefebvre resisted the Adaptation; the Red Chinese bishops, on the other hand, *exemplify* it.

But it is even worse than this. According to an Open Letter of protest to Cardinal Sodano and other members of the Vatican apparatus, published by the Cardinal Kung Foundation, priests of the CPA—a schismatic Communist-controlled pro-abortion "church"—have been given *canonical missions and priestly faculties in American dioceses*. Thus, these Communist priests celebrate Mass and hear confessions of Roman Catholic faithful in their local parishes where these agents of a Communist government learn the secret sins of innumerable Americans which may provide material for blackmail to the Communist masters in China. This was confirmed by Archbishop Levada of San Francisco, who claims that the Vatican—and no doubt Cardinal Sodano was involved in this decision—has authorized the granting of "an apostolic mission" to these priests of the pro-abortion, Communist-controlled, schismatic CPA.[6]

Here is a literal, visible penetration of Communist power into the body of the Church. There could not be a more dramatic demonstration of the Adaptation. But the presence of these Communist-controlled priests in American parishes is only an icon of the whole process that began in Metz, France, back in 1962, when the drawbridge of the Church was let down and the forces of the world, the Church's sworn enemies, began to march into the Church, leading even Pope Paul VI to speak of the invasion of the Church by worldly thinking.

## The Adaptation of the Message of Fatima

Nowhere can one find a sadder example of the Adaptation of the Church than what occurred on October 8, 2000: a ceremony at the Vatican "entrusting" various things to Mary—an "entrustment" for the masses, to take their minds off the consecration of Russia. During this ceremony "all peoples", the world, the unemployed, even "youth in search of meaning"—anything and everything but Russia—were "entrusted" to Our Lady. The day before this ceremony the praying of the Rosary in Saint Peter's Square was broadcast around the world by satellite. But one thing was missing: the Fatima prayers. No one at the Vatican would pray: "O my Jesus, forgive us our sins, save us from the fires of hell. Lead all souls to Heaven, especially those most in need." One decade of the Rosary, however, was recited by Sister Lucy for the cameras in the convent in Coimbra. Looking perfectly miserable, Sister Lucy did recite the Fatima prayers—in Portuguese. She had been reduced to a prop in a publicity stunt.

Here we see the Sergianization of the Message of Fatima, the Adaptation of Fatima to the world. Our Lady of Fatima becomes Our Lady of the Unemployed, Our Lady of Youth in Search of Meaning; and the Rosary is stripped of the Fatima prayers.

And this brings us to early 2001. The year 2000 had been a busy year for the Adaptation, but there was some mopping up to do. Father Gruner was still conducting his very effective Fatima apostolate. So on February 16, 2001, Cardinal Castrillón Hoyos wrote to Father Gruner to renew his threat of excommunication of the previous June. If Father Gruner did not stop what he was doing, then there will be "definitive measures that would be painful for all concerned."

In the same letter Cardinal Castrillón provided another demonstration of the new orientation at work on the Message of Fatima. According to Cardinal Castrillón "the Blessed Mother appeared to the three little visionaries in the Cova da Iria at the beginning of the century, and *marked out a program for the New Evangelization* which the whole Church finds itself engaged in, which is even more urgent at the dawn of the third millennium."[7] Our Lady of Fatima was now Our Lady of the New Evangelization—about which She had said not a single word at Fatima!

Our Lady did not come to Fatima to announce "the New Evangelization," a slogan that describes a novel and ineffectual campaign to stimulate the dying faith of those who are already Catholics.[8] Nor did Our Lady come to announce any of the other obscure slogans that have overrun the Church in the past forty years: "ecumenical dialogue," "interreligious dialogue," "solidarity," "the civilization of love," "inculturation," and so forth. She came to announce the *Old* Evangelization, the perennial Gospel of Jesus Christ, Who is the same yesterday, today and forever—the selfsame Christ who warned the world that "He who believes and is baptized shall be saved; he who believes not shall be condemned." As a group of Father Gruner's supporters protested in their reply to the Cardinal:

> Your Eminence, where can one find *any* of these elements in your rendering of the Message of Fatima? Where is Heaven and where is hell, for you speak only vaguely of "Ultimate Realities"—a term any Mason would find acceptable? Where is the *triumph* of the Immaculate Heart?

Where are the consecration and *conversion* of Russia? Where are the warnings of Our Lady? Where indeed is the Message of Fatima at all?

Our Lady of Fatima had uttered no slogans at all but only the simple Catholic truth: that many souls are burning in hell for lack of the Catholic Faith; that to save souls God ordains it necessary to establish *in the world*—not just among those who are already Catholics—devotion to Her Immaculate Heart; that Her Immaculate Heart must *triumph* through the Consecration of Russia to that Heart; that only by this means can there be true peace in our time. And Our Lady of Fatima also gave us a warning about the consequences of failing to heed Her requests: wars and persecution of the Church, the martyrdom of the good, the suffering of the Holy Father, the suffering of the whole world—all of which are occurring at this very moment in history—and then, if we continue to ignore Her requests, the annihilation of various nations.

The Message of Fatima had, quite simply, been written out of existence, transformed into slogans of the Adaptation. And in line with this Stalinist Adaptation of the Church there would be censorship of anyone who hearkened to the former understanding of the old terms. In the same letter of February 16, Cardinal Castrillón Hoyos had demanded that Father Gruner "publicly retract" certain opinions in his apostolate's magazine that the Cardinal deemed objectionable. In a Church teeming with heretical literature which has undermined the faith of millions and endangered their souls, Cardinal Castrillón Hoyos wished to censor the *Fatima Crusader* magazine! And why? Because the magazine had dared to criticize, not Catholic teaching on faith and morals, but the prudential decisions of Cardinal Sodano and his collaborators—including their press conferences and dinners with the likes of Mikhail Gorbachev, their cozy relations with the schismatic CPA and their attempt to bury the Message of Fatima under a mountain of false interpretations.

The case of Father Gruner, the Priestly Fraternity of St. Peter, Archbishop Lefebvre, the Society of St. Pius X, and other perceived obstacles to the new orientation of Vatican II illustrates that the post-conciliar epoch presents a situation very much like that lamented by St. Basil at the height of the Arian heresy: "Only one offense is now vigorously punished: an accurate observance of our fathers' traditions. For this cause the pious are driven from their countries and transported into deserts."

Only one offense is now vigorously punished today: an accurate observance of the Church's constant pre-conciliar traditions—summed up in the Message of Fatima. Strange to say, none other than Cardinal Ratzinger made the following observation about the so-called "Lefebvre schism" in his 1988 address to the Bishops of Chile:

> That which previously was considered Most Holy (the form in which the Liturgy was handed down) suddenly appears to be the most forbidden of all things, the one thing that can safely be prohibited. It is intolerable to

criticize decisions which have been taken since the Council. On the other hand, if men make question of ancient rules or even of the great truths of the Faith, for instance the corporal virginity of Mary, the bodily resurrection of Jesus, the immortality of the soul, etc., nobody complains or only does so with the greatest of moderation. All this leads a great number of people to ask themselves if the Church of today is really the same as that of yesterday or if they have changed it for something else without telling people.

Stranger still, Cardinal Castrillón Hoyos has made the same admission. In the aforementioned interview in *30 Days* he said: "The great emergency of our time is to show people that the Church of today is the same as the Church has always been." But why is there such an "emergency" in the first place? When in the entire history of the Catholic Church did it ever have to be *demonstrated* that the Church was still the same as before? Why would such a demonstration even be necessary if there were not a very good reason to believe that the Church has been changed?

And there *is* a very good reason, as we have shown: Since Vatican II the Catholic Church has undergone an Adaptation precisely along the lines predicted, plotted and carried out by her worst enemies. And those in charge of the Church today *refuse to recognize* what has happened, even if they are not conscious agents of destruction themselves. They are, as Our Lord said of the Pharisees: "blind, and leaders of the blind. And if the blind lead the blind, both fall into the pit." (Mt. 15:14)

As Sister Lucy herself said: "This is why the devil has waged such a war against it [the Rosary]! *And the worst is that he has succeeded in leading into error and deceiving souls having a heavy responsibility through the place which they occupy ...! They are blind men guiding other blind men ...*"[9]

And, as Saint Paul declared concerning the same type of stiff-necked persons: "There are none so blind as those who will not see." It is also written in Sacred Scripture: "For the heart of this people is grown gross, and with their ears have they heard heavily, and their eyes they have shut; lest perhaps they should see with their eyes, and hear with their ears, and understand with their heart, and should be converted, and I should heal them." (Acts 28:27) They blindly and stubbornly defend the Adaptation as if it were a dogma of the Faith, while the real dogmas of the Faith are being undermined throughout the Church before their very eyes, while they do nothing.

# Chapter 10

## Naming Names

It is now opportune for us to summarize what the evidence has shown so far, and whom it implicates in the crime at issue.

Thus far the evidence has shown the following:

- The Message of Fatima is a divinely given prophecy for our time, authenticated by an unprecedented public miracle and vouched for by a series of Popes, including the currently reigning Pope.
- The prophetic warnings in the Message have mostly come to pass, save for especially the annihilation of nations that would be the consequence of failing to effect the Consecration of Russia in time.
- God has already demonstrated the benefits of a national consecration to the Immaculate Heart in the case of Portugal in 1931, whose miraculous overnight transformation from an atheistic, Masonic republic into a Catholic country was seen by the Portuguese hierarchy itself as a foretaste of what God would bestow upon the world after the Consecration of Russia.
- Instead of following the path marked out at Fatima, the leaders of the Catholic Church chose a different path—the path of a new orientation of the Church initiated at Vatican II, including an "opening to the world" and "reforms" of the Church which have fulfilled the dreams of Her worst enemies, who admitted that their goal was to bring about precisely such changes in the Church.
- In taking this path of a new orientation, the Church's leaders have disregarded the repeated warnings of the pre-conciliar Popes (including Blessed Pius IX, Leo XIII, St. Pius X, Pius XI and Pius XII) that the Church's enemies were plotting to remake Her in the very manner She has in fact been remade in the post-conciliar period.
- The changes began in 1960—the very year in which Sister Lucy had insisted the Third Secret be revealed, because it would be clearer then.
- The result of these changes has been a catastrophic loss of faith and discipline in the Church which appears to be foretold in that part of the Great Secret of Fatima which begins with the words: "In Portugal the dogma of the Faith will always be preserved etc."—a phrase that remains mysteriously incomplete, despite the Vatican's claimed disclosure of the entirety of the Third Secret.
- Rather than admitting these incalculable blunders and their ruinous consequences for the Church, the current Vatican apparatus has

obstinately pursued the new orientation, which is obviously inconsistent with the expressly Catholic imperatives of the Fatima Message: namely, the establishment of devotion to the Immaculate Heart in the world, the consecration of Russia to the Immaculate Heart, the conversion of Russia to the Catholic Faith, and the triumph of the Immaculate Heart, accompanied by a period of world peace in a Catholic social order.

- To the contrary, the Vatican apparatus has willfully and deliberately refused to consecrate Russia by name to Mary's Immaculate Heart, but has instead conducted a systematic campaign to neutralize the Message of Fatima in order to subjugate it to the Church's new orientation—her Adaptation to Masonic and Communist ideals—while persecuting loyal Catholics who do not follow the Party Line.
- The Vatican apparatus, led by the Secretary of State, deliberately scorns the prophecies, imperatives and warnings of the Fatima Message in favor of "enlightened" new ecclesial policies, which include avoiding any offense to Russia by a public consecration of that nation.
- In consequence of these monumental errors of judgment, Russia has failed to convert, the Church is suffering an unprecedented crisis of faith and discipline, and the world continues to spiral downward in a cycle of violence and rebellion against God and His Holy Church—in response to which, the Vatican apparatus only redoubles its efforts to follow the utterly fruitless new orientation of the Church.

Especially in view of the events of June 26-27, 2000 and during the months following, the proof now suffices to identify the four men we must in conscience accuse in this book. They are:

**Cardinal Angelo Sodano**
**Cardinal Joseph Ratzinger**
**Archbishop Tarcisio Bertone**
**Cardinal Dario Castrillón Hoyos**

Why these four men and not others? As we have already shown, it is these men who have taken the lead in attempting nothing less than the murder of the Message of Fatima, and with it the Heaven-sent hope of the world in our time. They have combined and conspired, and then acted publicly, to impose upon the Church a version of the Fatima Message that bears no resemblance to the Catholic prophecy the Mother of God delivered to the world for the aid of all humanity. While these four men obviously have many collaborators in what Pope Paul VI rued as the "auto-demolition" of the Church, it is they who have specialized, as it were, in the demolition of Fatima. Thus they deserve to be identified as the principals of the crime we allege here.

But there is much more evidence of this crime, and our case is far from complete. We will now examine in more detail the basic elements of proof we have outlined so far. We will begin, in the next chapter, with a more detailed examination of Cardinal Ratzinger's "interpretation" of the Third Secret of Fatima, a key element of the effort to bury the Fatima Message once and for all.

# Chapter 11

## Cardinal Ratzinger's Message of Fatima

In a previous chapter we showed how, in keeping with the Church's new post-conciliar orientation, the Vatican has published a "commentary"—a Party Line—on the Message of Fatima that seeks to obliterate any specific prophetic content of the Message of Fatima for our time. We noted how even a secular newspaper, the *Los Angeles Times*, could see that the purpose of *TMF* was an attempt to "gently debunk" what it called "the cult of Fatima."

The reader should bear with us if confronted with an occasional polemical comment in this more detailed theological exegesis of *TMF*, but we need not apologize for being polemical because polemics are a good thing when necessary. Today's society increasingly substitutes the Catholic Faith and replaces it with faith in the so-called "exact sciences." People of today, therefore, do not value the science and art of polemics whose purpose is to defend the Faith and the Church against the enemies of Christ, Who is the Truth. "Ho Polemics" is the ancient Greek word for war. Nothing is wrong with waging war in defense of Christ and the Catholic Faith; but people who do not have the faith, or if their faith is weakened, will not understand this because they give too much faith to the so-called "exact sciences."

### The "Introduction"

Already the second paragraph of the introduction of the Bertone/Ratzinger commentary on the Third Secret contains a piece of Vatican politics that seems to be oblivious of both recent history and Moral Theology:

> The Twentieth Century was one of the most crucial in human history, with its tragic and cruel events culminating in the assassination attempt on the "sweet Christ on earth."

That even an attempt to assassinate the Supreme Pontiff is a heinous crime, no person in his right mind will doubt. It is indeed under the punishment of excommunication, even in the rather liberal Code of Canon Law of 1983. However, the statement shows a tragic lack of proportion. That the "tragic and cruel events" would have been *"culminating"* in the attempt on the Pope's life, is definitely out of proportion and in grave disregard of Stalin's sixty million victims, plus the victims of all wars of the outgoing century and the fifty-five million victims of abortion every single year! The lack of proportion is infinitely worse in its disregard of the supernatural aspect such as the real "sweet Christ on earth" in the tabernacle, Whose Real Presence is distributed in the hands and dropped on Saint Peter's Square[1] as it happens in thousands of other places. There is a purpose in this statement and it lies in *downplaying the importance of the Third Secret* in Cardinal Ratzinger's comments.

The Introduction of *TMF* states on the next page that "there is only one manuscript, which is here reproduced photographically." This would be a rather misleading, but literal truth, if it is meant that only one of the manuscripts has been photographically reproduced, but in the light of Cardinal Ratzinger's statement, that the Secret has been published in its "entirety" (*TMF*, pp. 32, 39), it has to be considered a lie. There is a mountain of evidence that there are indeed *two* parts of the Third Secret, the first one being the vision of the "Bishop dressed in White" taken from the archives of the former Holy Office and published on June 26, 2000, and the second one in the Pope's apartment. The evidence is marshaled in compelling fashion in an article by Mr. Andrew Cesanek (cf. Chapter 12). As Mr. Cesanek points out, the published text contains no words of Our Lady. Thus, the Ratzinger/Bertone presentation of the Third Secret is wholly lacking in credibility.

Without any illicit accusation of a deliberate sin against the Eighth Commandment, we are nevertheless facing the fact of a printed lie. As there has been no public statement to the contrary so far, it is virtually impossible to talk about error as to the number of manuscripts. Who and how many people are involved in this lie is of no importance, but the published lie as such is of a theological importance: even if it *were* only an error, it would affect the entire theological interpretation presented in the document. If it is a lie, which is what we firmly believe, then it means that the theological and historical interpretations presented are deliberately leading towards a wrong conclusion or message. Commonly this is called fraudulent. It affects a lot more than the theology visible in the published commentaries, as we shall see.

It is also of theological importance to see the quotation marks for both the "secret" and "Our Lady." If an "apparition" says that all religions are pleasing to God, which is heresy and blasphemy[2], we should put "Our Lady" in quotation marks, as we know the "apparition" to be someone else, most probably a demon. But to place quotation marks around Our Lady regarding an apparition that has been approved by several Popes and been proven by a definite miracle in front of 70,000 witnesses conveys a message: namely, the possibility that it was not Our Lady after all. As one piece in this jig-saw of truths, half-truths, and lies, this is of great significance.

The following pages of *TMF*'s Introduction reiterate the lie that the Consecration has been done, especially p. 8 which cites an unsigned letter by "Sister Lucy" which, as we showed in a previous chapter, is a manifest fake, as shown also by Father Paul Kramer.[3] *The Fatima Crusader* has sufficiently dealt with this lie in the past and there is no need for repetitions here. In the present document the old quotations from this fake letter, however, present an explanatory context for the new lies.

Finally, we note again the incredible statement by Archbishop Bertone on p. 9 of the Introduction in *TMF*:

> The decision of His Holiness John Paul II to make public the third part of the "secret" of Fatima brings to an end a period of history marked by tragic human lust for power and evil, yet pervaded by the merciful love of God and the watchful care of the Mother of Jesus and of the Church.

Various articles already published have sufficiently explained the absurdity of this statement in the historical sense.[4] Indeed, historically seen, this is an idiotic statement, bordering on lunacy.

Now, Archbishop Bertone, Secretary of the Congregation for the Doctrine of the Faith, is neither an idiot nor a lunatic. This statement must, therefore, be of a theological nature. Father Gruner rightly suggested that according to Msgr. Bertone we are supposed to believe that "the so-called 'fall of communism' means that Fatima is no longer relevant to world politics and the conversion of Russia is no longer to be mentioned."[5] This is not only a political interpretation concerning the continuation of Cardinal Casaroli's *Ostpolitik* and the Pope's strangely close relationship to the propagator of genocide, Gorbachev, but it is a clear analysis of a changed theology which is central to the Church's new orientation, a theology called Ecumenism.

For the moment the questions resulting from these observations will have to wait, as that can be understood better in the light of Cardinal Ratzinger's theology.

## The "Secret"

As far as the authenticity of the published text is concerned, while Father Gruner seems to be convinced of its authenticity,[6] certain questions present themselves: Why does Sister Lucy—who by 1944 had surely read Holy Scripture and many "devotional books," as Cardinal Ratzinger calls them—say that the Holy Father "prayed for the *corpses* he met on his way" (*cadaveres* in Portuguese)? Throughout the history of salvation one speaks of the "souls of the dead or defunct," as one can find in the Creed (... resurrection of the dead ...). Only in the Old Testament can one find the term "corpse", and it is found in the context of apostates or lost souls.

It is equally strange in the context of the First and the Second Secret that the seer would speak about a "Bishop dressed in White," when the events of 1939 were clearly prophesied with the terms "pope" and even his name: Pius XI. A "Bishop dressed in White" could be the Abbot of Brixen in South Tyrol, any bishop in the tropics, or an impostor in Rome who pretends to be pope—as the sedevacantists claim. We cannot and shall not venture an answer, but the phrase "Bishop dressed in White" is strangely vague in the historical context of all the events since 1917.

There will be more to be said about this aspect in the conclusion of this chapter. For the moment we will continue as if the published text were authentic.

## The Interpretation of the "Secret"

### A. The Pope's Letter to Sister Lucy

In this letter, dated April 19, 2000, which is cited in *TMF*, the Pope says:

> Since on that day [the Beatification of Francisco and Jacinta, May 13, 2000] there will be time only for a brief greeting and not a conversation, I am sending ... Archbishop Bertone ... Archbishop Bertone ... will come in my name to ask certain questions about the interpretation of "the third part of the secret."

We conclude that His Holiness has no time for a conversation with Sister Lucy. The ever-vigilant defender of Pope John Paul II might object to this conclusion by reminding us that it is not in our power to advise the Pope about his schedule, nor to challenge his decisions in discipline and Church government, *in rebus ... quae ad disciplinam et regimen Ecclesiae ... pertinent* (D.S. 3060).

This is certainly true. But we are allowed to ask an obvious question: Why is it that the Pope's advisors and assistants scheduled His Holiness to receive the Masons of the Trilateral Commission,[7] the aforesaid Mikhail Gorbachev, the Jewish High Masons of the B'nai B'rith,[8] to preach from the pulpit of Rome's Lutheran Church,[9] to visit Rome's Synagogue,[10] to meet with the Buddhist "patriarch" Vasana Tara,[11] the Dalai Lama,[12] Yassir Arafat,[13] and allowed the schismatic and heretical Patriarch Dimitrios I of Constantinople[14] to stand next to him on the Papal Loggia of St. Peter's Basilica in Rome (!), but they could not find the time to schedule the Pope to talk to Our Lady's personal and perhaps most important of all messengers in this century?

We do not know the answer and cannot venture to give it, but the theological connection to the Vatican's downplaying the Third Secret is obvious.

### B. "The Conversation with Sister Lucy ..."

This unsigned account of an alleged conversation (in April 2000) between Archbishop Bertone and Sister Lucy, commencing on p. 28 of *TMF*, is a remarkable piece of deception, probably written by Archbishop Bertone himself. As Father Paul Kramer rightly pointed out, Msgr. Bertone not only failed to ask Sister Lucy if the Consecration of Russia had been done, but he also juxtaposes two logically separate statements, namely Sister Lucy's affirmation that the figure in white was a Pope, although she *does not know the name* (!), and her agreement with the Pope's claim that it was "a mother's hand that guided the bullet's path" on May 13, 1981.[15]

There were many rather strange coincidences—or was it Providence?—in Ali Agca's assassination attempt, to consider a non-theological digression:

- Why did the gun jam after the third shot? It is not unusual for a semi-automatic pistol to jam, but it is almost impossible that Italy's best police force, the *Carabinieri*, would not find the cause after weeks of microscopic examination in their laboratories. Was it the

Guardian Angel's interference? That would be theologically highly probable.

- Why did Ali Agca not use hollow point bullets or the readily available *Federal Hydra-Shok* ammunition which would have accomplished his purpose to assassinate the Pope. Most sources claim that some organization or secret service was behind the attack. Were they all amateurs?
- Why did he choose St. Peter's Square and a small handgun, with no chances to escape, why not a rifle (easily available back then) and one of the many elevated positions around St. Peter's Square with at least a chance to escape? Was he just a dumb fanatic?

Probably, we will not know the truth about that day in our lifetime, but we do know the truth that this attempt to assassinate the Pope has nothing to do with the Third Secret, *because he was **not** killed*. The event was tragic, but it cost the Pope in his full activities less than one year—out of more than twenty. It is an insult to Divine Providence and to Our Lady to claim that this *relatively* unimportant event would be at the core of a prophecy about hell, two World Wars, Communism, and the punishment still to come.

Finally, we must ask: Why would the 1981 incident be better understood after 1960, as Sister Lucy said the Third Secret would be? Anyone in the 20th Century would have understood it as we do. Would the generation that had fought in World War II and in Korea have better understood the role of soldiers in this vision only *after* 1960? Sister Lucy's insistence on disclosure in the year 1960, that "Our Lady wishes it so", can only mean that Lucy knew something was going to happen around 1960 or shortly after that would make the Secret clearly understandable as a prophecy of future events. The Secret clearly has no connection with the assassination of President Kennedy, but what about John XXIII's encyclical *Pacem in Terris*, published in 1963, or Vatican II which was opened in 1962, *but announced January 25, 1959*?

### C. The "Announcement made by Cardinal Angelo Sodano ..."

The deception continues in the Secretary of State's statement that the text of the Third Secret must be interpreted "in a symbolic key". The purpose of this suggestion becomes evident when Cardinal Sodano distorts the actual vision by saying: "He [the Pope] too falls to the ground, apparently dead." As we discussed in a previous chapter, the words "apparently dead" are the exact contrary to Sister Lucy's word "killed."

This is followed by pushing the message into the past, be it by pointing at the event in 1981 or with the ridiculous declaration that 1989 ended Communism and the spreading of atheism. Gorbachev's "glasnost" and "perestroika" have been sufficiently dealt with in past issues of *The Fatima Crusader* and there is no need to repeat these analyses here. It is sad to see, however, that the Secretary of State does not shrink from using a decade-old lie to debunk a message from Our Lady.

## D. Cardinal Ratzinger's "Theological Commentary"

### i) Introductory Downplay

The very second line of this Commentary (*TMF*, p. 32) already contains the claim that the "so-called third 'Secret' of Fatima" has been "published here in its entirety." This lie is repeated later on (*TMF*, p. 39). The quoted article by Andrew Cesanek produces sufficient proof that this is a lie (see next chapter). We will deal with this deception at the conclusion of this chapter.

The next statement is cynical to say the least:

> No great mystery is revealed: nor is the future unveiled. We see the Church of the martyrs of the century which has just passed represented in a scene described in a language which is symbolic and not easy to decipher.[16]

If no great mystery is revealed, then why did Our Lady bother to make it a secret in the first place? Possibly—as we shall see later—the future is revealed in the other part of the Third Secret which has evidently been withheld from us, the part which contains the words of Our Lady following "In Portugal the dogma of the Faith will always be preserved etc." In any case, to claim that the vision of soldiers shooting the Pope dead is merely a symbol of the past, especially in the connection with the unusually clear messages of the rest of the Fatima Message, is preposterous.

In comparison to most prophecies—one thinks of the difficulties in interpreting the Apocalypse—the secrets of Fatima are indeed unusually clear and to the point; why would the Third Secret be "symbolic and not easy to decipher"? Why would the *Twentieth* Century end in nineteen hundred and ninety-nine?

In the year 1900 Kaiser Wilhelm II of Germany *decreed* this to be the beginning of the Twentieth Century, which is mathematically impossible. It would seem that Cardinal Ratzinger's mathematics, as well as his theology, is dependent on authority instead of the Truth. To say this is not to engage in "cheap polemics" in the light of a rather remarkable change of mind between 1984 and 2000. In 1984, when discussing the content of the Third Secret, Cardinal Ratzinger talked about "the last times" and "religious prophecy" and said:

> ... but the things contained in this third secret correspond to what is announced in Sacred Scripture and are confirmed by many other Marian apparitions themselves in their known contents.[17]

Cardinal Ratzinger's statement of 1984 is in direct contradiction to his downplaying of the Third Secret in *TMF*. Father Paul Kramer[18] collects the most important Marian messages from the other Marian apparitions on this point. They are quite frightening, and certainly—at least in a part of the prophecy—predict events yet to come.

We are once again faced with the same basic tenor of the entire publication, which is profoundly dishonest in trying to trivialize the Third Secret into an insignificant prediction of a failed attempt on the Holy Father's life. May we call the failed attempt on the Pope's life an "insignificant" prediction? Yes! We have said so already and it is the truth: The attempt *failed*, and even if it had killed the Pope, this would have had nothing to do with the Third Secret. In Roman dialect we say: *"Morto un Papa, se ne fa un'altro"*: with the death of a pope, one makes another.

Another point arises: Why has nobody in the Vatican bothered to suggest that the Third Secret may deal with the untimely death of Pope John Paul I? Was he a completely insignificant figure? No Pope is, but God never *knew* the future—He *knows*. The failed attempt on a Pope's life is indeed "no great mystery" as Cardinal Ratzinger cleverly formulates it, but the actual—and quite mysterious—death of a Pope has been conveniently forgotten.

The prophecy and the three seers' comments make it abundantly clear "that the Holy Father will have much to suffer." In the context of *two* world wars and—as we shall see—much worse, it borders on idolatry to enhance one Pope's importance to the point of making a few months in the hospital *the* Third Secret. What the Pope had to suffer in Rome's Gemelli Hospital is something that one would not even wish to contemplate. However, with today's medicine, the Pope's suffering at that time does not even compare to the average priest's fate in the Nazi concentration camps—not to mention the fate of many more priests and bishops behind the Iron Curtain.

Most telling of all, if the Third Secret predicts only that a Pope will survive an assassination attempt, then why did Cardinal Ratzinger say in 1984 that the Secret had not been disclosed to avoid "confusing religious prophecy with *sensationalism*." What would be sensational in 1984 about a prophecy concerning a *failed* assassination attempt that had taken place three years earlier? Obviously, nothing. On this point alone, Cardinal Ratzinger's gross contradiction of his own prior testimony is fatal to his credibility. His current version of the Third Secret is what the lawyers call a recent fabrication. The "sensational" content he had in mind in 1984 clearly could not have been the 1981 assassination attempt.

### ii) On Public and Private Revelations

Cardinal Ratzinger significantly sets the entire phenomenon of Fatima in the context of "private revelations"—one ought to call them either "fake" or "extraordinary," depending on their authenticity. Cardinal Ratzinger states that the Message of Fatima, like all "private revelations" approved as authentic by Church authorities, "can be a genuine help in understanding the Gospel and living it better at a particular moment in time; therefore it should not be disregarded. It is a help which is offered, but *which one is not obliged to use*." In other words, according to Cardinal Ratzinger, no one in the Church is obliged to follow the Message of Fatima—not the Pope, not the bishops, not the priests, not the members of the laity. Fatima—including the consecration of

Russia and the Five First Saturdays devotion—is purely optional. If we prefer, we can simply ignore it completely—as if the Miracle of the Sun had never happened; as if the requests of the Virgin of Fatima had been made by a ghost! Fatima is a mere "help" that we can take or leave at our pleasure.

One of the most erudite popes in history, Benedict XIV, rightly says that these revelations cannot be held with the assent of Faith, but "rather an assent of human faith in keeping with the requirements of prudence which puts them before us as probable and credible to piety." But Cardinal Ratzinger's quotation of Benedict rather shrewdly ignores what is so extraordinary about Fatima, and what takes it out of the category of other "private" revelations: the astounding Miracle of the Sun that proves Fatima to be a bit more than just "credible to piety."

Cardinal Ratzinger takes this approach, it seems, with all of the extraordinary revelations of the past two centuries. For example, he reduces the extraordinary revelations about the Corpus Christi Feast and the Sacred Heart to St. Margaret Mary Alacoque to an event that merely had an "*effect* even on the liturgy." This borders on blasphemy when we consider the fate of France after Louis XIV's impertinent and disastrous refusal to obey the request of Christ for the Consecration of France to the Sacred Heart, conveyed to St. Margaret Mary in the same "private" revelations.[19]

Cardinal Ratzinger's erroneous conception of prophecy is scandalously clear in the following statement:

> ... it should be kept in mind that prophecy in the biblical sense does not mean to predict the future but to explain the will of God for the present, and therefore show the right path to take for the future. A person who foretells what is going to happen responds to the curiosity of the mind, which wants to draw back the veil on the future.

This is tantamount to a denial of *all* prophecy, which is commonly called one of the highest of all freely given graces, the *gratiae gratis datae*. Prophecy often involves the correct interpretation of the past and the present, but is as such understood as a prediction of the future. Either Isaias, David, Christ, and St. Paul "responded to the curiosity of the mind" and the Church Fathers and many Doctors of the Church just wanted "to draw back the veil of the future," or Cardinal Ratzinger is wrong again. May we leave the answer to you?

Cardinal Ratzinger reduces prophecy to "the signs of the times," perhaps because he fails to see the real signs of the times, namely: empty churches, heresy, apostasy, blasphemy, sexual perversion and impurity, neo-paganism, and in fact, a total disagreement among many bishops and priests on anything in the Catholic Church. The only thing agreed upon among the leading powers in the Vatican is to hate traditional Catholic theology, which is scorned by them, along with whole idea of the conversion of Russia to the Catholic Faith—again, the very conflict of ecclesial visions which gave rise to the crime we are discussing here.

Cardinal Ratzinger has to pretend that these real signs of the times have nothing to do with that event known as the Second Vatican Council, wherein it is claimed that the Holy Spirit came a second time. That is obviously false, as we can see from the Council's bitter fruits.

While we may be accused of "polemics," in the light of the Church's teaching on prophecy and the importance that St. Paul (following Christ's example!) and the Church Fathers attributed to this Divine gift, Cardinal Ratzinger's statement borders on heresy and blasphemy, to say the least. To reduce everything between the Psalms and Don Bosco or Fatima to a "responding to the curiosity of the mind" is tantamount to declaring Holy Scripture, the Church Fathers, Tradition, and almost all extraordinary revelation of the future as a sort of clerical Rainbow Press on the level of the lowest publication at the local supermarket's cash register. The implication that the future predictions of divine prophecies are merely objects of idle human curiosity is an insult to God and the Saints; and this cannot ever be taken lightly.

On p. 38 of *TMF* Cardinal Ratzinger again refers to Cardinal Sodano's trivializing the significance of the vision:

> [they] do not describe photographically the details of future events, but synthesize and compress against a single background of events, facts which extend through time in an unspecified succession and duration.

That all of these events are in the past and no great mystery is the evident message of these eminent Cardinals.

### iii) Cardinal Ratzinger's "Attempt to Interpret ..."

The first question that arises here concerns Cardinal Ratzinger's surprise. In *TMF* (p. 39) he states that the Virgin's message that devotion to Her Immaculate Heart is the way to salvation is surprising to "the Anglo-Saxon and German cultural world." Why does Cardinal Ratzinger say this? Are the English and the Germans too ignorant to have heard about the Sacred Heart,[20] St. Margaret Mary Alacoque, and St. Philip Benitius, let alone Pope Leo XIII, or are they too intelligent to fall for such an Italian or Spanish romanticism? Does the sober German tell his girl: "I love you with all my brain!", or would a determined Englishman communicate his passion with a dry reference to his faculty of the will? What is the purpose of such ludicrous statements? The answer may lie in the lines that follow this incomprehensible "surprise" of the Cardinal's.

Cardinal Ratzinger's "attempt to interpret the 'secret' of Fatima" completely fails to interpret what is not the secret as such anyway, as this has not been revealed, but he succeeds in debunking nothing less than the Immaculate Conception Herself. This eminent prince of the Church seems to have forgotten when Our Lady appeared at Lourdes She did not introduce Herself as "Immaculately Conceived," but rather said: "I am *the* Immaculate Conception." Only She, among all mere creatures, has ever been conceived without Original Sin *and* has never committed a sin. Only Her Heart—referring to the third faculty of the soul, not the internal organ but the heart which St. Thomas Aquinas calls the *sensus comunis* —therefore, is the Immaculate Heart. Cardinal Ratzinger does not shrink from inflating this term, reserved to the Mother of God, to include any "heart, which, with God's grace, has come to perfect interior unity and therefore 'sees God.'" He is not even ashamed to abuse the Gospel for his interpretation by citing Matthew 5:8, which only says: "Blessed are the clean of heart: for they shall see God." Christ talks about the clean of heart, not "perfect interior unity" and certainly not the only Immaculate Heart. If we follow this implicit denial of the exclusiveness of the Immaculate Heart by attributing it to all who are "clean of heart," then we might as well arrive at the logical conclusion that all priests have sacred hearts, as they are consecrated an *alter Christus* (another Christ), which might account for their Latin title of *Reverendus* (to be revered). But to say all priests have sacred hearts would be blasphemous, which is exactly what one ought to think of Cardinal Ratzinger's trivializing the Immaculate Heart.

Even the 'typically Protestant' objection "that we should not place a human being between ourselves and Christ" is answered by Cardinal Ratzinger in apparent ignorance of Our Lady: he quotes St. Paul's exhortation to "imitate" him, instead of explaining that it was Our Lord Himself Who placed a mere human being between Himself and us by making His Mother the *Mediatrix* of all graces!

In his examination of the single images in the vision of the "Bishop dressed in White", Cardinal Ratzinger says:

> In this way, the importance of human freedom is underlined: the future is not in fact unchangeably set, and the image which the children saw is in no way a film image of a future in which nothing can be changed. ... The purpose of the vision is not to show a film of an irrevocably fixed future.[21]

This is, again, the denial of prophecy: The children did not have an entirely conditional vision. Our Lady clearly distinguished the unchangeable future from the consequences that would follow *if* Her wishes were not heeded. To declare the real future as such, whatever will actually take place, as changeable is against the Church's Teaching on Divine Providence and Predestination. The eternal plan of Divine Providence is unchangeable, because God is unchangeable, and nothing can happen independently from Providence.[22] In His Divine Wisdom God knows the entire future, which is, therefore, unchangeable, as Vatican I authoritatively taught. (D.S. 3003).

If Cardinal Ratzinger's statement is to mean what it says, he would be at least a material heretic; if it is to mean that we can change the future, by following Our Lady's requests, then his concept of future is warped. If a man decides to become a priest instead of a father of children, he does not "change" his future, which was set before he was born; rather, he has changed his mind.

Cardinal Ratzinger's statement is either an expression of a subjectivist or heretical mind. The latter seems to be the case, when we consider the statement: "There is no immutable destiny".[23]

The Cardinal's subjective certitude in denying any kind of "film image" (seen by the three Fatima children) shows whom he appears to believe to be the real prophet of Fatima—himself, and certainly not Our Lady of Fatima.

Sister Lucy finally is discredited as a seer, when Cardinal Ratzinger says that the vision incorporates images which she "may have seen in devotional books".[24] This is tantamount to declaring the whole vision a product of fantasy, and fits snugly into the plan of dissolving Fatima "into nothing more than generic Catholic piety and platitudes, involving events that are over and done with," as Father Gruner in his article so aptly describes the Bertone/Ratzinger commentary.[25]

As we discussed in a previous chapter, the last page of *TMF* again declares everything in the Secret to be part of the past, including Our Lady's words: "My Immaculate Heart will triumph"—from which the Cardinal deliberately strips the words *In the end.* The Cardinal reduces all of Fatima to "the *fiat* of Mary, the word of Her heart, [that] has changed the history of the world".[26] This is a patently ridiculous and clumsy effort to eliminate Fatima entirely from the scene.

### iv) The Leaven of Ratzinger

Cardinal Ratzinger's attempt to dismantle the Message of Fatima under the guise of a learned "interpretation" reminds one of Our Lord's admonition to His disciples to "Take heed and beware of the leaven of the Pharisees and Sadducees." (Mt. 16:6) At first the disciples, who were eating bread at the moment, did not understand. What did this talk of leaven in bread have to do with the Pharisees? Soon, however, they grasped Our Lord's meaning: "Then they understood that he had not said that they should beware of the leaven of bread, but of the *doctrine* of the Pharisees and Sadducees." (Mt. 16:12)

As Archbishop Alban Goodier, S.J. explained in his classic commentary on this passage in Scripture, Our Lord was teaching the disciples to be on their guard against the *subtleties* of the Pharisees, which were far more dangerous than any open opposition to Christ:

> It was not so much their opposition that He feared for His own, it was their [the Pharisees'] *subtlety*. Before the Pharisees had blamed Him for His miracles and other good deeds; He knew that this would not take His friends away from Him. Now this morning they [the Pharisees] had come, with an affected simplicity, a show of desire to know the truth, an appeal to the *prophets, a zeal for tradition, a respect for law and order and obedience to the powers that be*; and all this, He knew, would be likely to affect His own *more than any open enmity*. Like leaven, unless they were careful, it would spread unconsciously among them.[27]

The Virgin of Fatima, like Our Lord Himself, was quite straightforward in Her message. But Cardinal Ratzinger, like the Phrarisees of old, is full of subtleties and citations to Scripture which, artfully arranged, obscure the simplicity of God's truth. And like the Pharisees, the Cardinal presents his obfuscation with a great show of respect for the Messenger and the Message; but beneath the appearance of respect is a thinly disguised contempt. By the time the Cardinal is done with his pharisaical "tribute" to Fatima, nothing is left of it. For him, the matter is all very *subtle*—so subtle that it vanishes away.

But the apparitions at Fatima are not so subtle. They were given to little children, who could not read, for the edification and guidance of the wise and the learned of this world, including theologians at the Vatican. Either Our Lady appeared at Fatima or She did not. Either She gave a distinct message to the children, which they could remember and repeat just as they had heard it, or She did not. Either She intended this message to be passed on to the world or She did not. Either She insured that Her message would be accurately transmitted or She did not. Either She guaranteed beyond any shadow of reasonable doubt, by the Miracle of the Sun, that it was indeed She, the Queen of Heaven and Earth, Who came, Who spoke and Who commanded, or She did not. The answer in each case is, obviously, that She did, for She is the Mother of God.

Like the disciples in their encounter with the Pharisees, we must be on guard against Pharisaical subtleties which have spread like poisonous leaven through the Church over the past forty years. Now the latter day leaven of the Pharisees seeks to penetrate the Message of Fatima, as Cardinal Ratzinger tells us that any heart can be like the Immaculate Heart, and that "*in the end* My Immaculate Heart will triumph" means the Annunciation 2,000 years ago. The Pharisees of old were dangerous precisely because they seemed to have a genuine respect for the truth. Today a feigned respect for the Message of Fatima conceals its most determined opponents.

## Conclusion

In one of the stranger events in an already very strange post-conciliar Church, we are faced with quite a few questions which arise from the unorthodox comments on the vision in the Third Secret provided by Cardinal Ratzinger and Msgr. Bertone:

- Why are the actual words of Our Lady, the real Third Secret, written down on a single sheet and—most probably still in the Papal safe—withheld from the public and even denied?
- Why is the published vision, which obviously deals with the murder of a Pope in the future, associated with the 1981 attempt at the Pope's life which failed?
- Why is the lie that the Consecration of Russia has been done repeated?

- Why the absurd statement that: "The decision of His Holiness Pope John Paul II to make public the third part of the 'secret' of Fatima *brings to an end a period of history marked by tragic human lust for power and evil*"?
- Why do the Pope's assistants and advisors make His Holiness available for hundreds of political meetings but virtually no time for Sister Lucy?
- Why is the lie about the fall of Communism in 1989 repeated?[28]
- Why is the Secret, long kept secret, belittled as "no great mystery," and reduced to symbolism?
- Why is prophecy's prediction of the future denied?
- Why is the Immaculate Heart belittled and equated with the "clean of heart"?
- Why is the unchangeable future—and with it God's Providence—denied, at least implicitly?
- Why is Sister Lucy's vision belittled by mentioning "devotional books" as the possible source?
- Why do the prelates fail to explain the line "In Portugal the dogma of the Faith will always be preserved *etc.*"?
- What is the purpose of publishing the vision of the Third Secret in the first place, when the words of Our Lady are withheld and the vision reduced to nothingness?

The evidence points to one answer for all these questions: Whenever we are faced with any kind of sin, such as a lie, we have to ask the question: *Cui bono?*—to whose benefit?

The Vatican's fabrications and incoherencies about the Third Secret and Fatima as such, cannot be a silly play by a few bored prelates. There must be an important purpose to the fabrication of lies that can be unmasked with no great difficulty. Why risk this exposure, unless for an important purpose?

As it is evident that the Third Secret is not abused to predict some politically correct or convenient visions for the future, but—on the contrary—is reduced to the past *and* deprived of any real importance, the only purpose of the entire act of publication must be a strategic diversion from the actual words of Our Lady: a vision and a prophecy are turned into deception or—as the intelligence communities like to call it—perception management.

This answer is far from being a mere speculation. Every piece of evidence we have discussed so far, including the Third Secret vision itself and other approved apparitions referred to by Cardinal Ratzinger himself in 1984, points to the conclusion that the *real* Third Secret must be the words of Our Lady withheld from the public, and, possibly, the *authentic* text of the supposedly published vision.

We conclude this chapter with some further questions raised by the evidence:

Why has the international press—mainly without comment or objection—published the "vision"? Usually they are quite efficient in ridiculing, doubting, denying, and slandering the sacred. Just consider the international reaction to the Vatican's announcement to beatify Pope Pius IX. We admit that this is not a strictly theological argument. The consideration of probability, however, has been accepted by St. Thomas Aquinas whose common sense is—as G.K. Chesterton points out—"the sense for the probable."

Why would we be so sure about the authenticity of the published text or "Sister Lucy's personal" affirmations as to their authentic interpretations? Two of the highest prelates of the Vatican do not hesitate in their jointly presented "commentary" to declare that the Third Secret contains "no great mystery". They present to us a collection of absurd and self-contradictory statements which range from insulting our intelligence to proximate heresy (to say the least) and blasphemy.

In view of this, can we be so sure that "Sister Lucy's" lines are not the product of software capable of reproducing someone's handwriting and available for less than one hundred dollars? Who, in that case, would be allowed to ask Sister Lucy about the publication? Certainly none of us.

This is not mere paranoia, but only prudent doubt regarding the habitual truthfulness of persons who have told us demonstrable lies. One is not paranoid if one has doubts about inconsistencies and self-contradictions.

There cannot be many reasons for withholding a message from Our Lady, if ever: It would be conceivable that the message is sufficiently terrifying to cause panic, such as the prophecy of a locally limited catastrophe, a flood or a nuclear attack. Or the message might be too symbolic to comprehend, as might be the case with a few lines in the Apocalypse. Or the message could be quite explicit and clear, but highly embarrassing for the ones who hold power over its publication.

It seems evident that the first two possibilities are out of character with Fatima and most Marian apparitions, which leads us to the third possibility as our conclusion: *The Vatican has something to hide that would be extremely embarrassing*. We recall the testimony of Father Joaquin Alonso, who for sixteen years was the official archivist of Fatima:

> It is therefore completely probable that the text makes concrete references to the crisis of faith within the Church and to the negligence of the pastors themselves [and the] internal struggles in the very bosom of the Church and of grave pastoral negligence of the upper hierarchy.[29]

This is entirely congruent with the 1846 apparition and message of Our Lady at *La Salette,* the apparition of 1634 of Our Lady of Good Success, Quito, and a few others. And possibly we might know the actual text of the Third Secret: There is the story of some years ago of a supposedly reliable French priest who heard a supernatural message, while listening to a recording in a sort of Oratory. He claims to have heard the following lines:

> There will be a wicked council planned and prepared that will change the face of the Church. Many will lose the Faith and confusion will reign everywhere. The sheep will in vain search for their shepherds. A schism will tear apart the tunic of My Son.—This will be the end of times, announced in the Holy Scriptures and recalled to memory by Me in many places. The abomination of abominations will reach its peak and it will bring the chastisement announced in La Salette. My Son's arm, which I will not be able to hold back anymore, will punish this poor world, which has to expiate its crimes.—One will not talk but about wars and revolutions. The elements of nature will be unchained and will cause anguish, even with the best (the most courageous). The Church will bleed from all her wounds. Blessed are they who will persevere and search for refuge in My Heart, because in the end My Immaculate Heart will triumph.

Of course, there is absolutely no proof for the authenticity of this text. We must not claim this to be the real Third Secret. However, it makes a great deal more sense than anything contained in the Vatican's "interpretation" of the visional part of the Third Secret.

The heresies and the apostasy following Vatican II are of such a tragic and widespread importance that common sense demands to believe this to be the Third Secret, or part of it. Is it possible that Our Lady knew about the end of World War I, the beginning of World War II under Pius XI, Russia spreading her errors, Russia being the instrument of chastisement, a future Pope being shot by soldiers, but nothing about the cataclysmic developments in the Church beginning with Vatican II, an event that spiritually pales all wars into insignificance? We have already mentioned that no less than Pope Paul VI said:

> The Church finds herself in an hour of unrest, of self-critique, one might say, even of auto-destruction! It is like an internal, acute, and complicated revolution, for which no one was prepared after the Council (Dec. 7, 1968).

He also mentioned "the smoke of Satan" that had entered the Church. Even Pope Paul VI, who found himself at the center of the crisis, perceived the disaster to a point. Is it conceivable that Our Lady of Fatima had nothing to say about it when other approved apparitions, as even Cardinal Ratzinger admits, speak of dangers to the faith? Clearly this is impossible!

And so while there is no proof—we say it again—for the authenticity of the above-quoted message the French priest claims to have received, there is no logical alternative to the Third Secret being *something* along these lines. This can only mean that there is a text pertaining to the Third Secret which the Vatican has yet to disclose—a text that follows the words about the dogma of the Faith being preserved in Portugal. We discuss this in the next chapter.

# Chapter 12

## Does the Third Secret Consist of Two Distinct Texts?

Despite their best efforts to close the book on Fatima, the Sodano/Ratzinger/Bertone alliance had not succeeded with the June 26, 2000 press conference. Knowledgeable Catholics the world over simply did not believe that a wordless, ambiguous vision of "a Bishop dressed in White" could be all there was to a secret the Vatican had kept under lock and key for forty years.

The best witness in support of the claim that something had to be missing was, ironically enough, Cardinal Ratzinger himself, speaking in 1984 in the *Jesus* magazine interview we have already pointed out. What had happened to the "religious prophecy" the Cardinal had mentioned back then, concerning "dangers to the faith and the life of the Christian, and therefore (the life) of the world"? What about his statement in 1984 that "the things contained in this 'Third Secret' correspond to what has been announced in Scripture and has been said *again and again in many other Marian apparitions*, first of all that of Fatima"? Nothing in the vision of the "Bishop dressed in White" repeats what has been said in many other Marian apparitions, for in this vision Mary *says nothing at all.* And if, as Cardinal Ratzinger 2000 was now claiming, the "Bishop dressed in White" was John Paul II escaping death in 1981, why had Cardinal Ratzinger in 1984 not simply revealed this and declared the Third Secret to have been fulfilled?

The inescapable conclusion for many completely loyal Catholics was that there had to be another document to go along with the vision. Perhaps the height of the Vatican's embarrassment on this score came on May 16, 2001, nearly a year after the "Fatima is over" press conference. On that date Mother Angelica—who is, if anything, a staunch defender of the Vatican apparatus—expressed the common sense of millions of Catholics on her live television show:

> As for the Secret, well I happen to be one of those individuals who thinks *we didn't get the whole thing*. I told ya! I mean, you have the right to your own opinion, don't you, Father? There, you know, that's my opinion. *Because I think it's scary*. And I don't think the Holy See is going to say something that does not happen, that might happen. And then what does it do if it doesn't happen? I mean the Holy See cannot afford to make prophecies.[1]

The question we must confront in this chapter—the question raised by such Catholics as Mother Angelica—is whether the Third Secret of Fatima is completely contained within the single document published in June 2000, or whether it is comprised of two documents: the vision published in June 2000, and a separate text containing the words of Our Lady which explain the vision—words which probably follow immediately after the phrase "In Portugal the dogma of the faith will always be preserved etc." in Lucy's Fourth Memoir.

The conviction grows that there are indeed two documents containing the Third Secret. But what evidence is there to support the existence of a second document?

As we noted in Chapter 4, the existence of two documents—one being a letter written on a single sheet of paper and sealed in an envelope, the other being in a notebook that Sister Lucy turned over along with the envelope—is clearly suggested by the testimony of various credible witnesses, including Sister Lucy. A more detailed discussion of their testimony can be found in Frère Michel's book *The Whole Truth About Fatima - Volume III: The Third Secret*. The 20,000 copies of the French edition of Volume III were published in 1985 and 1986 (after more than 4 years of research), and 50,000 copies of the English edition were published in 1990. To our knowledge this book has never been questioned as to either the authenticity or thoroughness of its research. Volume III alone has over 1,150 footnotes, citing numerous documents, witnesses, and testimonies. Likewise, Frère Michel's sources and his own testimonies have never been questioned; thus, Frère Michel himself is also to be considered a valid and credible witness.[2]

We now turn to the business of proving from the available evidence, some of which we have laid out in the preceding chapters, that there are indeed two original manuscripts by Sister Lucy pertaining to the Third Secret, and that both documents eventually found their way to the Vatican. We recall what Sister Lucy wrote to Bishop da Silva on January 9, 1944:

> I have written what you asked me; God willed to try me a little, but finally this was indeed His will: [the text] is sealed in an envelope and it [the sealed envelope] is in the notebooks ...[3]

Examination of the original Portuguese reveals that Sister Lucy means to say that the Secret proper is in the envelope, and that the envelope is in one of her notebooks which she also consigned to Archbishop Manuel Maria Ferreira da Silva (the Archbishop of Gurza) for carrying to Bishop da Silva of Fatima in June of 1944. As Frère Michel further states:

> The seer discreetly handed the Bishop of Gurza *the notebook* in which she had slipped the *envelope* containing the Secret. That same evening, the bishop placed the envelope into the hands of Bishop da Silva ..."[4]

But what happened to the notebook? Surely it contains some text relevant to the Third Secret. Why else would Sister Lucy have entrusted both the sealed envelope *and* the notebook to the Bishop of Fatima?

The following table summarizes eleven different facts pointing to the existence of two manuscripts for the Third Secret of Fatima: one in the envelope, containing the words of Our Lady, and another in the notebook, probably containing the vision of the "Bishop dressed in White" which was revealed on June 26, 2000. We will examine these facts in the subsequent sections. We must emphasize at the outset, however, that one cannot discount the possibility that the text in the envelope has been lost or destroyed and that it may, in fact, never be produced.

| | **Third Secret Text #1**<br>**Alluded to by Various Witnesses**<br>**(see Chapter 4)** | **Third Secret Text #2**<br>**Published by the Vatican**<br>**June 26, 2000** |
|---|---|---|
| (1) | Text contains words of Our Lady. | Text does not contain any words of Our Lady. |
| (2) | Text transferred to Holy Office - April 16, 1957. | Text transferred to Holy Office - April 4, 1957. |
| (3) | Written on a single sheet of paper. | Written on 4 sheets of paper. |
| (4) | About 25 lines of text. | 62 lines of text. |
| (5) | Text was ready on January 9, 1944. | Text was ready on January 3, 1944. |
| (6) | Pope John Paul II read the text in 1978. | Pope John Paul II read the text on July 18, 1981. |
| (7) | Pope John Paul II consecrated the world on June 7, 1981 after reading the text in 1978 but before reading the 4-page text which he only read on July 18, 1981. | This text was not read by the Pope prior to his act of consecrating the world on June 7, 1981. |
| (8) | Written in letter form (addressed and signed). | Not written in letter form (not addressed or signed), but as an entry in Sister Lucy's notebook. |
| (9) | Stored by the Pope's bedside. | Stored in the Holy Office building. |
| (10 | The single sheet of paper has margins on each side of three quarters of a centimeter. | The 4 sheets of paper have no margins. |
| (11) | Explains the vision. | Describes the vision. |

## Fact #1:
## Supporting Documentation for Fact #1 – Text #1 Contains the Words of Our Lady

In Chapter 4 we noted the Vatican announcement in the February 8, 1960 communiqué of the Portuguese news agency A.N.I. (at Rome), which admits that the text of the Third Secret (i.e. Text #1 referred to in the table) contains the actual words of Our Lady:

It has just been stated, in very reliable Vatican circles, to the representatives of United Press International, that it is most likely that the letter will never be opened, in which Sister Lucy wrote down *the words which Our Lady confided as a secret* to the three little shepherds in the Cova da Iria.[5]

We also have Sister Lucy's own testimony that the Third Secret contains Our Lady's actual words, not simply a wordless vision. Frère Michel reports:

> ... in her third Memoir, written in July-August, 1941, Sister Lucy had been content to mention the existence of a third part of the Secret, but as yet she had said nothing about it. A few months later, in her fourth Memoir, written between October-December, 1941, she decided to say more. She recopied almost word for word the text of the third Memoir, but adding after the final words—"... and a certain period of peace will be granted to the world"—the new sentence: "Em Portugal se conservara sempre o dogma da fe etc."[6]

This new sentence translates into: "In Portugal the dogma of the Faith will always be preserved etc."—directly quoting words of the Virgin of Fatima. Frère Michel also reports:

> Indeed in 1943, when Bishop da Silva had asked her to write down the text [of the Third Secret], and she was encountering insurmountable obstacles in obeying this order, she declared that it was not absolutely necessary to do so, ***'since in a certain manner she had said it'***.[7] Undoubtedly Sister Lucy was alluding to the ten words she had discreetly added in December, 1941 to the text of the great Secret—but added so discreetly that almost nobody noticed them.[8]

It is very telling that these discreetly added words—"In Portugal the dogma of the Faith will always be preserved etc." are the very ones *TMF* tries to avoid by demoting them to a footnote, as if they were of no consequence, and by relying on the *Third* Memoir for the text of the Great Secret, which does not contain these added words.

We repeat the question we asked earlier: Why would Cardinal Sodano, Cardinal Ratzinger and Msgr. Bertone choose the *Third* Memoir when the Fourth Memoir offers a more complete text of the Fatima Message? The answer, clearly, is that they chose the Third Memoir in order to avoid any discussion of the momentous phrase "In Portugal the dogma of the Faith will always be preserved etc." By this expedient they deftly navigated around an obvious indication that the Message of Fatima includes further words of the Virgin embraced within the "etc.", and that these missing words must pertain to the Third Secret. If it were not so, then Sodano/Ratzinger/Bertone would not have displayed such an aversion to this phrase. They would simply have used the Fourth Memoir, including that phrase, in *TMF*'s discussion of the first two parts of the Great Secret of Fatima. One can only conclude that the phrase to which they were so averse is indeed the gateway into the Third Secret of

Fatima, and that they did not wish the faithful or the world at large to focus on this gateway, for it raises too many questions about what lies beyond it.

Here it should also be noted that in its English translation of the phrase "Em Portugal se conservara sempre o dogma da fe etc." in the aforementioned footnote, *TMF* makes subtle changes to the Portuguese original: "In Portugal, the dogma of the faith will always be preserved, etc. ...".

Notice that a comma has been added after the word "preserved" and an ellipsis after the word "etc.". *Neither the comma nor the ellipsis appears in the Portuguese original.* This subtle tinkering is no accident. By putting a comma before "etc." *TMF* creates the false impression that the "etc." comes from the authors of *TMF* themselves, to indicate that Sister Lucy completed the sentence in her Fourth Memoir and that the rest of the sentence is found in that memoir. By inserting an ellipsis after "etc.", the authors augment the false impression of a sentence that was completed by Sister Lucy in her Fourth Memoir. But in truth, Sister Lucy wrote exactly this and nothing more in her own handwriting: "Em Portugal se conservara sempre o dogma da fe etc." The rest was not recorded in the Fourth Memoir but in the later text at issue, the missing text of the Third Secret which explains the vision of the "Bishop dressed in White".

In fact, the authors of *TMF* neglect to mention that immediately after "In Portugal the dogma of the faith will always be preserved etc." we find in the Fourth Memoir: "Tell *this* to no one. Yes, you may tell Francisco." Now, if "this" referred only to the Faith always being preserved in Portugal, Our Lady would hardly have directed the seers to hide this heavenly compliment to the Portuguese people. Hence, "this" clearly involves a reference to how the dogma of the Faith would *not* always be preserved in other places—*many* other places. That is the very conclusion the authors of *TMF* have attempted to hide by demoting the key phrase to a footnote, and by adding a comma and ellipsis which are not in the original handwritten Portuguese.

As we pointed out in Chapter 4, these ten words—"Em Portugal se conservara sempre o dogma da fe etc."—introduce a new, and incomplete, thought into the Secret of Fatima. The phrase suggests, as every reputable Fatima scholar concluded, that there is more to follow and that the "etc." is but a placeholder for the third part of the Secret. But the Vatican's June 2000 manuscript of the Third Secret (i.e. Text #2 referred to in the table on page 143), published in *TMF*, contains no words of Our Lady; it describes only the vision of the Secret seen by the three children of Fatima. This text does not explain the new sentence in the Fourth Memoir, nor does it provide the words embraced within the "etc."

Did Our Lady's actual words, spoken personally by the Mother of God, end with "etc."? Certainly, they did not. There is undoubtedly more text after the "etc." What happened to it?

### What Can Be Concluded Regarding Fact #1

These facts demonstrate that there must be two documents: one containing the words of Our Lady, the other containing the vision seen by the three children, but with no words at all which are attributed to Our Lady.

### Fact #2:

### Supporting Documentation for Fact #2 – Different Dates of Transfer

Frère François tells us when the text of the Third Secret was transferred to the Holy Office (now known as the Congregation for the Doctrine of the Faith):

> Arriving at the Vatican on April 16, 1957, the Secret undoubtedly was placed by Pope Pius XII in his personal desk, inside a small wooden box, bearing the inscription *Secretum Sancti Officii* (*Secret of the Holy Office*).[9]

It is important to recall what we noted earlier: that the Pope was the head of the Holy Office prior to Pope Paul VI reorganizing the Roman Curia in 1967. Therefore, it was quite appropriate for the Pope to retain the Third Secret in his possession and for the box containing it to be labeled as "Secret of the Holy Office." With the Pope being the head of the Holy Office, this box became part of the Holy Office archives.

The Vatican commentary, however, states that Sister Lucy's original manuscript of the Third Secret was transferred to the Holy Office on April 4, 1957. Furthermore, Archbishop Tarcisio Bertone, Secretary of the Congregation for the Doctrine of the Faith, tells us:

> The sealed envelope was initially in the custody of the Bishop of Leiria. To ensure better protection for the 'secret' the envelope was placed in the Secret Archives of the Holy Office on 4 April 1957.[10]

### What Can Be Concluded Regarding Fact #2

This difference of dates supports the conclusion that there are two documents: one document containing the vision was transferred to the Secret Archives of the Holy Office on April 4, 1957; the other document, containing the words of Our Lady of Fatima, was transferred to the Pope's apartment, which can be considered a part of the Holy Office, on April 16, 1957.

### Fact #3:

### Supporting Documentation for Fact #3 – Text #1 is a Single Sheet of Paper

As we showed in Chapter 4, Cardinal Ottaviani, as Prefect of the Congregation for the Doctrine of the Faith in 1967, stated that he had read the Third Secret and that it was written on a *single sheet* of paper. He testified to this fact on February 11, 1967, at a press conference during a meeting of the Pontifical Marian Academy in Rome:

> And then, what did she [Lucy] do to obey the Most Holy Virgin? She wrote on *a sheet of paper*, in Portuguese, what the Holy Virgin *had asked her* to tell ...[11]

Cardinal Ottaviani is a witness to this fact. In the same press conference, he states:

> I, who have had the grace and the gift to read the text of the Secret—although I too am held to secrecy because I am bound by the Secret ...[12]

Note well: Cardinal Ottaviani read the Third Secret. Cardinal Ottaviani later said it was written on *a sheet* of paper. But the text of the vision produced by the Vatican on June 26, 2000 is on *multiple* sheets. If the Third Secret sealed in the envelope—the one read by Cardinal Ottaviani—had been on multiple sheets, *he would have said so.*

By way of corroboration, Father Alonso reports that both Sister Lucy and Cardinal Ottaviani state that the Secret was written on a single sheet of paper:

> Lucy tells us that she wrote it *on a sheet of paper*. Cardinal Ottaviani, who has read it, tells us the same thing: 'She wrote it *on a sheet of paper* ...'.[13]

We also have the testimony of Bishop Venancio, who was then the Auxiliary Bishop of Leiria-Fatima, that he was ordered by Bishop da Silva (the Bishop of Leiria-Fatima) in mid-March 1957 to bring copies of all Sister Lucy's writings—including the original of the Third Secret—to the Apostolic Nuncio at Lisbon for transferral to Rome. Before bringing Lucy's writings to the Nuncio, Bishop Venancio looked at the envelope containing the Third Secret while holding it up to the light and saw that the Secret was "written on *a small sheet* of paper".[14] Frère Michel was a first-hand witness to this highly probative testimony:

> However, thanks to the disclosures of Bishop Venancio, at the time Auxiliary Bishop of Leiria and intimately involved with these events, we now have many reliable facts which we will take care not to neglect. *I myself received them from the mouth of Bishop Venancio* on February 13, 1984, at Fatima. The former Bishop of Fatima repeated to me on this subject, almost word for word, what he had already said previously to Father Caillon, who gave a very detailed account of it in his conferences.[15]

Here is Bishop Venancio's testimony, according to Frère Michel:

> Bishop Venancio related that once he was by himself, he took the great envelope of the Secret and tried to look through it and see the contents. In the bishop's large envelope he discerned a smaller envelope, that of Lucy, and inside this envelope *an ordinary sheet of paper* with margins on each side of three quarters of a centimeter. He took the trouble to note the size of everything. Thus the final Secret of Fatima was written on a small sheet of paper.[16]

The Vatican's June 2000 manuscript of the Third Secret is written on four sheets of paper. Something is seriously amiss.

### What Can Be Concluded Regarding Fact #3

Once again, the evidence points to the existence of two documents: one consisting of a single sheet of paper, the other consisting of four sheets of paper.

### Fact #4:

### Supporting Documentation for Fact #4 – Text #1 is 25 Lines of Handwritten Text

In addition to the evidence cited in support of Fact #3, regarding the Third Secret being written on just one single sheet of paper, Frère Michel and Frère François both agree that the text of the Third Secret contains only 20 to 30 lines:

> ... we are just as certain that the twenty or thirty lines of the third Secret ...[17]

> The final Secret of Fatima, written on a small sheet of paper, is therefore not very long. Probably twenty to twenty-five lines ...[18]

> (Bishop Venancio looked) at the envelope [containing the Third Secret] while holding it up to the light. He could see inside a little sheet of which he measured the exact size. We thus know that the Third Secret is not very long, probably 20 to 25 lines ...[19]

On the other hand, the Vatican's June 2000 manuscript of the Third Secret contains 62 lines of handwritten text. Again, something is seriously amiss.

### What Can Be Concluded Regarding Fact #4

This discrepancy demonstrates that there are two documents: one with 20 to 30 lines of text on one sheet of paper, the other with 62 lines of text on four sheets of paper.

### Fact #5:

### Supporting Documentation for Fact #5 – Text #1 Was Not Ready by January 3

As we showed in Chapter 4, Lucy first attempted to write down the text of the Third Secret in October 1943. From that mid-October until early January 1944, Lucy was prevented from obeying a formal order to write down the Third Secret by an unspeakable anguish.

We noted also that the order to write down the Secret came after Sister Lucy came down with pleurisy in June of 1943, which caused Canon Galamba and Bishop da Silva to fear that she would die without having revealed the final part of the Great Secret of Fatima. Canon Galamba later convinced Bishop da Silva to suggest to Sister Lucy that she write down the Secret.

However, Sister Lucy would not comply without a formal order from the Bishop, which was finally given in mid-October 1943.

Even then Sister Lucy was unable to obey for another two and a half months, until the Blessed Virgin Mary appeared to her on January 2, 1944, confirming that it was God's will that she commit the Secret to writing. Only then was Lucy able to overcome her fear and anguish and write down the Secret.[20] But it was not until January 9, 1944, that Sister Lucy wrote the following note to Bishop da Silva, informing him that the Secret was finally written down:

> I have written what you asked me; God willed to try me a little, but finally this was indeed His will: [the text] is sealed in an envelope and it is in the notebooks ...[21]

The Vatican's manuscript of the Third Secret, however, was completed on January 3, 1944, as shown by the date appearing at the end of Sister Lucy's 4-page handwritten document.[22] Furthermore, Archbishop Bertone tells us:

> The third part of the "secret" was written "by order of His Excellency the Bishop of Leiria and the Most Holy Mother ..." on 3 January 1944.[23]

## What Can Be Concluded Regarding Fact #5

Considering that Sister Lucy had finally written down the Secret after an apparition of the Blessed Mother, why would she not have immediately informed Bishop da Silva as soon as the document was ready, given the Mother of God's assurance that it was God's will that she deliver the document? Why would Sister Lucy, trained in obedience, wait *another* six days after obeying *Heaven's command* to write down the Third Secret—from January 3 to January 9—before informing her bishop? From this we may conclude that the text of the Third Secret was not ready until January 9, 1944 or very shortly before.

This difference of dates lends further support to the existence of two documents: one containing the vision, completed on January 3, 1944; the other containing Our Lady's words which explain that vision, completed on or very shortly before January 9, 1944.

Admittedly, this conclusion is dependent on circumstantial evidence; but Fatima scholars must rely on this kind of evidence because the anti-Fatima establishment has, since 1976, blocked publication of the works of Father Joaquin Alonso, consisting of over 5,000 documents in 24 volumes which are the result of his 11 years of research up to that time. As we have noted, Fr. Alonso was official archivist of Fatima for sixteen years.

All other conclusions in this article, except possibly the conclusion regarding Fact #11, are not dependent on circumstantial evidence.

**Fact #6:**

## Supporting Documentation for Fact #6 – Different Dates for When Pope First Read Secret

On July 1, 2000, *The Washington Post* reported that Vatican officials recently provided contradictory dates for when Pope John Paul II read the Third Secret for the first time:

> On May 13, Vatican spokesman Joaquin Navarro-Valls said the Pope *first read the secret within days of assuming the papacy* in 1978. On Monday, an aide to Cardinal Joseph Ratzinger, prefect of the Vatican's Congregation for the Doctrine of the Faith, said that the Pope *first saw it in the hospital* after his attack.[24]

An article in the June 26, 2000 edition of *The New York Times* identified the aide to Cardinal Ratzinger:

> "John Paul II *read for the first time the text* of the third secret of Fatima *after the attack*," a top aide to Ratzinger, Monsignor Tarcisio Bertone, told journalists during a news conference to present the document.[25]

According to the Vatican's commentary, Pope John Paul II did not read the Third Secret until July 18, 1981. Archbishop Bertone tells us:

> John Paul II, for his part, asked for the envelope containing the third part of the 'secret' following the assassination attempt on 13 May 1981. On 18 July 1981 Cardinal Franjo Seper, Prefect of the Congregation, gave two envelopes to Archbishop Eduardo Martinez Somalo, Substitute of the Secretariat of State: one white envelope, containing Sister Lucy's original text in Portuguese; the other orange, with the Italian translation of the 'secret'. On the following 11 August, Archbishop Martinez returned the two envelopes to the Archives of the Holy Office.[26]

### What Can Be Concluded Regarding Fact #6

All these statements are true and can be reconciled if there are two documents: In 1978 the Pope read the one-page document originally sealed in the envelope, containing the words of Our Lady; and then on July 18, 1981 His Holiness read the 4-page document describing the vision of the "Bishop dressed in White."

**Fact #7:**

## Supporting Documentation for Fact #7 – Text #1 Inspired Pope to Consecrate World

Immediately following the statement of Archbishop Bertone quoted in support of Fact #6, the Archbishop goes on to tell us:

> As is well known, Pope John Paul II immediately thought of consecrating the world to the Immaculate Heart of Mary and he himself composed a prayer for what he called an 'Act of Entrustment', which was to be celebrated in the Basilica of Saint Mary Major on 7 June 1981 ...[27]

## What Can Be Concluded Regarding Fact #7

How could Pope John Paul II be moved by the Third Secret to consecrate the world to the Immaculate Heart of Mary on *June 7*, 1981, when, according to Archbishop Bertone, the Pope did not actually read the Third Secret until *July 18*, 1981—six weeks later?

Again, both statements can be reconciled if there are two documents: the Pope read the one-page document containing the words of Our Lady in 1978—and this is the text that moved him to consecrate the world on June 7, 1981—and then he read the four-page document describing the vision on July 18, 1981. As we have already shown in Chapter 6, Pope John Paul II's own statements demonstrate that he views these acts of consecration of the world as setting the stage for when he finally feels free to perform the Consecration of Russia.

## Fact #8:
## Supporting Documentation for Fact #8 – Text #1 is a Letter

Sister Lucy, herself, tells us that the Third Secret was written *as a letter*. We have the written testimony of Father Jongen who, on February 3-4, 1946, interrogated Sister Lucy:

> 'You have already made known two parts of the Secret. When will the time arrive for the third part?' 'I communicated the third part in a *letter* to the Bishop of Leiria,' she answered...[28]

As Canon Galamba testified:

> When the bishop refused to open the *letter*, Lucy made him promise that it would definitely be opened and read to the world either at her death or in 1960, whichever would come first.[29]

In February 1960, the Patriarch of Lisbon declared:

> Bishop da Silva enclosed (the envelope sealed by Lucy) in another envelope on which he indicated that the *letter* had to be opened in 1960 by himself, Bishop Jose Correia da Silva, if he was still alive, or if not, by the Cardinal Patriarch of Lisbon.[30]

Father Alonso tells us:

> Other bishops also spoke—and with authority—about the year 1960 as the date indicated for opening the famous *letter*. Thus, when the then titular Bishop of Tiava, and Auxiliary Bishop of Lisbon, asked Lucy when the Secret was to be opened, he always received the same answer: in 1960.[31]

In 1959, Bishop Venancio, the new Bishop of Leiria, declared:

> I think that the *letter* will not be opened before 1960. Sister Lucy had asked that it should not be opened before her death, or not before 1960. We are now in 1959 and Sister Lucy is in good health.[32]

Finally, the Vatican announcement of February 8, 1960 through the A.N.I. press agency also tells us that the text of the Third Secret was written *as a letter*:

> ... it is most likely that the *letter* will never be opened, in which Sister Lucy wrote down the *words which Our Lady confided* as a secret ...[33]

Now, the text of the vision of the Third Secret has also been identified as a letter in the Vatican's commentary. However, that text is plainly not a letter, as it is:

- not addressed to anyone;
- is dated at the end, even though, according to custom in Portugal since the 18th Century, no letter is dated at the end but only at the beginning;
- is *not signed by Sister Lucy* or anyone else; and
- clearly, therefore, is anything but a letter.

Copies of letters written by Sister Lucy have been included in her published memoirs. These letters *all have an addressee, a date, and her signature*.

Thus, we can expect that the one-page document that was available on January 9, 1944 is a letter addressed to someone (Sister Lucy told Father Jongen in February 1946 that she sent it to the Bishop of Leiria), and is signed by Sister Lucy.

Here it is important to note that Sister Lucy was offered the option to write the Third Secret in the form of a letter or in her notebook, and that she decided to write it as a letter. According to Father Alonso, Sister Lucy wrote to Bishop da Silva on January 9, 1944:

> I have written what you asked me; God willed to try me a little, but finally this was indeed His will: it is sealed in an envelope and it is in the notebooks ...[34]

Again, as we have noted above, Frère Michel reports that, on June 17, 1944:

> The seer discreetly handed the Bishop of Gurza the notebook in which she had slipped the envelope containing the Secret. That same evening, the bishop placed the envelope into the hands of Bishop da Silva ...[35]

### What Can Be Concluded Regarding Fact #8

The evidence supports this highly probable conclusion: There are two documents—the text of the Third Secret containing Our Lady's words in the form of a one-page *letter*; and four pages of text *from the notebook.*

Moreover, as we have noted, the text of the vision is dated January 3, 1944, whereas Sister Lucy's letter to the Bishop of Fatima stating "I have written what you asked me; God willed to try me a little, but finally this was indeed His will: [the text] is sealed in an envelope and it is in the notebooks" is dated January 9, 1944. It is entirely possible that Sister Lucy's notebooks contain a number of other things pertaining to the Third Secret which she wrote during the period January 3-9, 1944. These other things may be lesser points pertaining to the Secret, leading up to the final disclosure of the most fearsome part of the Secret on January 9—namely, the Virgin's explanation of the Secret in Her own words. We recall here Father Schweigl's testimony that there are indeed two parts to the Secret: one pertaining to the Pope and the other representing the conclusion of the *words* "In Portugal the dogma of the Faith will always be preserved etc."

In this connection it is important to remember that Sister Lucy was given the choice of writing the Third Secret in her notebooks or on a sheet of paper. Evidently, she availed herself of both options. Again, why else would she have turned over *both* a sealed envelope *and* a notebook to the Bishop of Gurza for delivery to the Bishop of Fatima?

Is it not entirely likely, then, that the ambiguous vision—a "safer" part of the Third Secret—was written down in the notebook, whereas the concrete explanation of the vision in the words of the Virgin Herself—whose impact was quite terrible—had to be sealed in the envelope that Sister Lucy placed *inside* the notebook? There seems to be no other sensible explanation for why Sister Lucy, in response to the Bishop of Fatima's order to write down the Third Secret, provided him with both a sealed envelope and a notebook.

In short, the vision of the "Bishop dressed in White", whose text comprises four sheets of paper, was contained in the notebook, but the explanation—on the single sheet of paper that numerous witnesses have attested to—was sealed in the envelope. *That is why the notebook accompanied the sealed envelope.*

Thus, the four pages of text released by the Vatican on June 26, 2000 are possibly the *visional part* of the Third Secret contained in the notebook, *certainly not* the one-page letter that was sealed in the envelope.

### <u>Fact #9:</u>
### Supporting Documentation for Fact #9 – Text #1 Stored in Papal Apartment

Frère Michel reports the testimony of journalist Robert Serrou who, while doing a photo story at the Vatican on May 14, 1957,[36] about one month after the Third Secret had arrived at Rome on April 16, 1957, discovered that the

Third Secret was being stored in the Pope's apartment by his bedside. As Frère Michel tells us:

> ... we now know that the precious envelope sent to Rome by Msgr. Cento was not placed in the archives of the Holy Office, but that Pius XII wanted to keep it in his own apartment.
>
> Father Caillon received this information from the mouth of journalist Robert Serrou, who himself got it from Mother Pasqualina, in this way. Robert Serrou was doing a photo story for *Paris-Match* in the apartments of Pius XII. Mother Pasqualina—this woman of great common sense who directed the handful of Sisters acting as the Pope's housekeepers, and who sometimes received his confidences—was present.
>
> Before a little wooden safe placed on a table and bearing the inscription *'Secretum Sancti Officii'* (Secret of the Holy Office), the journalist questioned the Mother: 'Mother, what is in this little safe?' She answered: *'The third Secret of Fatima is in there ...'*
>
> The photograph of this safe, which we have reproduced here, was published in *Paris-Match* a year and a half later ...[37]

The photograph of this safe, published in the October 18, 1958 issue of *Paris-Match* (Issue No. 497, page 82), is shown here. The details of Serrou's testimony were later confirmed in a letter he wrote to Frère Michel on January 10, 1985. In this letter, Serrou states:

> It is exact that Mother Pasqualina did tell me, while showing me a little safe bearing a label with the mention, 'Secret of the Holy Office': 'In there is the third Secret of Fatima.'[38]

The Vatican's commentary, however, tells us that the Third Secret had been stored in the building which houses the Holy Office. Again, according to Archbishop Bertone:

> The sealed envelope was initially in the custody of the Bishop of Leiria. To ensure better protection for the 'secret' the envelope was placed in the Secret Archives of the Holy Office on 4 April 1957.[39]

In addition, we have also demonstrated in Fact #6 that Pope John Paul II read the text of the Third Secret (i.e. the one-page document containing the words of Our Lady) in 1978 and then he read the four-page document describing the vision on July 18, 1981. As discussed in Fact #6, the Holy Office records that Pope John Paul II asked for the Third Secret in 1981, *but there is no record of the Pope asking for the Secret in 1978* because he didn't need to—it was in the papal apartments.

### What Can Be Concluded Regarding Fact #9

These testimonies establish the fact that there are two documents stored in two different locations and in two different archives. In 1978 Pope John Paul II read the text of the one-page letter containing Our Lady's words, which was stored in his apartment, a document the Pope did not need to request from the Secret Archives of the Holy Office. But in 1981 Pope John Paul II read the four pages of text containing the description of the vision from Sister Lucy's notebook, which was stored in the Holy Office building. It was this text he had to request from the Secret Archives of the Holy Office.

### Fact #10:
### Supporting Documentation for Fact #10 – Text #1 has Margins of ¾ Centimenter on both sides

Here we have the testimony of Bishop John Venancio, the second Bishop of Fatima, who examined a silhouette of the text under a strong light and noted precisely the margin outlines of the page on which it was written.

> Bishop Venancio related [to Frère Michel] that once he was by himself, he took the great envelope of the Secret and tried to look through it and see the contents. In the bishop's large envelope he discerned a smaller envelope, that of Lucy, and inside this envelope *an ordinary sheet of paper* with margins on each side of three quarters of a centimeter. He took the trouble to note the size of everything. Thus the final Secret of Fatima was written on a small sheet of paper.[40]

Again, the four pages containing the Third Secret vision display no margins whatsoever—a small but very telling discrepancy to be added to all the other discrepancies.

## What Can Be Concluded Regarding Fact #10

This discrepancy also demonstrates that the text released by Cardinal Ratzinger and Msgr. Bertone on June 26, 2000 is not the text of the Third Secret contained in the envelope, and therefore we have not yet been given the complete text of the Third Secret, even though high Vatican officials claim the contrary.

## Fact #11:
## Supporting Documentation for Fact #11 – Text #1 Explains the Vision

In Sister Lucy's Fourth Memoir we read that, during the apparition of Our Lady on June 13, 1917, after Sister Lucy had asked Our Lady to take the three seers to Heaven, Our Lady responded:

> Yes, I will take Jacinta and Francisco soon. But you are to stay here some time longer. Jesus wishes to make use of you to make Me known and loved. He wants to establish in the world devotion to My Immaculate Heart. To whoever embraces this devotion I promise salvation ...[41]

Sister Lucy then proceeds to give us a description of the vision that the three seers were then graced to see immediately after Our Lady spoke the above words—words which *explain* the meaning of the vision:

> As Our Lady spoke these last words, She opened Her hands and for the second time, She communicated to us the rays of that immense light. We saw ourselves in this light, as it were, immersed in God. Jacinta and Francisco seemed to be in that part of the light which rose towards Heaven, and I in that which was poured out on the earth.[42]

Thus, we see that when Our Lady provides a vision to the children *She explains it as well.* Indeed, even in *TMF* we read Sister Lucy's description (taken from her "Third Memoir") of the vision of hell given to the three little shepherds during the apparition of Our Lady on July 13, 1917.

> Our Lady showed us a great sea of fire which seemed to be under the earth. Plunged in this fire were demons and souls in human form, like transparent burning embers, all blackened or burnished bronze, floating about in the conflagration, now raised into the air by the flames that issued from within themselves together with great clouds of smoke, now falling back on every side like sparks in a huge fire, without weight or equilibrium, and amid shrieks and groans of pain and despair, which horrified us and made us tremble with fear. The demons could be distinguished by their terrifying and repulsive likeness to frightful and unknown animals, all black and transparent. This vision lasted but an instant. How can we ever be grateful enough to our kind heavenly Mother, who had already prepared us by promising, in the first

Apparition, to take us to heaven. Otherwise, I think we would have died of fear and terror.[43]

Following that account, Sister Lucy then proceeds to tell us Our Lady's words *explaining* what this vision means, *even though it was quite obvious* that the vision was a vision of hell:

> *You have seen hell* where the souls of poor sinners go. To save them, God wishes to establish in the world devotion to My Immaculate Heart. If what I say to you is done, many souls will be saved and there will be peace.[44]

So, even though the children knew what they saw, nevertheless Our Lady tells them: "You have seen hell." Once again, we see that when Our Lady provides a vision to the children *She explains it as well.*

In contrast to the above-noted visions and the corresponding words of Our Lady explaining them, *TMF* provides only the text of an ambiguous vision, including the following:

> After the two parts which I have already explained, at the left of Our Lady and a little above, we saw an Angel with a flaming sword in his left hand ... Beneath the two arms of the Cross there were two Angels each with a crystal aspersorium in his hand, in which they gathered up the blood of the Martyrs and with it sprinkled the souls that were making their way to God.[45]

This text of the Third Secret contains no words of Our Lady. Why would Our Lady explain something as obvious as the vision of hell, but offer not one word to explain the highly ambiguous passage presented by the Vatican?

Here it must be noted that immediately following the words "In Portugal the dogma of the Faith will always be preserved etc.", Our Lady said to Sister Lucy: "Tell this to no one, yes you may tell it to Francisco." The "this" that can be told to Francisco refers to the last thing said during the vision. If it was only a vision, without an explanation, then Francisco didn't need to be told anything, because he had just seen it himself already. But if "this" refers to additional words of the Virgin by way of explanation of the vision, then Francisco would have to be told because, as we know, he could not hear Our Lady during the Fatima apparitions. Francisco *saw* but did not *hear*, and would thus have needed to be informed about what Our Lady had *said* about the vision.

Nor can one argue plausibly that "you may tell it to Francisco" refers merely to the words Our Lady spoke during the second part of the Secret. The phrase "Tell this to no one. Yes, you may tell it to Francisco" follows immediately after "In Portugal the dogma of the Faith will always be preserved etc."[46] Clearly, then, the "etc." indicates the words, not yet written down, that Sister Lucy could *tell* Francisco orally. Those words clearly belong to the Third Secret, which was finally written down in 1944 under orders from the Bishop of Fatima.

## What Can Be Concluded Regarding Fact #11

Where, then, are the words of Our Lady to *explain* this vision? If Our Lady said nothing to explain this vision, Her actions would have been inconsistent over the course of the apparitions. Given that the teaching authority of the Church—meaning a formal papal or conciliar pronouncement—is not imposing a specific interpretation on this vision, and if we have not been given any special grace to understand this vision on our own, then there is all the more reason to believe that Our Lady would explain to us the meaning of the vision of the Third Secret of Fatima. And there is obviously an absolute need for the true explanation by Our Lady Herself.

In fact, Cardinal Ratzinger admits in *TMF* that his own comments are merely an *attempt* at an interpretation of the vision of the Third Secret:

> In what follows, therefore, we can only *attempt* to provide a deeper foundation for *this interpretation*, on the basis of the criteria already considered.[47] [emphasis added]

Cardinal Ratzinger also confirmed that a specific interpretation is *not being imposed* on this vision. On July 1, 2000, *The Washington Post* reported:

> Ratzinger, asked to comment on the pope's reading of the vision, said there is '*no official interpretation*' and that the text is not dogma.[48]

Now, does it seem likely that the Virgin of Fatima would have given the three children a vision so obscure that even the head of the CDF can only "attempt" to interpret it, when the rest of the Message of Fatima is not only crystal clear, but fully explained by the *Virgin's own words* in *all* its visional aspects—even the obvious vision of hell?

Furthermore, the probability of Our Lady having provided a detailed explanation of the Third Secret vision rises to the level of certainty when one considers the patently fraudulent "interpretation" offered by Sodano/Ratzinger/Bertone—i.e. that the killing of a Pope and many other members of the hierarchy by soldiers is merely the failed assassination attempt on John Paul II in 1981. Then there is Cardinal Ratzinger's bogus—bordering on blasphemous—"interpretation" of *devotion* to the Immaculate Heart, which he demotes to the "immaculate heart" of any one who avoids sin, and the *triumph* of the Immaculate Heart, which he reduces to the *fiat* of the Virgin 2,000 years ago.

These are not only lies, but clumsy lies. Our Lady of Fatima certainly foresaw these lies and provided a definitive explanation of the vision to combat them. The Mother of God would never allow such a fraudulent interpretation of Her Message to stand. This makes all the more urgent the disclosure of the true interpretation which is found, we are morally certain, in the missing words of the Virgin—most probably indicated by the "etc."

## Overall Conclusion from the Evidence

In conclusion, the evidence overwhelmingly supports the existence of two documents:

One document consists of four sheets of paper (with no margins) containing 62 lines of text copied from Sister Lucy's notebook (not written as a letter), which describes a vision seen by the three children of Fatima but does not contain any words of Our Lady. This text was written down by Sister Lucy on January 3, 1944, transferred to the Holy Office on April 4, 1957, read by Pope John Paul II on July 18, 1981 (but it did not move him to consecrate the world to the Immaculate Heart of Mary on June 7, 1981), was stored in the Holy Office, and released by the Vatican on June 26, 2000.

The other document is a one-page letter (with ¾ centimeter margins) containing about 25 lines of Our Lady's own words and sealed in an envelope. This text was written down by Sister Lucy on or very shortly before January 9, 1944, transferred to the Holy Office on April 16, 1957, read by Pope John Paul II in 1978 (moving him to consecrate the world to the Immaculate Heart of Mary on June 7, 1981), was stored in the Pope's apartment by his bedside, and to this day remains unreleased by the Vatican.

Can we state all these conclusions with absolute certainty? No, but we can state them with the moral certitude that they are true, because they are supported by a mountain of evidence indicating that something is missing from what the Vatican apparatus disclosed on June 26, 2000. It is certain that *someone* is lying to us. Either all of the witnesses who spoke of the Third Secret's reference to an apostasy and breakdown of faith and discipline in the Church are lying, or Cardinals Sodano and Ratzinger and Archbishop Bertone are lying. Either Sister Lucy is lying to us or Sodano/Ratzinger/Bertone are lying to us. One cannot have it both ways. We can have the moral certitude that Sister Lucy is not the liar. Therefore, we can have the moral certitude that the lies are emanating from Sodano, Ratzinger and Bertone.

And who, after all, is the more credible witness? Cardinal Ratzinger, for example, who has dramatically changed his testimony since 1984, or Sister Lucia of Fatima, who was chosen by God to be a witness to the Message of Fatima and whose testimony has been unwavering?[49] Moreover, if a witness such as Cardinal Ratzinger changes his testimony without bothering to explain the change, is it not obvious that he is being deceptive? Even if this were not the case, we still have the right to question his change of testimony, and we are entitled to an explanation.

Are there good grounds to disbelieve them, and to demand an investigation? There certainly are. Probable cause exists to accuse those we have named of not only fraudulent misrepresentation of the Message of Fatima, but fraudulent concealment as well.

Indeed, these highly disturbing discrepancies are chief among the reasons that have made it impossible for the Vatican to bury the Message of Fatima. The skepticism of even loyalists like Mother Angelica is only the tip of an iceberg of doubt among the faithful that is growing with each passing day.

# Chapter 13

## The Third Secret Fully Revealed

If, as seems to be the case—and as millions of responsible Catholics believe—there is more to the Third Secret than an ambiguous vision of the "Bishop dressed in White" with no explanation by Our Lady of Fatima, then in what would the missing part of the Secret consist? We have already suggested an answer. In this chapter, we develop the answer in some detail.

### Every Witness Agrees

The testimony of every single witness who has spoken on the question points to only one conclusion: the missing part of the Third Secret of Fatima foretells a catastrophic loss of faith and discipline in the human element of the Church—that is, in short, a great apostasy. Let us recall the testimonies on this point, which we first presented in Chapter 4:

### Pope Pius XII

> I am worried by *the Blessed Virgin's messages to Lucy of Fatima*. This persistence of Mary about the dangers which menace the Church is *a divine warning against the suicide of altering the Faith, in Her liturgy, Her theology and Her soul. …*

### Fr. Joseph Schweigl

> I cannot reveal anything of what I learned at Fatima concerning the Third Secret, but I can say that it has two parts: one concerns the Pope; the other logically (although I must say nothing) would have to be the continuation of the words: 'In Portugal, the dogma of the Faith will always be preserved.'

### Father Fuentes

On December 26, 1957, with an imprimatur and the approbation of the Bishop of Fatima, Father Fuentes published the following revelations by Sister Lucy concerning the Third Secret:

> Father, the Most Holy Virgin is very sad because no one has paid any attention to Her message, neither the good nor the bad. The good continue on their way but without giving any importance to Her message. The bad, not seeing the punishment of God falling upon them, continue their life of sin without even caring about the message. But believe me, Father, God will chastise the world and this will be in a terrible manner. *The punishment from heaven is imminent.*

*Father, how much time is there before 1960 arrives*? It will be very sad for everyone, not one person will rejoice at all if beforehand the world does not pray and do penance. *I am not able to give any other details because it is still a secret. ...*

*This is the Third part of the Messsage of Our Lady which will remain Secret until 1960.*

Tell them, Father, that many times, the most Holy Virgin told my cousins Francisco and Jacinita, as well as myself, that many nations will disappear from the face of the earth. She said that Russia will be the instrument of chastisement chosen by Heaven to punish the world if we do not obtain beforehand the conversion of that poor nation.

Father, the devil is in the mood for engaging in a decisive battle against the Blessed Virgin. And the devil knows what it is that most offends God and which in a short space of time will gain for him, the greatest number of souls. *Thus, the devil does everything to overcome souls consecrated to God, because in this way, the devil will succeed in leaving souls of the faithful abandoned by their leaders, thereby the more easily will he seize them.*

That which afflicts the Immaculate Heart of Mary and the Heart of Jesus is *the fall of religious and priestly souls*. The devil knows that *religious and priests who fall away from their beautiful vocation drag numerous souls to hell. ... The devil wishes to take possession of consecrated souls*. He tries to corrupt them in order to lull to sleep the souls of laypeople and thereby lead them to final impenitence.

## Father Alonso

Before his death in 1981, Father Joaquin Alonso, who for sixteen years was the official archivist of Fatima, testified as follows:

It is therefore completely probable that the text makes concrete references to the crisis of faith within the Church and to the negligence of the pastors themselves [and the] internal struggles in the very bosom of the Church and of grave pastoral negligence of the upper hierarchy.[1]

In the period preceding the great triumph of the Immaculate Heart of Mary, terrible things are to happen. These form the content of the third part of the Secret. What are they? If 'in Portugal the dogma of the Faith will always be preserved,' ... *it can be clearly deduced from this that in other parts of the Church these dogmas are going to become obscure or even lost altogether.*[2]

Does the unpublished text speak of concrete circumstances? It is very possible that it speaks not only of a real crisis of the faith in the Church during this in-between period, but like the secret of La Salette, for example, there are more concrete references to the internal struggles of Catholics or to the fall of priests and religious. *Perhaps it even refers to the failures of the upper hierarchy of the Church.* For that matter, none of this is foreign to other communications Sister Lucy has had on this subject.[3]

## Cardinal Ratzinger

[A]ccording to the judgment of the Popes, it would add nothing to what a Christian must know from Revelation: a radical call to conversion, the absolute seriousness of history, *the dangers threatening the faith and life of the Christian, and therefore the world.* And also the importance of the last times. ... If it is not published—at least for the moment—it is to avoid confusing religious prophecy with sensationalism. But the things contained in this Third Secret correspond to what is announced in Scripture and are confirmed by many other Marian apparitions, beginning with the Fatima apparitions themselves in their known contents.[4] (11 November 1984)

## Bishop Amaral

Its content concerns only our faith. To identify the Secret with catastrophic announcements or with a nuclear holocaust is to deform the meaning of the message. *The loss of faith of a continent is worse than the annihilation of a nation*; and it is true that faith is continually diminishing in Europe.[5]

It is important to note that, as part of the general attempt to conceal and suppress the truth about Fatima, Bishop Amaral was pressured to withdraw his remarks shortly after they were made. But then, ten years later, and now safely retired, the bishop casually *reaffirmed his testimony* in a public interview in 1995, adding a crucial bit of evidence: "Before I asserted in Vienna (in 1984) that the Third Secret concerned only our Faith and the loss of Faith *I had consulted Sister Lucy and first obtained her approval.*"[6] Thus, Sister Lucy herself indirectly confirmed, yet again, that the true and complete Third Secret of Fatima predicts apostasy in the Church.

## Cardinal Oddi

It [the Third Secret] has nothing to do with Gorbachev. The Blessed Virgin was alerting us against the apostasy in the Church.

## Cardinal Ciappi

To these witnesses we must add the testimony of two others. The first is Cardinal Mario Luigi Ciappi, who was nothing less than Pope John Paul II's own personal papal theologian. In a personal communication to a Professor Baumgartner in Salzburg, Cardinal Ciappi revealed that:

In the Third Secret it is foretold, among other things, that the great apostasy in the Church will begin *at the top*.[7]

## Father Valinho

Then there is Father Jose dos Santos Valinho, who is Sister Lucy's own nephew. In a book by Renzo and Roberto Allegri entitled *Reportage su Fatima*

[Milan 2000], published—providentially enough—very shortly before the disclosure of the Third Secret vision and the publication of *TMF* by Ratzinger/Bertone, Father Valinho expressed the view that the Third Secret predicts apostasy in the Church.[8]

In short, every single witness on the issue—even Cardinal Ratzinger in 1984—has testified to the same effect: the contents of the Third Secret of Fatima pertain to a crisis of faith in the Catholic Church, an apostasy, with grave consequences for the whole world. Not a single witness has ever denied that this is what the Third Secret portends. Nor has Sister Lucy ever corrected any of these testimonies, even though throughout her life she has not hesitated to correct those who misrepresented the contents of the Message of Fatima.

## Pope John Paul II Has Twice Revealed the Essence of the Secret

As if all this were not enough, on two occasions, in his own sermons at Fatima, Pope John Paul II himself has confirmed the essential contents of the Third Secret. It is apparent that Pope John Paul II told us essential elements of the Third Secret in his sermon at Fatima on May 13, 1982, as well as in his sermon during the beatification ceremony of Blessed Jacinta Marto and Blessed Francisco Marto at Fatima on May 13, 2000.

On the first occasion the Pope asked in his sermon: "Can the Mother who, with all the force of the love that She fosters in the Holy Spirit and desires everyone's salvation, can She remain silent when She sees the very bases of Her children's salvation *undermined*?" The Pope then answered his own question: "No, She cannot remain silent." Here the Pope himself tells us that the Fatima Message concerns Our Lady's warning that *the very bases of our salvation* are being undermined. Notice the striking parallel between this testimony and that of Pope Pius XII, who spoke of the suicide of altering the Faith in the Church's liturgy, theology and Her very soul.

Then, on May 13, 2000, the Pope in his sermon during the beatification ceremony warned the faithful as follows:

> "Another portent appeared in Heaven; behold, a great red dragon" (Apoc. 12: 3). These words from the first reading of the Mass make us think of the great struggle between good and evil, showing how, when man puts God aside, he cannot achieve happiness, but ends up destroying himself. ...
>
> The Message of Fatima is a call to conversion, alerting humanity ***to have nothing to do with the "dragon" whose "tail swept down a third of the stars of Heaven***, and dragged them to the earth" (Apoc. 12:4). ...
>
> Man's final goal is Heaven, his true home, where the heavenly Father awaits everyone with His merciful love. God does not want anyone to be lost; that is why 2,000 years ago He sent His Son to earth, "to seek and to save the lost" (Lk. 19:10). ...

> In Her motherly concern, the Blessed Virgin came here to Fatima to ask men and women "to stop offending God, Our Lord, who is already too much offended". It is a mother's sorrow that compels Her to speak; *the destiny of Her children is at stake*. For this reason She asks the little shepherds: "Pray, pray much and make sacrifices for sinners; *many souls go to hell because they have no one to pray and make sacrifices for them*".

We have already noted that His Holiness cited Chapter 12 verses 3 and 4 of the Book of the Apocalypse, and that the reference in those verses is commonly interpreted to mean one-third of the Catholic clergy being swept down from their exalted state through loss of faith or moral corruption—and we are certainly seeing both among the Catholic clergy today. Notice the exact coincidence of the Pope's sermon with Sister Lucy's warning to Father Fuentes about how "The devil knows that religious and priests who *fall away* from their beautiful vocation *drag* numerous souls to hell."

Therefore, it seems perfectly clear that Pope John Paul II was trying to tell us that the Third Secret relates to the great apostasy foretold in Sacred Scripture. Why did the Pope not say these things directly and explicitly, but rather in a somewhat hidden manner, in language only the more learned would grasp? *It seems likely that he was sending a signal to the more astute about what he thought was going to be revealed very soon—namely, the whole of the Third Secret.* As it turned out, of course, we received only the vision of the "Bishop dressed in White" and the so-called "commentary" in *TMF*. Perhaps the Pope recognized the strength of the resistance posed by Cardinal Sodano and his collaborators, and hoped that he would at least be able to disclose in his sermon the essence of the Secret in the hope that sooner or later the whole truth would come out. Perhaps the Pope does not feel that he can speak freely, precisely because he had allowed himself to be surrounded by clerics, religious, bishops and Cardinals whom he has discovered now to be untrustworthy but whom he feels unable to replace, *who are* still in office and *who are* undermining the Faith, *who are* part of that one-third of the consecrated souls swept down from their high stations by the devil. Perhaps the Pope either does not know who they are, or he does know but does not think he can speak out publicly and survive for long. (We recall here the sudden death of John Paul I.) Whatever the reason, the Pope is not speaking very clearly—yet clearly enough that one can discern his meaning. As Jesus told His disciples on one occasion: "He who has ears to hear, let him hear."

So, not only is every witness, from the future Pius XII in the 1930s through Sister Lucy's own nephew in the year 2000, unanimous on this point, but the reigning Pope adds his own voice to theirs: the Third Secret foretells a widespread loss of faith and fall from grace among the Catholic clergy of various ranks.

Now, the first two parts of the Secret of Fatima say absolutely nothing about apostasy in the Church. Likewise, the visional portion of the Third Secret, concerning the "Bishop dressed in White", says absolutely nothing about an apostasy. If every witness says that the Third Secret speaks of apostasy in the Church, yet those portions of the Message of Fatima revealed to date, including the vision of "a Bishop dressed in White", say nothing about it, the inescapable conclusion is that some portion of the Third Secret has been withheld. What does this portion actually say?

The logical place to begin is with the telltale phrase that the Vatican apparatus has been at great pains to demote and obscure as if it were a mere footnote to the Message of Fatima: "In Portugal the dogma of the Faith will always be preserved etc." This phrase is the only evident reference to a coming apostasy in the published portions of the Message (although we hasten to add, that even without this phrase, it would still be clear from all the evidence that the Third Secret relates to an apostasy in the Church). Here, *and only here*, the revealed portion of the integral Message of Fatima touches upon the question of the *dogmas* of the Faith, and how they will be *preserved* in Portugal.

What would be the point of Our Lady mentioning the *preservation of dogma* in Portugal if not to warn us that dogma was *not* going to be preserved elsewhere in the Church? And, as we have earlier suggested, the "elsewhere" is undoubtedly described in the words comprised within Sister Lucy's "etc."

Given that the vision published on June 26, 2000 contains no further words of Our Lady, it can only be concluded that the missing words of Our Lady are found in the "sound track", as it were, of the Third Secret, in which Our Lady would explain the vision. The vision, it would seem, is the end result of this catastrophic loss of faith: The Pope and remaining hierarchy are being hunted down and killed outside the half-ruined city of Rome, perhaps (we can only speculate since the words of Our Lady are missing) after a nuclear holocaust.

This, indeed, fits perfectly with Cardinal Ratzinger's admission in 1984 that the Third Secret relates to "dangers to the faith and the life of the Christian, and therefore *of the world.*" On the figurative level, the corpses surrounding the Pope as he walks haltingly toward the hill where he is executed by soldiers would represent the victims of apostasy, and the half-ruined city the condition of the Church during this time of apostasy.

## The Greatest Threat of All:<br>The Loss of Catholic Dogma

When Mother Angelica stated on national television on May 16, 2001 that she believes "we didn't get the whole thing" [i.e., the whole Third Secret] because "I think it's scary," she was surely correct. There is nothing more frightening than the danger of a widespread loss of Faith in the Church, especially when the danger emanates "from the top" as Cardinal Ciappi, the Pope's own personal theologian, said concerning the Third Secret. The result of this danger, if it is not averted, will be the eternal damnation of millions of souls. And who knows how many have been lost already for lack of the Third Secret's salutary warnings and advice?

The vision published on June 26, however, simply does not express anything that frightening. The vision, in fact, expresses *nothing* so terrible that the Vatican would have kept it under lock and key for forty years. Indeed, Cardinal Ratzinger would have us believe that the Third Secret, as represented by the vision alone, contains "no great surprises". That is because the surprises follow the still-hidden conclusion of the phrase "In Portugal the dogma of the Faith will always be preserved etc"—again, the very phrase the Cardinal's "commentary" has removed from the integral text of Our Lady's words in Sister Lucy's Fourth Memoir.

Now, when the Pope spoke of "the very bases of our salvation undermined" in his Fatima sermon in 1982, he certainly meant the undermining of the Catholic Faith. We know this from the constant teaching of the Catholic Church. For example, the Athanasian Creed says: "Whoever wishes to be saved must before all else adhere to the Catholic faith. He must preserve this faith whole and inviolate; otherwise he shall most certainly perish in eternity." The foundation of our salvation is belonging to the Catholic Church and holding on to our Catholic Faith whole and inviolate. The loss of this foundation must be what the Third Secret concerns. Every witness says so, John Paul II says so, and the telltale phrase "In Portugal the dogma of the Faith will always be preserved etc." also says so.

As Our Lord warned us: "What does it profit a man to gain the whole world if he loses his own eternal soul?" If a person loses his soul for the new orientation of the Church, the New World Order, the One World Religion, or the promise of peace and prosperity in the world, it profits him nothing, for he will burn in hell for all eternity. For this reason alone, the Third Secret is vitally important to us. It could not be any more important, because it concerns the salvation of our own individual souls. It also concerns the salvation of the souls of the Pope, Cardinals, bishops, priests, and indeed of every living person. Thus, the Third Secret concerns every man, woman and child on the face of the earth, and particularly Catholics.

We recall again that in 1984 Cardinal Ratzinger admitted that if the Secret was not published "at least for now" it was to "avoid confusing religious *prophecy* with sensationalism"—a far cry from his claim today that, according to Sodano's Party Line, the Third Secret culminated in 1981 with the failed assassination attempt. Further, the Third Secret is a prophecy that began to be realized in 1960, which Sister Lucy said was the year by which the prophecy will be "much clearer" (*mais claro*). As Frère Michel points out, a prophecy that starts to be realized obviously becomes much clearer. The prophecy, therefore, started to be realized at least by 1960. It is, therefore, a prophecy that tells us *about our time*. It is a loving warning from Our Lady, and also advice on how to respond to the clear and present danger in the Church.

Now let us look more closely at the essence of the Third Secret. As Cardinal Ratzinger admitted 18 years ago—again, before Cardinal Sodano issued the Party Line on Fatima—the Third Secret concerns, first of all, the dangers to the Faith. St. John tells us what it is that overcomes the world: he says it is our faith. *Therefore, in order for the world to overcome the Church, it first has to overcome our faith as Catholics*.

The Third Secret's essence then concerns the world's attempt to overcome our Catholic Faith. As we have demonstrated abundantly in the previous chapters, the forces of the world have conducted a major assault on the Catholic Faith since 1960. There is simply no question about this, based on the overwhelming evidence which we have only outlined here.

Still more particularly, the Secret concerns the *dogma* of the Faith. Our Lady of Fatima spoke about the *dogma* of the Faith always being preserved in Portugal, not simply "the Faith." Why did Our Lady focus on Catholic *dogma*? Clearly, She did so because the Secret is a prophecy that Catholic dogma, *specifically*, would be the target of those who would attack the Church from within and without. As Our Lord Himself warned us in Sacred Scripture: "For false Christs and false prophets shall rise, and shall show signs and wonders, to seduce, if it were possible, even the elect" (Mk. 13:22). As the Arian crisis demonstrates, these false prophets can include even priests and bishops. We recall here Cardinal Newman's description of that time in Church history: "The comparatively few who remained faithful were discredited and driven into exile; the rest were either *deceivers or deceived."* In such times of crisis, Catholics must adhere to the dogmas of the Faith.

What is dogma? Dogma is what has been *infallibly defined by the Church.* Dogma is what Catholics must believe in order to be Catholic. The dogmas of the Faith are what is contained in the solemn, infallible definitions of the Magisterium—namely, the Pope alone, speaking in a way that clearly binds the Universal Church to believe in what he is pronouncing, or an ecumenical council of all the Catholic bishops presided over by the Pope which issues such binding pronouncements, or those things taught by the Ordinary and Universal Magisterium of the Church.

What is meant by the *infallible* definition of dogma? The word infallible means *"cannot fail"*. Therefore, the definitions of the Faith, solemnly defined by the Church, cannot fail. We know what the Faith is, what the dogmas of the Faith are, by means of the *infallible* definitions. *If we believe and hold fast to these infallible definitions, then we cannot be deceived in those matters so defined.*

How do we know that a matter has been defined infallibly as an article of the Catholic faith? We know it from the manner in which the teaching is presented.

## Four Sources of Infallible Teaching

There are four principal ways Church teaching is presented to us infallibly:

First, through the promulgation of *creeds* by the Popes and ecumenical councils, which provide a summary of what Catholics must believe in order to be Catholic.

Second, by means of solemn *definitions* containing such phrases as "We declare, pronounce and define," or some similar formula indicating that the Pope or the Pope together with an ecumenical council clearly intend to bind the Church to believe in the teaching. Such definitions are usually accompanied by *anathemas* (condemnations) of those who would in any way deny the defined teaching.

Third, the definitions of the Ordinary and Universal Magisterium.

Fourth, there are definitive judgements of the Pope, usually *condemned propositions*, which are those propositions a Catholic is *forbidden* to believe. When a Pope, or a Pope and council together, solemnly condemn a proposition, we can know infallibly that it is contrary to the Catholic Faith.

An example of a *creed* is the Profession of Faith promulgated by the Council of Trent. We present it here, conveniently arranged in the form of points, with the language unaltered:

- I, N., with firm faith believe and profess each and every article contained in the Symbol of faith which the holy Roman Church uses; namely:
- I believe in one God, the Father almighty, maker of heaven and earth, and of all things visible and invisible; and in
- one Lord Jesus Christ, the only-begotten Son of God, born of the Father before all ages; God from God, light from light, true God from true God; begotten not made, of one substance (consubstantial) with the Father; through whom all things were made;
- who for us men and for our salvation came down from heaven, and was made incarnate by the Holy Spirit of the Virgin Mary, and was made man.
- He was crucified also for us under Pontius Pilate, died, and was buried; and
- He rose again the third day according to the Scriptures, and ascended into heaven;
- He sits at the right hand of the Father, and He shall come again in glory to judge the living and the dead, and of His kingdom there will be no end.
- And I believe in the Holy Spirit, the Lord, and giver of life, who proceeds from the Father and the Son; who equally with the Father and the Son is adored and glorified; who spoke through the prophets.
- And I believe that there is one, holy, Catholic, and apostolic Church.
- I confess one baptism for the remission of sins; and I hope for the resurrection of the dead, and the life of the world to come. Amen.
- I resolutely accept and embrace the apostolic and ecclesiastical traditions and the other practices and regulations of that same Church.
- In like manner I accept Sacred Scripture according to the meaning which has been held by holy Mother Church and which she now

holds. It is Her prerogative to pass judgement on the true meaning and interpretation of Sacred Scripture. And I will never accept or interpret it in a manner different from the unanimous agreement of the Fathers.

- I also acknowledge that there are truly and properly seven sacraments of the New Law, instituted by Jesus Christ our Lord, and that they are necessary for the salvation of the human race, although it is not necessary for each individual to receive them all.
- I acknowledge that the seven sacraments are: Baptism, Confirmation, Eucharist, Penance, Extreme Unction, Holy Orders, and Matrimony; and that they confer grace; and that of the seven, Baptism, Confirmation, and Holy Orders cannot be repeated without committing a sacrilege.
- I also accept and acknowledge the customary and approved rites of the Catholic Church in the solemn administration of these sacraments.
- I embrace and accept each and every article on Original Sin and justification declared and defined in the most holy Council of Trent.
- I likewise profess that in the Mass a true, proper, and propitiatory sacrifice is offered to God on behalf of the living and the dead, and that the Body and Blood together with the Soul and Divinity of our Lord Jesus Christ is truly, really, and substantially present in the most holy Sacrament of the Eucharist, and that there is a change of the whole substance of the bread into the Body, and of the whole substance of the wine into the Blood; and this change the Catholic Church calls transubstantiation.
- I also profess that the whole and entire Christ and a true Sacrament is received under each separate species.
- I firmly hold that there is a purgatory, and that the souls detained there are helped by the prayers of the faithful.
- I likewise hold that the saints reigning together with Christ should be honored and invoked, that they offer prayers to God on our behalf, and that their relics should be venerated.
- I firmly assert that images of Christ, of the Mother of God ever Virgin, and of the other saints should be owned and kept, and that due honor and veneration should be given to them.
- I affirm that the power of indulgences was left in the keeping of the Church by Christ, and that the use of indulgences is very beneficial to Christians.
- I acknowledge the holy, Catholic, and apostolic Roman Church as the mother and teacher of all churches; and

- I promise and swear true obedience to the Roman Pontiff, vicar of Christ and successor of Blessed Peter, Prince of the Apostles.
- I unhesitatingly accept and profess all the doctrines (especially those concerning the primacy of the Roman Pontiff and his infallible teaching authority[9]) handed down, defined, and explained by the sacred canons and ecumenical councils and especially those of this most holy Council of Trent (and by the ecumenical Vatican Council I). And at the same time:
- I condemn, reject, and anathematize everything that is contrary to those propositions, and all heresies without exception that have been condemned, rejected, and anathematized by the Church.
- I, N., promise, vow, and swear that, with God's help, I shall most constantly hold and profess this true Catholic faith, outside which no one can be saved and which I now freely profess and truly hold. With the help of God, I shall profess it whole and unblemished to my dying breath; and, to the best of my ability, I shall see to it that my subjects or those entrusted to me by virtue of my office hold it, teach it, and preach it. So help me God and His holy Gospel.

As for solemn and infallible *definitions* of Catholic dogma, one recent example is the Apostolic Letter of Pius XI, *Ineffabilis Deus* (1854), infallibly defining the dogma of the Immaculate Conception of Mary:

> We *declare, pronounce, and define* that the doctrine which holds that the most Blessed Virgin Mary, in the first instance of Her conception, by a singular grace and privilege granted by Almighty God, in view of the merits of Jesus Christ, the Savior of the human race, was preserved free from all stain of Original Sin, is a doctrine revealed by God and therefore to be believed firmly and constantly by all the faithful.
>
> Hence, if anyone shall dare—which God forbid!—to think otherwise than as has been defined by us, let him know and understand that *he is condemned by his own judgment; that he has suffered shipwreck in the faith*; that he has separated from the unity of the Church; and that, furthermore, by his own action he incurs the penalties established by law if he should dare to express in words or writing or by any other outward means the errors he think in his heart.

Here we recall that in *TMF* Cardinal Ratzinger blatantly undermined this dogma—and the Message of Fatima—by daring to claim that "According to Matthew 5:8, the 'immaculate heart' is *a* heart which, with God's grace, has come to perfect interior unity and therefore 'sees God.'" No, no, no! The Immaculate Heart is not "a" heart, but *the* heart—the one and only heart—of the Blessed Virgin Mary, Who is the only merely human being Who was conceived without Original Sin and Who never committed even the slightest personal sin during Her glorious life on this earth.

Finally, there is the *condemned proposition.* A prime example of this is the *Syllabus of Errors* of Blessed Pius IX, wherein this great Pope enumerated the many errors of liberalism in the form of propositions which he solemnly, definitively and infallibly condemned as errors against the Faith,[10] including proposition #80 (which we mentioned earlier): "The Roman Pontiff can and ought to reconcile himself and come to terms with progress, liberalism and modern civilization."

As we have shown, here too Cardinal Ratzinger has sought to undermine prior Church teaching, telling us that the teaching of Vatican II was a "countersyllabus" which was "an attempt at an official reconciliation with the new era inaugurated in 1789" and an effort to correct what he dared to call "the *one-sidedness* of the position adopted by the Church under Blessed Pius IX and Saint Pius X in response to the situation created by the new phase of history inaugurated by the French Revolution ..."[11] To make his rejection of the solemn, infallible teaching of Blessed Pope Pius IX even more explicit, Cardinal Ratzinger declares that at Vatican II, "the attitude of critical reserve toward the forces that have left their imprint on the modern world is to be replaced by a *coming to terms* with their movement."[12] This opinion of Cardinal Ratzinger's flatly contradicts the teaching of Blessed Pope Pius IX that the Church *must not* "come to terms" with "progress, liberalism and modern civilization."

Ratzinger's outrageous abuse of the dogma of the Immaculate Conception and his arrogant dismissal of the *Syllabus* as "one-sided" exposes the very core of the post-conciliar crisis in the Church: an assault on *the infallible definitions* of the Magisterium.

Now, for the most part, this assault has been rather indirect. The infallible definition is usually not directly denied, but rather *undermined* through criticism or "revision." The innovators in the Church are not so stupid as simply to declare that an infallible Church teaching is wrong. And, in their supposed "enlightenment" these innovators may actually think they are "deepening" or "developing" Catholic teaching for the good of the Church—again, we are not judging their subjective motivations. But the *effect* of what they do is obvious: the undermining of the infallibly defined teachings of the Magisterium.

Another example of this undermining is the attack on the dogma that outside the Catholic Church there is no salvation. The Tridentine creed, quoted in full above, states: "I shall most constantly hold and profess this true Catholic faith, outside which no one can be saved ..." In Chapter 6 we show how, over and over again, the Magisterium has solemnly defined the dogma that there is no salvation outside the Catholic Church. Yet today, the dogma is denied and *undermined* by an "ecumenism" which declares that neither the Protestant heretics nor the Orthodox schismatics need return to the Catholic Church, because this is "outdated ecclesiology."[13] And in many places today, the dogma is directly denied, and in other places it is not directly denied but in practice it collapses from insidious, repeated, indirect attacks and, as a result, it is no longer believed and followed in those places.

It is undeniable that since Vatican II a host of novel notions has been passed off in the Church as "development" of Catholic doctrine, even though these novelties at least implicitly (and somtimes explicitly) contradict and undermine the infallible definitions. The idea, for example, that the Council document *Gaudium et Spes* is a "countersyllabus" that counters the solemn condemnations of Blessed Pius IX[14] undermines the whole integrity of the infallible Magisterium. Such talk is an assault on the very credibility of the teaching office of the Church, and is thus, in the end, an assault on Catholic dogma itself.

## There Cannot be a "New Understanding" of Catholic Dogma

This post-conciliar attack on dogma through undermining and implicit contradiction cannot be justified as a "development" or "new insight" into dogma. As the First Vatican Council solemnly taught: "For, the Holy Spirit was not promised to the successors of Peter that they might disclose *new doctrine*, but that by His help they might guard sacredly the revelation transmitted through the apostles and the deposit of faith, and might faithfully set it forth."[15]

Further, as Vatican I taught, there cannot be any "new understanding" of what the Church has already infallibly defined:

> [T]hat understanding of its sacred dogmas must be *perpetually retained,* which Holy Mother Church has once declared; and there must never be a recession [moving away] from that meaning under the specious name of a deeper understanding.[16]

Thus, it is a matter of Catholic Faith that we believe that *no new doctrine has been revealed by God since the death of the last Apostle, Saint John* and that *no new understanding of doctrine* has arisen because of Vatican II or otherwise.

Therefore, this "new" doctrine or "counter"-doctrine we have heard so much about since Vatican II can only be pseudo-doctrine. This pseudo-doctrine is being taught very subtly. When pseudo-doctrine contradicts doctrines that have been infallibly defined, then Catholics must cling to the infallible doctrines and reject the "new" doctrines.

The dogma of the Faith *cannot* fail, but novelties can fail us. Men can fail; lay people can fail; priests can fail; bishops can fail; Cardinals can fail; and even the Pope can fail in matters which do not involve his charism of infallibility, as history has shown us with more than one Pope who taught or appeared to teach some novelty.

For example, Pope Honorius was posthumously condemned by the Third Council of Constantinople in 680 A.D. for aiding and abetting heresy,[17] and that condemnation was approved by Pope Leo II and repeated by later Popes. As another example, John XXII, back in the 14th Century (1333 A.D.), gave sermons (but not solemn definitions) in which he insisted that the blessed departed do not enjoy the Beatific Vision until the day of General Judgment. For this he was denounced and corrected by theologians, and he finally retracted his heretical opinion on his deathbed.

In the case of John XXII, knowledgeable Catholics (in this case theologians) knew that John XXII was wrong in his teaching about the Particular Judgment. They knew that something was wrong with John XXII's teaching because it contradicted what the Church had always believed, even if there had not yet been an infallible definition. Catholics who knew their faith in the 14th Century did not simply say: "Oh, the Pope has given a sermon, therefore we must change our belief." Looking at the Church's constant teaching that the Blessed departed enjoy the Beatific Vision immediately after Purgatory, the theologians knew John XXII was wrong, and they told him so.

As it turned out, the immediacy of the Beatific Vision was solemnly and infallibly defined by John XXII's successor in 1336. This placed the matter beyond all further dispute—which is precisely why an infallible definition was needed. The same is true with every other matter infallibly defined by the Church. We can, and must, rely on these infallible definitions with absolute certainty, rejecting all opinions to the contrary—even if contrary opinions were to come from a Cardinal or even a Pope.

There are other examples of Popes failing. Even the first Pope, St. Peter, failed, as shown in Sacred Scripture—not by what he said but by the example he gave. Peter refused to sit at table with Gentile converts, in Antioch about 50 A.D. By shunning these converts he gave the false impression that the First Council of Jerusalem was wrong in its infallible teaching that the Mosaic ceremonial law, including the prohibition against Jews eating with "unclean" Gentiles, was not binding on the Catholic Church. This was the incident for which St. Paul rebuked St. Peter to his face in public. (Gal. 2:11)

Another example is Pope Liberius in 357 A.D. (or thereabouts), who failed by signing a Creed which the Arians proposed to him, leaving out any reference to the Son being consubstantial with the Father. He did this after two years in exile and under the threat of death. And he also failed (under duress while in exile) by wrongly condemning and excommunicating—in reality, only giving the appearance of excommunicating—St. Athanasius, who was defending the Faith in this matter. Pope Liberius, the first Pope not to be proclaimed a saint by the Church, was wrong because Athanasius was teaching the Catholic doctrine—the true doctrine, the infallible doctrine—taught infallibly by the Council of Nicea in 325 AD. It was that infallible definition, not the defective teaching of Pope Liberius, that had to be followed in that case.

From these examples in Church history we learn that *everything* proposed to us for our belief must be judged by those definitions. And so if a Cardinal, a bishop, a priest, a layman *or even the Pope* teaches us some novelty that is contrary to any definition of the Faith, we can know that the teaching is wrong and that it must be rejected for the salvation of our immortal souls. Yes, even the Pope can fail, *and he does fail* if he expresses an opinion that is contrary to a solemn, infallible definition of the Catholic Church. This does not mean the *Church* fails when this happens, but only that the Pope has made a mistake without imposing it on the whole Church. And, of course, if even the Pope can make a mistake in teaching some novelty, then certainly Cardinals, bishops and priests can make mistakes in their teaching and opinions.

And so, when Our Lady speaks about the "dogma of the Faith", She indicates to us that the danger to the Faith—and to "the life of the Christian and therefore (the life) of the world", to recall Cardinal Ratzinger's admission—will arise when solemn dogmatic definitions of the Catholic Faith are contradicted or undermined; for it is these definitions which are the very foundation of the Catholic Faith, and therefore the foundation of our salvation, to recall the Pope's 1982 sermon at Fatima.

To the objection that mere priests, or mere lay people, cannot disagree with high-ranking prelates like Cardinal Ratzinger, or even (in the kind of extraordinary case for which we have just given examples) the Pope, one must reply: That is why the Church has infallible definitions. It is by measuring any given teaching against solemn, infallible definitions that one can know that a teaching is true or false—not by what rank in the clergy a person has. As St. Paul taught: "But though we, or an angel from Heaven, preach a gospel to you besides that which we have preached to you, let him be anathema." (Gal. 1:8) The faithful are to regard *even an Apostle* as anathema—accursed, cut off from the Church, worthy of hellfire—if he contradicts the infallible teaching of the Church. That is why theologians were able to correct Pope John XXII in his erroneous teaching from the pulpit; and it is why Catholics today can tell right from wrong teaching, even if they have a rank lower than the prelate who is committing the error.

A prime historical example of this is found in the case of a lawyer named Eusebius, who pointed out that Nestorius, a high-ranking Archbishop in Constantinople, the highest ranking prelate after the Pope, was wrong when he denied that Mary is the Mother of God. Eusebius stood up in his pew on Christmas Day, during Mass, and denounced Nestorius for preaching heresy. Yet all the "high-ranking" priests and bishops had remained silent in the face of Nestorius' heresy. Thus, a mere layman was right and all the rest of them were in error. The Council of Ephesus was called to hear the matter, and it was solemnly and infallibly defined that Mary is the Mother of God. And since Nestorius refused to recant, he was deposed and declared a heretic. Nestorius was excommunicated!

To summarize, truth is not a matter of numbers or rank; truth is a matter of what Christ and God have revealed in Sacred Scripture and Tradition, what has been solemnly defined by the Catholic Church, and what the Catholic Church has always taught—taught *always*, not just since 1965!

## The Disastrous Effects of Tampering With Infallible Definitions

History likewise provides us with a prime example of what can happen to the Church when even one dogma is contradicted on a wide scale. The heresy of Arianism caused catastrophic confusion in the Church from 336 A.D. to 381 A.D. Arianism was condemned in 325 A.D.; and yet in 336, it arose again. Beginning around 336, the heresy eventually claimed about 90% of the bishops before it was finally defeated about fifty years later. In the resulting confusion and loss of faith, even the great St. Athanasius was "excommunicated" by the Pope in 357. By 381 Arianism had been defeated by the First Council of Constantinople. However, it was still in full bloom for some time between 360 and 380. The results were utterly devastating to the Church.

The Arian crisis has more to teach us about the probable contents of the missing text of the Third Secret. One reason the Arians were able to succeed for a time, was that they "successfully" attacked a *dogma* that had been solemnly and infallibly defined at the Council of Nicea in 325 —that Christ is God from God, Light from Light, true God from true God; begotten not made, *consubstantial with the Father*. This solemn and infallible definition is in the Credo of the Council of Nicea, which we say every Sunday at Mass.

The Arians overturned the definition by getting many of the "faithful" to argue for replacing it with a false definition that was not infallible. In 336 they replaced the Greek word *Homoousion* with another word *Homoiousion*. The word *Homoousion* basically means "consubstantial" with the Father. For God the Son to be consubstantial with the Father, the Son must not only be God but the *same* one God as the Father, so that the substance of the Father *is* the substance of the Son, even though the Person of the Father is not the Person of the Son. Thus, there are three Persons in one God—Father, Son and Holy Ghost—but there is only one God, with one *substance,* in three Persons. That is the mystery of the Trinity. The new word *Homoiousion*, however, means "of *similar* substance" to the Father. Thus, the critical phrase in the dogma—"consubstantial with the Father"—was changed to "of similar substance with the Father" or "like the Father."

Thus the Arians brought about mass confusion in the Church by adding *one letter* to the word *Homoousion* to create a new word with a new meaning: *Homoiousion*. They attacked a solemn definition, claiming that their new definition would be better than the solemn definition. But, of course, the new definition could not be better than the solemn definition, because the solemn definition of the Council of Nicea was infallible.

By adding *one letter to one word,* the Arians got rid of an infallible definition. This opened the way for the Arians and the semi-Arians, leading to actual warfare. People were martyred, persecuted, driven out into the desert, driven into exile over this *one* change to *one* infallible dogma. St. Athanasius was driven into exile five different times by the Synod of Egypt (and spent at least 17 years in exile as a result.) But he was right and the heretical bishops of that Synod were all wrong.

## Infallible Definitions Are Higher than Any Learning or Rank in the Church

Why did Athanasius know he was right? Because he clung to the infallible definition, no matter what everyone else said. Not all the learning in the world, nor all the rank of office, can substitute for the truth of one infallibly defined Catholic teaching. Even the simplest member of the faithful, clinging to an infallible definition, will know more than the most "learned" theologian who denies or undermines the definition. *That is the whole purpose of the Church's infallibly defined teaching*—to make us independent of the mere opinions of men, however learned, however high their rank.

Now, in 325 the solemn definition of the Council of Nicea *was* infallible, but many people then did not fully realize that solemn definitions of the Faith were infallible. That is, at this time in Church history the Church had not yet issued the solemn definition teaching that the definitions of Faith are infallible. But in 1870, the First Vatican Council solemnly and infallibly defined the infallibility of the Church's solemn definitions. Now we know, infallibly, that solemn definitions are infallible. Once again: they cannot fail—*ever*.

## The Infallible Definitions Are Under Attack in Our Time

In our day, therefore, there is no excuse for being taken in by heresy and giving up the defense of solemn definitions. But that is precisely what is happening today, just as in the time of Arius. *Churchmen are judging things in light of the Second Vatican Council instead of judging the Second Vatican Council in light of the infallible definitions.* They have forgotten that the infallible definitions, not Vatican II, are the unchanging standard by which one measures every doctrine, just as a 36-inch yardstick is the unchanging standard for measuring a yard. One does not suddenly decide that the new standard for measuring a yard is a 35-inch stick. Likewise, the Church cannot suddenly decide that Vatican II is the new yardstick of the Faith.

And so we arrive again, after a more detailed examination, at the crux of the Third Secret. *This* is why it begins with Our Lady's reference to the *dogma* of the Faith. This is why Sister Lucy said the Third Secret would be "much clearer" after 1960. And here it must be noted that we are clearly living in the midst of the period of calamity the Third Secret predicts. How do we know this? Because the Virgin has told us that the Secret would "be clearer" as of 1960 and She has also told us that *in the end* Her Immaculate Heart will triumph. Since the Triumph of the Immaculate Heart is obviously not yet upon us, we must be living in the interim period between 1960 and that final Triumph—that is, the period encompassed by the prophecy of the Third Secret.

Now what we have seen since the Second Vatican Council is, again, an attack—a very subtle, indirect attack—on the solemn definitions of the Church. We have had a so-called *pastoral* council that refused to speak with solemn definitions and—in the view of some—actually went against certain solemn definitions. But the Council, as we have seen, wished to be "pastoral", to avoid solemn definitions, to avoid condemnations of error, as Pope John XXIII declared in his opening speech.

Well, what is wrong with that? What is wrong is that by the subtle mistake of refusing to make solemn definitions, the door is opened for a Council to use language that could undermine *existing* solemn definitions—exactly this trick was used by the Arians in the Fourth Century in order to bring about confusion in the Church. And they almost succeeded in overcoming the whole Church.

This same process has been occurring again since the opening of the Second Vatican Council. But the faithful have a remedy for the problem: Vatican II is not authoritative to the extent it did not exercise its supreme Magisterium, its power to define doctrine and its power to anathematize error. Since it did not exercise this authority, everything taught by Vatican II that had not been taught infallibly *before* Vatican II has to be examined in light of the infallible dogmatic definitions and teachings of the Catholic Church.

However, that is not what is happening today. What is happening today is people are redefining "the faith" in light of Vatican II. It is surely this process that Our Lady of Fatima speaks about when, going right to the heart of the matter, She says that the *dogma* of the Faith will always be preserved in Portugal—but clearly lost in many other places—telling Sister Lucy that this warning must be made known *by 1960*, by which time the Council had been announced.

This conclusion is confirmed by the Pope's sermons at Fatima in 1982 and 2000. In 1982 the Pope said that the bases of our salvation were being *undermined*. And in 2000, in his sermon during the beatification of Blessed Jacinta and Blessed Francisco, Pope John Paul II warned us about the dangers to our salvation *today* by telling us that "The Message of Fatima is a call to conversion, alerting humanity *to have nothing to do with the 'dragon' whose 'tail swept down a third of the stars of heaven, and dragged them to the earth'* (Apoc. 12:4)." Again, where do we find this in the revealed parts of the Fatima Message? Nowhere. It must, therefore, be in the Third Secret. The Pope is telling us that the Third Secret concerns dangers to the Faith and that one-third of the Catholic clergy are involved.

## The Attack is From *Within* the Church

Now we will focus on yet another particular of the Third Secret's essence. The Pope also pointed out that the attack on the Catholic Faith is coming from *within*. He said in 1982: "Can the Mother with all the force of the love that She fosters in the Holy Spirit and who desires everyone's salvation, can She remain silent when She sees the very basis of Her children's salvation *undermined*?" The word *undermine* implies a weakening of the foundation of our salvation from within. An external enemy of the Church attacks from without, an infiltrator from within. In the latter case, the attack is not expected and everyone's guard is down; the attacker is viewed as a "friend."

So we have Pope John Paul II telling us that the Catholic Faith is being undermined from within (May 13, 1982: "the very basis of Her children's salvation undermined") by the Catholic clergy (May 13, 2000: "one-third of the stars of heaven").

We conclude this point by noting that there is another source from which we can glean this aspect of the Third Secret. In 1963 the German publication *Neues Europa* revealed what was purported to be part of the Third Secret: that Cardinal would oppose Cardinal, bishop oppose bishop. We know that when asked whether the *Neues Europa* account should be published, Cardinal Ottaviani, who also had read the Third Secret—who had a very dry personality and was pretty much indifferent to most apparitions—exclaimed very emphatically: "Publish 10,000 copies! Publish 20,000 copies! Publish 30,000 copies!"[18]

Then we have the testimony of the late Father Malachi Martin that the message of Garabandal contains the Third Secret or parts of the Third Secret. Father Martin, who knew the Third Secret because he had read it himself, and who also read the message of Garabandal, said that because the Vatican chose not to release the Third Secret in 1960, Our Lady had appeared at Garabandal in 1961 in order to disclose the Third Secret. What is in the Garabandal message? The Garabandal message says, among other things: "many Cardinals, bishops, and priests are on the road to hell and 'dragging' many more souls with them". Notice yet again the concept of *dragging* souls down into hell. The same terminology appears in Sister Lucy's remark to Father Fuentes that "The devil knows that religious and priests who fall away from their beautiful vocation *drag* numerous souls to hell,"[19] and in the Pope's sermon on May 13, 2000, which refers to the scene in the Book of the Apocalypse in which the tail of the dragon drags one-third of the stars (consecrated souls) from Heaven.

While the Garabandal apparitions are not formally approved, the Bishop with jurisdiction over Garabandal—that is, the Bishop of Santander—said that nothing in the message was contrary to the Catholic Faith.

## The Attack Includes Bad *Practices* As Well As Bad Doctrine

Here it must be noted that whether a member of the clergy (or the laity) is good or bad is not determined solely by whether he verbally upholds or does not uphold the Faith. Besides comparing the teaching (i.e. the words) of a priest, a bishop, a Cardinal or the Pope to the infallible teaching of the Magisterium, one needs to see if the person is also upholding the orthodox *practices* of the Catholic Church by his words (written and spoken), by his actions and by the Christian conduct of his life. One needs to know if the person (priest, bishop, Cardinal or Pope) is engaging in *heteropraxis*—practices contrary to the Faith—such as disrespect for the Blessed Sacrament.

The Faith can be attacked by *actions* done in either an obvious or a subtle manner. *Our actions must support our words.* We uphold the Faith by upholding the doctrines in our thoughts, words, and writings and also by upholding the pious practices of the Church that support our adherence to the Faith. By introducing novel practices into the local parish (or the local diocese or the local ecclesiastical province, or even into the Universal Church as Catholic Doctors have written it is possible to happen) that give the *impression* that the defined Faith is not to be believed, one scandalizes the little ones and even some learned souls by this *heteropraxis*.

For example, we know by the solemn definitions of the Council of Trent that God guarantees to us that the consecrated Host is indeed His Real Presence—that is, the Body and Blood of Our Lord Jesus Christ, together with His Soul and Divinity. Now, the Protestant rebels wanted to deny this article of the Faith and they wanted to influence others to do the same. So they reintroduced the practice of Communion in the hand (it had been originally introduced as a widespread practice by the Arian heretics of the Fourth Century to deny that Jesus is God). By this symbolic action, their denial would be clear to all.

*Heteropraxis* has been used in our day by the enemies of the Church to scandalize many Catholics into losing their Faith in the Real Presence. That is why the abuse of Communion in the hand was forbidden by the universal law of the Church for many centuries and is still forbidden by the law of the Church to this day. The recent indult [i.e. permission] to go against the letter of the law is only allowed if this practice does not lead to the lessening of the Faith in the Real Presence and does not lead to less respect for the Real Presence. But it *always does,* as we can see from our own everyday experience with this form of heteropraxis.[20]

The practices which *uphold* orthodox doctrine, on the other hand, are referred to as *orthopraxis* (i.e. orthodox Catholic practices). These include: genuflecting in the presence of the Blessed Sacrament, distributing/receiving Communion on the tongue, maintaining the tabernacle with the Blessed Sacrament as the primary focus of attention (and worship) in the center of the sanctuary; and the solemn behavior of the clergy within the sanctuary, showing due reverence to the Presence of God in the Blessed Sacrament. These examples of *orthopraxis* (orthodox actions upholding the Faith) testify to the truth of the dogma that the Blessed Sacrament *is* the Real Presence of God—the Body, Blood, Soul and Divinity of Our Lord Jesus Christ under the appearance of bread—as well as the proper respect of man to God.

Examples of *heteropraxis* against the dogma of the Real Presence include Communion in the hand. This form of *heteropraxis* conveys the erroneous message to the faithful that the Blessed Sacrament is just not that important, that It is just bread, and promotes the heresy that It is not the Real Presence of God—the Body, Blood, Soul and Divinity of Our Lord Jesus Christ under the appearance of bread. Another example of *heteropraxis* in this area is the permanent removal of the tabernacle with the Blessed Sacrament from the sanctuary to a side room or broom closet, so that the primary focus of attention (and worship) in the sanctuary becomes the chair of the "celebrant" or "Presider" over the "assembly". The message is subtly given, and received, that the person sitting in the chair is more important than the Blessed Sacrament. And since the "Presider" (or president of the "assembly") represents the people, then subtly the message is given that God is less important than the people.

These examples remind us yet again of the words of Pope Pius XII, quoted earlier:

> Suppose, dear friend, that Communism [one of "the errors of Russia" mentioned in the Message of Fatima] was only the most visible of the instruments of subversion to be used against the Church and the traditions of Divine Revelation ... I am worried by the Blessed Virgin's messages to Lucy of Fatima. This persistence of Mary about the dangers which menace the Church is a divine warning against the suicide of altering the Faith, in Her *liturgy, Her theology and Her soul.* ... A day will come when the civilized world will deny its God, when the Church will doubt as Peter doubted. She will be tempted to believe that man has become God ... In our churches, Christians will search in vain for the red lamp where God awaits them, like Mary Magdalene weeping before the empty tomb, they will ask, "where have they taken Him?"[21]

From Pope Pius XII's words, it seems then that these above-mentioned forms of *heteropraxis* against the Blessed Sacrament were explicitly mentioned in the Third Secret of Fatima, because while Pope Pius XII relates them to the Fatima Message, they are not mentioned in *any* part of the Message that has been published. That is why they must be mentioned in the Third Secret—that is, the part that is not yet published. Pope Pius XII clearly says that it is *Our Lady of Fatima* who warns us against "the suicide of altering the Faith in Her *liturgy*, Her *theology* and Her soul." Therefore, the Third Secret warns us about *both* false doctrine and *heteropraxis* as attacks upon "the dogma of the Faith."

## The Attack Includes the Moral Corruption of the Clergy Which We Now Witness

As we see today, with the eruption of a massive, worldwide scandal involving the sexual misconduct of members of the priesthood, there is a third line of attack on the Church during this time of great crisis: the moral corruption of many consecrated souls. The tail of the dragon sweeps souls from the heavens—down from their consecrated state—not only through heterodoxy and heteropraxis, but also through immorality. Let us recall the statements of Sister Lucy to Father Fuentes:

The devil wishes to take possession of consecrated souls. He tries to corrupt them in order to lull to sleep the souls of lay people and thereby lead them to final impenitence.

That which afflicts the Immaculate Heart of Mary and the Heart of Jesus is the fall of religious and priestly souls. The devil knows that religious and priests who fall away from their beautiful vocation drag numerous souls to hell.

Today we see widespread corruption among the Catholic clergy which is now being manifested in sexual scandals of an unspeakable nature in dioceses throughout North America, Europe and Africa. The tail of the dragon has dragged many members of the clergy down into the rankest forms of immorality.

As a result, the credibility of the many priests who do honor their vows and keep the faith is being destroyed, along with the very credibility of the Church as an institution. Even if there is good doctrine and good practice, the benefits of these often are negated when moral corruption undermines the credibility of the Church.

## Who Is Responsible?

Now the question arises: But *who* is identified in the Third Secret as being responsible for the undermining of the Faith through heterodoxy, heteropraxis and the moral corruption and fall of consecrated souls? First of all, it is members of the Vatican apparatus itself. We note again the revelation of Cardinal Ciappi, Pope John Paul II's official papal theologian, that "In the Third Secret it is foretold, among other things, that the great apostasy in the Church will begin *at the top*." Thus, the responsibility lies first and foremost with men in the Vatican. In this, we see the fulfillment not only of the Third Secret, but also the warning of Pope St. Pius X in his 1907 encyclical *Pascendi*, wherein he writes: "The partisans of error are to be sought not only among the Church's open enemies; but ... *in her very bosom, and are the more mischievous the less they keep in the open.*" These enemies are lay people and priests "thoroughly imbued with the poisonous doctrines taught by the enemies of the Church", and who put themselves forward "*as reformers of the Church*".[22]

St. Pius X insists:

> "The Church has no greater enemies. For they put into operation their designs for Her undoing, not from without but from within. Hence, the danger is present almost in the very veins and heart of the Church, whose injury is the more certain from the very fact that their knowledge of Her is more intimate."[23]
>
> "They seize upon professorships in the seminaries and universities, and gradually make of them chairs of pestilence."[24]
>
> "It is time to tear away the mask from these people and to show them to the Church such as they are."[25]

But then it will be asked: "How do we know which of the clergy are part of the one-third of the stars alluded to by John Paul II; how do we know who the partisans of error are?" The answer again lies in what has been infallibly defined. Those who uphold the Faith, who hold fast to the doctrine of Jesus, are friends. (Apoc. 12:17) Those who do not are foes. As Our Lord said, "By their fruits you shall know them." (Mt. 7:16) One can tell whom to trust by whether they are upholding the Catholic Faith as defined by the solemn definitions. Another sign is that they are living their Catholic Faith as well.

In conclusion, when Paul VI lamented in 1967 that "the smoke of Satan has entered the Church" and in 1973 that "the opening to the world has become a veritable invasion of the Church by worldly thinking" he was only confirming the contents of the Third Secret; so was John Paul II in his more veiled statements in 1982 and 2000. The first two parts of the Great Secret of Fatima warn of the spread of Russia's errors throughout the world. The Third Secret, in its full contents, is surely a warning that those errors will infiltrate the Church itself, and especially taking hold through the "opening to the world" at Vatican II. The infiltration of the Catholic Church by Masonic, Communist, neo-modernist and homosexual elements is seen in the ruinous results of their activities and the loss of faith among Catholics in the pew.

To those who scoff at the claim that such a disaster has befallen the Church in our time, we can only say that they are blind, and that they have ignored the Church's own history, which shows that something very similar has happened before. As Cardinal Newman wrote concerning the Arian heresy in his book *On Consulting the Faithful in Matters of Doctrine*:

> The body of bishops failed in their confession of the Faith. ... They spoke variously, one against another; there was nothing, after Nicea, of firm, unvarying, consistent testimony, for nearly sixty years. There were untrustworthy Councils, unfaithful bishops; there was weakness, fear of consequences, misguidance, delusion, hallucination, *endless, hopeless, extending into nearly every corner of the Catholic Church*. The comparatively few who remained faithful were discredited and driven into exile; the rest were either *deceivers or deceived*.[26]

The point of Cardinal Newman's book was that it was the laity, clinging to the defined dogma of the Faith along with a few good bishops such as Athanasius, who kept the Faith alive during the Arian crisis. So it is today.

But one of the great differences between the Arian crisis and the current crisis in the Church is that the Virgin Mary not only gave us a warning many years in advance of the current crisis, but also the means to avoid it by following Her requests at Fatima. To have deprived the Church of the warning contained in the Third Secret, to have covered up the prophecy of apostasy that implicates the very men who have imposed a ruinous new orientation upon the Church and allowed her to be invaded by the enemy, to have thus prevented the faithful from understanding the cause of it all and arming themselves against it, is another key element of the great and terrible crime in question here.

Yet the cover-up has not succeeded. The Message of Fatima has not been buried; disbelief in the completeness of the purported disclosure of the Third Secret is widespread and growing. Recognizing this, the members of the Vatican apparatus we have identified attempted yet another burial on November 17, 2001, thus aggravating their crime against the Church and the world. We will now consider this development.

# Chapter 14

## Let Us Hear the Witness, for Heaven's Sake

Few revelations have been as unconvincing as the Vatican's version of the Third Secret of Fatima. Those who thought, or hoped, that the June 2000 unveiling of the CDF's booklet, *The Message of Fatima* ended matters are probably surprised by the recent tumult over Fatima in the press. There should be no surprise. For over forty years nearly every tactic—silence, intimidation, bad theology, disinformation—has been used to bury the real Message of Fatima. Yet the cork continues to bob to the surface. The terrorist attacks on September 11, 2001 triggered a chain reaction of Fatima stories. The buzz in the press and on the Internet was that the attacks were part of the Third Secret of Fatima, which had still not been fully revealed.

How exasperating for the drafters of the CDF's *The Message of Fatima (TMF)*, who insist the entire secret of Fatima is contained inside its covers. They simply are not believed, in part because they are not believable, but also because of a certain collective awareness, a shared sense of our impending doom. Deep down we know that a "civilization of love" is utopian nonsense. It has never existed. The real Message of Fatima implicitly confirms this: hell is real and many souls are going there because there is no one to pray and make sacrifices for them. Heaven's remedy is *not* well-publicized inter-religious prayer meetings, but the consecration and conversion of Russia, devotion to the Immaculate Heart of Mary, and the Rosary. The real Message of Fatima is not a request for more papal apologies. It is a plea to Jesus to "forgive us our sins," to "save us from the fires of hell". We are not experiencing the new advent of humanity. We are on the Titanic as it slides into the blackness, and the world senses the impending doom even as it continues to heap judgment on itself.

Yet not even the events of September 11, 2001 had deterred the Vatican apparatus from implementing Sodano's Party Line that Fatima "belongs to the past." On the contrary, the effort to impose the Sodano Interpretation of Fatima on the Church only intensified, as if Cardinal Sodano, *et al.* had recognized that the events of September 11 might actually jolt Catholics into an awareness that—just a moment!—Fatima is *not* finished, because we are obviously not witnessing anything like the triumph of the Immaculate Heart and the promised period of peace. Some sort of bold action to reassert the Party Line was needed.

On September 12, 2001, literally within hours of the fall of the Twin Towers, the Vatican Press Office released its top bulletin for the day: a "Declaration" from the Congregation for the Clergy concerning, not the terrorist attacks, not the horrendous scandals erupting almost daily from the ranks of the priesthood, not the profusion of heresy and disobedience among the clergy over the past forty years, but Father Nicholas Gruner, "the Fatima priest." The Declaration stated that it had been issued "by mandate of *a* higher authority"—Vatican-speak for the Secretary of State, Cardinal Sodano, not the Pope (who is *the* highest authority).

The Declaration warned the entire Catholic world about a serious threat to the good of the Church; a threat of such magnitude that the Congregation for the Clergy could not even wait until the dust had settled over the former Twin Towers. The threat consisted of *a conference on world peace and Fatima* in Rome, sponsored by Father Gruner's apostolate.

Yes, the Vatican's top priority within hours of the worst terrorist attack in world history was to tell everyone to shun a conference on world peace and Fatima. Why? Because, said the "Declaration", the conference "does not enjoy the approval of legitimate ecclesiastical authority." Of course, the issuer of the Declaration knew quite well that no "approval" for conferences of clergy and laity is necessary under Church law. The Code of Canon Law promulgated by Pope John Paul II (Canons 212, 215, 278, 299) recognizes the natural right of the faithful to meet and discuss issues of concern in the Church today without any "approval" by anyone. Indeed, the Vatican issues no announcements about the lack of "approval" for innumerable conferences conducted by advocates of women's ordination and uncountable other heresies, even though the participants in these conferences are abusing their natural right and causing grave harm to the Church. One might as well say that the apostolate's Rome conference had not been approved by the American Medical Association. What of it?

But that was not the worst of it. The Declaration also stated that Father Gruner had been "suspended" by the Bishop of Avellino. Suspended for *what*? For nothing, apparently, since no grounds were stated. The reason for this curious omission was clear to anyone with a knowledge of Father Gruner's canonical proceedings: the "grounds" were so flimsy that to state them publicly would be to invite laughter.

As we have already noted, the only pretext ever given for the "suspension" was that Father Gruner must return to Avellino, Italy (where he was ordained in 1976) or be suspended. Why? Because he had "failed" to find another bishop to incardinate him. But the "Declaration" failed to mention that three successive friendly bishops had offered to incardinate Father Gruner with express permission to continue his apostolate, and that all three incardinations had been blocked (or declared "non-existent") by the same Vatican bureaucrats who had now announced the resulting "suspension". That is, Father Gruner had been "suspended" for failing to "obey" an order *his accusers themselves had prevented him from obeying.* (Not to mention that the Bishop of Avellino by September 12, 2001 had absolutely no authority over Father Gruner—since Father Gruner was now incardinated in another diocese.)

Nearly forty years after the "springtime" of Vatican II began, the Consecration of Russia—not the world, not "youth in search of meaning," not "the unemployed," but *Russia*—remains undone. The world is convulsed by regional wars, Islamic terrorism and the holocaust of abortion, as it becomes clearer by the hour that we are heading for an apocalypse. The Islamic fundamentalists, whom Vatican diplomats now like to call "our Muslim brothers", hate us and wish to subjugate or kill us in accordance with the dictates of their Koran. After forty years of utterly useless "ecumenical dialogue," the Protestant sects are even more decrepit than when they began, and the Orthodox are more adamant than ever in rejecting submission to the Vicar of Christ. The Church is gravely wounded by heresy and scandal in dioceses throughout the world, where She has lost all credibility because of the corruption of Her human members. The new orientation of Vatican II is a total debacle; a ruinous failure. Yet in the midst of all this death, chaos, heresy, scandal, and apostasy, all now reaching their respective apogees, the Vatican had considered it imperative—right *now*!—to alert the world to the "menace" of Father Nicholas Gruner.

So, one day after September 11, 2001, Father Gruner—who had committed no offense against faith and morals, who had kept his vows for the entire 25 years of his priesthood, who had not molested any altar boys or women, who had not stolen any money or preached any heresy—was publicly condemned before the entire Church in a Declaration that gave no grounds for the condemnation, and which cited the "mandate" of an anonymous "higher authority" who did not even have the courage to name himself. In the living memory of the Church, nothing like this had ever happened to a faithful Catholic priest. The Secretary of State's obsession with destroying Father Gruner—symbol of resistance to the Party Line—had reached the level of obscenity.

Why? It could only be a deep-seated antipathy toward the Message of Fatima and all that it implies for the new orientation of the Church, which Cardinal Sodano (friend of Gorbachev) and his collaborators implement so unswervingly. Fatima, it seems, alarms them more than the current state of the Church and the world. And yet the state of the Church and the world would surely change radically for the better if only Father Gruner's persecutors would simply *do* what Our Lady requested at Fatima: "If My requests are granted, many souls will be saved and there will be peace."

But Cardinal Sodano had surely miscalculated. The issuance of this baseless condemnation of "the Fatima priest" within hours of September 11 had such a stink about it that many who might otherwise have been disposed to accept the "Declaration" at face value began to wonder about its grotesquely inappropriate timing. *In a Church being undermined and disgraced by clerical traitors in every nation, why was the Vatican apparatus so concerned about this one priest, who was not even accused of any specific wrongdoing*?

The scapegoating of Father Gruner would be no more successful than the other anti-Fatima stratagems. Contrary to what some Vatican prelates seem to be hoping, the Fatima controversy cannot be reduced to the status of one priest. In the weeks following the "Declaration" on Father Gruner, other prominent Catholics began to express serious doubts about Sodano's Party

Line on the Third Secret. It was not only Mother Angelica who believed that "we didn't get the whole thing."

On October 26, 2001, the story "broke wide open", as reporters say, when *Inside the Vatican* news service (along with various Italian newspapers) ran an article entitled: "The Secret of Fatima: More to Come?" The article reported that: "News has just emerged that Sister Lucia dos Santos, the last surviving Fatima visionary, several weeks ago sent Pope John Paul II a letter reportedly warning him that his life is in danger. *According to Vatican sources*, the letter, claiming that events spoken of in the 'Third Secret' of Fatima had not yet occurred, was delivered sometime after September 11 to John Paul by the bishop emeritus [retired] of Fatima, Alberto Cosme do Amaral."

When asked about the letter, the current Bishop of Fatima, Serafim Ferreira de Sousa, "*did not deny that Sister Lucia had sent a letter to the Pope*, but said [drawing a Jesuitical distinction] 'there are no letters from the seer that express fear for the life of the Pope.'" The *Inside the Vatican* report further revealed that "Sources have also suggested that Sister Lucia's letter encourages the Pope to fully reveal the Third Secret," and that Sister Lucy's letter to the Pope "is said to contain this warning: 'Soon there will be great upheaval and punishment.'"

The *Inside the Vatican* article reports on yet another secret encounter with Sister Lucy behind the convent walls—only this one does not follow the Bertone/Ratzinger line. According to *Inside the Vatican*, an Italian diocesan priest, Father Luigi Bianchi, "claims to have met Sister Lucia dos Santos last week at her cloistered Carmelite convent in Coimbra, Portugal." Echoing the suspicions of Mother Angelica, Father Bianchi "speculated on the possibility that the Vatican *did not reveal the full secret* to avoid creating panic and anxiety in the population; to not scare them."

Concerning Bertone/Ratzinger's ludicrous "interpretation" of the Secret as a prophecy of the 1981 attempt on the life of John Paul II, Father Bianchi stated that "The message doesn't speak only about an attempt on the pontiff, but speaks of 'a Bishop dressed in White' who walks amongst the ruins and bodies of murdered men and women ... This means that the Pope will have to suffer greatly, that some nations will disappear, that many people will die, that we must defend the West from becoming Islamicized. That is what is happening in these days."

*Inside the Vatican* was careful to point out, as has *The Fatima Crusader*, that Sister Lucy "*is not allowed to speak with anyone* who has not received prior permission from the Vatican ..." Accordingly, *Inside the Vatican* hedged its bets by stating that "it is not immediately clear whether Bianchi received that approval, circumvented the need for it, or did not actually meet Sister Lucia as he maintains." But no one, including Sister Lucy herself, has ever denied that the meeting with Father Bianchi took place.

That at least some of *Inside the Vatican's* sources are within the Curia itself was suggested by Cardinal Ratzinger's response to these developments. *Inside the Vatican* quoted him as having said that the "recent rumors of a letter are only the continuation of 'an old polemic fed by certain people of dubious credibility,' with the objective of '*destabilizing the internal equilibrium of the Roman Curia* and of troubling the people of God.'" Notice, however, that neither does Cardinal Ratzinger actually deny the existence of the letter from Sister Lucy to the Pope.

Cardinal Ratzinger's remark is quite telling. How could people of "dubious credibility" destabilize the "internal equilibrium of the Roman Curia"? If their credibility is so dubious, the Roman Curia would hardly be destabilized by what they say. And just who are these people of "dubious credibility"? The *Inside the Vatican* piece suggested that Cardinal Ratzinger might have been referring to Father Gruner. But what about Mother Angelica? What about Father Bianchi? What about *Inside the Vatican* itself, whose editor, Robert Moynihan, is, if anything, beholden to the Vatican apparatus, as the title of his magazine suggests? And what about the millions of other Catholics who harbor the well-founded suspicion that Msgr. Bertone and Cardinal Ratzinger are not being entirely forthcoming in their claim that the prophecies of the Message of Fatima, including the Third Secret, "belong to the past," and that its warning of a great chastisement of the Church and the world need no longer concern us? Indeed, what serious Catholic really believes this in his heart, given the perilous state of the world today?

Despite a determined effort to impose Sodano's Party Line (an effort that now included a Soviet-style declaration that Father Gruner is to be regarded as a "non-person" in the Church), Catholics the world over continue to wonder what has happened to the words which follow the key phrase "In Portugal the dogma of the Faith will always be preserved etc." Why had *TMF* run away from this phrase by removing it from the Message of Fatima and placing it in a footnote? *What has happened to the missing words of the Virgin? Where is the promised conversion of Russia? Why has there been no period of peace in the world, as the Virgin promised?*

In the face of these questions that would not go away, the Vatican apparatus made yet another attempt to put a lid on the rising speculation of a cover-up, before the pot boiled over and became uncontainable. Indeed, Cardinal Ratzinger's statement about a destabilized curia would indicate that the Party Line on Fatima was now meeting with resistance from within the Roman Curia itself, perhaps in view of the increasing destabilization of the world at large, which hardly squares with the Ratzinger/Bertone/Sodano notion that Fatima's warnings belong to the past.

The stratagem this time would be another secret interview of Sister Lucy in her convent in Coimbra. The interview was conducted on November 17, 2001 by Archbishop Bertone, but for some reason its results were not revealed for more than a month. It was not until December 21, 2001 that *L'Osservatore Romano* (Italian edition) published Msgr. Bertone's brief communiqué about the interview, entitled "Meeting of His Excellency Mons. Tarcisio Bertone with Sister Maria Lucia of Jesus and the Immaculate Heart." This was followed by an English translation in *L'Osservatore Romano*'s English edition on January 9, 2002.

The substance of the communiqué was that, according to Msgr. Bertone, Sister Lucy says that the 1984 consecration of the world sufficed for a consecration of Russia, and that "everything has been published; there are no more secrets." As we demonstrated in Chapter 6, the former statement contradicts everything Sister Lucy has said to the contrary for the better part of seventy years. The latter statement is presented as Sister Lucy's answer to a question about the Third Secret—but the question, oddly enough, is not provided.

Now, when a newspaper or magazine publishes an interview with a person of note, the reader rightly expects a series of complete questions followed by complete answers, so that the reader can see for himself—in its full context—what the interviewee had to say in his or her own words. Not in this case. Although we are informed that Msgr. Bertone and Sister Lucy conversed for "more than two hours," Msgr. Bertone had provided only his summary of the conversation, sprinkled with a few words attributed to Sister Lucy herself. No transcript, audiotape or videotape of the two-hour session has been produced. In fact, *less than ten percent* of what Sister Lucy is quoted as saying had anything to do with the stated purpose of the interview, namely, to address continuing doubts in the minds of millions of Catholics about the Consecration of Russia and the completeness of the Vatican's disclosure of the Third Secret.

Perhaps we should have become accustomed to suspicious irregularities in the way the Vatican apparatus handles Sister Lucy, and this belatedly disclosed, elliptical "interview" was no exception. The Msgr. Bertone communiqué demonstrates that Sister Lucy is still being treated as if she were a member of the federal Witness Protection Program. Yes, of course, she is a cloistered nun. But an interview is an interview, and two hours of talk is two hours of talk. Where is the interview, and what happened to the two-hour conversation? And how can one square this curious substitute for a real interview with the claim that Sister Lucy has told us everything there is to know about the Message of Fatima? If she has told us all she knows, then there is nothing to hide. If there is nothing to hide, why not publish everything she was asked and all that she answered during those two hours? Indeed, why not simply allow Sister Lucy to speak to the world herself, and lay all the questions to rest?

Yet despite publication of *TMF*, which was supposedly the last word on Fatima, revealing all that remains to be known, Sister Lucy was still being kept far away from open microphones and neutral witnesses. She was completely invisible during the process of "revealing" the Third Secret in May-June of 2000, and she remains invisible today, even though—so the Party Line goes—Fatima "belongs to the past."

Before addressing the particulars of the "interview" of November 2001—including the grand total of *forty-four words* attributed to Sister Lucy herself during an alleged *two hours* of conversation about the matters in controversy—it must be noted that Msgr. Bertone's communiqué undermines its own credibility immediately with the following claim: "Going on to discuss the problem of the third part of the secret of Fatima, she [Sister Lucy] says that she has read attentively and meditated upon the booklet published by the Congregation for the Doctrine of the Faith [i.e., *The Message of Fatima (TMF)*], and confirms *everything* it says."

This could not possibly be anything but a deception. To begin with, Msgr. Bertone is asking the faithful to believe all of the following:

- Sister Lucy "confirms" *TMF*'s contention that the vision contained in the Third Secret incorporates images Sister Lucy "may have seen in devotional books" and her own "intuitions of the faith". In other words, Sister Lucy "confirms" that she made it up.[1]
- Sister Lucy "confirms" Cardinal Ratzinger's praise of the modernist Jesuit Edouard Dhanis as an "eminent scholar" on Fatima, even though Dhanis dismissed as "unconscious fabrications" every prophetic aspect of the Message of Fatima—from the vision of hell, to the prediction of World War II, to the consecration and conversion of Russia. (This is discussed more fully below.)
- Sister Lucy "confirms," in essence, that she could very well be a sincere and pious fake, who only imagined that the Virgin Mary called for the consecration and conversion of Russia, so that *TMF* was quite correct in ignoring these key elements of the Message of Fatima, treating them as if they did not exist.

One must be sensible about this. When a Vatican functionary, no matter what his stature, comes out of a locked convent and declares that a 94-year-old nun inside "confirms everything" in a forty-page document he has co-authored, reasonable minds expect a bit more in the way of corroboration. All the more so when the forty-page document politely suggests that the nun in question concocted a pious fable that has held the Church in suspense, needlessly, for more than 80 years.

On these grounds alone one must conclude that the latest secret Sister Lucy interview is but another attempt to manipulate and exploit a captive witness, who has yet to be allowed to come forward and speak at length to the faithful in her own unfiltered words. The last surviving Fatima visionary is still being subjected to closeted interviews during which she is surrounded by handlers, who then report her "testimony" in little bits and pieces—an answer without the question, a question without the answer. And now the faithful were being asked to swallow the whopper that Sister Lucy, the divinely chosen seer of Fatima, agrees with "everything" in 40 pages of neo-modernist "commentary" which, as even the *Los Angeles Times* could see, "gently debunks the Fatima cult."

While it is clear on these grounds alone that the "interview" of November 17, 2001 is highly suspect, there is still an obligation to demonstrate the point more amply for the historical record.

To begin with, the Bertone interview was expressly conducted to squelch growing doubt among the faithful about the Vatican's blatant campaign to consign the Message of Fatima to the dust-bin of history. As Msgr. Bertone's communiqué admits:

> In recent months, above all after the sad event of the terrorist attack of last September 11th, in foreign and Italian newspapers have appeared articles regarding presumed new revelations of Sister Lucy, announcements of warning letters to the Supreme Pontiff, apocalyptic reinterpretations of the Message of Fatima. Moreover, emphasis has been given to the suspicion that the Holy See has not published the integral text of the third part of the 'secret', and some 'Fatimist' movements have repeated the accusation that the Holy Father has not yet consecrated Russia to the Immaculate Heart of Mary. *For this reason ... it was considered necessary to organize a meeting with Sister Lucy.*

We recall here that the Message of Fatima contains both promises, if the Virgin's requests are obeyed, and warnings about the consequences of a failure to obey:

**The Promises:**

If Russia *is* consecrated to the Immaculate Heart—

- the Immaculate Heart will triumph,
- Russia will be converted,
- many souls will be saved from hell (which the three seers were shown in a terrifying vision),
- and a period of peace will be granted to mankind.

**The Warnings:**

If Russia is *not* consecrated to the Immaculate Heart—

- Russia will spread its errors throughout the world,
- raising up wars and persecutions against the Church;
- the good will be martyred,
- the Holy Father will have much to suffer,
- and *various nations will be annihilated.*

While the *eventual* fulfillment of the Fatima prophecies is inevitable—"In the end, My Immaculate Heart *will* triumph. The Holy Father *will* consecrate Russia to Me, which *will* be converted, and a period of peace *will* be granted to mankind"—the question for us today is whether the world will first have to suffer the predicted chastisements in full, including the annihilation of nations, an event clearly suggested in the half-ruined city outside of which the Pope is executed in the Third Secret vision. We recall Sister Lucy's warning to the Pope (one year after the assassination attempt in St. Peter's Square) in the purported letter dated May 12, 1982, reproduced in *TMF* itself:

> And if we have not yet seen the complete fulfillment of the final part of this prophecy, *we are going towards it with great strides.*[2] If we do not reject the path of sin, hatred, revenge, injustice, violations of the rights of the human person, immorality and violence, etc. And let us not say that it is God who is punishing us in this way; on the contrary *it is people themselves who are preparing their own punishment*.

The Bertone interview, however, had failed to address continued public concern in the Church concerning the Fatima warnings. Quite the contrary, Msgr. Bertone had staked his entire position, and indeed the fate of the world, on the Party Line, to which he had adhered quite faithfully with his preposterous claim in *TMF* (his own commentary) that "The decision of His Holiness Pope John Paul II to make public the third part of the 'secret' of Fatima brings to an end a period of history marked by tragic human lust for power and evil ..." Thus, the Bertone interview had one aim: to persuade the world that peace is at hand, that the Fatima saga is over and can now safely be considered a part of history.

Let us examine the circumstances of the interview with reference to the standards of credibility even godless civil tribunals require for the acceptance of testimony from an important witness. We do not suggest that Sister Lucy ought to be subjected to anything like the indignity of a civil trial, but only that the proponents of "Sister Lucy's" latest "testimony" should be held to these minimal standards in asking us to believe it.

***Suspicious Circumstance #1*:** Although Sister Lucy is available to testify in person, she has never been produced by the party who controls access to her, namely Joseph Cardinal Ratzinger.

The Bertone communiqué reveals that Sister Lucy *could not even speak to Archbishop Bertone* without permission from Cardinal Ratzinger. This confirms what *The Fatima Crusader* has been reporting for years and what the aforesaid article in *Inside the Vatican* also noted: no one may speak to Sister Lucy without the Cardinal's permission. That is a very curious restriction on the liberty of a witness who, so we are told, has nothing to add to what she has already said.

Under the minimal standards of trustworthiness in civil proceedings, witnesses are required to testify in person if they are available, so that the parties to the case, whose rights may be affected by the testimony, will have the opportunity to pose questions to the witness. If one party has control over a witness but fails to produce him or her, civil judges instruct juries that they may draw the conclusion that *the witness' testimony would have been unfavorable to that party*. This is only common sense: a party would not fail to produce a favorable witness, but would very likely fail to produce an unfavorable one.

Sister Lucy is available to "take the stand" before the bar of history in the Fatima Case. She is not bedridden, crippled or otherwise unable to make an appearance. On the contrary, the Bertone communiqué claims that on the date of the secret interview Sister Lucy "appeared in great form, lucid and vivacious." Why is this lucid and vivacious witness, who is available to testify, never produced by the party who controls all access to her? Why was her latest "testimony" obtained behind closed doors and presented second-hand in a communiqué from Archbishop Bertone?

What would happen in a civil case if one of the parties offered a fragmentary report of a key witness' testimony when the witness herself could readily testify in person? The jury would rightly conclude that something was being hidden. In the Fatima Case, the inference can and should be drawn that Sister Lucy has been kept "off the stand" because her live, uncontrolled testimony would contradict Sodano's Party Line. If Sister Lucy could be counted on to hew to the Party Line, then she would have been produced long ago to testify in person, and at length, before the Church and the world. Instead, it is *Msgr. Bertone*, not the witness herself, who testifies.

But even if we assume that Sister Lucy were bedridden or otherwise unavailable to testify, the other circumstances of the purported interview could not fail to raise suspicion in the mind of any reasonable person. Let us proceed.

***Suspicious circumstance #2***: The interview of this 94-year-old nun was conducted in secret by Archbishop Bertone, an authority figure with a clear motive to manipulate the witness.

In a civil law context, undue influence is presumed when someone in a position of authority or dominance over a very elderly person extracts a statement from that person, such as a will or power of attorney. In this case, Archbishop Bertone is clearly a dominant party with the imposing authority of a Vatican title, whereas Sister Lucy is not only very elderly but has vowed to submit in holy obedience to the requests of her superiors, by whom she was surrounded during the two-hour session.

Furthermore, Msgr. Bertone was clearly intent on using the "interview" to defend his own credibility against mounting public skepticism toward the Party Line that Fatima is finished. Given recent world events, Archbishop Bertone was obviously suffering a massive loss of face over his utterly indefensible statement in *TMF* that the *decision to publish* the Third Secret vision "brings to an end a period of history marked by tragic human lust for power and evil ..." Msgr. Bertone, being only human, would have every motive to induce Sister Lucy to confirm his ridiculous claim of a world at peace due to the great "fulfillment" of the Third Secret in 1981, when the Pope survived the assassination attempt. (Even the secular radio commentator, Paul Harvey, was openly contemptuous of the Ratzinger/Bertone "interpretation" of the Third Secret.)

Under these circumstances, Msgr. Bertone conducting the "interview" and then reporting its results was akin to a prosecutor interviewing a key witness and then testifying in place of the witness, who is kept out of the courtroom. Objectively speaking, Msgr. Bertone was the last person who should have conducted the interview. The Church and the world are entitled to hear from this vital witness directly, rather than receiving reports from a partisan interrogator with an axe to grind.

***Suspicious Circumstance #3***: The Bertone communiqué is extremely brief, occupying a mere quarter-page in *L'Osservatore Romano*. Yet the communiqué states that the interview went on "for more than two hours."

What did Bertone and Sister Lucy discuss for more than two hours, given that the entire communiqué can be read in less than two minutes? By way of comparison, a one-hour address delivered at a normal rate of speech would require roughly 14 single-spaced typewritten pages to transcribe; a two-hour address would require about 28 pages, or approximately 14,000 words.

Yet Bertone's communiqué concerning an alleged two-hour interview provides *a mere 463 words*[3] purportedly from the mouth of Sister Lucy herself. These 463 words break down as follows:

- **165 words**: A verbatim quotation of Cardinal Ratzinger's opinion in *TMF* (the June 26, 2000 Ratzinger/Bertone commentary) that the phrase "My Immaculate Heart will triumph" (from which, as we have mentioned, the Cardinal conspicuously deletes the words "In the end") does not refer to future events but to Mary's *fiat* in consenting to be the Mother of God 2,000 years ago.

Here we are asked to believe that Sister Lucy now "confirms" that when Our Lady of Fatima predicted four future events—"In the end, My Immaculate Heart *will* triumph. The Holy Father *will* consecrate Russia to Me, which *will* be converted, and a period of peace *will* be granted to the world."—She was referring to the Annunciation in 1 B.C.! Bertone's Lucy apparently also "confirms" Cardinal Ratzinger's removal of the key words "In the end" from Our Lady's prophecy.

We note that the verbatim quotation (of 165 words) from *TMF* includes Cardinal Ratzinger's parenthetical citation to John 16:33. Either Sister Lucy has developed a photographic memory at age 94, or someone added the entire quotation to her "answer"—along with the parenthetical Scripture citation. (Or perhaps *TMF* was placed in front of Sister Lucy for her to read aloud in "obedience" to her superiors.)

- **100 words:** The significance of the heart Sister Lucy saw in the left hand of the Virgin during the apparitions at Fatima.

The Bertone communiqué informs us that this is "an unpublished particular" which Sister Lucy has added to the Message of Fatima. That is very interesting, but what does it have to do with the subject of the interview for which Bertone traveled to Portugal on such an emergent basis?

Notice also that the Bertone communiqué announces this new detail with great excitement—in italics, no less. Suddenly, Sister Lucy is the reliable visionary again, as opposed to Cardinal Ratzinger's impressionable child who makes things up from what she has read in devotional books. Of course, this detail is a calculated distraction from the issue at hand.

- **69 words**: Sister Lucy denies press accounts that she is "very worried about recent events" and that she "can no longer sleep and is praying night and day."

Again, this is beside the point. But at any rate, Bertone's Lucy gives this rather flippant answer: "How could I pray during the day if I did not rest at night?" Obviously, no one had actually claimed that she never sleeps at all. Another distraction.

Sister Lucy is said to have added: "How many things they are putting in my mouth! How many things they make me seem to do!" Yes, but who is it that is falsely putting words in Sister Lucy's mouth and ascribing to her actions she has never taken? The objective witnesses we have previously quoted, who spoke to Sister Lucy openly and during unguarded moments, or the authority figures who surrounded Sister Lucy during Bertone's secret two-hour interrogation?

The reader will notice that Bertone's Lucy never denies that she is very worried about recent events. Who in his right mind would not be? Most tellingly, she *is never asked about her urgent letter to the Pope* (we mark this as the ***First Glaring Omission*** in the interview) *or her face-to-face meeting with Father Bianchi*, during which, according to Bianchi, she cast doubt on the Bertone/Ratzinger interpretation of the Third Secret (this is ***Glaring Omission* #2**).

- **39 words**: The effect the Fatima apparitions had on Sister Lucy's life.

What do these reminiscences have to do with the stated purpose of the emergency secret interview in the convent? Sister Lucy has covered this subject exhaustively in her voluminous memoirs. For *this* a Vatican functionary traveled to Portugal for a two-hour encounter?

- **34 words**: Sister Lucy denies that she has received any new revelations.

Oddly enough, while Bertone's Lucy denies any further revelations from Heaven, in the same communiqué she declares—contrary to all her prior testimony—that the 1984 consecration of the world "has been accepted in Heaven." (See her alleged words regarding this on a later page in this chapter under the heading **"21 words on the Consecration of Russia"**.) How would she know this, absent any new revelations?

- **12 words:** Sister Lucy says the Carmelite community has rejected the petition forms Father Gruner's apostolate is circulating for the Consecration of Russia.

What of it? What about the Consecration of Russia? Is it done or not?

Thus far we have accounted for 419 of the 463 words attributed to Sister Lucy in the communiqué's purported verbatim quotations. Only 44 words remain to deal with the questions being posed by millions of Catholics.

Yes, incredibly enough, the loudly trumpeted Bertone communiqué contains only *forty-four words* of "Sister Lucy" concerning the very matters—the Consecration of Russia and the disclosure of the Third Secret—that supposedly prompted Bertone to travel all the way to the convent in Coimbra on an emergent basis. Here is how the forty-four words break down:

- **9 words** concerning (so we are told) the Third Secret: *"Everything has been published; there are no more secrets."*

The question that elicited this answer is not provided. Instead, Bertone's communiqué declares: "To whoever imagines that some part of the secret has been hidden she replied: ..."—followed by the nine quoted words.

Replied to what? What *exactly* was Sister Lucy asked about the Vatican's disclosure of the Third Secret? What was the full context of the question and the answer? And why was Sister Lucy not asked the one question millions of people around the world were asking: *Where are* the words of Our Lady which follow the phrase "In Portugal the dogma of the Faith will always be preserved etc."? We mark this as ***Glaring Omission #3.***

Notice also that here, at the very crux of the matter, we are not shown that Sister Lucy was asked even one precise question, such as:

- *What are* the words of Our Lady following "In Portugal the dogma of the Faith will always be preserved etc."
- Were any words spoken by Our Lady to explain the vision of the "Bishop dressed in White" seen in the Third Secret?
- Does the Third Secret include a separate text that explains the vision of the "Bishop dressed in White"?
- What does Sister Lucy say about the testimony of numerous witnesses (including the Bishop of Fatima and Cardinal Ottaviani) that the Third Secret was written on a single sheet of paper, as opposed to the four sheets on which the vision of the "Bishop dressed in White" is written?

All such particulars are studiously avoided. We are not even given the wording of the one question that *was* asked. This is ***Glaring Omission #4***.

- **14 words on the Bertone/Ratzinger interpretation of the Third Secret**: "That is not true. I fully confirm the interpretation [of the Third Secret] made in the Jubilee Year."

Here Sister Lucy allegedly denies press reports that she expressed doubts to Father Luigi Bianchi and Father Jose Santos Valinho about *TMF*'s interpretation of the Third Secret. Yet Bertone *never asked Sister Lucy about her letter to the Pope*, as reported by Father Bianchi, nor does she deny that she met face-to-face with Father Bianchi at the convent in Coimbra and that they discussed Sodano's interpretation of the Third Secret.

We are thus expected to believe that Lucy agrees that the Third Secret was fulfilled with the failed assassination attempt against John Paul II on May 13, 1981, even though her own letter to the Pope on May 12, 1982—a year later—says nothing about the attempt but rather demolishes the Party Line by warning that "we have *not yet seen* the complete fulfillment of the final part of this prophecy." And, once again, in the same letter Sister Lucy makes no connection between the assassination attempt and the Third Secret.

- **21 words on the Consecration of Russia**: "I have already said that the consecration desired by Our Lady was made in 1984, and has been accepted in heaven."

These words were allegedly uttered by Sister Lucy in answer to the question: "What do you say to the persistent affirmations of Father Gruner who is gathering signatures in order that the Pope may finally consecrate Russia to the Immaculate Heart of Mary, which has never been done?"

First of all, that the Secretary of the CDF would travel to Coimbra to obtain comments about Father Gruner for publication to the entire Church is a dramatic demonstration that the Vatican apparatus views Father Gruner's apostolate as a prime locus of opposition to the Party Line.

Furthermore, what does "Sister Lucy" mean by the curious affirmation that a consecration of the world was "accepted" in Heaven as a consecration of Russia? Is "Sister Lucy" seriously claiming that Heaven "accepted" a compromise imposed by Vatican diplomats? Since when does Heaven accept a human substitute for a precise act that God has commanded? Further, how would "Sister Lucy" know what Heaven has "accepted" if, as Msgr. Bertone claims, she also said there have been no new revelations to her?

Now, it may be that God "accepts" our refusal to comply with His will in the sense that He will allow us the freedom to disobey Him in this life. But that does not mean that what God has "accepted" is pleasing to Him.

What is more, by saying that the act of consecration of the world in 1984 was "accepted", is not Sister Lucy saying nothing more than that it was "accepted" in the same sense as the 1942 consecration by Pius XII, which shortened WWII even though it did not fulfill the request of Our Lady of Fatima? Was Sister Lucy perhaps attempting to answer the question in a way that satisfied her questioner, Msgr. Bertone, yet still signaling that while what was "accepted" might confer some benefit on the world, it would not be the period of world peace that the Virgin of Fatima promised if Her precise request were honored? Indeed, where is the period of peace She promised? That we have not seen it only demonstrates that even if Heaven "accepted" the 1984 ceremony for what it was worth, Heaven has not deemed that ceremony to be the fulfillment of Our Lady of Fatima's specific request. No matter what the authority of Msgr. Bertone and his Vatican collaborators, they cannot simply declare the existence of something that our own senses tell us does not exist: the conversion of Russia and the worldwide epoch of peace that would follow a proper consecration of that nation to the Immaculate Heart of Mary.

In any case, we have already demonstrated abundantly that Sister Lucy testified repeatedly, in widely reported statements, that the consecration ceremonies of 1982 and 1984 did not suffice to honor Our Lady's request, because on neither occasion was Russia mentioned, nor did the world episcopate participate. According to the Bertone interview, however, the witness has reversed her testimony, and now testifies that the 1984 consecration ceremony "has been accepted in heaven."

What "accepted in heaven" means is anybody's guess. Did Heaven decide to "accept" something less than what Our Lady of Fatima had requested after negotiations between Heaven and Cardinal Sodano?

In any case, notice that *Sister Lucy is not questioned about her many prior statements to the contrary*, and is not asked to explain her purported change of testimony. This is ***Glaring Omission #5***. We are evidently supposed to assume that nothing Sister Lucy ever said before carries any weight, and that only when she speaks *in secret* to Msgr. Bertone does she tell the truth about this matter.

Quite significant is that Bertone's Lucy does not tell us *when, where or to whom* she has "already said" that the 1984 consecration she once deemed unacceptable is now acceptable. Why such vagueness, when Msgr. Bertone had every opportunity to nail down this issue by eliciting specific testimony? Why did he not ask her, for instance, to authenticate any of the various computer-generated letters which began mysteriously to appear over her purported signature in 1989, the letters which assert the consecration had been accomplished in 1984?

And this is most suspicious: As we have noted, *TMF* relies entirely on one of these dubious letters, dated November 8, 1989, as proof that the consecration has already been accomplished. We noted also that this letter's credibility was extinguished by its false statement that Pope Paul VI consecrated the world to the Immaculate Heart during his brief visit to Fatima in 1967—a consecration that never happened. *Why did Bertone make no effort to have Sister Lucy authenticate this hotly disputed letter, when it was the only evidence cited in TMF?*

Most telling in this connection is that Father Gruner's Fatima apostolate had published proof that the letter (whose addressee, Walter Noelker, is not even revealed in *TMF*) is an obvious fake. The proof was published in Issue No. 64 of *The Fatima Crusader*, of which there were some 450,000 copies in circulation as of the date of the Bertone interview in November of 2001.

Now Msgr. Bertone was surely aware that *The Fatima Crusader* had exposed the fraudulence of the 1989 letter, yet he failed to ask Sister Lucy to authenticate the letter and thereby deliver a serious blow to the credibility of Father Gruner's apostolate. This failure could not have been an oversight, since an attempt to refute the position taken by Father Gruner and his apostolate was *the very reason* Msgr. Bertone had conducted the interview of Sister Lucy in the first place.

Why would Msgr. Bertone pass up a golden opportunity to use Sister Lucy, his "star witness", to refute Father Gruner's claim that the 1989 letter was a fake? Obviously, because Msgr. Bertone must have known that it *was* a fake, and thus he would not have dared to ask Sister Lucy to authenticate it during the interview. We must mark this is as ***Glaring Omission #6.***

This, then, is the sum total—forty-four words—of what Sister Lucy is alleged to have said during a two-hour interview on one of the greatest controversies in the history of the Church. We are asked to accept these forty-four words from a closeted witness as the end of the story of Fatima. These words are supposed to allay all the doubts, questions and fears of millions of the faithful—even though Russia has manifestly failed to convert and the gathering forces of violence and rebellion against God and His law loom larger by the day.

**Suspicious Circumstance # 4:** No tape recording or transcript of the interview has been made available.

Why has no transcript, audio tape, video tape or any other independent record of the interview been produced in order to show the precise questions Msgr. Bertone asked, the full answers Sister Lucy gave, the sequence of the questions and answers, and any comments or suggestions Msgr. Bertone and others might have made to Sister Lucy during the "more than two hours" they were in the same room together? *Where is the give and take one always sees in published interviews*?

Further, why did Msgr. Bertone require more than two hours to extract forty-four words from Sister Lucy about the matters at issue? Assuming it took Sister Lucy a full minute to utter those 44 words, what did she say, and what did Msgr. Bertone, Father Kondor and the Mother Superior say, during the remaining 119 minutes of the encounter? Was Sister Lucy reminded of her duty of "obedience"? Was it implied that the whole Church was depending on her to give the answers that would end this "divisive" controversy? Was it suggested that loyalty to "the Holy Father" required that she accept the Party Line, even though her own purported 1982 letter to the Pope contradicts it? Was she told how important it was to the Church that she assure everyone that Russia has been consecrated, despite everything she has said to the contrary throughout her life? Was she given the impression that to say otherwise would be to contradict the Pope himself?

Or did Sister Lucy perhaps give many answers that were unsatisfactory to her questioner, only to be asked the same questions repeatedly and in different ways until she got the answers "right"? To what subtle, or not-so-subtle, importuning was the witness subjected during the two hours she was surrounded by imposing authority figures in a closed room?

Surely, if there was nothing to hide Msgr. Bertone would have made certain that such a crucial interview with the only surviving witness of the Fatima apparitions, age 94 at the time, was recorded on audio or video tape, or at least transcribed *verbatim* by a stenographer so that the witness' testimony could be preserved in case of her death—which at her age is certainly very near. We would wager, however, that there is no recording, no transcript, no independent record whatsoever of the Bertone interview. For it seems there is a terrible fear of allowing this witness to speak at length, in her own words, in response to a series of simple and direct questions. Every one of the forty-four words from "Sister Lucy" which appear in the Bertone communiqué is carefully measured out, as if from an eyedropper.

No doubt the risk of creating such a record was too great. What if Sister Lucy consistently gave the "wrong" answers? What if the answers she did provide had to be extracted through leading questions or subtle persuasion by the interviewer or the others in attendance? What could be done with a record that revealed such things? How could it be kept from the public or only partially released? How could it be hidden or destroyed once it was created?

We would be happy to be proven wrong. Perhaps there *is* a tape or transcript of the entire two-hour session. But if there is, it will be most telling if the Vatican refuses to produce it.

***Suspicious Circumstance #5:*** The Italian communiqué purports to be signed by both Msgr. Bertone and Sister Lucy, but the English version drops her "signature."

In the first place, why is Sister Lucy signing *Msgr. Bertone's* statement in Italian about what she allegedly told him in *Portuguese*? Why is Sister Lucy not making and signing *her own* statement in her own language? If Sister Lucy really spoke with Msgr. Bertone for more than two hours, why not simply prepare a faithful transcript of her own words in Portuguese and then have her sign that, instead of Msgr. Bertone's self-serving communiqué?

Further, why was Sister Lucy's "signature" dropped from the English translation of the communiqué? In fact, to what document was her "signature" actually affixed in the first place—the Italian communiqué or a Portuguese original of the same document that has not yet been produced?

Of what value, in any case, is Sister Lucy's "signature" on a document written in a language she does not speak, which partially quotes her testimony, but only in Italian translation (Sister Lucy does not speak Italian) and without setting forth the full questions she was asked or the full answers she gave?

The inescapable conclusion is this: *Msgr. Bertone and the Vatican apparatus have no intention of ever allowing Sister Lucy to give her own statement at length, entirely in her own words, about the major questions which remain concerning the Message of Fatima.* This is borne out by the next suspicious circumstance.

***Suspicious Circumstance #6***: Sister Lucy's just-published 303-page book on the Message of Fatima completely avoids any of the subjects supposedly covered in the secret Bertone interview.

In October 2001 the Vatican Library publishing house published a book by Sister Lucy entitled *The Appeals of the Message of Fatima.* Sister Lucy's introduction to the book, which was reviewed and approved by the Congregation for the Doctrine of the Faith, states that it is intended to be "an answer and a clarification of *doubts and questions* addressed to me." The preface, by the current Bishop of Leiria-Fatima, likewise observes that Sister Lucy had asked the Holy See's permission to write a book on Fatima in order to "answer *multiple questions* in a global manner, not being able to answer every person individually."

Yet despite the book's stated purpose, its 303 pages fail to address *any* of the prevailing "doubts and questions" about the Message of Fatima. The errors of Russia, the Triumph of the Immaculate Heart, the consecration and conversion of Russia, the period of peace promised by the Virgin as the fruit of the Consecration, and the Third Secret *are not even mentioned* in the book, let alone discussed. Not even the vision of hell is mentioned in Sister Lucy's discussion of eternal life and seeking God's pardon. In short, the book presents a thoroughly expurgated Fatima message, stripped of every one of its prophetic and admonitory elements—precisely in keeping with the Party Line. The version of Fatima presented in this book hardly required a Miracle of the Sun to confirm it.

Now this is very curious: When Sister Lucy is allowed to write a 303-page book to address "doubts and questions" concerning the Message of Fatima, she says nothing about the doubts and questions millions of people really have. Only when she is interviewed *in secret* by a self-interested questioner, who happens to be an imposing authority figure, is "Sister Lucy" allowed anywhere near these doubts and questions. But even then her answers are fragmentary and do not come from her directly, in her own language. Instead, they are conveyed by Archbishop Bertone, who provides us with forty-four relevant words out of two hours of conversation with his captive witness.

Now let us sum up the suspicious circumstances surrounding the handling of the key witness in the Fatima Case:

- No one may speak to the witness without the permission of one party to the case, who controls all access to her, even though we are told she has nothing further to say.
- When doubts arise about official versions of the witness' testimony, she is subjected to a secret interview at the age of 94, conducted by an imposing authority figure who then presents her fragmentary answers to his questions in a communiqué to which her signature is affixed, even though the communiqué is not in her own language.
- One version of the communiqué purports to bear the witness' signature below that of her interrogator, but her signature is removed from another version, on which only the interrogator's signature appears.
- The communiqué fails to provide the full questions asked and the answers given by the witness, in their full context.
- Out of 463 words attributed to the witness in the communiqué, only 44 relate to the matters in controversy—out of two hours of conversation!
- No transcript or other independent record of the witness' testimony is provided.
- The secretly elicited, fragmentary testimony contradicts many prior statements by the same witness.
- No effort is made by the witness, or by anyone else, to explain her prior inconsistent statements.

- During the secret interview of the witness, no attempt is made to have her authenticate "letters" attributed to her whose authenticity is clearly in doubt, nor is any effort made to authenticate the very "letter" *on which the interrogator himself had placed sole reliance* as proof of the witness' alleged change of testimony [regarding the Consecration of Russia].
- The secret examination of the witness avoids any specific questions about widely known major discrepancies in the case of which the witness has peculiar knowledge—including the six glaring omissions set forth here.
- When the witness is allowed to publish an entire book to address "doubts and questions" she has received regarding the Message of Fatima, the book contains no references to any of the doubts and questions that actually concern millions of people, which doubts and questions are addressed only in a secret interview for which there is *no transcript or other independent record*.

Archbishop Bertone and Cardinal Ratzinger are men with high offices in the Church. With all due respect to their offices, however, nothing can overcome the reasonable suspicion that these circumstances and glaring omissions engender in reasonable minds. No court on earth would accept the testimony of a witness fraught with so many indications of unreliability. Surely in the Church we can expect at least that measure of openness and disclosure a civil judge would require. *Let us hear the witness, for Heaven's sake*!

We must, in candor, state the conclusion that would be obvious to any neutral observer of the mysterious handling of Sister Lucia of Jesus and the Immaculate Heart: There is every reason to believe that a fraud is being perpetrated; that a key witness—in fact the last surviving witness—is being tampered with. This fraudulent witness tampering is another element of the crime at issue.

But why? Beyond the motive we have already demonstrated—that of furthering at all costs the new orientation of the Church, which collides with the Message of Fatima—we believe a further motive exists, at least in the case of Cardinal Ratzinger. We base this conclusion on what we discussed in a preceding chapter: Cardinal Ratzinger's express approbation in *TMF* of the views of Edouard Dhanis, S.J.—the neo-modernist "debunker" of Fatima. With his endorsement of Dhanis as an "eminent scholar" on Fatima, Cardinal Ratzinger has made it perfectly clear that he, with Dhanis, holds that the prophetic elements of the Message concerning Russia and so forth—again, what Dhanis belittled as "Fatima II"—are little more than fabrications by a simple and well-intentioned, but seriously misguided person.

As we noted earlier, Cardinal Ratzinger followed the line of Dhanis by stating in *TMF* (the Ratzinger/Bertone commentary) that the Third Secret itself may be largely a concoction: "The concluding part of the 'secret' uses images which Lucia may have seen in devotional books and which draw their inspiration from long-standing intuitions of faith." If that were true of the Third Secret, it would also be true of the entire Message of Fatima. What other conclusion could the Cardinal have intended to suggest?

We recall also that the Cardinal himself reduced the culmination of the Message of Fatima—the triumph of the Immaculate Heart—to nothing more than the Virgin Mary's *fiat* 2,000 years ago. In like manner, the Cardinal deconstructed the Virgin's prophecy that "To save them [i.e. souls from hell], God wishes to establish *in the world* devotion to My Immaculate Heart." Under the Cardinal's interpretation (which would surely please Dhanis), devotion to the Immaculate Heart means nothing more than acquiring—and here we are confronted once again with a blasphemy—an "immaculate heart" of one's own. To quote *TMF* again: "According to Matthew 5:8, the 'immaculate heart' is a heart which, with God's grace, has come to perfect interior unity and therefore 'sees God'. To be 'devoted' to the Immaculate Heart of Mary *means therefore* to embrace this attitude of heart, which makes the *fiat*—'your will be done'—the defining centre of one's whole life." It is Cardinal Ratzinger who removes the initial capitals from "Immaculate Heart" in order to reduce it to an 'immaculate heart' that anyone can have by simply conforming himself to God's will. With this exercise in clearly deliberate reductionism, the Cardinal completed his systematic removal of every bit of the Message of Fatima's explicitly Catholic prophetic content.

Here we arrive at the precise additional motive in the Cardinal's case: Given his evident disbelief in the authentic prophecies of the Message of Fatima—a disbelief he shares with Dhanis, the only Fatima "authority" the Cardinal cites—it would appear that Cardinal Ratzinger does not think that what he is doing is a fraud at all. He may well believe that the suppression of Sister Lucy's full and unfettered testimony is actually a service to the Church. What we mean by this is that Cardinal Ratzinger *does not really believe* in the prophetic elements of the Message of Fatima concerning the need for the consecration and conversion of Russia and the triumph of the Immaculate Heart in our time, or the disastrous consequences to the Church and the world in failing to heed these elements of prophecy. The Cardinal, therefore, would consider the suppression of these elements as the suppression of dangerous falsehoods that are "troubling" the faithful, however much Sister Lucy may believe them to be true.

It is clear enough from everything the Cardinal himself has said, that the Prefect of the Congregation for the Doctrine of the Faith, like Dhanis, places little or no credence in the testimony of Sister Lucy that the Virgin requested the consecration and conversion of Russia in order to bring about the triumph of the Immaculate Heart of Mary in the world. The Cardinal evidently does not believe that with the Miracle of the Sun God authenticated this testimony beyond any doubt. What other conclusion can one draw from the Cardinal's prominent endorsement of the very "theologian" who attempted to debunk the entire Fatima prophecy?

Here, then, is a secondary motive for it all: In the Cardinal's mind, he is protecting the Church from the disruption caused for too long by a "private revelation" to which he, agreeing with Dhanis, gives no great weight. Thus, to revise or suppress Sister Lucy's testimony in these matters would not, from the Cardinal's perspective, be wrong. Quite the contrary, the Cardinal may well perceive it to be his duty. But then he owes it to the Church and mankind to be up front about it. It seems that he may be like the rest of elitist insiders who think that the faithful are too stupid to know what's best for them. That may be why he does not tell us his prejudices and he asks us to trust his "good" judgement.

In sum, it seems impossible to avoid the conclusion that the Message of Fatima is now in the custody of those *who simply do not believe in it* and who wish to have done with it once and for all, as they set their sights on the Vatican's new policies of ecumenism, "interreligious dialogue", a world brotherhood of religions and a "civilization of love" under the guidance of the United Nations. But as the world descends ever more quickly into violence and moral depravity, as the evidence of Russia's failure to convert mounts higher in the sight of an avenging God, we, the simple faithful, as well as priests and bishops, must continue to ask the simple questions and to work and pray for that day when the men who control the levers of power at the Vatican will finally allow the Pope to do precisely what the Mother of God requested of him 73 years ago. May God deliver the Church from their bad governance, and soon! To hasten that day we, the faithful, have the God-given right to petition the Supreme Pontiff for the removal from office of the accused and their collaborators in this debacle—a remedy we discuss in the final chapter.

Sister Lucy's diaries record that at Rianjo, Spain in August 1931 Our Lord, speaking of a protracted failure of His ministers to consecrate Russia, told her: "Make it known to My ministers, given that they follow the example of the King of France in delaying the execution of My command, like him they will follow him into misfortune."

Jesus also said, "They will repent, and will do it, but it will be late." How late it will be, how much more the world and the Church will have to suffer, depends upon those who have custody of the Message of Fatima and who control all access to the last surviving witness of its delivery from Heaven.

And to some extent it depends on each of us to do our part to expose and oppose the fraud that is being perpetrated on the world and endangering billions of souls.

That is why we have written this book.

# Chapter 15
## Counting the Cost

"In the end, My Immaculate Heart will triumph. The Holy Father will consecrate Russia to Me, and she will be converted, and a period of peace will be granted to the world." So the Mother of God promised at Fatima.

But something has gone wrong. The Fatima prophecies, fulfilled unerringly in every other respect, have not been fulfilled here. Did the Mother of God mislead us? Or is it, rather, certain men who have misled us?

On March 3, 2002, *Time* magazine reported that "a month after the Sept. 11 attacks, top federal officials feared a nuclear weapon obtained from the Russian arsenal was being smuggled into New York. The White House's Counterterrorism Security Group, part of the National Security Council, was alerted to the danger through a report by an agent code-named DRAGONFIRE, according to the magazine, but New York officials and senior FBI officials were not informed in an effort to avoid panic."

Although the report later proved to be inaccurate, in Washington, D.C. a "shadow government" has been installed in underground bunkers, and nuclear detectors have been arrayed at key locations throughout the United States in anticipation of what the President and his advisors believe to be an inevitable, and far more deadly, attack by Islamic terrorists. As *The Washington Post* reported on March 3, 2002: "Alarmed by growing hints of al Qaeda's progress toward obtaining a nuclear or radiological weapon, the Bush administration has deployed hundreds of sophisticated sensors since November to U.S. borders, overseas facilities and choke points around Washington. It has placed the Delta Force, the nation's elite commando unit, on a new standby alert to seize control of nuclear materials that the sensors may detect."

Based on fallible human intelligence reports, political leaders show sufficient prudence to prepare for the worst, which they know is coming. But the Fatima revisionists in the Vatican apparatus, following the Sodano Party Line, tell us that we may safely disregard heavenly intelligence from an infallible source, which warns us of the annihilation of nations. Worse, they hide from the Church a vital portion of that heavenly intelligence report—the still-missing words of the Third Secret—while assuring us that everything has been revealed. And it seems that as the world hurtles towards disaster, there is no short supply of useful idiots in the Church, who are only too happy to parrot the Party Line while helpfully denouncing anyone who questions it.

Consider that as of this writing, it has been eighteen years since the supposed consecration of Russia on March 25, 1984—in a Vatican ceremony from which any mention of Russia was deliberately omitted. Over the past eighteen years there has been no triumph of the Immaculate Heart, and Russia has not converted. Quite the contrary, during the same period of time the Vatican apparatus has openly repudiated, as "outdated ecclesiology", any attempt to seek Catholic converts in Russia.

In Russia and throughout the world the abortion holocaust burns ever higher in the sight of God. There have been at least 600 million victims of the war on the unborn since the "consecration" of 1984, the blood of every victim crying out to Heaven for vengeance.

Not even the catastrophe of September 11, 2001, or the threat of worse to come, could deter the Vatican apparatus from its pursuit of the new "post-Fatima" orientation of the Church. Instead of the consecration of Russia, the Vatican staged another pan-religious prayer meeting: the World Day of Prayer for Peace at Assisi on January 24, 2002. Catholics, Orthodox, Protestants, Hindus, Muslims, Jews, African animists, Buddhists, Shintoists, Confucians, Tenrikyoists and Zoroastrians were shuttled from the Vatican to Assisi in what *L'Osservatore Romano* called "a peace train." The "representatives of the world's religions", including a witch doctor, all gave sermons on world peace from a large wooden pulpit set up in the lower plaza of the Basilica of Saint Francis. As part of the event, each non-Christian "religion" was given a room in the Sacred Convent of Saint Francis to perform pagan rituals and offer prayers for peace to various gods and spirits. At the end of the event, the "representatives of the world's religions" placed little burning oil lamps on a table to symbolize their supposed commitment to interreligious brotherhood and world peace, and then went home.

Afterwards there was, of course, no peace. On the very next day the Israelis began bombing Palestinian targets, as the Arab-Israeli conflict continued to hurtle toward all-out war, while India tested a nuclear missile. Over the next few weeks, the Hindus and Muslims whose "representatives" had gone to Assisi to deposit their oil lamps on the table began slaughtering each other in Western India; the death toll in just three days of riots was nearly 300.[1]

No peace in the world, and no peace in Russia. Rather, as Pope John Paul II said at Fatima in 1982, we are confronted with "almost apocalyptic menaces looming over the nations and mankind as a whole." This is the consequence of ignoring the warnings in the heavenly intelligence report conveyed to the world at Fatima.

And what of peace within the Church herself? Here too the Virgin of Fatima gave us a warning. Here too it was disregarded by the men who tell us that the Third Secret of Fatima "belongs to the past." Today the corruption and collapse of the Church's human element over the past forty years is erupting into full view for the entire world to chronicle daily and mock to scorn. This is happening because churchmen themselves have spurned the Message of Fatima, which gave us the means to know in advance and take measures to avoid the homosexual infiltration of the priesthood that is now raging out of control.

It has long been known that the majority of Catholics, the victims of decades of senseless liturgical and ecumenical "reforms", no longer possess a faith in the Holy Eucharist and no longer regard their Church as any different in essence from a Protestant denomination; nor do they feel obliged to follow the Church's teaching on marriage and procreation. But in the year 2002 the Church would suffer another devastating blow to her credibility.

As this book was nearing completion, the press has exposed the massive pedophile scandal in the Archdiocese of Boston—where Cardinal Law had been hiding the activities of priestly predators for decades. Evidently in a panic over potential liability, diocese after diocese in North America has suddenly begun submitting lists of priests suspected of sexual abuse to law enforcement authorities—after years of hiding this information from the victims and their families and shifting the perpetrators from one place to another. The diocese-by-diocese review of priestly sexual abuse of little boys was provided in cover stories by *Newsweek* and *National Review* and in a host of stories in national and local newspapers. One can only imagine what lies beneath the tip of this iceberg.

The seminaries and convents of North America and Europe are practically empty or closed, except for those operated by small "traditionalist" orders (like the SSPX and the Priestly Fraternity of Saint Peter) which follow "the old ways". There are not nearly enough vocations to replace the older priests who are dying or retiring in the "mainstream" Church. And it is widely known that among the few men who do enter "mainstream" seminaries that adhere to the post-conciliar "reforms", a very large percentage is homosexual. Father Donald Cozzens, head of Saint Mary's Seminary in Cleveland, Ohio, was only admitting what everyone can see when he observed in his book *The Changing Face of the Catholic Priesthood* that:

> At issue at the beginning of the 21st century is the growing perception that the priesthood is, or is becoming, a gay profession ... Heterosexual seminarians are made uncomfortable by the number of gays around them. ... The straight seminarian feels out of place and may interpret his inner destabilization as a sign that he does not have a vocation for the priesthood. ... The sexual contacts and romantic unions among gay seminarians create intense and complicated webs of intrigue and jealousy.[2]

The plague of sexual abuse and perversion among the priesthood is hardly limited to North America. England, France and Spain have their own scandals involving homosexual and pedophile priests, and even a leading Polish Archbishop has been turned over to the Vatican by the fellow priests he has sexually extorted and abused. And in Africa, a vast scandal involving the sexual abuse of nuns by African priests has been reported in the world press and admitted by the Vatican. Vatican spokesman Father Bernardo Cervellera (director of Fides, the Vatican's missionary news service) offered the outrageous defense that "the problem was limited to sub-Saharan Africa and related to negative cultural views there of women and of the value of celibacy ... These are not cases of 'psychopathic' violence against women, but instead a 'cultural way of living' that is common throughout the region ..." The abuse of nuns by African priests is "a cultural way of living" in Africa! African priests simply don't appreciate the "value" of celibacy! According to Reuters, the Vatican is "monitoring the situation ... but no direct action has been taken."[3]

No direct action by the Vatican against priests who sexually abuse nuns; but Father Nicholas Gruner has been declared "suspended" in the Congregation for the Clergy's *only public announcement* concerning the "discipline" of any of the Church's 260,000 diocesan priests in 2001—for the crime of spreading the authentic Fatima Message. Such are the Vatican's priorities in the new orientation of the Catholic Church.

Although the Church's new orientation is a disastrous failure in every respect, producing nothing but the bitterest of fruits, the members of the Vatican apparatus who hound Father Gruner persevere in their pursuit of ruinous novelties. So far as they are concerned, there will be no return to the "model" of the Church represented by the Message of Fatima. There will be no "embarrassing" public consecration of Russia. There will be no "outdated" conversion of Russia to the Catholic Faith. There will be no triumph of the Immaculate Heart, for this would be a setback to "ecumenical dialogue" with the Protestants and the Orthodox. And so Russia has not converted, and there is no peace in the world, and the Catholic Church remains in a state of near-chaos—no doubt as predicted in the Third Secret.

In Russia, after some forty years of feckless "ecumenical dialogue," the Russian Orthodox are fiercer than ever in their rejection of the papal primacy and their opposition to the Catholic Church. The Russian Orthodox hierarchy exploded in outrage when the Vatican announced in February 2002 that its "apostolic administrations" in Russia would be designated as dioceses. These would not even be dioceses in the traditional Catholic sense. There will, for example, be only an "Archdiocese of the Mother of God *at* Moscow"; and the Archbishop in charge of this structure will not be called the Archbishop of Moscow, lest the Vatican give offense to the Russian Orthodox Partriarch of Moscow, the ex-KGB agent, Alexy II.

After creation of the Catholic "dioceses", the anti-Catholic rage of the Russian Orthodox hierarchy—illicit heirs of Catholic parishes and Catholic believers stolen from the true Church at gunpoint by Josef Stalin—has become uncontainable. Cardinal Kasper's visit to Moscow was cancelled in protest over the creation of the dioceses. In his written statement announcing the cancellation, Orthodox Metropolitan Kyrill of Smolensk, who was to lead the Russian Orthodox delegation in yet another round of futile "ecumenical" negotiations, angrily declared that "we have nothing to say to each other." A fitting conclusion to an enterprise that was worthless to begin with. On March 2, 2002, the Pope conducted a Saturday prayer service that was broadcast from the Vatican by satellite into Russia. The broadcast was totally blacked out by the same Russian television networks now under Vladimir Putin's thumb. Only by shipping special equipment into the country (that was held up at customs until the last moment) could a few thousand Catholics see the Pope on television screens set up at Assumption Cathedral in Moscow. The BBC reported that "Patriarch Alexy of the Russian Orthodox Church said it (the satellite broadcast) was an 'invasion of Russia' and referred to the Polish occupation of Moscow in the early 17th Century. John-Paul is of Polish origin."[4] After 40 years of *Ostpolitik* and "ecumenical dialogue", the Orthodox hierarchy will not even tolerate a video image of the Pope in Russia. *This* is the conversion of Russia promised by Our Lady of Fatima?

Trying to put a happy face on the debacle in Russia, Archbishop Tadeusz Kondrusiewicz, the new head of the "Archdiocese of the Mother of God *at* Moscow", claimed that "It's all a misunderstanding." The Catholic Church has no intention of making converts among the Orthodox; no intention of seeking the conversion of Russia. After all, this was the same Archbishop Kondrusiewicz who had publicly declared in 1998 (as we have noted) that "The Second Vatican Council has declared that the Orthodox Church is our Sister Church and has the same means for salvation. So there is no reason to have a policy of proselytism." An Associated Press story on Kondrusiewicz's reaction to Orthodox hostility noted that "Parishioners have come to Kondrusiewicz in tears recently, complaining that the indignant rhetoric by Orthodox leaders on national newscasts since Feb. 11 has made them afraid to practice their faith."[5] While Orthodox prelates blast the Catholic Church on national newscasts, "ultranationalists have joined forces with the Russian Orthodox Church in criticizing the Catholic Church for its 'proselytism' [and] a parliamentary panel plans an investigation."[6]

It is not as if the Orthodox prelates of Russia were defending a vibrant Church of their own. Nearly all of those who designate themselves Russian Orthodox do not practice their religion. *The Economist* notes that "Russia is suffering a crisis of faith. According to the magazine, 94% of Russians aged 18-29 do not go to church."[7] The moral degeneration of Russian society we have already mentioned continues unabated: two abortions for every live birth (an average of five to six abortions for each Russian woman), rampant alcoholism and premature death from disease and violent crime, a burgeoning AIDS epidemic following the legalization of homosexuality by Boris Yeltsin, a flourishing child pornography industry, and so forth.

But the Catholic Church will not be allowed to fill the spiritual vacuum that Russian Orthodoxy cannot fill. Russia's 1997 law on "freedom of conscience" continues to grant special legal status to Russian Orthodoxy, Judaism, Islam and Buddhism, while forbidding Catholic "proselytism" and requiring registration of Catholic churches with local bureaucrats. The Catholic Church keeps such a low profile in Russia that the Moscow office from which Archbishop Kondrusiewicz conducts Church affairs is "tucked behind a military commandant's office and bears no signs saying it houses the Catholic Church's Russian leadership."[8]

As of the year 2002, Catholics remain a tiny, benighted minority in Russia. There are perhaps 500,000 nominal Catholics in a nation of 144 million people. The small percentage of Catholics who even go to Mass on Sunday (most of them in Siberia) is dependent almost entirely on non-Russian priests, who are allowed into Russia only with visitor's visas that require a departure from the country every three months to seek renewal, which can be denied at any time and for any reason or for no reason at all. The very secretary of the Catholic Bishops' Conference in Russia, Father Stanislaw Opiela, was denied an entry visa three times without explanation: "I don't think I'll try again. It's just not worth it," he said. "Maybe there will be some kind of protest."[9] And then, in April of 2002, Bishop Jerzy Masur, assigned by the Vatican to administer to the vast (but sparsely populated) region of Siberia was expelled from Russia, his entry visa confiscated without explanation. Bishop Masur learned that he had been added to a secret "list" of those who are considered "undesirables" and will no longer be allowed to enter Russian territory.

All of these developments in Russia prompted Archbishop Kondrusiewicz to issue a formal protest on behalf of the Conference of Catholic Bishops of Russia, entitled "Religious Liberty in Russia Is in Serious Danger." The protest declares:

> Catholics in Russia ask themselves: What will happen next? Are the constitutional guarantees valid also for them, including liberty of conscience and of the right to have their own pastors, which comprises inviting them from abroad, not forgetting that for 81 years the Catholic Church was deprived of the right of forming and ordaining its own priests? Perhaps the State really considers Catholics second-class citizens? Are they (the State) returning to the times of persecution of the faith? ... The expulsion of a Catholic bishop who has not violated any law, surpasses all imaginable limits of civilized relations between the State and the Church. ... With grave worry, we express our decisive protest in respect to violation of the constitutional rights of Catholics.[10]

So, while Cardinal Sodano and the followers of his Party Line insist that Russia was consecrated to the Immaculate Heart some 18 years ago and that the current state of affairs in Russia is the "miracle" of "conversion" brought about by this "consecration," the leading Catholic prelate in Russia publicly decries *the persecution of the Church in Russia* and warns that religious liberty for Russian Catholics is in serious danger. The only word to describe this situation is insane.

It is even worse for the Catholic Church in the neighboring "former Soviet republics." In Romania, at least eleven Catholic parishes stolen by Stalin have been bulldozed to the ground rather than returned to their rightful owners after the "fall of communism" in 1990.[11] In Belarus, Catholic World New Service reported on January 10, 2002 that there are "disturbing new indications of hostility to the Catholic Church" and that "the broadcasting of Sunday Mass on the state radio service has been canceled without warning."

As CWN noted, "Belarus is officially a secular state ... [I]ts authoritarian President Aleksandr Lukashenko, although he proclaims himself to be an atheist, nevertheless looks to the Orthodox Church for support in his policy of *the 'integration' of Belarus with Russia*." The examples of persecution of the Catholic Church in Belarus, Kazakhstan, Moldova, Romania, Transylvania and elsewhere in "the former Soviet Union" could be multiplied endlessly.

And where is Russian President Vladimir Putin in all of this? He has been busy reassembling the never-quite-dismantled elements of a Soviet-style dictatorship. As reported by the *London Times* online edition of January 12, 2002, "Russia's last independent television station was closed yesterday, leaving the country's entire broadcast media under Kremlin control"—the same broadcast media that have been denouncing the Catholic Church over the question of dioceses in Russia. As if by a prearranged schedule, the same thing is happening in the Ukraine. On December 21, 2001 WorldNetDaily reported that "The torch of liberty has grown dimmer in the former Soviet republic of Ukraine—*as it has across most of the territory of the old USSR*—with the government's silencing of the last independent media outlet and the continuing controversy surrounding the murder of a popular outspoken journalist." There have been many murders and fatal "accidents" involving journalists since the "fall of communism."

In conjunction with his systematic takeover of the mass media under the guise of "debt collection" and "tax evasion", Putin has restored the Soviet national anthem, consolidated Kremlin control over Russian provinces and signed a military and diplomatic "friendship" treaty with Red China. Putin has even ordered the production of a commemorative calendar glorifying the Soviet era, Lubyanka Prison (capstone of the Soviet gulag) and the Soviet-era butcher Felix Dzerzhinsky, who founded the KGB, authorized the torture and execution of Catholic priests, and presided over Lenin's liquidation of the Russian middle class. The calendar is for use in the offices of the KGB, which has been strategically renamed the FSB.

As if by magical coincidence, a national cult of Vladimir Putin is "spontaneously" emerging. As reported in the *Electronic Telegraph* of May 8, 2001:

> [T]he cult of President Putin received new impetus yesterday when thousands of students celebrated the first anniversary of his inauguration under the Kremlin walls. The rally, where many wore T-shirts decorated with Mr. Putin's face, plumbed new depths of grovelling to the former KGB colonel, who is already immortalized in children's books, sculpture and obsequious coverage in the media. Speakers tried to outdo each other in their praise of the great leader. Their rhetoric yielded new insights into the thinking of Putin loyalists, who now dominate the bureaucracy, parliament and state broadcasting.

All of these developments were summed up by Yelena Bonner, widow of the Soviet dissident physicist Andrei Sakharov: "Under Putin, a new stage in *the introduction of modernized Stalinism* has begun. Authoritarianism is growing harsher, society is being militarized, the military budget is increasing." Bonner warned that "under the present government our country can expect, in the foreseeable future, destructive upheavals that could affect surrounding countries as well." She also drew clear parallels between "converted" Russia and Stalinist Russia: "about a third of the population worked for either nothing or symbolic wages during the Stalin era. In modern Russia two thirds of the population are on the verge of poverty. The health care system is worse today than it was in the Fifties. Stalin murdered about 20 million [actually more like 50 million] people, while in today's Russia the population is falling by a million people a year."[12]

Everywhere—in the Church, in Russia, in the world—the practitioners of Cardinal Sodano's Party Line on Fatima see the evidence of its failure. Yet Sodano's collaborators in the Vatican apparatus, and their Fatima revisionist dupes throughout the Church, continue to insist that Russia was consecrated to the Immaculate Heart 18 years ago, that recent events in Russia are "a miracle", that the Third Secret and the Message of Fatima as a whole "belong to the past" and need no longer concern us. Catholics like Father Gruner, who continue to point out the obvious, are being subjected to the equivalent of a Stalinist purge for their lack of fidelity to the Party Line. They are denounced as "disobedient", "schismatic", and their "loyalty to the Pope" is questioned, even though the Pope has never personally endorsed or imposed Sodano's Party Line on Fatima but has rather given compelling indications of its utter falsity.

How does one count the cost of the insane conspiracy to do away with the prophecies of the Mother of God at Fatima? The cost in temporal suffering and harm to souls is already beyond all human calculation: the misery of the Russian people and the continuing State persecution of Russian Catholics; the holocaust of abortion in every nation; a rising tide of violence throughout the world; the loss of countless souls through destruction of their Catholic Faith and the corruption of the Catholic clergy now on display before the whole world. And yet all of this was undoubtedly predicted in that part of the Third Secret we have not been allowed to see; and *all of it could have been avoided if the men who rule the Church today had followed, rather than despised, the Virgin of Fatima's simple requests*.

But what will be the cost in the coming days, if the course which the accused have set for the Church is not corrected soon? Our Lady of Fatima has already answered that question: wars and persecution of the Church, the martyrdom of Catholics, the suffering of the Holy Father, the annihilation of nations, the loss of millions more souls.

Those who have engineered the Church's new orientation and imposed the Party Line on Fatima insist that we ignore these divine warnings, even though they were delivered by the Mother of God Herself and authenticated by a public miracle without precedent in human history. No, we cannot ignore the warnings. *The time has come to declare that it is not the Message of Fatima, but the all-too-fallible human advice of these men that we must ignore.* By their fruits ye shall know them, and the fruits of their policies and judgments are there for all to see: the Church is in the depths of her worst crisis in 2,000 years, and the world is headed toward an apocalypse.

We have made our case as best we can; we have discharged our duty of conscience before the Church and the bar of history. Now, we submit, a duty descends upon you, the reader. We ask you to consider the evidence we have presented and render your verdict—a verdict that good cause exists to ask that the highest authority in the Church judge the actions of these men, correct the damage they have done, and do justice to the Church and the world.

But while we wait for justice to be rendered, we must do whatever is in our power to protect ourselves, our loved ones, our fellow Catholics, and the world at large from further harm.

This means, first of all, that we must reject the false counsel of those in authority who have tried to replace the words of the Mother of God with their own words, and Heaven's plan for peace with their own plan. We have seen the ruinous results of their fallible human wisdom, which they continue to try to impose upon the Church against the evidence of our senses, the dictates of our reason and the very words of the Mother of God Herself. With all due respect to their offices in the Church, we must say of these men that insofar as the Message of Fatima and its implications for the Church and the world are concerned, they have forfeited their own credibility. We should no longer follow them.

As we have seen in Cardinal Newman's apt description of the Arian crisis, the present crisis in the Church would not be the first time in her history that the laity were left to carry on the Faith without the help of the upper hierarchy or even most bishops, relying instead on their own *sensus catholicus* and a few good priests and prelates who did not succumb to the reigning confusion. During the Arian crisis nearly the entire hierarchy lost sight of something as fundamental as the divinity of Christ, and the laity, for the safety of their own souls, had to cease following those in authority for at least 40 years. It is manifest that a comparable situation has arisen today. Can anyone looking objectively at the present condition of the Church seriously deny that she is undergoing a crisis of faith and discipline no less severe than that in the time of Arius?

In *Reform of the Roman Liturgy*, the renowned liturgist Msgr. Klaus Gamber, lamenting the ecclesial destruction caused by the liturgical "reforms" of Paul VI, observed as follows:

> Great is the confusion! Who can still see clearly in this darkness? Where in our Church are the leaders who can show us the right path? Where are the bishops courageous enough to cut out the cancerous growth of the modernist theology that has implanted itself and is festering within the celebration of the most sacred mysteries, before the cancer spreads and causes even greater damage? What we need today is a new Athanasius, a new Basil, bishops like those who in the Fourth

Century courageously fought against the Arian heresy when almost the whole of Christendom had succumbed to the heresy.[13]

Until such leadership emerges in the Church, until the current crisis has ended and things are set right again, we must educate ourselves and others about the Faith, defending it as best we can. In our time, this task requires that we also defend the Message of Fatima; for as Saint Thomas teaches, in every age God sends prophets, not to give a new doctrine, but to remind the faithful of what they must do to save their souls. The great prophet of our age is Our Lady of Fatima. As Sister Lucy herself said in the famous interview with Father Fuentes in 1957:

> Father, the Most Holy Virgin is very sad because no one has paid any attention to Her Message, neither the good nor the bad. The good continue on their way, but without giving any importance to Her Message. ...
>
> Tell them Father, that many times, the Most Holy Virgin told my cousins Francisco and Jacinta, as well as myself, that *many nations will disappear from the face of the earth*. She said that Russia will be the instrument of chastisement chosen by Heaven to punish the whole world if we do not beforehand obtain the conversion of that poor nation.

The conversion of Russia has not been obtained. Anyone with any sense can recognize this. That being the case, the annihilation of nations is surely coming, unless the men who govern the Church change course, abandon their destructive novelties, and simply do what the Mother of God requested at Fatima. We simply can no longer risk relying on the advice of those who are determined to ignore the true signs of the times; the signs of a gathering apocalypse foretold by the Virgin at Fatima. Imploring the grace of God, we will have to advance the cause of true peace in the world without the help of our own superiors, so many of whom have been blinded in their pursuit of a new and alien vision of the Church.

In this undertaking we must gather together under the mantle of Our Lady of Fatima, praying incessantly for Her intercession in this time of great confusion, and never forgetting Her unbreakable promises to the Church and the world.

Our Lady of Fatima, Pray for Us!

# Chapter 16
## Framing an Indictment

Great is the calamity that now afflicts Holy Church and the world at large. In these extraordinary times, just as in the time of the Arian crisis, the laity must shoulder burdens that in ordinary times would not be theirs.

As members of the Mystical Body of Christ, we have a duty to combat the current crisis. We must reject the advice of those who tell us to indulge in the gross presumption that "God is in charge of the Church", by which they mean that we must do nothing to oppose error and injustice perpetrated by members of the hierarchy, but rather blindly submit to every decision of authority, no matter how destructive its consequences.

### Our Duty in Justice and Charity

That is not the Catholic way. That is not what the laity and faithful clergy did during the Arian crisis, and it is *not* what we should do today. Our silence and acquiescence in the face of this ongoing disaster would, first of all, be an injustice to the Church and a betrayal of our solemn duty in justice as confirmed Catholics, as soldiers of Christ.

Then, too, there is our obligation in charity toward our fellow Catholics, including our superiors in the hierarchy. *We have a duty in charity to our superiors to oppose what is happening in the Church, even if that means taking the extraordinary step of having to rebuke our own superiors in public.*

As Saint Thomas Aquinas taught: "if the faith were endangered, a subject *ought* to rebuke his prelate even publicly." Why is it both just and *charitable* for a subject to rebuke his prelate, even publicly, in such cases? St. Thomas here observes that the public rebuke of a prelate "would seem to savor of presumptuous pride; but *there is no presumption in thinking oneself better in some respect*, because, in this life, *no man is without some fault.* We must also remember that when a man reproves his prelate charitably, it does not follow that he thinks himself any better, but merely that he offers his help to one who, 'being in the higher position among you, *is therefore in greater danger,*' as Augustine observes in his Rule quoted above."[1] Of course, there is also danger to our fellow Catholics—the gravest possible danger—from the current course of destructive innovation being followed by certain members of the Vatican apparatus, who have turned their backs not only on the Message of Fatima but on the Church's entire past.

The teaching of Saint Thomas on the duty to rebuke our superiors when their actions threaten harm to the faith reflects the unanimous teaching of the Saints and Doctors of the Church. As St. Robert Bellarmine, Doctor of the Church, taught in his work on the Roman Pontiff, *even the Pope* may be rebuked and resisted if he threatens harm to the Church:

> Just as it is licit to resist the Pontiff that aggresses the body, it is also licit to resist the one who aggresses souls or who disturbs civil order, or, above all, who attempts to destroy the Church. I say that it is licit *to resist him by not doing what he orders and by preventing his will from being executed*; it is not licit, however, to judge, punish or depose him, since these acts are proper to a superior.[2]

Likewise, the eminent Sixteenth Century theologian Francisco Suarez (whom Pope Paul V praised as *Doctor Eximius et Pius*, or "Exceptional and Pious Doctor") taught as follows:

> And in this second way the Pope could be schismatic, if he were unwilling to be in normal union with the whole body of the Church, as would occur if he attempted to excommunicate the whole Church, or, as both Cajetan and Torquemada observe, if he wished to *overturn the rites of the Church based on Apostolic Tradition.* ... If [the Pope] gives an order contrary to right customs, he should not be obeyed; *if he attempts to do something manifestly opposed to justice and the common good, it will be lawful to resist him*; if he attacks by force, by force he can be repelled, with a moderation appropriate to a just defense.[3]

If even the Pope may legitimately be resisted when he takes actions that would harm the Church, all the more so the prelates whom we must accuse here. Quite simply, as Pope St. Felix III declared: "Not to oppose error is to approve it; and not to defend truth is to suppress it." Members of the laity and lower-ranking clergy are not exempt from that injunction. All the members of the Church are subject to it.

We thus have a duty to speak out. We have a duty to bring to the Pope's attention what we believe in conscience is a well-founded accusation that the prelates named in this book (and their many collaborators) have caused, and imminently will cause, grave harm to the Church and the world by their attack on the Message of Fatima. We have a duty to petition the Holy Father for redress of the crime that we believe these men have committed.

We are about to submit our case for your consideration as fellow members of the Holy Catholic Church. We will now summarize briefly what the evidence has shown in general, and what it shows as to the particular actions of those we have accused here.

In general, we have proven the following:

First, the Message of Fatima is a true and authentic prophecy of vital importance for the Church and the world in this epoch of human history. The Message was delivered in person by the Mother of God, authenticated by indisputable public miracles witnessed by tens of thousands of people, has been pronounced worthy of belief by the Church, and has received the explicit endorsement of a series of Popes, including Pope John Paul II. In short, *the Message of Fatima simply cannot be ignored.* As Pope John Paul II himself has said, the Message of Fatima imposes an obligation on the Church.

Second, the Message of Fatima calls for the establishment in the world of devotion to the Immaculate Heart—and thus *the Catholic Faith*—throughout the world. To that end, *God Himself* has decreed these things for our time: the solemn public consecration of Russia—specifically and only Russia—to the Immaculate Heart by the Pope and the bishops together, the conversion of Russia to Catholicism, and the consequent Triumph of the Immaculate Heart in Russia and elsewhere.

Third, the Third Secret of Fatima (in that portion yet to be revealed) predicts what Catholics see all around them today: a catastrophic loss of faith and discipline in the Church—heresy, scandal, apostasy reaching into nearly every corner of the Catholic world. Aside from the mountain of other evidence we have presented on this point, one piece of evidence standing alone proves this: the crucial phrase in the Message which the accused have buried and tried to make everyone forget: "In Portugal the dogma of the Faith will always be preserved etc."—in Portugal, yes, but not in other countries, as we have seen.

Fourth, Sister Lucy insisted that the Third Secret be made public by 1960, because in that year it would be "much clearer."

Fifth, by 1960 the Second Vatican Council had been called. The men who have governed the Church since 1960 have given the human element of the Church an entirely new orientation. They have done this by means of an "opening to the world" through which "dialogue" with heretics, schismatics, Communists, atheists and other opponents of the one true Church has *de facto* replaced the Church's once fierce opposition to error and Her obligation to pass on to all the following generations the Catholic Faith whole and inviolate, as Christ commanded them to do. Not content with ignoring their own solemn duty to keep and pass on the Faith, they also persecute those who seek to adhere to that duty.

Sixth, as early as 1973 Pope Paul VI was forced to admit that "the opening to the world has become a veritable invasion of the Church by worldly thinking"—that is, by liberalism. This invasion of the Church by liberalism, and the consequent collapse of faith and discipline within the Church, represents the cherished goal of organized Masonry and Communism: not the complete overthrow of the Church, which they know is impossible, but the *adaptation* of the Church to liberal ideas. The present state of the Church is precisely what these forces boldly predicted they would achieve, and precisely what a long line of pre-conciliar Popes warned was the object of their conspiracies.

Seventh, instead of fighting against the new orientation that adapts the Church to liberal ideas, post-conciliar churchmen, including those we accuse here, have unswervingly pursued the new orientation by taking and implementing decisions in the name of Vatican II, including (a) *Ostpolitik*, a policy by which many members of the Church are made to avoid any condemnation of or active opposition to Communist regimes; (b) the "ecumenical venture" and "interreligious dialogue", which *de facto* abandon both the conversion of non-Catholics to the one true religion and the dogma that the Catholic Church is the one true Church, outside of which there is no salvation; (c) the introduction of novel and ambiguous terminology in conciliar and post-conciliar documents which (like the formulas of the Arians in the 4th Century) undermine belief in the dogmas of the Faith; (d) a totally unprecedented "reform" of the liturgy by abandoning the traditional Latin Rite; (e) permission or toleration for various forms of heteropraxis (unsound practices) such as communion in the hand, altar girls, removal of the tabernacle from the altar, etc., which undermine belief in the Holy Eucharist and the sacrificial priesthood.

Eighth, the Message of Fatima, with its simple call for the public consecration of Russia to the Immaculate Heart by the Pope and bishops, the conversion of Russia to Catholicism and the Triumph of the Immaculate Heart (and with it the Catholic Church) throughout the world, cannot be reconciled with the new orientation of the Church, in which *Ostpolitik*, "ecumenical dialogue" and "interreligious dialogue" prevent the Church from publicly declaring that Russia must be consecrated and converted to the true religion for the good of that nation and the world.

Ninth, the churchmen who implement the new orientation, including the accused, have attempted to revise the Message of Fatima to make it conform to the new orientation. They have done this by insisting upon an "interpretation" of the Message that eliminates (a) any consecration of Russia by name (which they regard as an intolerable "ecumenical" offense or "provocation" to the Russian Orthodox), (b) any conversion of Russia to the Catholic Faith (which they have expressly abandoned as "outdated" ecclesiology), and (c) any Triumph of the Immaculate Heart throughout the world (which they regard as "triumphalistic", embarrassing and "non-ecumenical").

Tenth, the present Vatican Secretary of State, Cardinal Sodano, who has assumed *de facto* control of the daily governance of the Church since the reorganization of the Roman Curia by the Masonic Cardinal Jean Villot (Secretary of State of Pope Paul VI), has dictated a Party Line on Fatima, according to which the Message of Fatima in general, and the Third Secret in particular, are to be buried by means of an "interpretation" that eliminates its prophecies of future events, converting them into past events, and reduces its specifically Catholic content to mere generic "Christian" piety that will not offend the Russian Orthodox or the Protestants.

Eleventh, the Secretary of State's Party Line on Fatima was cited no less than four times in the commentary on the Message of Fatima and the Third Secret published by Cardinal Ratzinger and Monsignor Bertone on June 26, 2000.

Twelfth, in accordance with the Party Line on Fatima, the Third Secret has been only partially disclosed, and the vision of the "Bishop dressed in White" being executed by soldiers outside a half-ruined city has been "interpreted" to mean nothing more than the failed attempt on the life of John Paul II by a lone assassin 21 years ago.

Thirteenth, that portion of the Third Secret which contains the "words of the Virgin" referred to by the Vatican itself in 1960—the words which almost certainly follow the incomplete phrase "In Portugal the dogma of the Faith will always be preserved etc."—has been withheld from the faithful.

Fourteenth, the Third Secret has in fact been revealed in its essence not only by the testimony of numerous witnesses, but by Pope John Paul II himself, who has twice (in sermons at Fatima) explicitly linked the Message of Fatima to the Book of the Apocalypse, and in particular to the fall of one-third of the stars (consecrated souls) from Heaven after they are dragged down by the "tail of the dragon" (Apoc. 12:3,4)—an event nowhere seen in the first two parts of the Message, and therefore undoubtedly seen in the Third Secret.

Fifteenth, in a vain attempt to quell legitimate doubts about the Party Line on Fatima, the Vatican apparatus has conducted a secret "interview" of Sister Lucy—for which there is no transcript or other complete record—in which it appears that she was essentially induced to "agree" that she likely concocted those elements of the Fatima Message that contradict the Party Line, and was further induced to repudiate (without the slightest explanation) her unwavering testimony for 60 years that the Consecration of Russia requires explicit mention of Russia and the participation of both the Pope and the world's bishops in a joint public ceremony.

Sixteenth, those who do not hew to the Church's new orientation, including the Party Line on Fatima, are subjected to persecution and "purging" by means of "suspension", threats of "excommunication" and other forms of unjust discipline, while those who are faithful to the new orientation and the Party Line on Fatima are left alone, or even rewarded, even if they are promoting heresy, engaging in open disobedience to liturgical or other Church laws, or committing unspeakable sexual scandal. As in the time of the Arian heresy, we are facing the same situation lamented by Saint Basil the Great: "Only one offense is now vigorously punished: an accurate observance of our fathers' traditions. For this cause the pious are driven from their countries and transported into deserts."

Seventeenth, as the direct result of this concerted effort to revise, obscure and bury the Message of Fatima in favor of the new orientation, Russia has not been consecrated, Russia has not converted but has only further degenerated, the Church is in the depths of an unprecedented crisis, many souls are at risk. For the Virgin of Fatima said: "If people do what I ask, many souls will be saved." And Our Lady also said: "Many souls go to hell because they have no one to pray and make sacrifices for them." Regarding her own mission, Sister Lucy said to Father Fuentes on December 26, 1957: "my mission is not to indicate to the world the material punishments which are certain to come if the world does not pray and do penance beforehand. No! My mission is to indicate to everyone the imminent danger we are in of losing our souls for all eternity if we remain obstinate in sin." In consequence, the world is facing the annihilation of various nations that Our Lady of Fatima warned would be the consequence of spurning Her requests.

Now, as to the prelates we have been compelled to accuse by name before the Church, the following has been established by substantial evidence:

### As to Cardinal Angelo Sodano

**First,** as Vatican Secretary of State, Cardinal Sodano is literally the most powerful figure in the Church today, given the reorganization of the Roman Curia under Pope Paul VI; and, as such, Cardinal Sodano is the *de facto* ruler over the daily affairs of the Church, especially given the failing health of the Supreme Pontiff.

**Second,** owing to the same curial reforms of Pope Paul VI, Cardinal Sodano stands at the head of every Vatican dicastery, including the Congregation for the Doctrine of the Faith (CDF), which (when it was called the Holy Office) was formerly headed by the Pope.

**Third,** it is Cardinal Sodano who has dictated what we have called the Party Line on Fatima: i.e., the falsehood that the Message of Fatima, including the Third Secret, belongs entirely to the past, and that no one may request any longer the Consecration of Russia. We know this because,

- it was Cardinal Sodano, not the Pope, who announced to the world on May 13, 2000 that the Third Secret would be revealed, but only after a "commentary" had been prepared by the CDF, which, again, is subordinate to him, and
- it was Cardinal Sodano's "interpretation" of the Third Secret that was cited no fewer than four times in the CDF's commentary *The Message of Fatima* (*TMF*).

**Fourth,** Cardinal Sodano, as the *de facto* ruler of daily Church affairs, has vigorously enforced the new orientation of the Church in the matter of Fatima. We know this because,

- Sodano took control of the "interpretation" of the Third Secret and its false reduction to a thing of the past, along with the rest of the Fatima Message.
- One day after the publication of *TMF*, Sodano pointedly demonstrated his adherence to the new orientation by inviting Mikhail Gorbachev, the pro-abortion, ex-Soviet dictator, to the Vatican for a bogus "press conference" (no questions allowed), during which Cardinal Sodano, Gorbachev and Cardinal Silvestrini sat together to heap praise on a key element of the new orientation, developed by Cardinal Sodano's predecessor, Cardinal Casaroli: namely, *Ostpolitik*, under which the Church "dialogues" with Communist regimes rather than opposing them, and observes diplomatic silence in the face of Communist persecution of the Church.

- Cardinal Sodano's representative, Cardinal Cassidy, negotiated the Balamand Declaration (1993) which declares that the return of the Orthodox to Rome is "outdated ecclesiology"—as is, therefore, (according to Cardinal Sodano) the conversion of Russia to the Catholic Faith called for by Our Lady of Fatima.
- Cardinal Sodano has overseen the persecution of Father Nicholas Gruner, perhaps the Church's leading exponent of the authentic Fatima Message, as shown by the following facts:
  - ➢ Father Gruner's groundless "suspension" was announced "by mandate of a higher authority" (the Vatican term for the Secretary of State) on September 12, 2002.
  - ➢ Documents falsely denouncing Father Gruner and pressuring priests and bishops to shun his apostolate's conferences have been circulated throughout the world over the years by apostolic nuncios, who are ecclesial "diplomats" attached to the Secretary of State.
  - ➢ The persecution of Father Gruner began in 1989, with what his bishop at the time called "worried signals" from the Vatican Secretary of State.

### As to Cardinal Joseph Ratzinger

**First,** Cardinal Ratzinger, in his capacity as head of the CDF, has on innumerable occasions stated his commitment to the new orientation of the Church, which he described as "demolition of bastions" in a book published after he had become head of the CDF.

**Second**, in accordance with this "demolition of bastions", Cardinal Ratzinger has openly declared his view that Blessed Pius IX and St. Pius X were "one-sided" in their solemn, infallible condemnations of liberalism, and that their teaching was "countered" by Vatican II. He further declares that the Catholic Church no longer seeks to convert all the Protestants and schismatics, and that it has no right to "absorb" their "churches and ecclesial communities," but must make a place for them in a "unity of diversity"—a view that is obviously irreconcilable with the consecration and conversion of Russia to the Catholic Faith. Cardinal Ratzinger's view is, to say the least, suspect of heresy.

**Third**, one of the "bastions" Cardinal Ratzinger has sought to "demolish" is the traditional Catholic understanding of the Message of Fatima.

**Fourth**, Cardinal Ratzinger sought to demolish the bastion of Fatima in *TMF*, which he published under the control of Cardinal Sodano.

**Fifth**, *TMF* attempts to destroy the authentic Catholic prophetic content of the Message by the following exegetical frauds:

- Cardinal Ratzinger removed the words "In the end" from the Virgin's prophecy "*In the end,* My Immaculate Heart will triumph."

- Cardinal Ratzinger also cropped the immediately following words from the Fatima prophecy: "The Holy Father *will* consecrate Russia to Me, and it *will* be converted, and a period of peace *will* be granted to the world."
- Having deliberately tampered with the words of the Mother of God, Cardinal Ratzinger then declared that the (predicted future) Triumph of the Immaculate Heart means only Mary's *fiat*, 2,000 years ago, in consenting to be the Mother of the Redeemer.
- Cardinal Ratzinger thus deliberately ignored the Virgin's prophecy of *four* future events surrounding the consecration and conversion of Russia, and deliberately reduced them all to one event—Her *fiat* in 1 B.C.
- Concerning devotion to the Immaculate Heart, which Our Lady of Fatima announced that God wills to establish *in the world*, Cardinal Ratzinger dared to say that devotion to the one and only Immaculate Heart of Mary means nothing more than following Mary's example by achieving *an "immaculate heart" of one's own*, through "interior unity" with God.
- By means of this grotesque and blasphemous "interpretation", Cardinal Ratzinger debases the Mother of God Herself in order to sever any link between devotion to the Immaculate Heart *in the world*, and Our Lady of Fatima's call for the conversion of Russia to the Catholic religion, which must precede true devotion to the Immaculate Heart in that nation since the Russian Orthodox religion does not recognize the dogma of the Immaculate Conception.

**Sixth,** Cardinal Ratzinger, following Cardinal Sodano's Party Line, stated in *TMF* that "we must affirm with Cardinal Sodano: '... the events to which the third part of the 'secret' of Fatima refers now seem part of the past'", and (according to Sodano's "interpretation") that the Third Secret culminated with the failed assassination attempt in 1981.

**Seventh,** in adopting the Sodano Party Line on the Third Secret, Cardinal Ratzinger flatly contradicted his own testimony in 1984—three years *after* the assassination attempt—that the Third Secret is a "religious prophecy" concerning "dangers to the faith and the life of the Christian, and therefore the world", on which occasion Cardinal Ratzinger made no suggestion that the Secret pertained to the 1981 assassination attempt or any other past event.

**Eighth**, in furtherance of the Party Line, Cardinal Ratzinger went out of his way to criticize Father Nicholas Gruner at the press conference of June 26, 2000, advising the world press that Father Gruner "must be submissive to the Magisterium" and accept the alleged 1984 consecration of the world as a consecration of Russia. That is, according to Ratzinger, Father Gruner must submit to Cardinal Sodano's Party Line. Ratzinger's claim is false because there has been no binding, authoritative pronouncement of the

Magisterium—not the Pope, not a Council, not the Ordinary and Universal Magisterium.

**Ninth**, in sum, Cardinal Ratzinger, carrying out the Party Line, deliberately used his position as head of the CDF to lend the false appearance of theological weight and validity to a shameless "deconstruction" of the Message of Fatima—an effort so blatant that even the *Los Angeles Times* sub-headlined its coverage of *TMF* and the June 26, 2000 press conference as follows:

> The Vatican's Top Theologian Gently Debunks a Nun's Account of Her 1917 Vision That Fueled Decades of Speculation.

## As to Monsignor Tarcisio Bertone

In his capacity as Secretary of the CDF, Msgr. Bertone also carried out the Party Line dictated by Cardinal Sodano.

**First**, Msgr. Bertone perpetrated a demonstrable fraud by asserting in *TMF* that "Sister Lucia personally confirmed that this solemn and universal act of consecration [of the world in 1984] corresponded to what Our Lady wished ('*Sim, està feita, tal como Nossa Senhora a pediu, desde o dia 25 de Março de 1984*': 'Yes it has been done just as Our Lady asked, on 25 March 1984': Letter of 8 November 1989). Hence any further discussion or request [for the Consecration of Russia] is without basis."

**Second**, the fraud is demonstrable since the cited "letter of 8 November 1989" was printed out by a computer that the aged Sister Lucy does not use, and contains an error of fact that Sister Lucy could not have made—namely, that Paul VI performed a consecration of the world during his visit to Fatima in 1967, when Pope Paul never consecrated anything during his fleeting appearance at the Cova da Iria.

**Third**, Msgr. Bertone deliberately relied solely upon the patently bogus "letter of 8 November 1989", even though he (and the rest of the Vatican apparatus) had complete access to Sister Lucy in April-May 2000 and could have asked her to confirm that the 1984 consecration of the world sufficed for a consecration of Russia—contrary to her consistent testimony for decades.

**Fourth**, Msgr. Bertone, truckling to the Sodano Party Line that Fatima "belongs to the past", dared to state in *TMF* that "the decision of His Holiness Pope John Paul II" to publish the Third Secret on June 26, 2000 "brings to an end a period of history marked by tragic human lust for power and evil"—a reckless, preposterous and fraudulent claim that ignores reality and contributes to the present endangerment of the Church and the whole world.

**Fifth,** in response to growing public doubt about the completeness of the Vatican's disclosure of the Third Secret and the Consecration of Russia, Msgr. Bertone staged a secret "interview" of Sister Lucy at her convent in Coimbra, the alleged results of which were not produced for more than a month.

**Sixth**, although the "interview" is alleged to have lasted more than two hours, Msgr. Bertone offered only *forty-four words* from Sister Lucy related to the Consecration of Russia and the Third Secret, which words are presented without any surrounding context, so that it is impossible to tell exactly what Sister Lucy was asked, and how exactly she answered.

**Seventh**, among other incredible things, we are asked to believe that during this two-hour interview, of which we are given only forty-four relevant words,

- Sister Lucy repudiated a lifetime of unwavering testimony that Our Lady asked for the Consecration of *Russia* by the Pope and all the world's bishops, not the consecration of the world by the Pope and a few bishops.
- Sister Lucy "confirms everything that is written" in *TMF*, including its suggestion that she concocted the Third Secret vision from things she had seen in books, and that Edouard Dhanis is an "eminent scholar" on Fatima, even though Dhanis asserted that Sister Lucy concocted virtually every prophetic element of the Fatima Message.
- Sister Lucy "confirms" that the Triumph of the Immaculate Heart has nothing to do with the consecration and conversion of Russia, but only the Virgin Mary's *fiat* 2,000 years ago.

**Eighth**, no transcript or other record of the two-hour "interview" has been produced, but only an Italian-language summary in *L'Osservatore Romano*, signed by Bertone and (purportedly) by Sister Lucy, who does not even speak Italian. (Sister Lucy's "signature" does not appear on the English translation of the "summary.")

**Ninth**, Bertone conducted the "interview" even though he had a vested interest in coercing Sister Lucy to support the Party Line, and to defend his own preposterous claim that the press conference of June 26, 2000 "brings to an end a period of history marked by tragic human lust for power and evil ..."

## As to Cardinal Dario Castrillón Hoyos

The principal role of Cardinal Castrillón Hoyos in this matter has been to carry out the Party Line and serve the new orientation of the Church by seeking, in his capacity as head of the Congregation for the Clergy, to crush the Fatima apostolate and destroy the reputation of Father Nicholas Gruner, who represents the largest pocket of "resistance" to the effort to bury the Message of Fatima. The evidence shows that,

**First**, the new orientation of the Church has allowed the Catholic clergy to be thoroughly infiltrated with homosexuals, pederasts and heretics who bring disgrace upon the Church—to the detriment of the many good priests who, like Father Gruner, have kept their vows and kept the faith.

**Second**, despite a crisis in faith and discipline among the clergy that is raging on every continent, Cardinal Castrillón Hoyos has issued public condemnations, notices of "suspension" and even a threat of excommunication regarding only one priest in the entire Catholic Church: Father Nicholas Gruner, who has committed no offense against faith or morals, has kept his vow of celibacy, has kept the faith, and has done absolutely nothing to warrant any punishment, let alone the cruel and unusual punishment imposed upon him by Cardinal Castrillón Hoyos under the direction of Cardinal Sodano, who has arrogated the papacy to himself *de facto*.

**Third**, the only priests Cardinal Castrillón Hoyos has subjected to immediate and harsh disciplinary measures during his tenure are "traditionalist" priests he deems insufficiently "inserted" into the "ecclesial reality of today" and "the present-day Church"—i.e. the new orientation, which he enforces far more diligently than the doctrinal or moral integrity of the priesthood.

**Fourth**, in his letter to Father Gruner of June 5, 2000, Cardinal Castrillón Hoyos threatened Father Gruner with excommunication—only days before the June 26, 2000 press conference called to "gently debunk" the Message of Fatima, under the direction of Cardinal Sodano.

**Fifth,** on February 16, 2001, Cardinal Castrillón Hoyos sent Father Gruner another letter, renewing the threat of "excommunication" and demanding that he "publicly retract" criticism of Cardinal Sodano, and other matters of free opinion in the Church, found in certain articles in *The Fatima Crusader*—an unprecedented demand, and one that is quite ludicrous considering the profusion of heretical literature promoted by unfaithful priests and even bishops today, about which Cardinal Castrillón Hoyos does nothing.

**Sixth**, in the same letter, Cardinal Castrillón Hoyos revealed his motive of furthering the Party Line when he castigated Father Gruner for not accepting the new version of Fatima: "the Blessed Mother appeared to the three little visionaries in the Cova da Iria at the beginning of the century, and *marked out a program for the New Evangelization* which the whole Church finds itself engaged in, which is even more urgent at the dawn of the third millennium."

**Seventh,** Our Lady of Fatima said nothing about any "New Evangelization", but only the consecration of Russia, the conversion of Russia to Catholicism, and the triumph of Her Immaculate Heart—all of which Cardinal Castrillón Hoyos studiously ignores, along with the other accused.

**Eighth,** in a Church beset by widespread clerical corruption that he generally tolerates, Cardinal Castrillón Hoyos has attempted to destroy the life's work and good name of Father Nicholas Gruner, a faithful priest, simply and only because Father Gruner will not accept a counterfeit of the Message of Fatima, dictated by Cardinal Sodano.

### As to All of the Accused

The evidence we have presented shows that all four of the accused—Cardinal Angelo Sodano, Cardinal Joseph Ratzinger, Msgr. Tarcisio Bertone, and Cardinal Dario Castrillón Hoyos—have combined and conspired to take various actions that make no sense unless they are viewed through the prism of the motive we have proven here: the motive of eliminating the

Message of Fatima, understood in a traditional Catholic sense, from the memory of the Church, in order to make way for a new ecclesial orientation that cannot coexist with what the authentic Message says.

The accused have attempted to dispose of the Message of Fatima at precisely that moment in history when the Church's correspondence to its requests would avert what anyone can see is a coming global catastrophe. The civil authorities of the world, armed with only the fallible intelligence reports of their human operatives, are wise enough to prepare for the worst. But the accused, who are in possession of an infallible heavenly intelligence report about the coming annihilation of nations, tell us that the report mentions only past events, is probably not reliable, and can in any event be safely disregarded.

At the same time, the evidence is overwhelming that the accused are still concealing from us a part of that heavenly intelligence report pointing directly at their own actions and omissions as the cause of an unprecedented crisis in the Church, a crisis whose terrible effects are now visible to the entire world, which looks on with a mixture of mockery and contempt.

## Eleven Lies

The evidence shows that the accused have perpetrated at least eleven distinct lies. These lies have already caused grave harm to the Church and mankind at large, and they imminently threaten even graver harm to every man, woman and child, as the Virgin of Fatima Herself has warned us.

These lies are as follows:

**Lie #1:** The vision of the "Bishop dressed in White" published on June 26, 2000, is all there is to the Third Secret of Fatima.

This lie criminally deprives the Church and the world of the obvious prophetic warnings in the vision, which can only be explained by the missing words of the Blessed Virgin. The missing words would not only explain the vision but also tell us how to avoid the future catastrophe it depicts, which includes the execution of a Pope (or a bishop dressed in white) by a band of soldiers outside a half-ruined city.

In a display of gross duplicity, the accused tell us, on the one hand, that the vision must be interpreted "figuratively" (as representing the persecution of the Church during the 20th Century), while on the other hand they themselves interpret it literally as a depiction of the failed assassination attempt against the Pope in 1981. They simply ignore Sister Lucy's own explanation in the published text of the vision that "the Pope *is killed*". They also ignore Sister Lucy's purported letter of May 12, 1982—which they themselves offer as evidence in *TMF*! In that letter, supposedly written a year *after* the assassination attempt, Sister Lucy warned: "And if we have *not yet seen* the complete fulfillment of the final part of this prophecy, *we are going towards it with great strides.*"

By withholding the words of the Virgin which are clearly missing from the Third Secret, the accused deprive us of precious heavenly guidance in this time of unprecedented crisis in the Church, while attempting to hide their own role in causing the crisis, which the Secret in its entirety no doubt reveals.

**Lie #2:** The Third Secret depicts events that "belong to the past," including the failed attempt on the life of Pope John Paul II.

The effort to "interpret" the vision of a future disaster befalling the Pope and the hierarchy (including a public execution) as nothing more than a *failed* assassination attempt more than 20 years ago is the most blatant fraud involved in the crime at issue. As we have shown abundantly, this lie is the most dangerous aspect of the crime, since it would lead the entire Church down the primrose path to ruin by telling all the faithful to have no concern any longer about vitally prophetic warnings—including the annihilation of various nations—which have clearly not yet come to pass.

This fraud—almost laughable in its audacity—is exposed by none other than Cardinal Ratzinger's own description of the contents of the Third Secret in 1984. At that time the Cardinal said nothing of his current "interpretation" (clearly dictated by Cardinal Sodano) that the Third Secret culminated in the 1981 assassination attempt. This "interpretation" is obviously a recent fabrication designed by Cardinal Sodano (and carried out by the other accused) to misdirect and mislead the faithful.

**Lie #3:** The Message of Fatima offers no specific prescription for the current crisis in the Church and the world beyond generic piety in the form of prayer and penance and being "pure of heart."

The accused and their collaborators wish to pretend that Our Lady of Fatima did not specifically request, *by the will of Almighty God Himself*: the Consecration of Russia to the Immaculate Heart of Mary by the Pope together with all the Catholic bishops of the world at the same time; and the Five First Saturdays devotion, including the Holy Communions of Reparation for man's sins against Our Lady's Immaculate Heart, numbered among which are all of man's blasphemies against the Immaculate Heart.

The evidence shows that these requests from Heaven have been buried and ignored by the accused and their collaborators because such things are too explicitly Catholic for the new "ecumenical" and worldly orientation of the Church which they obstinately pursue and promote. Thus the very means God has ordained to obtain special graces in our time for the salvation of souls from hell are criminally removed from view.

**Lie #4:** The requests of the Virgin of Fatima have all been honored.

On the contrary, Her requests have been spurned by the accused. The accused and their collaborators have arrogantly substituted a consecration of the world, in which very few bishops participated, for the Consecration of

Russia which must be done by the Pope together with all the world's Catholic bishops in a solemn public ceremony. They have "adjusted" what the Mother of God requested on the authority of Her divine Son in order to fit their failed and worthless human plans and initiatives, including an utterly fruitless "ecumenism" that has produced nothing but continued contempt for the Pope on the part of an unconverted, Kremlin-controlled Russian Orthodox hierarchy.

Instead of seeking the conversion of Russia, the Triumph of the Immaculate Heart, and reparation for sins as God commanded them at Fatima, the accused have participated in the fraudulent repackaging of the Message of Fatima as a bland and meaningless "program for the new Evangelization" (to recall Cardinal Castrillón's ridiculous assertion in this regard).

As we have shown, "the new Evangelization" abandons the constant teaching of the Church that not only the Russian Orthodox but also all schismatics and heretics must return to the Catholic Church, and that Moslems, Jews and pagans also need conversion, faith in Jesus Christ and Baptism to be saved from hell. "The new Evangelization"—much in the manner of Communist slogans—means the opposite of what it says. That is, "the new Evangelization" means *no* evangelization—of anyone!—and thus no honoring of the Virgin's requests concerning the conversion of Russia.

**Lie #5:** The alarming state of the Church and the world is the best we can expect from the falsely claimed "obedience" to the Message of Fatima.

It is criminal to attempt to deceive the faithful by telling them that the current state of Russia and the world at large represents in any way the fulfillment of the promises of the Mother of God at Fatima. The Church and the world are thus robbed of the untold temporal and spiritual benefits that God would bestow if the Message of Fatima were respected and obeyed. We have been given a demonstration of those benefits in the case of Portugal, a nation miraculously transformed into a Catholic social order following its consecration to the Immaculate Heart in 1931—a result the head of the Portuguese hierarchy explicitly declared would occur throughout the world if Russia were likewise consecrated. It also savors of blasphemy to attribute the horrendous spiritual and moral condition of Russia and the world to the triumph of the Immaculate Heart.

**Lie #6:** The Message of Fatima offers no concrete solution to the crisis in the Church and the world beyond prayer and penance.

Here the specific requests of the Mother of God are deliberately and fraudulently concealed so that no one will petition Church authorities to undertake them. This fraudulent concealment of Heaven's prescribed spiritual helps for our time has caused untold losses to the Church and the world.

**Lie #7:** We can do nothing to avoid the great chastisement foretold by Our Lady of Fatima, including the annihilation of various nations, besides offering individual prayer and penance.

The accused thus deliberately and willfully hide from the Church and the world two precise means that Heaven has ordained for protection from temporal harm and the obtainment of extraordinary graces in this epoch of Church history: namely, the Consecration of Russia and the widespread practice of the First Saturdays devotion.

The accused thus coldly, deliberately and ruthlessly place the Church and civil society alike on the same path as that followed by the unfortunate kings of France, who failed to heed Our Lord's command that France be consecrated to His Sacred Heart in a solemn public ceremony.

The execution of the King of France by French revolutionaries in 1793 mirrors the fate that awaits the Pope and many members of the hierarchy, as seen in the Third Secret vision: that is, the execution of the Pope and his ministers by soldiers, outside the half-ruined city. This future event the accused criminally attempt to misrepresent as a *failed* assassination attempt against the Pope alone more than 20 years ago!

**Lie #8:** The Message of Fatima is a mere "private revelation" that does not impose any obligation on the members of the Church to believe it or to follow it.

As Cardinal Ratzinger claims in *TMF*, the Message of Fatima is nothing more or less than "a help which is offered, but *which one is not obliged to use*." That is, Ratzinger openly declares that the Church is not obliged to heed the requests of the Virgin of Fatima—including the Consecration of Russia and the Five First Saturdays. The other accused agree.

Yet while the accused tell us that no one need believe or heed the Message of Fatima, the Pope himself has declared that the Message of Fatima "imposes an obligation on the Church." To demonstrate this, the Pope has had a Feast of the Virgin of Fatima inserted into the new Roman Missal, which the universal Church will celebrate on May 13 each year. Thus, according to the fraudulent claim of the accused, the Church celebrates a feast day in honor of an apparition in which no one has to believe!

To hold that heavenly warnings about a great chastisement, that "various nations will be annihilated" and the loss of millions of souls need not be given credence if we choose to disbelieve them—even though the warnings were authenticated by an unprecedented public miracle witnessed by 70,000 people—is the height of human folly. We will all suffer terrible chastisements including the annihilation of various nations—and have already suffered World War II, the Korean War, the Vietnam War, etc. as well as the war on the unborn with more than 800 million murders of innocent children—all of these and more are the consequences of this arrogant demotion of the counsels of the Mother of God at Fatima.

**Lie #9:** The Message of Fatima is ultimately of little importance in its prophetic particulars, while the Third Secret contains "no great mystery", "no surprises" and no warnings about the future.

By this lie the faithful are criminally deprived of heavenly warnings and prescriptions of utmost importance for the Church in our time. Had the Message of Fatima been heeded, incalculable temporal and spiritual harm could have been avoided. By continuing to perpetrate this lie, the accused leave the Church and the world powerless to avoid the great chastisement which will affect gravely every man, woman and child—namely the literal "annihilation of various nations" and the enslavement of the whole surviving populations of the world, not to mention the loss of millions of souls in hell for all eternity. Our Lady warned this would be the ultimate consequence of failing to heed Her requests.

**Lie #10:** The accused themselves are believers in the authentic Message of Fatima.

While they hide behind a false appearance of belief in the Message of Fatima, the objective words and deeds of the accused reveal a systematic attempt to undercut and destroy all credence in the explicitly Catholic prophetic content of the Message. They reveal their true intention by citing Dhanis as an "eminent scholar" on Fatima, when Dhanis cast doubt on every prophetic aspect of the Message. By citing Dhanis as their great authority, the accused signal their fellow "illuminated ones" (but not the uninformed general public) that they regard the Message of Fatima as essentially the pious concoction of Sister Lucy, whose claim to have spoken with the Virgin about the consecration and conversion of Russia, and so forth, cannot really be taken seriously by the "enlightened" men of the post-conciliar Church.

The failure of the accused to admit openly that they really do not believe in the authentic Message of Fatima, even as they purport to "interpret" it for us, is not only gross hypocrisy but an outrageous fraud upon the Church. Just as in the court of law, judges and potential members of the jury must disclose any possible prejudices they may have regarding the case at hand, so too should the accused reveal their prejudices openly before they pretend to be unbiased judges of the Fatima Message.

**Lie #11:** Catholics who do not agree with the accused concerning the Message of Fatima are "disobedient" to "the Magisterium."

By "Magisterium" the accused mean nothing more than their own opinions about the Message of Fatima, which opinions in fact contradict what the Pope himself has said and done to vouch for the authenticity of the Message—most recently with his institution of the Feast of the Virgin of Fatima in the Church's liturgical calendar.

Thus, ironically enough, it is the *accused* who are disloyal to the Magisterium when they seek to demote Fatima to the status of "private revelation" that may be disregarded by the entire Church with complete safety.

## A Crime Beyond Calculation

How can one assess the magnitude of the crime committed by those who would bury, in misrepresentation and concealment, a precious Message from Heaven, delivered by the Mother of God Herself for the temporal and eternal welfare of Her children? This crime is beyond all calculation, because it involves not only temporal calamity but also the loss of countless millions of souls, which could be avoided by heeding the Virgin's request for the Consecration of Russia and Her other requests at Fatima (including the First Saturday devotion, which the accused and their collaborators refuse to promote). The Virgin of Fatima Herself indicts them: "If My requests are granted, many souls will be saved and there will be peace." Her requests have not been granted, and these men (along with their collaborators) are responsible for the consequences to the Church, to the world, and to countless millions of souls who have been robbed of the graces Our Lady of Fatima came to provide them in the name of Her Son.

## A Mystery of Iniquity

Why are the accused and those who labor with them in pursuit of the Church's new orientation so adamant in their refusal to allow the Pope and the bishops to do the simple thing that Our Lady of Fatima requested? Why do they move mountains to prevent the utterance of one word—*Russia*—in a public consecration of "that poor nation"? What do we have to lose by carrying out the Virgin's request to the letter, without amendments imposed by Vatican diplomats and ecumenists? Nothing. What do we have to gain? Everything.

There is simply no legitimate explanation for such perverse resistance to the Consecration of Russia by name. Something unnatural is at work here. Without judging the subjective motives of the accused, one is driven to the conclusion that their otherwise inexplicable and seemingly senseless refusal to allow the utterance of one simple word—the one word Our Lady of Fatima requested—is the result of a *preternatural* intervention into the Church. It is an intervention by the Adversary himself, who, as Sister Lucy herself has said, is "in the mood for engaging in a final decisive battle against the Blessed Virgin." This final battle has involved the penetration into the Church of the organized forces that have long sought to bring her to ruin. In the face of this awful development, even Pope Paul VI was compelled to lament publicly that "the smoke of Satan has entered the temple of God."

Whether they subjectively intend it or not, the accused have acted in a way that only serves the aims of the Church's worst enemy. The results of their actions speak for themselves. "By their fruits ye shall know them." (Mt. 7:16) What are the fruits of their governance of the Church? Simply look at the condition of the Church today and you will know the answer.

Along with many others in high positions in the hierarchy, the accused have presided over the worst crisis of faith and morals in Church history. In their pursuit of the ruinous novelties that have brought on the crisis, the accused spurn a heavenly prescription that would restore the Church to health and bring peace to a warring world. Instead of listening to the advice of the Mother of God at Fatima, they press on with their utterly fruitless "ecumenism", "interreligious dialogue", and "dialogue with the world"; their hobnobbing with men of blood like Mikhail Gorbachev, whose presence desecrated the Vatican only one day after the accused attempted to dispose of the Message of Fatima. As the accused and their fellows palaver endlessly with the forces of the world, countless souls in need of the light of Christ for their salvation in Russia and elsewhere are allowed to remain in darkness. The enemies of the Church delight in seeing Her thus rendered almost powerless to oppose them.

The Church retreats as the forces of the world continue to advance against Her. Yet the accused and their collaborators persist in their suicidal attempt to embrace the world instead of conquering it spiritually for Christ the King, as Our Lady of Fatima would have them do. The men who control the Vatican apparatus today do not wish to offend the Russian Orthodox or anyone else with a show of Catholic militancy, which they view as embarrassing and "outdated"—to use one of their favorite words. The Church's abject retreat from battle warms the hearts of the Masons and the Communists, who labored for generations in the hope of seeing the Church reduced precisely to this pathetic condition.

And yet the accused and their collaborators are not without militancy of a sort. While over the past forty years they have done almost nothing to stop infiltrators of the Church from spreading heresy and moral corruption with virtual impunity, they relentlessly hound, denounce and ostracize anyone who opposes too effectively their disastrous policies of "reform", "openness" and "renewal." For the accused and the other members of the upper hierarchy who have presided over the post-conciliar debacle, it seems that the only remaining "heresy", the only offense warranting harsh punishment, is to question their judgment in imposing the new orientation upon the Church, an orientation from which they have utterly and definitively excluded the Message of Fatima in its traditional Catholic sense—or so they think.

## The Remedies to Which the Faithful Are Entitled

What is it that we seek from the Holy Father as remedies for the acts and omissions of the accused? We seek the following:

### First,<br>The Consecration of Russia—<br>There Is Still Time

By this we mean precisely what Our Lady of Fatima requested: The immediate Consecration of Russia—*by name and without equivocation*—to the

Immaculate Heart of Mary, in a solemn public ceremony by the Pope together with all the Catholic bishops of the world.

We ask the Pope to command under pain of excommunication all the Catholic bishops (except those prevented by imprisonment or serious illness) to consecrate solemnly, publicly and specifically Russia according to the requests of Our Lady of Fatima, together with the Pope on the same day and at the same hour specified by the Pope.

Some will say it is already too late to obtain the Consecration and that it is pointless to go on requesting it. That is simply not so. As Our Lord Himself revealed to Sister Lucy in the revelation at Rianjo in August of 1931:

> Make it known to My ministers that given they follow the example of the King of France in delaying the execution of My command, they will follow him into misfortune ... They [the ministers of the Catholic Church] did not want to heed My command. Like the King of France they will repent of it, and they will do it, but it will be late. Russia will already have spread her errors throughout the world, causing wars and persecutions of the Church. The Holy Father will have much to suffer.[4]

And yet, as Our Lord also revealed to Sister Lucy on that occasion: "*It will never be too late to have recourse to Jesus and Mary.*" That is, even though we are now suffering the consequences of delay in the execution of Heaven's command, the worst of those consequences, including the annihilation of various nations, may yet be avoided if the command to consecrate Russia is heeded, however belatedly.

It is outrageous that human respect—fear of offending the Russian Orthodox—has been allowed until now to prevent the Church's fulfillment of Heaven's plan for peace in our time. As members of the Church militant, we can no longer allow those who claim to speak for our ailing Pope to declare that "the Pope" has pronounced unequivocally, authoritatively, and definitively the consecration to be accomplished. We have shown how the Pope himself has publicly said quite the opposite. We must implore His Holiness to reject the manifestly bad advice he has been given by those who surround him, and to follow Heaven's advice instead.

## Second, Disclosure of the Full and Integral Third Secret of Fatima

This disclosure would have to include the text of the words of the Blessed Virgin explaining the vision that was published on June 26, 2000. That such a text exists has been proven to a moral certainty by a mountain of direct and circumstantial evidence, every piece of which points to a missing text of one page and some 25 lines in letter form, containing the words of the Virgin Herself.

The Church and the world have the right to know the contents of the Third Secret, which obviously contains salutary warnings about the current crisis in the Church. The Holy Father's clear indications that the Secret relates to the apostasy and fall of consecrated souls described in the Book of the Apocalypse tell us that he himself has been constrained not to reveal the Secret in its entirety, but rather has been reduced to hinting at its contents. Meanwhile, those who actually control the daily affairs of the Church—first and foremost Cardinal Sodano—continue to bury the truth about their own failed governance of the Church.

## Third, A Call for Daily Recitation of the Rosary

The Rosary is infinitely more powerful than any weapon devised by man. There is no difficulty that cannot be overcome, no battle that cannot be won, with the aid of the Holy Rosary. If enough Catholics pray the Rosary with the correct intention, the enemies of the Church will be routed from their strongholds within her and driven out. As Fatima itself shows us, by the will of God the Virgin Mary is our refuge and our strength in times of crisis. In this gravest of crises, the whole Church must seek recourse to Her through daily recitation of the Rosary.

While we need not wait, and should not wait to institute a perpetual Rosary Crusade at all levels in the Church where we can and as soon as possible, we also can petition the Pope to institute such a campaign throughout the Church by writing encyclicals on the Rosary every year like Pope Leo XIII, by appointing a dicastery headed by a Cardinal to promote the Rosary by various initiatives through the network of Catholic shrines and Marian priests (both religious and diocesan). Such initiatives, of course, must be entirely in keeping with authentic Catholic doctrine and practices promoting all the great privileges of Our Lady.

The Rosary should, of course, include the prayer prescribed by Our Lady of Fatima as an addition to the Rosary: "O my Jesus, forgive us our sins, save us from the fires of hell. Lead all souls to Heaven, especially those most in need." During the "entrustment" of the world to the Immaculate Heart in October of 2000, however, the public recitation of the Rosary at the Vatican conspicuously omitted this prayer. This is yet another sign of the new orientation, which abhors any reference to hell and damnation.

## Fourth, Promotion of the Five First Saturdays Devotion

The accused and the other elements of the Vatican apparatus who have undertaken to "revise" the Message of Fatima have attempted to bury in silence this part of the Message, along with all its other explicitly Catholic elements. Indeed, the whole concept of man making reparation to God and the Blessed Virgin Mary for blasphemies and other sins has been gravely diminished in the Church's new orientation. (One of the key elements obscured in the new liturgy is that the Mass is a *propitiatory* sacrifice to make reparation to God for sin, not merely a "sacrifice of praise.")

The First Saturday devotion is one of Heaven's chosen means to restore in our time a sense of the need for reparation for sin by the members of the

Church. Who can doubt that now, more than ever before, the Church must renew Her effort to offer reparation to God and to the Immaculate Virgin Mother of God, thus staying the execution of God's wrath? Yet the wrath of God is another thing of which we hear nothing from modern churchmen. By promoting the First Saturday devotion, the Holy Father will marshal the Church's power to offer reparation for sin at this critical time in world history.

## Fifth, Reestablishment Throughout the Church of Devotion to *the* Immaculate Heart of Mary

Cardinal Ratzinger's shameful attempt to equate the one and only Immaculate Heart to the heart of anyone who repents of his sins is only typical of the new orientation, which abhors the concept of Original Sin as much as it does hell and damnation.

Only the Immaculate Heart of Mary was preserved free from all stain of Original Sin and was never under the dominion of Satan. In contemplating the glory of the one and only sinless Immaculate Heart of Mary, we are drawn also to be aware of our own wretchedness and the need for Baptism and the other sacraments of the Church to preserve us in a state of grace.

The uniquely Catholic devotion to the Immaculate Heart of Mary is a rebuke to the new orientation of the Church, whose "ecumenism" downplays the dogma of the Immaculate Conception (and the Assumption) out of human respect for the sensibilities of non-Catholics. That is precisely why, as Our Lady of Fatima told us, God wishes to establish *in the world* devotion to Her Immaculate Heart. God wishes the world to see that it is the Catholic Church, and none other, which is the ark of salvation.

## Sixth, The Resignation of the Accused and Their Collaborators

As we have proven, Cardinal Sodano, Cardinal Ratzinger, Cardinal Castrillón and Archbishop Bertone have combined and conspired to do away with the Message of Fatima in its traditional Catholic sense. They have tampered with the meaning of the very words of the Mother of God, buried in silence and obscuration all of the explicitly Catholic and prophetic elements of the Message, and persecuted those who have offered a principled opposition to their revisionist program, their Party Line on Fatima. By so doing, the accused have already caused untold damage to the Church and have exposed both the Church and the world to the gravest possible dangers, including the loss of millions of souls and the annihilation of various nations. For as Our Lady of Fatima cautioned the Church: "*If* My requests are not granted, Russia will spread her errors throughout the world raising up wars and persecutions against the Church, the good will be martyred, the Holy Father will have much to suffer, and various nations will be annihilated." She also promised: "*If* My requests are granted, many souls will be saved and there will be peace." The course of conduct in which the accused obstinately persist imminently threatens the Church and the world with incalculable harm. For the good of the Church these men should be directed by the Holy Father to resign their offices, immediately.

Some will object, however, that it is the height of arrogance for mere members of the laity to petition the Pope for the removal of such high-ranking prelates. On the contrary, *it is our duty as Catholics* to petition the Pope for the removal of errant prelates who endanger the flock.

## The Example of St. John Gualberto

No less than a canonized saint of the Catholic Church gives us the example to follow when the faithful are confronted with a wayward prelate who is harming the Church.[5]

St. John Gualberto lived in the 12th Century. He is not only a saint but founder of the Val Ambrosian Benedictines. His feast day is July 12 in the old calendar. St. John's heroic Christian virtue is demonstrated by his having forgiven the murderer of his own brother. Encountering the weaponless and defenseless killer in a blind alley, St. John (who was not yet a monk) was moved to forgiveness when the man put up his arms in the form of a cross and asked for mercy for the sake of Christ crucified. St. John forgave the man even though he had been searching for him with a band of soldiers in order to exact vengeance. That very day, which was Good Friday, St. John saw the image of Christ on a crucifix come alive and nod His head toward St. John. At this moment, Our Lord imparted to St. John an absolutely extraordinary special grace, because he had forgiven his own brother's murderer. It was that moment of grace which led St. John to become a monk.

Now, as we can see, St. John Gualberto was the very model of Christian forgiveness. If he could forgive his brother's own murderer, he could forgive any offense. He was also a man of considerable importance in the hierarchy of the Church, having gone on to found a monastery and an order of monks that still exist to this day. The order had—and still has—charge of a church in Rome, the Church of St. Praxedes, wherein nothing less than the column at which Christ was scourged is to be found. The church, literally just around the corner from St. Mary Major, also contains a painting of St. John Gualberto forgiving his brother's murderer—clearly, a very significant event in Church history.

Yet despite his exemplary Christian mercy and forgiveness and his great stature in the Church, St. John Gualberto did not hesitate to seek the removal of a corrupt prelate of his own day. St. John went to the Lateran (where the Pope resided in those days before the creation of the Vatican enclave) to ask that the Archbishop of Florence be removed because he was unworthy of his office. The grounds for St. John's petition were that the Archbishop had paid money to certain persons of influence in order to have himself appointed Archbishop. That is, he had purchased his ecclesiastical office, which constitutes a grave sin of simony.

After the Pope's officials in the Lateran—including no less than St. Peter Damian—would take no action to remove the Archbishop, citing a supposed lack of proof, God gave St. John a special inspiration: In order to demonstrate that St. John was telling the truth about the Archbishop, God would give a sign. One of the brothers in St. John's order, Brother Peter, would walk through a bonfire from which he would emerge miraculously unscathed, to testify to the truth of St. John's accusation against the Archbishop. St. John called all the townspeople together and told them to construct a huge bonfire with a narrow passage in the middle. He explained to them what was about to happen and why. Then Brother Peter, under holy obedience, walked through the narrow, fiery passage and emerged at the other end without injury. For his own great faith, Brother Peter was beatified (his feast day is on February 8 in the Roman Martyrology). When the lay faithful saw this miraculous sign, they arose as one and literally drove the Archbishop out of Florence. The Archbishop had to flee for his life, and the Pope had to appoint an honest replacement.

## The Removal of Wayward Prelates in Our Own Time

What does this event in Church history tell us about our own situation today? It teaches us that the laity have the right and the duty to protect themselves from wayward prelates who are harming the Church and souls by their misconduct. And in this time of unparalleled crisis in the Church, we are hardly alone in seeking this extraordinary remedy from the Pope.

Consider that in March of 2002 the Pope received a canonical petition from various members of the faithful in the Archdiocese of San Antonio, seeking the removal of Archbishop Flores from his office on grounds that he had covered up criminal acts of sexual abuse by homosexual priests under his charge and paid millions of dollars in "hush money" to silence the victims of these predators. The petition to the Pope charges that Archbishop Flores has "been grossly negligent in the exercise of his episcopal office, has failed to protect the temporal goods of the archdiocese, and has *endangered the faith of the people entrusted to his care* by allowing sexual predators within the clergy free rein."[6] In like manner, thousands of members of the faithful have called for the resignation of Cardinal Law of the Archdiocese of Boston because of his complicity in shielding dozens of homosexual predators from exposure and punishment.[7]

Would anyone accuse the faithful of the Archdiocese of San Antonio or the Archdiocese of Boston of arrogance for exercising their canonical and God-given right to seek the removal of prelates whose acts and omissions have caused so much damage to the Church and to countless innocent victims? By what peculiar standard of justice, then, are prelates who work in the Vatican apparatus exempt from accountability to the Pope for their actions? Clearly, they are not exempt. And while the sexual abuse of members of the flock by their very pastors is among the gravest of scandals, justifying a movement of the laity against the priests who commit these unspeakable acts and the bishops, and even Cardinals, who shield the offenders, there is a scandal even greater than this. We mean the scandal of spurning the very prescriptions which the Mother of God Herself gave to the Church at Fatima—prescriptions which, had they been followed, would have prevented not only the sexual scandal now racking the Church but indeed the entire ecclesial and world crisis we now see. We mean also the scandal of a Vatican apparatus that does nothing to combat the true enemies of the Church in her very midst, while it persecutes faithful traditional clergy for the "offense" of being too staunchly Catholic for the "ecclesial reality of today"—to recall once again the telltale phrase of Cardinal Castrillón Hoyos. For no other reason than to prevent the collapse of faith and discipline which we now witness did Our Lady come to Fatima. Yet it is precisely the Message of Fatima which the accused have devoted so much time and effort to burying, while they do virtually nothing about the ecclesial crisis that is raging all around them.

The example of St. John Gualberto teaches us also that when God gives a sign through a chosen messenger, the laity are entitled to rely upon that sign, even if the highest prelates in the Church choose to ignore it. Such is the case with the Message of Fatima, for there could be no greater sign from Heaven than the Miracle of the Sun. The Message of Fatima clearly involves a warning of apostasy and malfeasance among the members of the upper hierarchy, as well as the fall of many consecrated souls from their stations. We are witnessing the fulfillment of that prophecy at this very moment. We are entitled to rely upon the sign of Heaven that authenticates that prophecy beyond all reasonable doubt, no matter what the Message of Fatima's "debunkers" in the Vatican may claim.

Knowing what Heaven has told us at Fatima, it is our duty as members of the Church to try to convince the Pope to remove the errant advisors who surround him, especially the accused, and to follow instead the advice of the Mother of God at Fatima. We must plead with the Pope to perform the consecration of Russia to the Immaculate Heart exactly in the manner She requested, *without alteration by any worldly-wise member of the Vatican apparatus*. Further, we should ask the Pope to remove from office, if necessary, any prelate in the Vatican who attempts to prevent the Pope from carrying out the Virgin's requests.

Likewise, we must petition the Pope to remove from office those, including the accused, who have conspired to prevent full disclosure of the Third Secret of Fatima. The Third Secret is obviously of the utmost importance in understanding and combating the crisis in the Church, while protecting ourselves from its devastating spiritual effects—of which the unspeakable crimes committed by so many priests are but one manifestation. *The faithful are entitled to know what Heaven itself wishes them to know for their own spiritual safety.* The conspiracy to prevent full disclosure of the Third Secret is a high crime against the Church, as well as an offense against Almighty God and against the Blessed Virgin Mary Herself.

## The Church's Urgent Need for Militant Prelates

Today the Church needs more than ever true soldiers of the Church—men possessed of an unabashed Catholic militancy, who are not afraid of a confrontation with the forces of the world, which invaded the Church while the accused and their many collaborators in the Vatican apparatus stood by and did nothing, except to encourage the invasion. The Church needs men who will act decisively to root out the pandemic heresy and scandal in the Church, instead of hounding and oppressing traditional Catholic clergy who decline to be "inserted" into Cardinal Castrillón's "ecclesial reality of today." The Church needs spiritual warriors, not practitioners of "dialogue", "ecumenism" and *Ostpolitik*.

The Message of Fatima itself is a call to spiritual warfare—to a battle that is to culminate in the consecration and conversion of Russia and the *triumph* of the Immaculate Heart of Mary. The accused regard such things with the squeamishness of those who consider themselves more enlightened than all the generations of Catholic saints, Popes, doctors and martyrs whose militancy down through the centuries is a living testament to the very words of Christ Himself:

> "If the world hates you, know ye that it has hated me before you. If you had been of the world, the world would love its own; but because you are not of the world, but I have chosen you out of the world, therefore the world hates you." (Jn. 15:18-20)

> "Do not think that I came to send peace upon earth: I came not to send peace, but the sword. For I came to set a man at variance against his father, and the daughter against her mother, and the daughter-in-law against her mother-in-law. And a man's enemies shall be they of his own household." (Mt. 10:34-36)

For too long the Church has suffered under the governance of those who would have us believe that there is no spiritual combat between Christ and His Church on the one hand, and the world on the other. For too long these men have been allowed to pursue and promote their false vision of a Church reconciled to the world, rather than a world reconciled to the Church. For too long these men have yoked the Church to the utopian notion of worldly peace among men of all religions or no religion at all, rather than the true peace that can come only when the souls of men are conquered by the grace of Christ the King, which He deigns to mediate to men through the Immaculate Heart of Mary and through the Holy Roman Catholic Church.

Fatima shows us the way to this true peace among men. The accused have blocked our progress along that way, exposing the Church and the whole world to the risk of an ultimate calamity. It is they, not we, who are lacking in vision. It is they, not we, who are narrow-minded. It is they, not we, who are being unrealistic. They must step aside for the good of all humanity.

# Chapter 17

## What Can Be Done in the Meantime?

While petitioning the Pope in the manner we have set forth is an important step, there is, of course, no guarantee that the men who surround the Pope will even allow him to read our petitions, especially given his steadily declining physical health which has caused him to rely more and more upon Cardinal Sodano to run the Church.[1] While we must not be deterred by this obstacle, nevertheless we must still deal with the crisis on our own until this Pope or his successor takes definitive actions to end it. We recall here Cardinal Newman's description of the state of the Church during the Arian crisis:

> The body of bishops failed in their confession of the Faith. ... They spoke variously, one against another; there was nothing, after Nicea, of firm, unvarying, consistent testimony, for nearly sixty years. There were untrustworthy Councils, unfaithful bishops; there was weakness, fear of consequences, misguidance, delusion, hallucination, *endless, hopeless, extending into nearly every corner of the Catholic Church*. The comparatively few who remained faithful were discredited and driven into exile; the rest were either *deceivers or deceived.*[2]

What, then, can we do in this time of darkness for the Church, as we wait for those who lead Her to put Her back on the proper course? We can do whatever it is in our power to do, according to our station in life.

### Above All, Prayer

First and foremost, there is the power of prayer—and particularly the most efficacious prayer of the Holy Rosary.

The importance of the Rosary and other forms of Catholic prayer in this struggle cannot be overemphasized. We are dealing with forces and circumstances that, humanly speaking, seem impossible to overcome. Our Pope is ailing, and a papal deathwatch is already underway. The Pope is surrounded by powerful men who have thus far successfully impeded fulfillment of the Message of Fatima. The next Pope will still have to contend with these men or like-minded successors in office, for the internal enemies of the Church are now legion.

How can we, simple members of the rank-and-file laity or clergy, hope to reverse the current course of events in the Church and the world? How can we secure the Consecration of Russia when so many of the high and powerful are so opposed to it? Humanly speaking, we cannot. But with the power of the Holy Rosary, we can. Is this not indeed why Our Lady of Fatima, with our present circumstances clearly in view, called for daily recitation of the Rosary? As Our Lady, speaking of Herself in the third person, declared: "Only Our Lady of the Rosary can help you!"

First of all, then, *pray the Rosary* for the intention of Our Lady's final triumph over the crisis in the Church and the world through fulfillment of Her requests at Fatima, and urge your friends, relatives and neighbors to pray for the same intention. If ten percent of the world's Catholics prayed the Rosary daily for this precise intention, the battle would be won. History records that ten percent of the population of Austria, by mounting a Rosary Crusade, brought about the miraculous and otherwise inexplicable withdrawal of an invading Soviet army after the end of World War II. Therefore, begin right now to organize a Rosary Crusade among your friends and relatives and in your parish—a Rosary Crusade for the Consecration of Russia and the Triumph of the Immaculate Heart of Mary.

In addition to the powerful prayer of the Rosary, Catholics must conduct spiritual works in other ways, including the Sacred Heart devotions (the Nine First Fridays, having sacred images of Jesus in our homes, and making frequent visits to the Blessed Sacrament) and, of course, the First Saturday devotions prescribed by Our Lady of Fatima. By these means we address spiritually the many sacrileges and outrages committed against Our Lord, particularly Our Lord in the Blessed Sacrament, Who has been abused innumerable times by the sacrilege of communion in the hand which is a part of the current crisis of faith and discipline in the Church. By making reparation in this way, we will hasten the coming of the Triumph of the Immaculate Heart.

Then, too, there are the sacramentals of the Church by which Catholics can gain spiritual favor for themselves and others. These include the Brown and Green scapulars—sacramentals bestowed by Heaven itself, which are all but forgotten in this time of diabolical disorientation in the Church.

Finally, of course, each of us must strive to live a holy life through frequent reception of the great Sacraments of the Holy Catholic Church, whose grace arms us for the battles ahead and keeps us from the pitfalls which have claimed so many others in this crisis.

In short, through prayer (especially the Rosary) and the sacramental life, we must do everything we can to become more fervent in the faith and to make others more fervent as well. For this struggle is, first and foremost, a spiritual combat in which every soul is needed, and every soul is at risk.

## In the Practical Realm

Naturally, Catholics must back up their prayer with good works. As St. Ignatius said, we must pray as though everything depends on God and work as though everything depends on us. What are some of the things Catholics can do in their respective stations in life?

### As simple members of the laity, we can—

- arm ourselves against the crisis by knowing our faith, and by informing ourselves about the Message of Fatima and what it really means;

- tell our fellow Catholics, and everyone else we meet, about the relation of the Message of Fatima to the crisis in the Church and the crisis in the world;
- provide by our lives an example of Christian faith and good morals;
- demand that local bishops and pastors of parishes provide sound Catholic doctrine and liturgy;
- *withhold financial support* from parishes and dioceses where doctrinal and moral corruption and liturgical abuse is allowed to fester;
- *call for the removal* of morally and doctrinally corrupt priests and bishops;
- pray—especially the Rosary, which can conquer all heresies and other threats to the Church;
- pray for the Holy Father, as Jesus urged Sister Lucy to do, that the Pope might be moved to vanquish the enemies of the Church and to fulfill the requests of Our Lady of Fatima.

**As priests and religious, we can—**

- preach and defend the traditional Roman Catholic Faith;
- make known to everyone the Message of Fatima and what it requires of the Church;
- provide by our lives an example of Christian faith and good morals;
- call upon our superiors, including the Pope, to honor the Message of Fatima and take other actions to end the moral and doctrinal crisis in the Church, including the rooting out of morally and spiritually corrupt leaders of whatever rank who are wolves among the sheep.

**As Catholic journalists, authors and publishers, we can—**

- write the truth about Fatima and make it as widely known as possible;
- write the truth about the current crisis in the Church and its causes, as we have discussed in this book;
- investigate, expose and condemn the conspiracy against Fatima;
- publish to the extent we can, by the various media available to us, the truth about Fatima including the truth contained in this book.

**As Catholic lay people; political leaders; captains of industry, commerce and finance; diplomats; and military leaders, we can—**

- implore the Pope to pursue *Heaven*'s plan for peace as given to us at Fatima, rather than the failed diplomacy and treaties of mere men, including Vatican diplomats such as Cardinal Sodano;

- support with our financial means those apostolates and apostolic initiatives which promote, advance and defend the authentic Fatima message.
- use our influence to prevail upon members of the hierarchy to cooperate in carrying out the imperatives of the Fatima Message for the good of the whole world.

## An Act of Justice and Mercy

No less than Pope Saint Gregory the Great declared "It is better that scandal arise than that the truth be suppressed." Whatever our station in life, each of us is a member of the Church militant, a soldier of Christ. As such, each of us has a duty to defend the Church according to his ability. As Pope Saint Felix III declared: "Not to oppose error, is to approve it, and not to defend truth is to suppress it, and indeed to neglect to confound evil men, when we can do it, is no less a sin than to encourage them."

It should be obvious to any Catholic that time is running out for the human element of the Church and for civilization at large. As Saint Paul warned us, God will not be mocked. If salvation history teaches us anything, it teaches that when men rebel against God on the massive scale such as we are now witnessing, then the world will be swiftly and terribly punished with a divine chastisement. The Message of Fatima is nothing if not a warning that such a chastisement is imminent in our time if man does not turn away from sin.

The Virgin of Fatima offered us the means to avoid that chastisement, yet we find that men of the Church have spurned the heavenly offer. Like the Kings of France, who spurned Our Lord's simple request for the consecration of that nation to His Sacred Heart, the men who control the Vatican apparatus today have charted a course toward disaster—a disaster vastly greater than the one that befell France.

But there is still time to change course. It is the supreme urgency of our situation that has moved us to write this book and to present the serious accusations it contains. The actions of the accused jeopardize the temporal safety of the Church and the world, and the eternal safety of countless souls. How can we remain silent in the face of this danger?

We have presented our case to you, not to engage in provocation for its own sake, and not merely for the justice of this cause, but also as *an act of mercy*—mercy not only for the victims of the great crime against Fatima but for the accused themselves, who are owed in charity an opportunity to be confronted with the magnitude of what they have done so that they might change their course and begin to make amends before it is too late for them—and for us. We recall here what Saint Thomas teaches: "We must also remember that when a man reproves his prelate charitably, it does not follow that he thinks himself any better, but merely that he offers his help to one who, 'being in the higher position among you, *is therefore in greater danger*' as Augustine observes ..."

## We Ask For Your Verdict

The time has come, then, for you to render what we have called your verdict. As we said at the beginning of our presentation, we do not and cannot ask for a verdict of guilty in the sense of a juridical pronouncement, for that is neither yours nor ours to render. We ask only for your agreement, as fellow sons and daughters of the Holy Catholic Church, that what the accused have done warrants a petition to the Supreme Pontiff, John Paul II, or his successor, to investigate and effectively remedy what is, objectively speaking, a crime against the Church and humanity.

We believe the evidence we have presented imposes a duty that cannot be ignored by Catholics of good will. It is no longer possible to remain neutral at this critical point in the battle for the Church and the world. We have shown you the evidence, and it is overwhelming. Having seen the evidence, you must make a decision.

We pray that your decision will be to join us in this effort, however humble, to begin to set right what has gone so terribly wrong. We ourselves are of little importance in the great drama of Fatima, but we labor in the cause of the One who, by the will of God, stands at its very center. She cannot fail in what She promised, if only Her children, freed from the designs of erring men, will do what little She asked of them: "If My requests are granted, many souls will be saved and there will be peace. ... In the end, My Immaculate Heart will triumph."

# Chapter 18

## What You Can Do Right Now!

Besides obeying Our Lady of Fatima's requests to you personally, among which is praying the Rosary every day, another practical action you can take is to photocopy and sign the following petition and send it to the publisher of this book, who will forward it to the Pope.

The petition also serves as a summary of the basic claims put forth in this book, and can be used to send photocopies to educate others who may not have the time or inclination to read the book in its entirety.

**Petition to the Supreme Pontiff, His Holiness John Paul II,**

**—concerning the actions of—**

**Cardinal Angelo Sodano, Cardinal Joseph Ratzinger, Cardinal Dario Castrillón Hoyos and Msgr. Tarcisio Bertone**

Holy Father:

We, being faithful members of the Holy Catholic Church, are compelled in conscience to submit this Petition to Your Holiness, who is the final judge of matters in controversy in the Church.

This Petition is an extraordinary action by Catholics who have no representative to intercede for them before Your Holiness in the midst of the unprecedented crisis of faith and discipline that has followed the Second Vatican Council.

This Petition is an exercise of our God-given right as baptized Catholics to make direct recourse to the Supreme Pontiff, without any intervening canonical procedures. (First Vatican Council - 1870 A.D., Dz. 1830, D.S. 3063; Second Council of Lyons - 1274 A.D., Dz. 466; 1983 Code of Canon Law, can. 212, can. 1417 § 1)

The grounds for this Petition are contained in the study entitled *The Devil's Final Battle*. This document presents compelling evidence and well-founded accusations against Cardinal Angelo Sodano, Cardinal Joseph Ratzinger, Cardinal Dario Castrillón Hoyos and Msgr. Tarcisio Bertone (the accused), all of whom belong to the Vatican apparatus which is supposed to assist Your Holiness in the just and prudent governance of the Church.

Having considered the evidence, we are persuaded to a moral certainty of the following things:

First, the Messsage of Fatima is a vital prophecy for our time, whose veracity has been placed beyond all doubt by the absolutely extraordinary circumstances of its revelation (including a public miracle witnessed by 70,000 people), its approval as authentic by competent Church authorities, its acceptance by and incorporation into the life of the Church, and by the very statements and actions of Your Holiness himself, including the institution of the Feast of Our Lady of Fatima on May 13 in the Church's liturgical calendar.

Second, the accused (and numerous collaborators) have combined and conspired to attempt to impose upon the Church, through misinterpretation, obscurantism and outright concealment, an understanding of the Message of Fatima that would deprive the Message entirely of its specifically Catholic prophetic content. In particular (and with the aid of a "theological commentary" by Cardinal Ratzinger), the accused have perpetrated an "interpretation" of the Message which:

(a) dispenses with the Consecration of Russia requested by Our Lady of Fatima and arbitrarily replaces it with a consecration of the world, from which any mention of Russia has been deliberately omitted for shallow political reasons.

(b) fraudulently represents that the Triumph of the Immaculate Heart, which the Virgin prophesied would follow the Consecration of Russia, means nothing more than the Virgin's *fiat* in agreeing to become the Mother of God 2,000 years ago.

(c) dares to equate the one and only Immaculate Heart of Mary with the heart of anyone numbered among the "pure of heart" in the limited sense of the Beatitudes, while reducing devotion to the Immaculate Heart (which Our Lady of Fatima said God wishes to establish in the world) to nothing more than seeking "interior union" with God.

(d) ludicrously asserts that the visional aspect of the Third Secret, which depicts the Pope and numerous members of the hierarchy being executed by a band of soldiers outside a ruined city, signifies nothing more than Your Holiness *escaping* death at the hands of a lone assassin some 21 years ago.

(e) concludes (based on these "interpretations") that the events depicted in the Third Secret, and thus the Message of Fatima as a whole, "belong to the past."

Third, the accused have acted with the motive of sacrificing the Message of Fatima, with its explicitly Catholic prophetic content, to a new worldly, liberalized, ecumenical, pan-religious orientation of the Church, which the accused and their many collaborators unswervingly promote in the name of Vatican II. The new orientation is the result of "the demolition of bastions" that Cardinal Ratzinger himself has praised.

Fourth, the accused and their collaborators have, above all, systematically prevented the Consecration of Russia to the Immaculate Heart of Mary, which the new orientation excludes as a needless "provocation" of the Russian

Orthodox Church and a threat to the newfangled "ecumenism" and "dialogue"—utter novelties that have produced no good fruits whatever, but only continued opposition to the Church in Russia and elsewhere.

Fifth, the new orientation represents the substantial attainment of the openly professed goal of the Church's worst enemies, as various Popes and prelates warned before the Council. That goal is to liberalize and "instrumentalize" the Church so that it will not only cease to resist effectively, but actually lend itself, to the process of universal secularization and apostasy that has destroyed much of former Christendom and now threatens to subjugate the whole world to a universal secular collective, in which the Church will cease to have any real authority or influence.

Sixth, not surprisingly, the "demolition of bastions" commended by Cardinal Ratzinger has produced only confusion, loss of faith and discipline, and ruin to the commonwealth of the Church, of which the current worldwide sexual scandal among priests and bishops is only one of innumerable manifestations. As even Pope Paul VI was forced to admit shortly after the Council: "The smoke of Satan has entered the Church. ... The opening to the world has become a veritable invasion of the Church by worldly thinking. We have perhaps been too weak and imprudent." The very state of affairs foreseen by Pius XII in the light of Fatima (see, Seventh) has, as anyone can see, come to pass.

Seventh, in an attempt to cover up the complicity of the Vatican apparatus in the current ecclesial debacle, the accused have fraudulently withheld from the Church and the world a text which appertains to the Third Secret of Fatima. This text in all likelihood contains the missing words of the Virgin following Her incomplete statement in the Fourth Memoir of Sister Lucia: "In Portugal the dogma of the faith will always be preserved etc."—words which we are convinced predict the current crisis in the Church and provide the means to avoid or end it. As the future Pope Pius XII predicted in light of the Message of Fatima:

> I am worried by the Blessed Virgin's messages to Lucy of Fatima. This persistence of Mary about the dangers which menace the Church is a divine warning against the suicide of altering the Faith, in Her liturgy, Her theology and Her soul. ... A day will come when the civilized world will deny its God, when the Church will doubt as Peter doubted. She will be tempted to believe that man has become God. In our churches, Christians will search in vain for the red lamp where God awaits them. Like Mary Magdalene, weeping before the empty tomb, they will ask, "Where have they taken Him?"

What Pius XII foresaw has happened. And given that he foresaw these developments in light of Fatima, they must have been mentioned in the Third Secret, since the portions of the Message of Fatima thus far disclosed say nothing about such events in the Church.

Your Holiness yourself seems to have alluded to the Third Secret in your sermon at Fatima on May 13, 2000, which warns the Church to beware of the tail of the dragon that drags one-third of the stars (commonly interpreted as the consecrated souls of priests and religious) from Heaven. It appears Your Holiness has been constrained by your advisors, including one or more of the accused, to confine yourself to this veiled reference to a hitherto undisclosed portion of the Third Secret, whose full disclosure your advisors have prevented Your Holiness from making.

Eighth, in their pursuit of the new orientation, the accused (with the particular assistance of Cardinal Castrillón, acting as head of the Congregation for the Clergy) have persecuted and attempted to ostracize from the community of the faithful Father Nicholas Gruner, who represents legitimate opposition to their attempt to do away with the Message of Fatima in its traditional Catholic sense. At the same time, the accused and their collaborators fail to impose any effective discipline upon the true enemies of the Church within her structure, who (to recall the lamentations of Pope Paul VI) have opened the Church to the smoke of Satan and led the invasion of the Church by worldly thinking.

Ninth, in an effort to maintain their false interpretation of the Message of Fatima, the accused have imposed an unjust regime of silence and secrecy upon Sister Lucy, while attempting to pressure her into embracing their false interpretation. Meanwhile, no objective party is allowed access to Sister Lucy in order to investigate alleged sudden "changes" in her unwavering testimony, for more than 60 years, that the Virgin of Fatima requested the consecration of Russia *only*, not the world, precisely because God wished the world to know that it was the power of His grace, mediated through the Blessed Virgin, which had miraculously converted Russia to the Catholic Faith. Further, nearly all of the 24 volumes of Fatima documents compiled by Father Alonso, which undoubtedly answer many questions about the Third Secret and the Message of Fatima as a whole, remain under lock and key more than 25 years after their completion.

Tenth, this veritable conspiracy of the accused to rob the Church of the benefits of the authentic Message of Fatima has prevented the Church from accomplishing what the Virgin of Fatima requested: the Consecration of Russia—by name—to the Immaculate Heart of Mary, the consequent conversion of Russia, the Triumph of the Immaculate Heart, the salvation of many souls, and peace in the world. ("If My requests are granted, many souls will be saved and there will be peace. … In the end, My Immaculate Heart will triumph. The Holy Father will consecrate Russia to Me, which will be converted, and a certain period of peace will be granted to the world.")

Eleventh, as the direct result of the actions of the accused, the Church and the entire world have suffered the loss of untold temporal and spiritual benefits, which are only faintly suggested by the miraculous transformation of

Portugal following the public consecration of that nation to the Immaculate Heart of Mary in 1931—benefits which the Patriarch of Portugal at the time and Sister Lucy both declared would spread throughout the world if Russia were likewise consecrated.

Twelfth, whatever their subjective intention may be, the accused have committed what is, objectively speaking, an incalculable crime against the Church and humanity. Their subversion of the Message of Fatima exposes us all to the imminent threat of wars, famine, further persecutions of the Church, further suffering for Your Holiness or your successor, the annihilation of various nations, and the loss of millions more souls—all of which Our Lady of Fatima warned would follow from a refusal to honor Her requests.

Thirteenth, for these reasons, the continued exercise of authority by the accused represents a clear and present danger to the Church and the world, which only Your Holiness can address.

Therefore, we urgently petition Your Holiness for the following relief:

- The immediate consecration of Russia, by name, to the Immaculate Heart of Mary, by Your Holiness together with all the world's bishops in a solemn public ceremony.
- The full disclosure of the Third Secret of Fatima, including the words of the Virgin that describe the vision published on June 26, 2000.
- An end to the silence and secrecy imposed upon Sister Lucia of Fatima, so that she may speak to objective witnesses, freely and without intimidation.
- The publication of Father Alonso's entire 24 volumes of documents pertaining to the Message of Fatima, which have been suppressed since 1975.
- The removal of the accused from their respective offices, and their replacement with prelates who will cooperate with the Holy Father in honoring the Virgin of Fatima's requests, rather than attempting to make the heavenly Message of Fatima conform to the fallible human decisions that have given us the ruinous new orientation of the Church.
- An end to the persecution of Father Nicholas Gruner, as well as other faithful priests who rightly persevere in the traditional teaching and practices of the Church, and who in conscience resist the new orientation (including the attempted de-Catholicization of the Message of Fatima).
- Immediate Vatican intervention, through apostolic visitations, investigations, and prompt disciplinary measures in order to punish the guilty, rather than the innocent, and restore the many elements

of Catholic tradition (including traditional seminary life and priestly formation) that have been abandoned in the pursuit of the new orientation since Vatican II. This process must obviously begin with real, effective action by the *Vatican* to rid Catholic seminaries, parishes and chancery offices of the homosexual and pedophile infiltrators who have injured countless innocent victims and brought disgrace to the Church.

- Promotion of the First Saturday devotion and the daily worldwide recitation of the Rosary for an end to the crisis in the Church and the world.

This is our Petition to Your Holiness. We submit it with all due respect and reverence for Your exalted office as Vicar of Christ, but also with all the insistence that our perilous situation demands. For the present suffering of the Church and the world are as nothing compared to what will ensue if there is no correction of the course charted by those who have despised the prophecy of Our Lady of Fatima.

Your faithful subjects in Christ,

# Footnotes

## Chapter 1

1. This chapter is largely taken verbatim from Frère François de Marie des Anges, *Fatima: The Astonishing Truth*, Book One of *Fatima: Intimate Joy World Event*, (English edition, Immaculate Heart Publications, Buffalo, New York, 1993) Chapter III, pp. 163-198.
2. English translation of text in Sister Lucy, "Fourth Memoir", *Fatima in Lucia's Own Words*, (Postulation Centre, Fatima, Portugal, 1976) p. 162. See also Frère Michel de la Sainte Trinité, *The Whole Truth About Fatima - Volume I: Science and the Facts*, (Immaculate Heart Publications, Buffalo, New York, U.S.A., 1989) pp. 181-182.
3. English translation of text in Sister Lucy, "Third Memoir", *Fatima in Lucia's Own Words*, p. 104. See also *The Whole Truth About Fatima - Volume I*, p. 182.
4. English translation of text in Sister Lucy, "Fourth Memoir", *Fatima in Lucia's Own Words*, (Postulation Centre, Fatima, Portugal, 1976) p. 162. See also Sister Lucy, *Memorias e Cartas da Irma Lucia*, (Porto, Portugal, 1973, edited by Father Antonio Maria Martins) pp. 340-341; in Sister Lucy's own handwriting there is no ellipsis after the "etc.". See also Frère Michel de la Sainte Trinité, *The Whole Truth About Fatima - Volume I: Science and the Facts*, p. 182.
5. Frère Michel de la Sainte Trinité, *The Whole Truth About Fatima - Volume I*, pp. 180-181.
6. Frère Michel de la Sainte Trinité, *The Whole Truth About Fatima - Volume II: The Secret and the Church*, (English edition, Immaculate Heart Publications, Buffalo, New York, U.S.A., 1989) pp. 357-358.
7. *O Seculo* of October 15, 1917.
8. Article of October 29, 1917, with additions made for the purposes of this book, including continuity and further explanation.
9. *Ilustração Portuguesa*, October 29, 1917.
10. Frère François de Marie des Anges, *Fatima: The Astonishing Truth*, pp. 171-172.
11. Ibid., pp. 172-173.
12. Ibid., p. 173.
13. Frère Michel de la Sainte Trinité, *The Whole Truth About Fatima - Volume I*, p. 337.
14. Frère François de Marie des Anges, *Fatima: The Astonishing Truth,* p. 178.
15. Ibid.
16. Ibid.
17. Ibid.
18. Ibid.
19. Ibid.
20. Ibid.
21. Ibid.
22. Ibid., pp. 178-179.
23. Ibid., p. 179.
24. Frère Michel de la Sainte Trinité, *The Whole Truth About Fatima - Volume I*, p. 337.
25. Ibid., p. 339.
26. Ibid., p. 340.
27. Ibid.
28. Frère François de Marie des Anges, *Fatima: The Astonishing Truth,* p. 179.
29. Ibid.
30. Ibid.
31. Frère Michel de la Sainte Trinité, *The Whole Truth About Fatima - Volume I*, p. 340. See also Father John de Marchi, I.M.C., *Fatima From the Beginning*, (Missoes Consolata, Fatima, Portugal, 1981, third edition, first published in 1950) p. 141; and Joseph A. Pelletier, A.A., *The Sun Danced at Fatima*, (Doubleday, New York, 1983) pp. 129-130.
32. John M. Haffert, *Meet the Witnesses*, (AMI International Press, Fatima, Portugal, 1961) p. 62. This book was published with an Imprimatur from the Bishop of Leiria, Portugal and provides us with credible direct testimonies of numerous witnesses to the Miracle of the Sun.
33. Ibid., p. 65.
34. Ibid., pp. 86-89.

35. *Documentaçáo Crítica de Fátima*, Volume II (Santuário de Fátima, 1999) 17 cases documented on pp. 277-372; and Father John de Marchi, I.M.C., *Fatima From the Beginning.*

*36.* Father John de Marchi, I.M.C., *Fatima From the Beginning*, p. 136. See also *Documentaçáo Crítica de Fátima*, Volume I (Santuário de Fátima, 1992) p. 408. See also Frère Michel de la Sainte Trinité, *The Whole Truth About Fatima - Volume I*, pp. 330-331.

37. Among the many reference works, see: Frère Michel de la Sainte Trinité, *The Whole Truth About Fatima - Volume I: Science and the Facts*; John M. Haffert, *Meet the Witnesses*; Father John de Marchi, I.M.C., *Fatima From the Beginning*, pp. 135-142.

38. We find the photographic reproduction of those three articles in *Fatima 50* of October 13, 1967, pp. 6-10; 14-15.

39. *Novos Documentos de Fatima*, Loyola editions, Sao Paulo, 1984, pp. 60-63.

40. The modernist Jesuit priest, Father Dhanis, who would later attempt to "debunk" the vision of hell and the prophetic elements of the Message, including the consecration and ultimate conversion of Russia. Father Dhanis refused the invitation of Sister Lucy herself to come to Fatima and study the Fatima archives. Father Dhanis will eventually be cited by key members of the Vatican apparatus in their attempt to revise the Message of Fatima according to a "commentary" published on June 26, 2000.

## Chapter 2

1. "And He shall judge the Gentiles, and rebuke many people: and they shall turn their swords into plowshares, and their spears into sickles: nation shall not lift up sword against nation, neither shall they be exercised any more to war." (Is. 2:4) Also, "and they shall beat their swords into plowshares, and their spears into spades: nation shall not take sword against nation: neither shall they learn war any more." (Micheas 4:3)

2. William Thomas Walsh, *Our Lady of Fatima,* (Image-Doubleday, New York, *Imprimatur* 1947) pp. 95-97.

3. Father John de Marchi, I.M.C., *Fatima From the Beginning,* p. 88.

## Chapter 3

1. Frère Michel de la Sainte Trinité, *The Whole Truth About Fatima* - Vol. III, p. 464.

2. Sister Lucy's words cited from Frère Michel de la Sainte Trinité, *The Whole Truth About Fatima - Vol. II: The Secret and the Church*, p. 462-465. See also Sister Lucy, *Memorias e Cartas da Irma Lucia*, (Porto, Portugal, 1973, edited by Father Antonio Maria Martins) pp. 463-465.

3. *Collective Pastoral Letter for the Jubilee of the Apparitions* in 1942, Merv. XX's, p. 338. Cited from *The Whole Truth About Fatima - Vol. II,* p. 410.

4. Salazar's influence in the Portuguese government had been growing since 1928. He became President of the Council in 1933. Later, Salazar received for his efforts the praise and blessing of Pope Pius XII. Pius said, "I bless him with all my heart, and I cherish the most ardent desire that he be able to complete successfully his work of national restoration, both spiritual and material." Cited from *The Whole Truth About Fatima - Vol. II*, p. 412.

5. Ibid., p. 415. (Salazar's own words).

6. Ibid., p. 421.

7. Ibid., p. 422.

8. Ibid., p. 428.

9. See *The Whole Truth About Fatima - Vol. II,* pp. 369-439.

10. Ibid., p. 428.

11. Ibid., p. 405. Cardinal Cerejeira spoke these words during the 1942 Jubilee celebration of the Fatima apparitions.

12. We trust the word of a Fatima believer such as Cardinal Cerejeira, rather than a Fatima debunker such as Cardinal Ratzinger. See later chapters.

13. Cardinal Cerejeira, Preface to *Jacinta* (1942), *Obras Pastorais*, Vol. II, p. 333. Cf. also his homily of May 13, 1942, Merv. XX's, p. 339. Cited from *The Whole Truth About Fatima - Vol. II*, p. 437.

## Chapter 4

1. *The Whole Truth About Fatima - Volume III: The Third Secret*, (English Translation, Immaculate Heart Publications, Buffalo, NY, 1990) p. 47.
2. Ibid., p. 47.
3. Father Joaquin Alonso, *La Verdad sobre el Secreto de Fatima*, Centro Mariano, Madrid, Spain, 1976, p. 60. See also Frère Michel, *The Whole Truth About Fatima - Vol. III*, p. 651.
4. *The Whole Truth About Fatima - Vol. III*, p. 725.
5. Ibid., p. 727.
6. Frère François de Marie des Anges, *Fatima: Tragedy and Triumph*, (Immaculate Heart Publications, Buffalo, New York, U.S.A., 1994) p. 45.
7. *The Whole Truth About Fatima - Vol. III*, p. 480.
8. Ibid., p. 481.
9. Ibid., p. 626.
10. *Fatima, Tragedy and Triumph*, p. 45.
11. Brother Michael of the Holy Trinity, *The Secret of Fatima ... Revealed*, (Immaculate Heart Publications, Buffalo, New York, U.S.A.) p. 7.
12. *Revue Mediatrice et Reine*, October 1946, pp. 110-112. See also *The Whole Truth About Fatima - Vol. III*, p. 470.
13. Father Alonso, *La Verdad sobre el Secreto de Fatima*, pp. 46-47. See also *The Whole Truth About Fatima - Vol. III*, p. 470.
14. Barthas, *Fatima, merveille du XXe siècle*, p. 83. Fatima-editions, 1952. It must be noted that Canon Barthas published this account after having the privilege of meeting Sister Lucy again, on October 15, 1950 in the company of Msgr. Bryant, O.M.I., vicar apostolic of Athabasca-Mackenzie. See *The Whole Truth About Fatima - Vol. III*, p. 472.
15. *Novidades*, February 24, 1960, quoted by *La Documentation Catholique*, June 19, 1960, col. 751. See also *The Whole Truth About Fatima - Vol. III*, p. 472.
16. Father Alonso, *La Verdad sobre el Secreto de Fatima*, p. 46. See also *The Whole Truth About Fatima - Vol. III*, p. 475.
17. Father Alonso, *La Verdad sobre el Secreto de Fatima*, p. 46. See also *The Whole Truth About Fatima - Vol. III*, p. 478.
18. *The Whole Truth About Fatima - Vol. III*, pp. 578-589.
19. *Fatima, Tragedy and Triumph*, p. 45.
20. *The Whole Truth About Fatima - Vol. III*, p. 710.
21. English translation of Sister Lucy interview with Father Fuentes taken from Frère Michel's *The Whole Truth About Fatima - Volume III*, pp. 503 to 508. Frère Michel explains that the text comes from Fatima scholar Father Joaquin Alonso's, *La Verdad sobre el Secreto de Fatima* (pp. 103-106). The interview of Sister Lucy with Father Fuentes was published with the Imprimatur of Archbishop Sanchez of Vera Cruz, Mexico.
22. *The Whole Truth About Fatima - Vol. III*, p. 704.
23. Ibid., p. 687.
24. Ibid., pp. 705-706.
25. Frère Michel de la Sainte Trinité, *The Whole Truth About Fatima - Volume III*, pp. 822-823. See also *Jesus* magazine, November 11, 1984, p. 79. See also *The Fatima Crusader*, Issue 37, Summer 1991, p. 7.
26. *Fatima, Tragedy and Triumph*, pp. 243-244. See also Frère Michel de la Sainte Trinité, *The Whole Truth About Fatima - Volume III*, p. 676.
27. See Father Gerard Mura, "The Third Secret of Fatima: Has It Been Completely Revealed?", the periodical *Catholic*, (published by the Transalpine Redemptorists, Orkney Isles, Scotland, Great Britain) March 2002.
28. These quotations are condensed from numerous letters Sister Lucy wrote in the early 1970's to two of her nephews who were priests, and to other religious she knew. See *The Whole Truth About Fatima - Vol. III*, pp. 754-758.
29. Roche, *Pie XII Devant L'Histoire*, pp. 52-53.

## Chapter 5

1. For a booklet on the connection between the Alta Vendita and the new orientation of the

Church since the Council, see John Vennari, *The Permanent Instruction of the Alta Vendita,* (TAN Books and Publishers, 1999).

2. 2nd volume, original edition, 1859, reprinted by Circle of the French Renaissance, Paris 1976; Msgr. Delassus produced these documents again in his work *The Anti-Christian Conspiracy*, DDB, 1910, Tome III, pp. 1035-1092.

3. Msgr. Dillon, *Grand Orient Freemasonry Unmasked*, pp. 51-56, full text of *Alta Vendita* — Christian Book Club, Palmdale, CA.

4. Michael Davies, *Pope John's Council*, (Angelus Press, Kansas City, MO, 1992) p. 166.

5. *The Catholic Encyclopedia,* Vol. 3, (New York Encyclopedia Press, 1913) pp. 330-331.

6. Rev. E. Cahill, S.J., *Freemasonry and the Anti-Christian Movement,* (Dublin: Gill, 1959) p. 101.

7. Bishop Graber, *Athanasius and the Church of Our Time*, (Christian Book Club, Palmdale, CA, 1974) p. 39.

8. Pope Leo XIII, *Humanum Genus*, (TAN Books and Publishers, Rockford, Illinois) para. 31.

9. Msgr. Dillon, *Grand Orient Freemasonry Unmasked*, pp. 51-56, full text of *Alta Vendita* (Christian Book Club, Palmdale, California).

10. Father Denis Fahey, *Mystical Body of Christ in the Modern World,* (Regina Publications, Dublin, Ireland, 1939) Chapter VII.

11. Ibid., p. 116.

12. Quoted from *The Catholic Doctrine,* Father Michael Muller, (Benzinger, 1888) p. 282.

13. Father Vincent Miceli, *The Antichrist*, (Roman Catholic Books, Harrison, New York, 1981) p. 133.

14. Pope Pius X, *Pascendi Dominici Gregis (On the Doctrine of the Modernists),* September 8, 1907.

15. *Pascendi.*

16. Father Vincent Miceli, *The Antichrist*, cassette lecture, Keep the Faith, Inc. Ramsey, NJ.

17. Raymond Dulac, *Episcopal Collegiality at the Second Council of the Vatican*, (Paris: Cedre, 1979) pp. 9-10.

18. *Athanasius and the Church of Our Time,* p. 34.

19. A full account of all of Roca's quotes here printed is found in *Athanasius and the Church of Our Time*, pp. 31-40.

20. "Joint Catholic-Lutheran Vespers at Vatican," CWNews.com, November 13, 1999: "Archbishops G.H. Hammar and Jukka Paarma—the Lutheran primates of Sweden and Finland, respectively—and Bishops Anders Arborelius of Stockholm and Czeslaw Kozon of Copenhagen joined with the Holy Father for the Vespers service. Several other Lutheran bishops from the Scandinavian countries were present for the ceremony, including two female bishops."

21. *Athanasius and the Church of Our Time,* p. 36.

22. See "The Secret Red Plan to Take Over the Catholic Church", published in Red China in 1959. Published in English in *The Fatima Crusader*, Issue 19, February-April, 1986, p. 6. See also "The Prophecy of Bella Dodd", a Fatima Perspective web column by Chris Ferrara (www.fatima.org/perspective235.htm); this prophecy is also found on pages 47-48 of this book. See also Father Paul Kramer, "The 'Party Line' in Relation to Fatima", *The Fatima Crusader*, Issue 69, Winter 2002, pp. 10ff.

23. "The Greatest Conspiracy", *Christian Order,* November 2000.

24. Another ex-Communist, Mr. Manning Johnson gave similar testimony. In 1953, to the House Un-American Activities Committee, Manning said: "Once the tactic of infiltration of religious organizations was set by the Kremlin ... The Communists discovered that the destruction of religion could proceed much faster through the infiltration of the Church by Communists operating within the Church itself." He then stated, "This policy of infiltrating seminaries was successful beyond even our

Communist expectations." Speaking of the infiltration of religious institutions in general, Manning Johnson further explained, "... the major plot to take over religious organizations was really hatched during that particular period (1935), and the fact that the Communists in headlines in the *Daily Worker,* can boast of 2,300 Protestant Ministers supporting them is the result of this part that began in the thirties when I was a member of the Communist party." Testimony of Manning Johnson, Investigation of Communist Activities in the New York City Area — Part 7, Hearing Before the Committee on Un-American Activities, House of Representatives, Eighty-Third Congress, First Session, July 8, 1953, (Published by the Government Printing Office, Washington, 1953) p. 2214. A collection of quotations from ex-Communists and the infiltration of the Church is found in John Vennari's "Heaven's Request for Reparation to the Holy Face of Jesus", Part III, *Catholic Family News*, August 2001.

## Chapter 6

1. A full account of this fascinating history is found in *The Whole Truth About Fatima - Vol. III* by Frère Michel of the Holy Trinity, pp. 257-304.
2. Ibid., p. 298.
3. Vicomte Leon de Poncins, *Freemasonry and the Vatican*, (Christian Book Club, Palmdale, California, 1968) p. 14.
4. L. Bouyer, *Dom Lambert Beauduin, a Man of the Church*, Casterman, 1964, pp. 180-181, quoted by Father Dilder Bonneterre in *The Liturgical Movement*, Ed. Fideliter, 1980, p. 119.
5. Jesuit Father Aparicio was Sister Lucy's confessor and spiritual director from 1926 to 1938. Then he was sent to Brazil as a missionary and corresponded with Sister Lucy over the years. In 1950 he returned to Portugal for a short while and visited Sister Lucy both in 1950 and in 1951 without difficulty. Father Aparicio testified that in August 1960, during a month-long visit to Portugal, he was not allowed to speak to Sister Lucy: "I have not been able to speak to Sister Lucy because the Archbishop could not give the permission to meet her. The *conditions of isolation in which she finds herself have been imposed by the Holy See.* Consequently, no one may speak to her without a licence from Rome. The Archbishop has only a very limited number of those licences." (*Fatima: Tragedy and Triumph*, Immaculate Heart Publications, 1994, pp. 33-34.)

   The situation has not changed since then. On January 16, 1983 Father Joseph de Sainte-Marie, O.C. wrote to the eminent Catholic layman Hamish Fraser to advise that: "Moreover, I remind you—she (Sister Lucy) herself reminded me recently in a request that I had addressed to her—that Sister Lucia (Lucy) cannot speak to anyone on the question of the apparitions without the express permission of the Sacred Congregation for the Doctrine of the Faith or of the Holy Father himself." (*The Fatima Crusader*, No. 13-14, p. 13) And on March 19, 1983 Sister Lucy told the Papal Nuncio to Portugal, Most Reverend Sante Portalupi, that she had not been able to comment earlier on the inadequacy of the 1982 consecration ceremony (of the world, not Russia) because the Holy See had not given her permission to speak: "The Consecration of Russia has not been made as Our Lady demanded. I could not say so (before) because I did not have permission of the Holy See." (*Ibid.* at p. 3, and *The Fatima Crusader*, Issue 16, Sept.-Oct. 1984, p. 22ff, reprinting the article by Father Pierre Caillon in *Fidelite Catholique*, first printed in 1983.)

   On February 19, 1990, Msgr. A. Duarte de Almeida, chaplain to the Coimbra Carmel, stated the following: "in order to meet Sister Lucy, it is necessary to obtain Cardinal Ratzinger's permission." (In David Boyce, "Fatima Inquest - August 1990", *The Fatima Crusader*, Issue 35, Winter 1990-1991, p. 13).

   As recently as the purported "interview" of Sister Lucy by Msgr. Bertone on November 17, 2001, Msgr. Bertone admitted (in his communiqué concerning the interview) that it had been conducted with the *consent* of Cardinal Ratzinger. Thus, as recently as 2001 even a high-ranking Vatican prelate needed the Holy See's permission to speak with Sister Lucy.

6. See Jean Madiran, "The Vatican-Moscow Agreement", *The Fatima Crusader*, Issue 16, September-October, 1984, p. 5. Also articles on pages 4, 7, and 11 in *The Fatima Crusader*, Issue 17, February-April, 1985. See also Atila Sinke Guimarães, "The Metz Pact", *Catholic Family News*, Sept. 2001.
7. Pope Pius XI, *Divini Redemptoris,* Encyclical on Atheistic Communism, March 19, 1937. See also quotation on p. 61 referenced by footnote 42 of this chapter.
8. A more complete account of this is found in *The Rhine flows into the Tiber,* Father Ralph Wiltgen, (New York: Hawthorne, 1967; TAN, 1985) pp. 272-278.
9. E.g., *The Rhine flows into the Tiber* by Fr. Ralph Wiltgen; *Pope John's Council* by Michael Davies (Angelus Press, Kansas City, Missouri); and even *Vatican II Revisited,* (see next footnote) which sings praises of the reform.
10. Most Reverend Aloysius Wycislo S.J., *Vatican II Revisited, Reflections By One Who Was There*, p. x, Alba House, Staten Island, New York.
11. Ibid., p. 33.
12. Ibid., p. 27.
13. *The Wanderer,* August 31, 1967, p. 7.
14. *Council Daybook,* National Catholic Welfare Conference, Washington, D.C., vol. 1, pp. 25, 27.
15. *Vatican II Revisited, Reflections By One Who Was There*, pp. 27-34.
16. Bishop Graber, *Athanasius and the Church of Our Time,* p. 54.
17. Atila Sinke Guimarães, *Animus Delendi (The Desire to Destroy)*, (Tradition in Action, Los Angeles, California, 2001) p. 128. The exact title is *Animus Delendi - I* (the first of two books with this title, the second is yet to be published).
18. Ibid.
19. "Vital life" seems to be just another term for the "Vital Imminence" condemned in Pope Pius X's encyclical against Modernism, *Pascendi.* See p. 8, English translation by Newman Press.
20. Greenstock, David, "Thomism and the New Theology", *The Thomist* (October, 1950). The entire article is well worth reading if one wishes to grasp the erroneous nature of the "New Theology".
21. Published in the *Angelicum* in 1946. First English translation published in *Catholic Family News*, August 1997, "Where is the New Theology Taking Us?"
22. *Animus Delendi - I,* p. 129.
23. Ibid., pp. 146-149.
24. These observations are from Msgr. Kelly's book *The Battle for the American Church,* quoted by John Vennari in "Vatican Praises Purveyor of Heresy", *The Fatima Crusader,* Spring/Summer 1998.
25. Ibid.
26. Cited from Guimarães, *Animus Delendi - I,* p. 60.
27. Ibid., p. 61.
28. Ibid., p. 59.
29. Ibid., p. 62.
30. Vatican I, Session III, Chap. IV, Faith and Reason.
31. Cited from *Open Letter to Confused Catholics*, pp. 88-89.
32. Yves Marsaudon, *Oecumènisme vu par un Maçon de Tradition* (pp. 119-120).
33. Cited from *Open Letter to Confused Catholics*, pp. 88-89.
34. Ibid., p. 100.
35. Bishop Graber, *Athanasius and the Church of Our Time,* p. 64.
36. Archbishop Marcel Lefebvre, *They Have Uncrowned Him*, (Kansas City, Missouri: Angelus Press, 1988) p. 229. Here Archbishop Lefebvre also notes that the Communist newspaper *Izvestia* demanded that Paul VI condemn him and his seminary at Ecône.
37. The progressivist *periti* at the Council are on record stating, "We will express it in a *diplomatic* way, but after the Council, we shall draw the conclusions implicit in it." In Father Ralph Wiltgen's book, *The Rhine flows into the Tiber*, p. 242.
38. The progressivist Archbishop Annibale Bugnini was the major architect of the liturgical revolution which culminated in the

New Mass (*Novus Ordo*). He was eventually banished from the Vatican to Iran because Pope Paul VI was shown documents demonstrating that Bugnini was a Freemason. Michael Davies devotes an entire chapter to Archbishop Bugnini in *Pope Paul's New Mass*, (Angelus Press, Kansas City, 1992) Chapter 24.

39. Cardinal Joseph Ratzinger, *Principles of Catholic Theology,* (Ignatius Press, San Francisco, 1987) p. 334.

40. Speech to the Lombard College, December 7, 1968.

41. Speech of June 30, 1972.

42. Pope Pius XI, *Divini Redemptoris,* Encyclical on Atheistic Communism, March 19, 1937.

43. Yves Congar, O.P., "Le Concile au jours le jours deuxieum section" ("The Council day by day, second session"), (Paris, Cerf, 1964) p. 115.

44. In truth, there can be no such thing as a "Counter-Syllabus", since Blessed Pope Pius IX's *Syllabus* of 1864 is plainly a solemn, definitive teaching binding on all Catholics. In Paragraph 6 of the Encyclical *Quanta Cura* which was issued with the *Syllabus* on Dec. 8, 1864, Blessed Pope Pius IX stated solemnly: "Amid, therefore, so great perversity of depraved opinions, We, well remembering Our Apostolic Office, and very greatly solicitous for Our most holy Religion, for sound doctrine and the salvation of souls which is entrusted to Us by God, and (solicitous also) for the welfare of human society itself, have thought it right to raise up Our Apostolic voice. *Therefore, by Our Apostolic Authority, We reprobate, proscribe and condemn all the singular and evil opinions and doctrines severally mentioned in this Letter, and will and command that they be thoroughly held by all children of the Catholic Church as reprobated, proscribed and condemned.* (Our emphasis) Taken from *The Popes Against Modern Errors,* (TAN Books and Publishers, Rockford, Illinois, 1999) p. 21.

45. Yves Congar, "La Crise d'Eglise et Msgr. Lefebvre", (Paris, Cerf, 1977) p. 54.

46. Cited from *Open Letter to Confused Catholics,* p. 100.

47. Cardinal Joseph Ratzinger, *Principles of Catholic Theology*, pp. 381-382.

48. Ibid., p. 191.

49. *L'Osservatore Romano*, English Weekly Edition, July 2, 1990, p. 5.

50. Ibid.

51. In the 1943 encyclical *Mystici Corporis*, Pope Pius XII taught that "the true Church of Jesus Christ ... is the One, Holy, Catholic, Apostolic Roman Church." This clearly means that the Church of Christ is not composed of the Catholic Church and other "Christian" denominations. Pope Pius XII reiterated this doctrine in his 1950 encyclical *Humani Generis*: "The Mystical Body of Christ and the Roman Catholic Church are one and the same thing."

52. Taken from *Vatican II, the Work That Needs to Be Done,* edited by David Tracy with Hans Küng and Johann Metz (Concillium, Seabury Press, NY, 1978) p. 91 (emphasis added).

53. *L'Osservatore Romano*, Italian edition, October 8, 2000, p. 4: "Quando i Padri conciliar sostituirono la parola 'è' con la parola 'subsistit' lo fecera con un scopo ben preciso. Il concetto espresso da 'è' (essere) è piu ampio di quello espresso da 'sussistere.' 'Sussistere' un modo ben preciso di essere, ossia essere come soggeto che esiste in sé. I Padri conciliari dunque intendevano dire che l'essere della Chiesa in quanto tale è un entità piu ampia della Chiesa cattolica romana."

54. See statements by Father Schillebeeckx in the Dutch magazine *De Bauzuin,* No. 16, 1965, quoted in the French translation in *Itineraires,* No. 155, 1971, p. 40.

55. *Frankfurter Allgemeine*, September 22, 2000; Italian translation in *L'Osservatore Romano*, October 8, 2000.

56. *Adista*, Feb. 26, 2001. English translation quoted from "Where Have They Hidden the Body?" by Christopher Ferrara, *The Remnant,* June 30, 2001.

57. The three *ex cathedra* pronouncements were: Pope Innocent III, Fourth Lateran Council, 1215; Pope Boniface VIII, Bull

*Unam Sanctam*, 1302; Pope Eugene IV, Bull *Cantate Domino*, 1442.

58. Bull, *Cantate Domino*, Eugene IV, Feb. 4, 1442, Council of Florence. (Dz. 714, D.S. 1351) See also *Mortalium Animos* by Pope Pius XI, 1928, and Pope Pius XII's "Decree on Ecumenism", 1950.

59. AAS 42-142.

60. "On the Ecumenical Movement," December 20, 1949.

61. (Emphasis added) *Theological Highlights of Vatican II*, Father Joseph Ratzinger [Paulist Press, New York, 1966], p. 65-66. This section of the book focuses on the deliberate ecumenical foundation on which is based the Council document *Lumen Gentium.* For a more complete discussion of Father Ratzinger's book, see "Vatican II vs. the Unity Willed by Christ," by J. Vennari, *Catholic Family News*, Dec. 2000.

62. Even if Cardinal Ratzinger would completely change his own personal views to a more orthodox position, the Council texts themselves remain ambiguous, imprecise, and appear to be oriented toward an unorthodox ecumenism which does not seek the conversion of non-Catholics to Catholicism.

63. E. Schillebeeckx, OP, *Igreja ou igrejas?,* in V.A. *Cinco problemas que desafiam a Igreja hoje,* pp. 26f. Cited from *In the Murky Waters of Vatican II,* Atila Sinke Guimarães, (Maeta, Metairie, 1997) p. 243.

64. SIDIC is an association identifying itself as Catholic that was "founded in Rome in 1965 at the request of a group of experts of the Second Vatican Council following the promulgation of *Nostra Aetate",* to promote Catholic-Jewish "dialogue". The Rome-based SIDIC has local representatives in the following countries: Australia, Belgium, Canada, England, France, Holland, Israel, Italy, United States.

65. The full quote reads, "Lefebvre's refusal to accept ecumenism originates in clear teachings from the Magisterium: the encyclical *Satis Cognitum* of Leo XIII (1896); the encyclical *Mortalium Animos* of Pius XI (1928); the Dec. 20, 1949, Instruction of the Holy Office regarding ecumenism. The only ecumenism accepted by Lefebvre and his followers is that which strives for the unconditional return of the members of other confessions to the one Church of Christ, the Roman Catholic Church. This hardened sectarianism is precisely the kind of logic which Vatican II, through profound reflection on the nature of the Church, refused to accept. Though rooted in Tradition [sic] the scope of the Council's reflection was without precedent in the history of Christianity. For integralists, ecumenism is one of the fundamental betrayals by Vatican II." (Emphasis added) *Service International de Documentation Judéo-Chrètienne*, Rome, [English edition from Washington, D.C.] Vol. XXXII, No. 3, 1999, p. 22.

66. The verbal ambiguity used by Vatican II to advance this false notion is found in *Lumen Gentium* 8 wherein it says "The Church of Christ subsists in the Catholic Church" rather than Pope Pius XII's definition that the Church of Christ *is* the Catholic Church [*Mystici Corporis*, Pope Pius XII]. See previous discussion and footnotes in this chapter concerning the origin and effect of this ambiguity, as admitted by Cardinal Joseph Ratzinger.

67. For a brief account of Father Popian's story, see "Vatican says, Do Not Convert to Catholicism", John Vennari, *Catholic Family News,* Dec. 2001. See also "Vatican says, 'You Must Not Become Catholic!'", John Vennari, *The Fatima Crusader*, Issue 69, Winter 2002. Father Popian's testimony on audio cassette entitled "Vatican's Ostpolitik and Ecumenism Tried to Prevent My Conversion to Catholicism" is also available from the Fatima Center, 17000 State Route 30, Constable, NY 12926.

68. "We are a Sign of Contradiction", interview with Bishop Bernard Fellay, SSPX, *Latin Mass* Magazine, Fall 2001, p. 11.

69. Balamand Statement, nn. 13 and 30. The Balamand Statement (1993) was cited approvingly by Pope John Paul II in *Ut Unum Sint,* n. 59.

70. Pope Pius XI, *Ubi Arcano Dei,* Encyclical Letter on the Peace of Christ in His Kingdom, December 23, 1922.

71. Ibid.

72. Pope Pius XI, *Quas Primas,* Encyclical on the Kingship of Christ, December 11, 1925.

73. Pope John Paul II's Message for World Day of Peace, January 1, 2001. "Dialogue Between Cultures for a Civilization of Love and Peace".

74. Addenda to *Lumen Gentium*, Explanatory Note of the Theological Commission, in Walter M. Abbott, S.J., ed., *The Documents of Vatican II,* (New York: America Press, 1966) pp. 97-98.

75. Bishop Morris' personal testimony reported in an article by Kieron Wood, *Catholic World News*, January 22, 1997.

76. *The Documents of Vatican II*, Editor Walter Abbott, S.J., p. 98.

77. Cited from *Open Letter to Confused Catholics*, p. 107.

78. Paul VI, General Audience of January 12, 1966, in *Inseganmenti di Paolo VI,* vol. 4, p. 700, cited from Atila Sinke Guimarães, *In the Murky Waters of Vatican II,* Metairie, Louisiana: Maeta, 1997; TAN 1999, pp. 111-112.

## Chapter 7

1. See, e.g., statistical analysis of the priesthood in *L'Osservatore Romano*, 13/20 August 1997, and "The Index of Leading Catholic Indicators," *The Latin Mass*, Winter 2000, presenting extensive data from the Vatican *Statistical Yearbook of the Church* and other standard reference works.

2. Cardinal Ratzinger, *Principles of Catholic Theology*, p. 391.

3. Ibid., p. 390.

4. Ibid., p. 391.

5. Audience Address of November 26, 1969.

6. Quoted from David Greenstock, "Thomism and the New Theology", *The Thomist*, Oct. 1950.

7. For example see: "Joint Catholic-Lutheran Vespers at Vatican", CWNews.com, November 13, 1999: "Archbishops G.H. Hammar and Jukka Paarma—the Lutheran primates of Sweden and Finland, respectively—and Bishops Anders Arborelius of Stockholm and Czeslaw Kozon of Copenhagen joined with the Holy Father for the Vespers service. Several other Lutheran bishops from the Scandinavian countries were present for the ceremony, including two female bishops." Likewise, at the beginning of the Jubilee Year, Pope John Paul II opened the Holy Doors of Saint Paul Outside the Walls with Anglican Archbishop Carey and schismatic Metropolitan Athanasios. Representatives of 20 other false confessions attended the ecumenical ceremony. See "Non-Catholics Joining Pope in Rite", *Los Angeles Times,* Jan. 19, 2000.

8. Cardinal Ratzinger, *Principles of Catholic Theology*, 1987.

9. Graber, *Athanasius and the Church of Our Time*, pp. 170-171.

10. Quote taken from *The Mystical Body of Christ in the Modern World*, Father Denis Fahey, (Regina Publications, Dublin, first printed in 1935) p. xi.

11. For further considerations on the fact that Our Lady of Fatima reinforced key Catholic doctrines that are denied today, see John Vennari, "A World View Based on Fatima", *The Fatima Crusader,* Spring 2000, Issue 64.

12. See *The Whole Truth About Fatima - Vol. III,* pp. 754-758.

## Chapter 8

1. "The Moscow Patriarchate and Sergianism" by Boris Talantov, from *Russia's Catacomb Saints*, (St. Herman of Alaska Press, Platina, California, 1982) pp. 463-486.

2. "The Moscow Patriarchate and Sergianism: An Essay by Boris Talantov," found at www.orthodoxinfo.com/resistance/cat_tal.htm.

3. Remarks of January 17, 1998 at Aid to Church in Russia Conference, www.catholic.net/rcc/Periodicals/Faith/1998-03-04/Russia.html. Reprinted in *The Catholic Dossier*, March/April 1998, p. 4.

4. *L'Osservatore Romano*, March 26-27, 1984, pp. 1, 6.

5. *Avvenire*, March 27, 1984, p. 11.

6. Father Fabrice Delestre, "Fatima: Why Isn't the Mother of God Being Obeyed as She Should Be?", *Angelus*, June 2000, Vol. 23, No. 6. See also Frère François de Marie des Anges, *Fatima: Joie Intime Événement Mondial,* (French edition, Contre-Réforme Catholique, France, 1991) pp. 363-364.

7. Father Maurer's remarks appeared in an interview in *Catholic World Report,* Feb. 2001. A synopsis and commentary on this interview was published in "The Myth of a Converted Russia Exposed", Marian Horvat, Ph.D., *Catholic Family News,* March 2001.

8. See Mark Fellows, "This Present Darkness" Part III, *Catholic Family News,* October 2000.

9. Regarding alcohol in Russia, researchers concluded: "Russia's rate of alcohol consumption, traditionally among the highest in the world, and rising significantly in the 1990s, is a major contributor to the country's health crisis ... alcoholism has reached epidemic proportions, particularly among males ... A 1995 Russian study found that regular drunkenness affected between 25 and 60 percent of blue-collar workers ... In 1994 some 53,000 people died of alcohol poisoning, an increase of about 36,000 since 1991." In the ten years since the alleged conversion of Russia, there has also been a sharp increase in illegal drug use: "In 1995 an estimated 2 million Russians used narcotics, more than twenty times the total recorded ten years earlier in the entire Soviet Union, with the number of users increasing 50 percent every year in the mid-1990s." From Mark Fellows, "This Present Darkness", Part II, *Catholic Family News,* Sept. 2000.

10. "Satanism on the Rise in Russia" compiled by John Vennari. See www.fatima.org/satanism. html.

11. "Russia Legalizes Homosexuality", *United Press International,* May 28, 1993. To quote the beginning of the article: "Russia's homosexual activists Friday celebrated a major victory for gay rights in post-Soviet Russia following the repeal of Article 121 of the Soviet criminal code, which outlawed consensual sex between men. 'This is great news for gays and lesbians in Russia,' said Vladislav Ortanov, editor of the Moscow gay magazine *Risk.*"

12. "Activist Says Child Porn Prosecutions Will be Difficult in Indonesia, Russia", Christine Brummitt, *Associated Press,* Aug. 9, 2001. (Emphasis added)

13. "Big Brotherski goes too far for Staid Russians", Mark Franchetti, *Sunday Times (London),* November 25, 2001.

14. "New Visa System Seen Choking Russia's Catholic Parishes", *Russia Reform Monitor,* No. 485, July 28, 1998. Also, "Catholic Clergy in Siberia Face Growing Visa Difficulties", *Catholic World News,* November 19, 1997.

15. Sarah Karush, "Foreign Priests Spark Controversy", *Associated Press,* February 12, 2002.

16. *Radio Free Europe Report,* June 20, 2001.

17. Ibid. See also Catholic News Service, February 17, 2002.

18. *Fatima: Tragedy and Triumph,* pp. 189-190.

19. For a good treatment of the falsehood of the Noelker letter, see Mark Fellows, "This Present Darkness" Part II, *Catholic Family News,* Sept. 2000.

20. The principle which requires that authority be exercised at the lowest possible level to avoid tyranny through excessive centralization of government. For example, the budget of a town should be determined by the town Fathers, not by the state or federal government.

21. Under the old structure, before 1967, the Pope presided over the Roman Curia. Under the new structure, since 1967, it is the Vatican Secretary of State who presides over the Roman Curia. The reader is invited to check the *Annuario Pontificio* both before and after 1967 to see the change in the structure of the Roman Curia.

22. A French priest showed the Masonic document to, among others, the American priest Father Paul Kramer.

23. Paul Fisher, *Their God is the Devil,* (American Research Foundation, Washington, D.C., 1990) p. 40.

24. See Francis Alban and Christopher A. Ferrara, *Fatima Priest*, Fourth Edition (Good Counsel Publications, Pound Ridge, New York, 2000).

25. For the details of the long and tortuous "proceedings" to silence Father Gruner, the reader may consult: *Fatima Priest* (Fourth Edition), *A Law for One Man* (both available from the Fatima Center, 17000 State Route 30, Constable, New York 12926) or visit the Fatima web site at www.fatima.org.

26. Regarding the on-again, off-again beatification ceremony and related matters, see: the daily newspaper *Correio da Manhã* of 14 October 1999, the article on p. 12; the weekly newspaper *Jornal de Leiria* of 14 October 1999, p. 24; the weekly newspaper *A Ordem* on 21 October 1999, p. 1; the official weekly of the Patriarchate of Lisbon *Voz da Verdade* on 31 October 1999, on p. 6, the article entitled "The Beatification of the Little Shepherds Definitely Will Be At Rome"; the official weekly of the Patriarchate of Lisbon *Voz da Verdade* on 5 December 1999, entitled "The Pope Will Return to Portugal; Fatima is the Place of the Beatification"; article in *Euronoticias* on 24 March 2000, p. 8, entitled "Bishop of Leiria-Fatima" March 21 press conference; weekly *Euronoticias* of 24 March 2000, on p. 8, "Crisis: The Bishop of Leiria-Fatima Creates A Mystery Around the Visit of the Pope Without Telling the Patriarch What It Concerns, Will the Pope Reveal the Third Secret?"; *Euronoticias* of 24 March, an article on p. 9 entitled "Analysis: Persons Who Have Studied the Apparitions Say That the Third Secret Could Concern the Destruction of the Faith. A Crisis in the Interior of the Church Would be the Third Secret".

27. Father Herman Bernard Kramer, *The Book of Destiny*, (first published 1955, republished by TAN Books and Publishers, Inc., Rockford, Illinois, 1975) pp. 279-284.

28. Ibid.

29. Ibid.

30. On this point we refer the reader again to the following articles: in *Euronoticias* on 24 March 2000, p. 8, entitled "Bishop of Leiria-Fatima" March 21 press conference; weekly *Euronoticias* of 24 March 2000, on p. 8, "Crisis: The Bishop of Leiria-Fatima Creates A Mystery Around the Visit of the Pope Without Telling the Patriarch What It Concerns, Will the Pope Reveal the Third Secret?"; *Euronoticias* of 24 March, an article on p. 9 entitled "Analysis: Persons Who Have Studied the Apparitions Say That the Third Secret Could Concern the Destruction of the Faith. A Crisis in the Interior of the Church Would be the Third Secret".

31. Dhanis' entire thesis against Fatima is explained and critiqued in Frère Michel, *The Whole Truth About Fatima - Volume I*, Part II, Chapter 1. All quotations concerning his false theory are from this source.

32. Ibid.

33. William Thomas Walsh, *Our Lady of Fatima,* (Image-Doubleday, New York, *Imprimatur* 1947) p. 221. Emphasis in the original.

34. *Il Pellegrinaggio Della Meraviglie*, p. 440. Rome, 1960. This same work, published under the auspices of the Italian episcopate, affirms that this message was communicated to Pope Pius XII in June. Also, Canon Barthas mentioned that apparition in his communication to the Mariological Congress of Lisbon-Fatima, in 1967; see *De Primoridiis cultus marianae, Acta congressus mariologici-mariana in Lusitania anno 1967 celebrati*, p. 517. Rome, 1970. See *Fatima: Tragedy and Triumph,* pp. 21 and 37.

35. *Fatima: Tragedy and Triumph,* p. 165.

36. Reported within an article by Father Pierre Caillon of Centre Saint Jean 61500 Sees, (Orne) France. This article was published by the monthly periodical *Fidelite Catholique*, B.P. 217-56402. Auray Cedex, France. English translation from *The Fatima Crusader*, Issue 13-14, (Oct.-Dec., 1983) p. 3.

37. *Fatima: Tragedy and Triumph*, p. 172.

38. See *Fatima e o Coraçao de Maria*, pp. 101-102.

39. *Fatima: Tragedy and Triumph,* pp. 172-173.

40. Ibid., pp. 167-168.

41. *La Verdad sobre el Secreto de Fatima, Fatima sin mitos,* Father Joaquin Alonso, (2nd edition, Ejercito Azul, Madrid, 1988) p. 78. English translation by Joseph Cain. Original Spanish reads: "*... podriamos decir que Lucia ha pensado siempre que la "conversión" de Rusia no se entiende solo de un retorno de los pueblos de Rusia a la religion cristiano-ortodoxa, rechazando el ateismo marxista y ateo de los soviets, sino que se refiere pura y llanmente a la conversion total e integral de un retorno a la unica y verdadera Iglesia, la catolica-romana.*"

42. *Sol de Fatima,* September 1985.

43. *Chrètiens-Magazine,* March 1987, #8. Cited from *Fatima: Tragedy and Triumph,* p. 189.

44. Father Laurentin, "*Multiplication des apparitions de la Vierge aujourd'hui*, p. 45, *Fayard,* September, 1988. Cited from *Fatima: Tragedy and Triumph*, p. 189.

45. This testimony of Sister Lucy was reported in the early August (1987) edition of *Para Ti* published in Argentina. See *World Enslavement or Peace ... It's Up to the Pope,* Father Nicholas Gruner (Immaculate Heart Publishing, 1989), pp. 212-213.

46. For more testimony, see Chapter VI of *Fatima: Tragedy and Triumph.*

47. The reported November 17, 2001 interview between Archbishop Bertone and Sister Lucy is treated at length in Chapter 14, "Let us Hear the Witness, For Heaven's Sake".

48. The Vatican translation "we are going towards it little by little with great strides" is clearly defective. The words "little by little" do not appear in the handwritten Portuguese original published on p. 9 of *TMF* provided by the Vatican itself. We have thus provided our own accurate translation.

49. Marmion, *Canto 6*, stanza 17.

50. It should be noted that Cardinal Ratzinger himself said regarding the Vatican's interpretation of the Third Secret, "The Church does not want to impose an interpretation". This quotation was reported in: "Final Secret of Vatican Published by Vatican", *Boston Herald,* June 27, 2000; "Vatican's Secret is Out", *The Express,* June 27, 2000; "Vatican Unease as it Reveals the Full Third Secret of Fatima", *Financial Times (London),* June 27, 2000; "Fatima 'Snapshot of Martyr's Past Century'", *The Irish Times,* June 27, 2000.

51. News of June 27, 2000 press conference. "Gorbachev Helps Introduce Casaroli Memoirs", *Catholic World News*, June 27, 2000.

52. In September 1995, Gorbachev held his "State of the World Forum" in San Francisco. Over 4000 of the world's "elite" paid $5,000 per person to attend the 5-day event. In a closing plenary session of the forum, a philosopher/author named Sam Keen provided a summary and concluding remarks on the conference. It reveals the Forum's anti-life, anti-Christian ethos. To the conference participants, Keen said: "there was very strong agreement that religious institutions have to take the primary responsibility for the population explosion. We must speak far more clearly about sexuality, about contraception, about abortion, about the values that control the population, because the ecological crisis, in short, is the population crisis. *Cut the population by 90 percent and there aren't enough people left to do a great deal of ecological damage.*" See "World's elite gather to talk depopulation," John Henry Western, *The Interim*, April 1996.

53. See interview with Afghan official Abdul Shams in *Review of the News*, July 1985.

54. Photograph published in *Catholic Family News,* January 2001, p. 13.

## Chapter 9

1. Letter to the General Chapter of the Priestly Fraternity of Saint Peter, June 29, 2000.
2. *30 Days* magazine, No. 11, 2000, p. 17.
3. Zenit, September 19, 2000.
4. *CWN News Brief*, September 18, 2000.
5. While it is true that in normal circumstances a bishop should not make a new bishop without explicit permission or authorization from the Pope, nevertheless it is foreseen both in law and in practice over the centuries in Church history that a bishop can and sometimes must consecrate—that is, make—another bishop without explicit

permission and even to go against a specific direct order of the Pope. Canon Law recognizes the right of a subject to go against an explicit order of a higher authority—even that of a Pope—in a specific instance, after due reflection and prayer, to go directly contrary if his conscience, informed by Catholic doctrine, persuades him that he must do so. (See Canon 1323, especially Section 4; and Canon 1324, especially Section 1 subsection 8, and Section 3.) Furthermore, in law it is not *ipso facto* an act of schism for one to disobey in a specific instance while being subject to the authority of the Pope in general—but at most it is an act of disobedience.

But even it is not an act of disobedience, at least subjectively, if one does not feel bound to obey the higher authority because the preservation of the Faith and the good of the Church demands it. The act of Archbishop Lefebvre on June 29, 1988 in consecrating four priests to the rank of bishop is beyond the scope of this book, but there are very learned articles by canonists and theologians which make a strong case for the subjective and objective defense of this act. (See articles by Patrick Valdrini, Dean of Canon Law, Institute Catholique, Paris, France and by Count Neri Caponi, Professor Emeritus of the Faculty of Canon Law, University of Florence, Italy.) Even various Cardinals in the Vatican have publicly, in various degrees, defended Archbishop Lefebvre in this act.

6. Cardinal Kung Foundation's *Open Letter to the Vatican*, Sec. III, March 28, 2000 (www.cardinalkungfoundation/cpa/openletter). In reply to the Kung Foundation (quoted in the *Open Letter*), Archbishop Levada reveals that the "apostolic ministry" of CPA priests "is being carried out according to directives received from the Holy See."
7. Letter to Father Nicholas Gruner, February 16, 2001.
8. The New Evangelization is described as an Evangelization that is "new in its ardor, new in its method, and new in its expression". It is under the umbrella of the "New Evangelization" that has "justified" the rowdy "Charismatic Movement" and Rock and Roll Eucharistic Congresses, World Youth Days nicknamed "Catholic Woodstock", and other present-day aberrations in the Church. For a full treatment of the subject, see John Vennari, "Catholicism Dissolved, The New Evangelization", (Four part series in *Catholic Family News* from Oct. 1998 to January 1999.
9. See Sister Lucy's quote in *The Whole Truth About Fatima - Vol. III,* p. 758.

## Chapter 10

There are no footnotes in this chapter.

## Chapter 11

1. Between 1986 and 1991 several *Sanpietrini*, the uniformed guards in St. Peter's Basilica in Rome, have directly told Father Gregorius Hesse (who worked for years in the Vatican) that after almost every single papal Mass in the Square, Sacred Hosts are found on the ground.
2. Only a religion in which one can be saved can be pleasing to God, and there is only one (which is a Dogma of the Faith), whence the contrary is heresy and it is also blasphemy, as God, Who is the Truth, cannot be careless about the Truth, whence to state the contrary is blasphemy.
3. *The Fatima Crusader*, Issue 64, p. 115.
4. Ibid., pp. 54ff.
5. Ibid., p. 55.
6. Ibid., p. 18.
7. Daniel Le Roux, *Petrus liebst du mich*? (Stuttgart 1990). *Peter, Lovest Thou Me*?, p. 110. The skeptic will find that I only referred to pictures which can be easily found in the English translation published by Instauratio Press, Yarra Junction, Australia, 1988.
8. Ibid., p. 112.
9. Ibid., p. 127.
10. Ibid., p. 155.
11. Ibid., p. 172.
12. Ibid., p. 177.
13. Ibid., p. 236.
14 Ibid., p. 144.
15. *The Fatima Crusader,* Issue 64, p. 31.

16. Joseph Cardinal Ratzinger, "Theological Commentary", *The Message of Fatima* (*TMF*), June 26, 2000, p. 32.

17. *The Fatima Crusader*, Issue 64, pp. 34f.

18. *The Fatima Crusader*, Issue 64, pp. 115ff.

19. See Bishop Emile Bougaud, *The Life of Saint Margaret Mary Alacoque* (originally published by Benzinger, 1890; republished by TAN Books and Publishers, 1990), Chapter XIV, "The Last Grand Revelation—The King of France, 1689".

20. In the 13th Century, St. Gertrude, a German, was a "herald of the Sacred Heart". See *St. Gertrude the Great*, published by the Benedictine Convent of Clyde, Missouri, republished by TAN Books and Publishers in 1979, pp. 26ff. Thus we do not understand why the "German cultural world" would find anything strange about Devotion to the Sacred Heart or the Immaculate Heart.

21. Joseph Cardinal Ratzinger, "Theological Commentary", *The Message of Fatima*, English edition, June 26, 2000, p. 40.

22. St. Thomas Aquinas, *Summa Theologiae*, 1.q.22, a.2.

23. Joseph Cardinal Ratzinger, "Theological Commentary", *The Message of Fatima*, p. 42.

24. Ibid.

25. *The Fatima Crusader*, Issue 64, p. 51.

26. Joseph Cardinal Ratzinger, "Theological Commentary", *The Message of Fatima*, p. 43.

27. Archbishop Goodier, S.J., *The Public Life of Our Lord Jesus Christ, Vol. I*, (Burns Oates & Washbourne Ltd., London, England, 1932) p. 462.

28. Cardinal Sodano, on May 13, 2000 at Fatima, said in his speech: "The successive events of 1989 led, both in the Soviet Union and in a number of countries of Eastern Europe, to the fall of the Communist regimes which promoted atheism."

29. Father Joaquin Alonso, *La Verdad sobre el Secreto de Fatima,* (Centro Mariano, Madrid, Spain, 1976) p. 73. In *The Whole Truth About Fatima - Vol. III,* p. 704. See also *The Fatima Crusader*, Issue 64, p. 121.

**Chapter 12**

1. *Mother Angelica Live*, May 16, 2001.

2. In some proofs, we are dealing with circumstantial evidence. There are two reasons for this: (1) over 5,000 original documents in 24 volumes compiled by Father Alonso—the result of 11 years of research by Father Alonso, then the official archivist of Fatima—have been prevented from being published since 1976 by religious authorities (i.e. the Bishop of Fatima and the Provincial of the Claretians based at Madrid, Spain), and (2) the continued imposition of a regime of silence upon Sister Lucy (in force since 1960), even though we are now told she has nothing further to reveal.

3. Quoted by Father Alonso, *Fatima 50*, October 13, 1967, p. 11. See also Frère Michel de la Sainte Trinité, *The Whole Truth About Fatima* ***(WTAF)*** *- Volume III: The Third Secret,* (Immaculate Heart Publications, Buffalo, New York, U.S.A., 1990) p. 47.

4. *WTAF - Vol. III*, p. 49.

5. Quoted by Father Martins dos Reis, *O Milagre do sol e o Segredo de Fatima*, p. 127-128. Cf. Father Joaquin Alonso, *La Verdad sobre el Secreto de Fatima* ***(VSF)***, Centro Mariano, Madrid, Spain, 1976, pp. 55-56. See also *WTAF - Vol. III*, p. 578.

6. *WTAF - Vol. III*, p. 684.

7. Father Alonso, *VSF*, p. 64. See also *WTAF - Vol. III*, p. 684.

8. *WTAF - Vol. III*, p. 684.

9. Frère François de Marie des Anges, *Fatima: Tragedy and Triumph* ***(FTT)***, Immaculate Heart Publications, Buffalo, New York, U.S.A., 1994, p. 45.

10. Archbishop Tarcisio Bertone, SDB., "Introduction", *The Message of Fatima* ***(TMF)***, June 26, 2000, p. 4.

11. *WTAF - Vol. III*, p. 725.

12. *WTAF - Vol. III*, p. 727.

13 Father Alonso, *VSF*, p. 60. See also *WTAF - Vol. III*, p. 651. Also, footnote no. 4 in *FTT*, p. 289.

14. *FTT*, p. 45. See also Brother Michael of the Holy Trinity, *The Secret of Fatima ... Revealed* ***(SFR)***, Immaculate Heart

Publications, Buffalo, New York, U.S.A., 1986, p. 7.

15. *WTAF - Vol. III*, p. 480. See also Father G. Freire's exposition, *O Segredo de Fatima, a terceira parte e sobre Portugal?*, pp. 50-51.

16. *WTAF - Vol. III*, p. 481.

17. *WTAF - Vol. III*, p. 626.

18. *FTT*, p. 45.

19. *SFR*, p. 7.

20. *WTAF - Vol. III*, pp. 38-46.

21. Quoted by Father Alonso, *Fatima 50*, p. 11. See also *WTAF - Vol. III*, p. 47.

22. Original text of Sister Lucy, "Third Part of the 'Secret'", *TMF*, p. 20.

23. Archbishop Tarcisio Bertone, SDB, "Introduction", *TMF*, p. 4.

24. Bill Broadway and Sarah Delancy, "3rd Secret Spurs More Questions; Fatima Interpretation Departs From Vision", *The Washington Post*, July 1, 2000.

25. The Associated Press, "Vatican: Fatima Is No Doomsday Prophecy", *The New York Times*, June 26, 2000.

26. Archbishop Tarcisio Bertone, SDB, "Introduction", *TMF*, p. 5.

27. Ibid.

28. *Revue Mediatrice et Reine*, October 1946, pp. 110-112. See also *WTAF - Vol. III*, p. 470.

29. Quoted by Father Alonso, *VSF*, pp. 46-47. See also *WTAF - Vol. III*, p. 470.

30. *Novidades*, February 24, 1960, quoted by *La Documentation Catholique*, June 19, 1960, col. 751. See also *WTAF - Vol. III*, p. 472.

31. *VSF*, p. 46. See also *WTAF - Vol. III*, p. 475.

32. *VSF*, p. 46. See also *WTAF - Vol. III*, p. 478.

33. Quoted by Father Martins dos Reis, *O Milagre do sol e o Segredo de Fatima*, pp. 127-128. Cf. Father Alonso, *VSF*, pp. 55-56. See also *WTAF - Vol. III*, p. 578.

34. Quoted by Father Alonso, *Fatima 50*, p. 11. See also *WTAF - Vol. III*, p. 47.

35. *WTAF - Vol. III*, p. 49.

36. Ibid., pp. 485-486.

37. Ibid., pp. 484-485.

38. Letter to Frère Michel de la Sainte Trinité of January 10, 1985. See also *WTAF - Vol. III*, p. 486.

39. Archbishop Tarcisio Bertone, SDB, "Introduction", *TMF*, p. 4.

40. *WTAF - Vol. III*, p. 481.

41. Sister Lucy, in an account written for her confessor, Father Aparicio, at the end of 1927.

42. Sister Lucy, "Fourth Memoir", December 8, 1941, p. 65. See also Frère Michel de la Sainte Trinité, *The Whole Truth About Fatima - Volume I: Science and the Facts (WTAF - Vol. I)*, Immaculate Heart Publications, Buffalo, New York, U.S.A., 1989, p. 159.

43. English translation of text in Sister Lucy's "Third Memoir" quoted in "First and Second Part of the 'Secret'", *TMF*, pp. 15-16. See also Sister Lucy, "Fourth Memoir", *Fatima in Lucia's Own Words*, (Postulation Centre, Fatima, Portugal, 1976) p. 162. See also Sister Lucy, *Memorias e Cartas da Irma Lucia*, (Porto, Portugal, 1973, edited by Father Antonio Maria Martins) pp. 338-341.

44. Sister Lucy quoted in *TMF*, p. 16. See also Sister Lucy, "Fourth Memoir", p. 162. See also Sister Lucy, *Memorias e Cartas da Irma Lucia*, pp. 340-341.

45. English translation of Sister Lucy, "Third Part of the 'Secret'", *TMF*, p. 21.

46. Father Fabrice Delestre, Society of St. Pius X, "June 26, 2000: Revelation of the Third Secret of Fatima or a Curtailed Revelation", *SSPX Asia Newsletter*, July-August 2000, p. 24.

47. Joseph Cardinal Ratzinger, "Theological Commentary", *TMF*, p. 39.

48. Bill Broadway and Sarah Delancy, *The Washington Post*.

49. Sister Lucy's testimony is discussed in detail in Chapter 14 of this book along with Msgr. Bertone's effort to change that testimony in a secret interview on November 17, 2001 for which no transcript has ever been produced.

**Chapter 13**

1. Frère Michel de la Sainte Trinité, *The Whole Truth About Fatima - Vol. III*, p. 704.

2. Ibid., p. 687.

3. Ibid., pp. 705-706.

4. *The Whole Truth About Fatima - Vol. III*, pp. 822-823. See also *Jesus* magazine, November 11, 1984, p. 79. See also *The Fatima Crusader*, Issue 37, Summer 1991, p. 7.

5. *The Whole Truth About Fatima - Vol. III,* p. 676.

6. *CRC*, December 1997.

7. See Father Gerard Mura, "The Third Secret of Fatima: Has It Been Completely Revealed?", the periodical *Catholic*, (published by the Transalpine Redemptorists, Orkney Isles, Scotland, Great Britain) March 2002.

8. Ibid.

9. The words in parenthesis in this paragraph are now inserted into the Tridentine profession of faith by order of Pope Blessed Pius IX in a decree issued by the Holy Office, January 20, 1877. (*Acta Sanctae Sedis*, X [1877], 71 ff.)

10. In Paragraph 6 of the Encyclical *Quanta Cura* which was issued with the *Syllabus* on Dec. 8, 1864, Blessed Pope Pius IX stated solemnly: "Amid, therefore, so great perversity of depraved opinions, We, well remembering Our Apostolic Office, and very greatly solicitous for Our most holy Religion, for sound doctrine and the salvation of souls which is entrusted to Us by God, and (solicitous also) for the welfare of human society itself, have thought it right to raise up Our Apostolic voice. *Therefore, by Our Apostolic Authority, We reprobate, proscribe and condemn all the singular and evil opinions and doctrines severally mentioned in this Letter, and will and command that they be thoroughly held by all children of the Catholic Church as reprobated, proscribed and condemned."* (Our emphasis) Taken from *The Popes Against Modern Errors*, (TAN Books and Publishers, Rockford, Illinois, 1999) p. 21.

11. Cardinal Joseph Ratzinger, *Principles of Catholic Theology,* (Ignatius Press, San Francisco, 1987) pp. 381-382.

12. Ibid., p. 380.

13. *The Balamand Statement*, No. 30, June 23, 1993.

14. See footnote 10 of this chapter.

15. Vatican Council I - 1870 A.D., see Denzinger (Dz.) 1836.

16. Vatican Council I, see Dz. 1800.

17. Through his negligence, Pope Honorius had been largely responsible for the spread of the Monothelite heresy by asserting that there is only one will in Christ, the divine will—an error that implicitly denies that Christ is both true God and true man—, although he understood this in a Catholic sense, namely that there could not be a conflict between the divine will and the human will of Christ. However, his formulation allowed the Monothelite heretics to assert that there was only one will in Christ and that the Pope agreed with them.

18. Personal testimony of retired Vatican Msgr. Corrado Balducci to Father Nicholas Gruner, Christopher Ferrara and various other witnesses. This fact is also attested to by Marco Tosatti in his book *Il Segreto Non Svelato* (The Secret Not Revealed), (Edizioni Piemme Spa, Casale Monferrato, Italy, May 2002), p. 86.

    Marco Tosatti writes: "Father Mastrocola, director of a religious newsletter 'Santa Rita', asked Cardinal Ottaviani the permission to reprint the prophecies made in 'Neues Europa'. The reply was encouraging, but in the light of the 'revealing' of the secret of June 26, 2000, embarrassing. 'Do it, do it'—replied the Cardinal custodian of the Third Secret—'publish as many copies as you want, because the Madonna wanted it to be published already in 1960.' And of that text Vatican Radio also spoke in 1977 on the occasion of the tenth anniversary of the trip of Pope Paul VI to Fatima. The text of 'Neues Europa' received great circulation and was republished even in the *L'Osservatore Romano* Sunday edition of October 15, 1978".

    The Italian original is as follows: "Padre Mastrocola, direttore di un foglio religioso, «Santa Rita», chiese al cardinale Ottaviani il permesso di riprendere l'anticipazione fatta da «Neues Europa». La risposta fu incoraggiante, ma alla luce dello «svelamento» del segreto del 26 giugno 2000, imbarazzante. «Fatelo, fatelo pure—rispose il porporato custode del terzo segreto—pubblicatene quante copie vi pare, perché la Madonna voleva che fosse reso noto già nel 1960». E di quel testo parlò anche la Radio Vaticana nel 1977, nel decennale del viaggio di Paolo VI a Fatima. Il testo di «Neues Europa» conobbe grande fortuna, e venne ripreso persino il 15 ottobre 1978 dall' «Osservatore della Domenica»".

19. See Francis Alban, *Fatima Priest*, First Edition, (Good Counsel Publications, Pound Ridge, New York, 1997) Appendix III, "A Prophetic Interview with Sister Lucy of Fatima", p. 312. See also *The Whole Truth About Fatima - Vol. III*, pp. 503-510 for the text of this interview together with further explanations by Freré Michel.
20. See *Fatima Priest*, Editions 1 and 2, Appendix V, "Regarding Communion in the Hand". See also *The Fatima Crusader*, Issue 28, June-July 1989, pp. 33ff, 34ff, 36ff; *The Fatima Crusader*, Issue 29, Sept.-Nov. 1989, p. 16; and *The Fatima Crusader*, Issue 7, Spring 1981, p. 11.
21. Pope Pius XII, quoted in the book *Pius XII Devant L'Histoire*, pp. 52-53.
22. Pope St. Pius X, *Pascendi Dominici Gregis,* para. no. 2.
23. Ibid., no. 3.
24. Ibid., no. 61.
25. Ibid., no. 3.
26. John Henry Newman, *On Consulting the Faithful in Matters of Doctrine* (Kansas City, Sheed and Ward, 1961), p.77.

## Chapter 14

1. On the contrary, as Father Alonso documents, Sister Lucy affirmed that "everything connected with the apparitions of the Lady was seen no longer as a simple recollection, but as a presence impressed upon her soul as though by fire. She herself points out to us these things remain impressed upon her soul in such a way that she could not possibly forget them. These reminiscences of Sister Lucia, therefore, are rather like re-reading inscriptions which are forever engraven in the deepest depths of the soul of the authoress. She appears to be 'seeing' rather than 'remembering'. The ease of her 'remembering' is indeed so great that she has only to 'read', as it were, from her soul." Father Joaquin Alonso, "Introduction", *Fatima in Lucia's Own Words*, p. 13.
2. See footnote 48 in Chapter 8.
3. Occasionally, when referring to or quoting the Bertone communiqué, this chapter sometimes uses the *Vatican Information Service* English translation of the December 2001 Italian original. Other times, the English translation used in *L'Osservatore Romano* English edition of January 9, 2002 is used. And very rarely, our own translation of the Italian version is used.

## Chapter 15

1. *New York Times*, March 2, 2002.
2. Donald Cozzens, *The Changing Face of the Catholic Priesthood,* (Liturgical Press, Collegeville, Minnesota, 2002) p. 135.
3. CNN, March 21, 2001.
4. BBC Online, March 2, 2002.
5. AP News, March 1, 2002.
6. Zenit News, February 17, 2002.
7. Zenit News, December 22, 2000.
8. AP report and photograph, February 28, 2002.
9. *Catholic News Service Report*, May 8, 2001.
10. *National Catholic Register* Online Web Edition, April 28 - May 5, 2002.
11. CWNews, March 2, 2002.
12. *Electronic Telegraph*, March 2, 2000.
13. Msgr. Klaus Gamber, *The Reform of the Roman Liturgy*, (Foundation For Christian Reform, Harrison, New York, 1993) p. 113.

## Chapter 16

1. ST, Q. 33, Art. V, Pt. II-II.
2. St. Robert Bellarmine, *De Romano Pontifice*, Book II, Chapter 29.
3. *De Fide*, Disp. X, Sec. VI, N. 16.
4. *The Whole Truth About Fatima - Vol. II: The Secret and the Church,* pp. 543-544.

See also *Toute La Vérite sur Fatima - Vol. II: Le Secret et L'Église*, pp. 344-345.

5. See Coralie Graham, "Divine Intervention", *The Fatima Crusader*, Issue 70, Spring 2002, p. 8ff.
6. "Abuse Victims File Petition Seeking Removal of Archbishop", *The Wanderer*, April 4, 2002.
7. "Internal church documents showed that from the mid-1980's and into the 90's Cardinal Law and his top aides were aware of the problems of Father Geoghan, who was eventually accused of molesting more than 130 children over 30 years. In February, he was sentenced to 9 to 10 years in prison for fondling a 10-year-old boy. After the church's role [that is, the Boston Archdiocese's officials' role] in protecting Father Geoghan became known, the Cardinal gave local prosecutors the names of more than 80 priests accused of sexual abuse over decades." Quoted from "As Scandal Keeps Growing, Church and Its Faithful Reel", *New York Times,* March 17, 2002.

## Chapter 17

1. See *Newsweek,* April 8, 2002, which notes (quoting a Vatican official) that the Pope has become so enfeebled that he "reads whatever they give him to read. Most of the time he signs ... whatever they give him to sign."
2. John Henry Newman, *On Consulting the Faithful in Matters of Doctrine*, p. 77.

# Selected Bibliography

## Books:


Alban, Francis (and Christopher Ferrara), *Fatima Priest,* Editions 1 through 4. Pound Ridge: Good Counsel Publications, 1997-2001. Italian Edition, *Il Sacerdote di Fatima,* New York: Good Counsel Publications, 2000.

Trinchard, Father Paul, *The Awesome Fatima Consecration*. Metairie: Maeta, 1992.

Alonso, Father Joaquin, *La Verdad sobre el Secreto de Fatima.* Madrid: Centro Mariano, 1976.

Benedictine Sisters of Clyde, Missouri, *Saint Gertrude the Great.* Rockford: TAN Books and Publishers, Inc., 1979.

Bougard, Bishop Emile, *The Life of Saint Margaret Mary Alacoque.* New York: Benzinger, 1890. (Republished by TAN, 1990).

Cahill, S.J., Rev. E., *Freemasonry and the Anti-Christian Movement.* Dublin: Gill, 1959.

*Catholic Encyclopedia,* New York: Encyclopedia Press, 1913.

*Council Daybook,* Washington: National Catholic Welfare Conference.

Cozzens, Donald, *The Changing Face of the Catholic Priesthood.* Collegeville: Liturgical Press, 2001.

Davies, Michael, *Pope John's Council.* Kansas City: Angelus Press, 1992.

———, *Pope Paul's New Mass,* Kansas City: Angelus Press, 1980; second printing, 1988.

De Poncins, Vicomte Leon, *Freemasonry and the Vatican.* Palmdale: Christian Book Club, 1968.

*Denzinger: The Sources of Catholic Dogma.* Translated by Roy J. Deferrari. London: Herder, 1957.

De Marchi, I.M.C, Father John, *Fatima From the Beginning.* Fatima: Missoes Consolata, 1981, third edition. (First published in 1950).

Dillon, Msgr. George E., D.D., *Grand Orient Freemasonry Unmasked.* Palmdale: Christian Book Club. (Originally published by M. H. Gill in Dublin, 1885).

*The "Divine Impatience".* (Speeches from the 1992 Fatima Conference.) Fort Erie: Immaculate Heart Publications, 2000.

*Documents of Vatican II,* edited by Walter M. Abbot, SJ. New York: American Press, 1966.

Fahey, C.S.Sp., Father Denis, *The Mystical Body of Christ in the Modern World.* Dublin: Regina Publications, 1939.

Fisher, Paul, *Their God is the Devil.* Washington: American Research Foundation, 1990.

François de Marie des Anges, (Frère) *Fatima: Intimate Joy World Event*, Book I, *Fatima: The Astonishing Truth.* Buffalo: Immaculate Heart Publications, 1993.

————, *Fatima: Intimate Joy World Event*, Book II, *Mary's Immaculate Heart and Your Salvation.* Buffalo: Immaculate Heart Publications, 1993.

————, *Fatima: Intimate Joy World Event*, Book III, *The Only Way to World Peace.* Buffalo: Immaculate Heart Publications, 1993.

————, *Fatima: Intimate Joy World Event*, Book IV, *Fatima: Tragedy and Triumph.* Buffalo: Immaculate Heart Publications, 1994.

Frère Michel, see Michel de la Sainte Trinité, (Frère).

Frère François, see François de Marie des Anges, (Frère).

Gamber, Msgr. Klaus, *The Reform of the Roman Liturgy*. Harrison: Foundation for Christian Reform, 1993.

*God's Endorsement of Fatima.* Fort Erie: Fatima Center, 2001.

Goodier, SJ, Archbishop Alban, *The Public Life of Our Lord Jesus Christ,* Vol. I. London: Burns, Oates and Washborne Ltd., 1932.

Graber, Bishop Rudolph, *Athanasius and the Church of Our Time*. Palmdale: Christian Book Club, 1974.

Gruner, Father Nicholas, *World Enslavement or Peace ... It's up to the Pope.* Fort Erie: The Fatima Crusader, 1988.

Guimarães, Atila Sinke, *Animus Delendi - I, "The Desire to Destroy".* Los Angeles: Tradition in Action, 2001

————, *In the Murky Waters of Vatican II.* Metairie: Maeta, 1997.

Haffert, John M., *Meet the Witnesses*. Fatima: AMI International Press, 1961.

Kelly, Msgr. George, *The Battle for the American Church.* Garden City, NY: Image Books, 1981.

Kramer, Father Herman Bernard, *The Book of Destiny*. Rockford: TAN, 1975.

Le Roux, Father Daniel, *Peter Lovest Thou Me?*. (English Edition) Yarra Junction: Instauratio Press, 1989.

Lefebvre, Archbishop Marcel, *Open Letter to Confused Catholics.* Kansas City: Angelus Press, 1992.

———, *They Have Uncrowned Him.* Kansas City: Angelus Press, 1988.

Leo XIII, Encyclical *Humanum Genus,* 1884.

Lucia dos Santos, Sister, *Fatima in Lucia's Own Words.* Fatima: Postulation Centre, 1976.

———, *Memorias e Cartas da Irma Lucia,* edited by Father Antonio Maria Martins. Porto, Portugal: Missoes Consolata, 1973, 1976.

Manifold, Deirdre, *Fatima and the Great Conspiracy.* Galway, Ireland: Firinne Publications, Seventh Edition, 1992.

*Message of Fatima, The,* Sacred Congregation for the Doctrine of the Faith, June 26, 2000.

Miceli, SJ, Father Vincent, *The Antichrist.* Harrison: Roman Catholic Books, 1981.

Michel de la Sainte Trinité, (Frère) *The Secret of Fatima ... Revealed.* Buffalo: Immaculate Heart Publications, 1986.

———, *The Whole Truth About Fatima,* Volume I, "Science and the Facts". Buffalo: Immaculate Heart Publications, 1989.

———, *The Whole Truth About Fatima,* Volume II, "The Secret and the Church". Buffalo: Immaculate Heart Publications, 1989.

———, *The Whole Truth About Fatima,* Volume III, "The Third Secret". Buffalo: Immaculate Heart Publications, 1990.

Muller, S.CC.R., Father Michael, *The Catholic Dogma.* New York: Benzinger, 1888.

Newman, Cardinal John Henry, *On Consulting the Faithful in Matters of Doctrine.* Kansas City: Sheed and Ward, 1961.

*Novos Documentos de Fatima.* Sao Paulo: Loyola editions, 1984.

*Our Lady's Urgent Appeal to us in the 1990s.* Fort Erie: Fatima Center, 1982.

Pelletier, A.A., Father Joseph A., *The Sun Danced at Fatima. New York: Doubleday, 1983.*

Pius IX, Pope, Encyclical *Quanta Cura,* 1864.

Pius X, Pope, Encyclical *Pascendi Dominici Gregis,* 1907.

Pius XI, Pope, Encyclical *Ubi Arcano Dei,* 1922.

———, Encyclical *Quas Primas,* 1925.

———, Encyclical *Divini Redemptoris,* 1937.

Pius XII, Pope, Encyclical *Mystici Corporis,* 1943.

————, Encyclical *Humani Generis,* 1950.

*The Popes Against Modern Errors,* 16 Papal Encyclicals. Rockford: TAN, 1999.

Popian, Father Linus Dragu, *I 24 Giorni Della Fuga*. Udine: Edizioni Segno, 1998.

Ratzinger, Joseph, *Theological Highlights of Vatican II.* New York: Paulist Press, 1966.

————, *Principles of Catholic Theology*. San Francisco: Ignatius Press, 1987.

Roche, Msgr. George, *Pie XII Devant L'Histoire.* Paris: Editions Robert Laffont, 1972.

Sister Lucia, See Lucia dos Santos, Sister.

Talantov, Boris, *Patriarchate and Sergianism.* Platina: St. Herman of Alaska Press, 1982.

Tosatti, Marco, *Il Segreto Non Svelato*. Casale Monferrato: Edizioni Piemme Spa, May 2002.

Tracy, David, Editor, (with Hans Küng and Johann Metz) *Vatican II, the Work that Needs to be Done.* New York: Seabury Press, 1978.

Vennari, John, *The Permanant Instruction of the Alta Vendita, A Blueprint for the Subversion of the Catholic Church.* Rockford: TAN, 1999.

Walsh, William Thomas, *Our Lady of Fatima.* New York: Doubleday, 1947.

Wiltgen, Father Ralph, *The Rhine Flows into the Tiber.* New York: Hawthorne, 1967. (TAN, 1985)

Wycislo, Most Reverend Aloysius, *Vatican II Revisited, Reflections by One Who Was There.* Staten Island: Alba House, 1987.

## Articles

"A World View Based on Fatima", John Vennari, *The Fatima Crusader,* Issue 64, Spring 2000.

"Abuse Victims File Petition Seeking Removal of Archbishop", *The Wanderer,* April 4, 2002.

"Activist Says Child Porn Prosecutions Will be Difficult in Indonesia, Russia", Christine Brummitt, *Associated Press,* August 9, 2001.

"Analysis: Persons Who Have Studied the Apparitions Say That the Third Secret Could Concern the Destruction of the Faith. A Crisis in the Interior of the Church Would be the Third Secret", *Euronoticias,* March 24, 2000.

"The Apparitions of Our Lady of Fatima, 1917", Father Nicholas Gruner. (Transcript of speech from Fatima Conference in Rome, October 2001).

"The Apparitions of Pontevedra/Rianjo/Tuy: The Consecration of Russia and the Five First Saturdays", Father Nicholas Gruner. (Transcript of speech from Fatima Conference in Rome, October 2001).

"Are There Two Original Manuscripts on the Third Secret?", Andrew M. Cesanek, *The Fatima Crusader,* Issue 64, Spring 2000.

"As Scandal Keeps Growing, Church and Its Faithful Reel", *New York Times,* March 17, 2002.

"Barbarism Then and Now", Thomas Woods, Ph.D. (Transcript of speech from Fatima Conference in Rome, October 2001).

"The Beatification of the Little Shepherds Definitely Will Be At Rome", *Voz da Verdade,* October 31, 1999.

"The Blessed Mother and the Return to Holiness", Cornelia Ferreira. (Transcript of speech from Fatima Conference in Rome, October 2001).

"Big Brother Goes too far for Staid Russians", Mark Franchetti, *Sunday Times (London),* November 25, 2001.

"Bishop of Leiria-Fatima," March 21 press conference; *Euronoticias,* March 24, 2000.

"Cardinal Ratzinger's Third Secret", Rev. Canon Gregorius D. Hesse, S.T.D., J.C.D. (Cand.), *The Fatima Crusader*, Issue 66, Winter 2001.

"Catholic Church Unveils 'Third Secret of Fatima'; The Vatican's Top Theologian Gently Debunks a Nun's Account of Her 1917 Vision That Fueled Decades of Speculation", Richard Boudreaux, *Los Angeles Times*, June 27, 2000.

"Catholic Clergy in Siberia Face Growing Difficulties", *Catholic World News,* November 19, 1997.

"Catholicism Dissolved, the New Evangelization" (Four part series), John Vennari, *Catholic Family News,* October 1998 to January 1999.

"Chronology of a Cover-up", Father Paul Kramer, *Catholic Family News* Special Supplement, April 2002. Also at www.fatima.org.

"Chronology of a Cover-up - Parts I, III and IV", Father Nicholas Gruner. (Transcripts of speech from Fatima Conference in Rome, October 2001).

"Chronology of a Cover-up - Part II: The Vatican Commentary, 'The Message of Fatima'." Christopher Ferrara. (Transcript of speech from Fatima Conference in Rome, October 2001).

"The Consecration of Russia: Our Lady of Fatima vs. the Culture of Death", Father Nicholas Gruner. (Transcript of speech from Fatima Conference in Rome, October 2001).

"Crisis: The Bishop of Leiria-Fatima Creates A Mystery Around the Visit of the Pope Without Telling the Patriarch What It Concerns, Will the Pope Reveal the Third Secret?", *Euronoticias,* March 24, 2000.

"The Coming Cashless Society" (Parts I & II), John Vennari. (Transcript of speech from Fatima Conference in Rome, October 2001).

"Defense of Father Gruner, The Right to Hold the Conference", Christopher Ferrara. (Transcript of speech from Fatima Conference in Rome, October 2001).

"Divine Intervention", Coralie Graham, *The Fatima Crusader,* Issue 70, Spring 2002.

"Fatima in Twilight", Mark Fellows. Series run in *The Remnant,* 1995 and *Catholic Family News,* 1995.

"Fatima Inquest", David Boyce, *The Fatima Crusader,* Issue 35, Winter 1990-1991.

"Fatima Snapshot of Martyr's Past Century", *The Irish Times,* June 27, 2000.

"Fatima: Why Isn't the Mother of God Being Obeyed as She Should Be?", Father Fabrice Delestre, *Angelus,* June 2000.

"Father Pierre De Smet, SJ: Missionary Hero of the 19th Century", John Vennari. (Transcript of speech from Fatima Conference in Rome, October 2001).

"Final Secret of Vatican Published by Vatican", *Boston Herald,* June 27, 2000.

"Foreign Priests Spark Controversy", Sarah Karush, *Associated Press,* February 12, 2002.

"Fundamentalism and Integralism: Christians Confronting Ecumenism", Pierre Lathuiliere, *Service International de Documentation Judeo-Chretienne (SIDIC),* Vol. XXXII, No. 3 - 1999, English Edition.

"Gorbachev Helps Introduce Casaroli Memoirs", *Catholic World News,* June 27, 2000.

"The Greatest Conspiracy", *Christian Order,* November 2000.

"Heaven's Request for Reparation to the Holy Face of Jesus" Part III, John Vennari, *Catholic Family News,* August 2001.

"The International Criminal Court", William Jasper. (Transcript of speech from Fatima Conference in Rome, October 2001).

"It Doesn't Add Up", John Vennari, *Catholic Family News,* February 2002 and *The Fatima Crusader,* Issue 70, Spring 2002.

"Jeremiah & Jude vs. Juvenile Naivety", Gerry Matatics. (Transcript of speech from Fatima Conference in Rome, October 2001).

"Joint Catholic-Lutheran Vespers at Vatican", CWNews.com, November 13, 1999.

"June 26, 2000: Revelation of the Third Secret of Fatima or a Curtailed Revelation?, Father Fabrice Delestre, *SSPX Asia Newsletter,* July-August 2000.

"Let Us Hear the Witness, For Heaven's Sake", Christopher Ferrara, *The Fatima Crusader,* Issue 70, Spring 2002.

"Lucy and the Pirates", Mark Fellows, *Catholic Family News,* February 2002 and *The Fatima Crusader,* Issue 70, Spring 2002.

"The Lying Press Conference of June 26, 2000", Father Paul Kramer. (Transcript of speech from Fatima Conference in Rome, October 2001).

"The Magnificent Promise for the Five First Saturdays", Brother Michael of the Most Holy Trinity. *The Fatima Crusader,* Issue 49, Summer 1995.

"The Metz Pact", Atila Sinke Guimarães, *Catholic Family News,* September 2001.

"The Myth of a Converted Russia", Marian T. Horvat, Ph.D., *Catholic Family News,* March 2001.

"New Visa System Seen Choking Russia's Catholic Parishes", *Russia Reform Monitor,* No. 485, July 28, 1998.

"Non-Catholics Join Pope in Rite", *Los Angeles Times,* January 19, 2000.

"Open Letter to the Vatican", Cardinal Kung Foundation, March 28, 2000.

"Our Lady, Conqueror of All Heresies: The Consecration of Portugal, 1931", John Vennari. (Transcript of speech from Fatima Conference in Rome, October 2001).

"Our Lady of Fatima vs. the Desire to Destroy our Catholic Heritage", John Vennari. (Transcript of speech, Fatima Rally Against Terrorism, New York, Nov. 2001).

"The 'Party Line' in Relation to Fatima", Father Paul Kramer, *The Fatima Crusader,* Issue 69, Winter 2002.

"Pope John Paul Gives us the Key to the Real Third Secret", (Three part series) Father Nicholas Gruner, *The Fatima Crusader,* Issues 67-69. Summer 2001, Autumn 2001, Winter 2002.

"The Pope Will Return to Portugal; Fatima is the Place of the Beatification", *Voz da Verdade,* December 5, 1999.

"Previous Attempts at the Consecration", Father Nicholas Gruner. (Transcript of speech from Fatima Conference in Rome, October 2001).

"The Prophecy of Bella Dodd", Christopher Ferrara, Fatima Perspectives (www.fatima.org).

"Russia Legalizes Homosexuality", *United Press International,* May 28, 1993.

"Satanism on the Rise in Russia!", John Vennari, Fatima News and Views (www.fatima.org).

"Satan's War Against Innocents", Michael Matt. (Transcript of speech, Fatima Rally Against Terrorism, New York, Nov. 2001).

"The Secret Red Plan to Take Over the Church", *The Fatima Crusader,* Issue 19, February-April 1986.

"The Stalinization of the Catholic Church", Christopher Ferrara. (Transcript of speech from Fatima Conference in Rome, October 2001).

"The Suicide of Altering the Faith in Her Liturgy", Father Paul Kramer. (Transcript of speech from Fatima Conference in Rome, October 2001).

"The Tail of the Dragon", Gerry Matatics. (Transcript of speech from Fatima Conference in Rome, October 2001).

"There is No Such Thing as the 'Global Community'", Thomas Woods, Ph.D. (Transcript of speech from Fatima Conference in Rome, October 2001).

"The Third Secret", Father Nicholas Gruner (Transcript of speech from Fatima Conference in Rome, October 2001).

"The Third Secret Handwritten Text Essential: An Interview with Fr. Paul Kramer", Fatima News and Views (www.fatima.org).

"The Third Secret of Fatima: Has it been Revealed", Father Gerard Mura, *Catholic,* March 2002.

"Third Secret Spurs More Questions; Fatima Interpretation Departs from Vision", Bill Broadway and Sarah Delancy, *The Washington Post,* July 1, 2000.

"This Present Darkness" (Four part series), Mark Fellows, *Catholic Family News,* August-November 2000.

"Thomism and the New Theology", Father David Greenstock, *The Thomist,* 1950.

"The Threat of U.N. Globalization - Panel", Cornelia Ferreira, William Jasper, John Vennari. (Transcript from Fatima Conference in Rome, October 2001)

"To Whom Shall We Go? - Concerning an Appeal to Pope John Paul II", Father Nicholas Gruner, *The Fatima Crusader,* Issue 66, Winter 2001.

"The United Nations: Chief Instrument of Russia's Errors", Cornelia Ferreira. (Transcript of speech from Fatima Conference in Rome, October 2001).

"The United Nations Exposed", William Jasper. (Transcript of speech from Fatima Conference in Rome, October 2001).

"Update on the Perestroika Deception", Cornelia Ferreira. (Transcript of speech from Fatima Conference in Rome, October 2001).

"Vatican's Ostpolitik and Ecumenism tried to Block My Conversion to Catholicism", Father Linus Dragu Popian. (Transcript of speech, Fatima Rally Against Terrorism, New York, Nov. 2001).

"Vatican Praises Purveyor of Heresy While it Hounds Apostle of Fatima", John Vennari, *The Fatima Crusader*, Issue 57, Spring/Summer 1998.

"Vatican Secret is Out", *The Express,* June 27, 2000.

"Vatican II vs. the Unity Willed by Christ", John Vennari, *Catholic Family News,* December 2000.

"Vatican Unease as it Reveals the Full Third Secret of Fatima", *Financial Times (London),* June 27, 2000.

"Vatican Says, You Must Not Become Catholic", John Vennari, *Catholic Family News,* December 2001 and *The Fatima Crusader,* Issue 69, Winter 2001.

"The Vatican-Moscow Agreement", Jean Madiran, *The Fatima Crusader,* Issue 16, September-October 1985.

"We are a Sign of Contradiction", interview with Bishop Bernard Fellay, SSPX, *Latin Mass Magazine,* Fall 2001.

"Where Have They Hidden the Body", Christopher Ferrara, *The Remnant,* June 30, 2001.

"Where is the New Theology Taking Us?", Father Reginald Garrigou-Lagrange, OP. First published in the *Angelicum,* 1946. English translation, *Catholic Family News,* August 1997.

"The Woman Clothed with the Sun: Fatima and Sacred Scripture", Gerry Matatics. (Transcript of speech from Fatima Conference in Rome, October 2001).

"World's Elite Gather to Talk Depopulation", John Henry Western, *The Interim,* April 1996.